Simmons

What to see – Where to stay

ABOUT THIS BOOK

If you want to find out about most aspects of travelling to and in London, turn to the part of this book called *Finding your Feet*, where there are details of tourist and travel information, and much practical advice about travel by public and private transport. This part of the book also has information on telephones, emergency services, lost property, etc. To find out where to go and what to do, consult the gazetteer which includes hundreds of places and things arranged under easy-to-find headings, such as art galleries, parks, churches, etc. Entries are referenced to the maps: the number (*eg* 15) refers to the map page number, the letter (*eg* 2B) refers to the grid square in which the place is located. Entries outside the Inner London map area are referenced to the district map. Opening details are believed to be correct at the time of printing, but it is always advisable to check before making a visit to avoid disappointment.

Cover: Mounting guard at Horseguards' Parade

Advertisement Sales: Tel. 0256 20123
Typesetters: Bookworm Typesetting
Printed and bound by: Richard Clay Ltd, Bungay, Suffolk

The Automobile Association would like to thank the following libraries for their assistance in the preparation of this book:
J Allan Cash Photolibrary: Cover Queens Life Guards
Spectrum Colour Library: 3 Lord Mayor's Coach, 5 & 6 Chelsea Flower Show, 6 Chinese New Year, 9 Notting Hill Carnival, London – Brighton Rally, Cenotaph.
All remaining photographs are held in the Automobile Association's own library (AA Photo Library).

Maps and plans produced by the Cartographic Department of The Automobile Association. The atlas section has been compiled and produced from the Automaps database utilising electronic and computer technology.
© The Automobile Association January 1991
Underground Map © London Transport

The contents of this publication are believed correct at the time of printing. Nevertheless the Publishers cannot accept responsibility for errors or omissions, or for changes in details given.

© The Automobile Association January 1991

All rights reserved. No part of this publication may be reproduced, stored in a retrieval system, or transmitted in any form or by any means – electronic, mechanical, photocopying, recording or otherwise – unless the written permission of the Publishers has been given beforehand.
ISBN 0 74950 166 9

Acknowledgements are due to the following:
Ann Halliday for editing *Shops and Markets*, *Villages and Favourite Haunts*, *Pubs* and *Eating Out*. Gerald Parsons at the London Tourist Board for his work on *Finding your Feet*.

Published by The Automobile Association, Fanum House, Basingstoke, Hampshire RG21 2EA

Produced by the Publishing Division of The Automobile Association

CONTENTS

The Lord Mayor's elaborately decorated coach

What to See	4
Central London Maps	11
Finding your Feet and District Map	33
Shops and Markets	49
Churches and Cathedrals	67
Palaces	73
Homes	78
Buildings	80
Villages and Favourite Haunts	84
Parks and Gardens	90
Waterside London	94
Statues and Monuments	98
Pubs	100
Art Galleries and Museums	103
Entertainment	118
Sport	126
Where to Stay Hotels, Guesthouses, Camping and Caravanning	132
Eating Out	149
Index of Places	157
Street Index to London Maps	165
Underground Map	Inside Back Cover

What to See

'No, Sir, when a man's tired of London, he is tired of life, for there is in London all that life can afford.'
SAMUEL JOHNSON 1709-1784

Modern London offers its 24 million annual visitors some extraordinary contrasts. Its ceremonial and historic ties continue in the annual enactments of events such as the Lord Mayor of Westminster's New Year's Day Parade, the Trooping the Colour and the State Opening of Parliament, while present-day London expands its imaginative riverside developments and tourist attractions in London Docklands and in the London Bridge City on the south bank of the Thames.

1990 saw the first International Covent Garden Festival, a biennial celebration of the contrasting characteristics of arts and commerce, and in the cobbled piazza of the Covent Garden central market, idiosyncratic shops and small cafés are the background to the street entertainers ranging from music students to conjurors.

Food has never been better or more diverse in this cosmopolitan capital and, when the fun of sightseeing and shopping has palled, there is a breath of fresh air in the three-mile swathe of parkland that cuts through London's West End.

The pages ahead will enable you to discover present-day London in detail.

Colourful exhibits at Chelsea Flower Show (opposite) include model gardens

Daily Events

(for full details please refer to the page numbers in brackets after the entries)
The Changing of the Guard *(p10)*
Ceremony of the Keys *(p10)*
Mounting Guard at Whitehall *(p10)*

Major Sightseeing Attractions

BUILDINGS
(Central London)
Banqueting House,
Whitehall *(p89)*
Buckingham Palace
(p73)
Houses of Parliament
(p74)
Kensington Palace
State Apartments *(p74)*
St Paul's Cathedral
(Evensong 5pm) *(p70)*
Tower of London
(p76)
Westminster Abbey *(p71)*

BUILDINGS
(outside Central London)
Hampton Court *(p74)*
Greenwich Palace *(p73)*
Kew Palace *(p75)*
Queen Charlotte's Cottage
(p75)
Syon Park *(p93)*
Thames Barrier *(p97)*
Windsor Castle *(p83)*

Occasional Events

Covent Garden Festival
(biennial, 1990, 1992, 1994 etc)

LONDON CALENDAR OF ANNUAL EVENTS

(For full details, please refer to the page numbers in brackets after the entries)

JANUARY
Lord Mayor of Westminster's New Year's Day Parade, *(p6)*
London International Boat Show, Earls Court SW5
Antiques Fair, Kensington Town Hall W8

FEBRUARY
Chinese New Year (sometimes late January) *(p6)*
Clown's Service *(p6)*
Gun Salute on Accession Day (6 February)

MARCH
Ideal Home Exhibition, Earl's Court SW5
Antiques Fair, Chelsea Old Town Hall SW3
London International Book Fair, Olympia W14
Head of the River Race *(p7)*
Oxford and Cambridge Boat Race *(p128)*

APRIL
Easter Parade *(p7)*
London Marathon *(p129)*
Gun Salute, Queen's Birthday (21 April)
Harness Horse Parade *(p7)*

MAY
Beating the Bounds (Ascension Day) *(p7)*
Rugby Cup Final Twickenham, Middlesex *(p131)*
Chelsea Flower Show, Royal Hospital, SW3 *(p7)*
SEP's Open Air Theatre, Regents Park *(p123)*
Wembley Football Association Cup Final, Wembley Stadium *(p126)*

JUNE
Greenwich Festival (various venues)
Spitalfields Festival, Christ Church E1
Royal Academy Summer Exhibition, Piccadilly *(p113)*
Beating Retreat, Horse Guards Parade, Whitehall *(p7)*
Queen's Official Birthday (17th June)
Trooping the Colour *(p7)*
Royal Ascot Race Meeting *(p7)*
Shoreditch Festival, Shoreditch Park N1
Wimbledon Lawn Tennis Championships *(p129)*
Derby Day, Epsom *(p7)*

JULY
Henley Royal Regatta, *(p8)*
Royal Tournament *(p8)*
Annual London International Festival of Street Entertainers, West Soho
The Promenade Concerts, Royal Albert Hall *(p120)*
Swan Upping, River Thames *(p8)*
Doggett's Coat and Badge Race *(p8)*

AUGUST
London Riding Horse Parade, Rotten Row, Hyde Park *(p8)*
Notting Hill Carnival *(p8)*

SEPTEMBER
Thamesday, Carnival and Festivities on the South Bank *(p8)*
Antiques Fair, Chelsea Old Town Hall SW3
Horseman's Sunday *(p8)*

OCTOBER
Horse of the Year Show, Wembley Arena, Wembley
Pearly Harvest Festival, St Martin-in-the-Fields *(p9)*
Punch and Judy Fellowship Festival, Covent Garden *(p55)*
Judges' Service *(p9)*
Trafalgar Day Parade *(p9)*

NOVEMBER
Guy Fawkes Night (5 November) *(p9)*
London to Brighton Veteran Car Run *(p9)*
State Opening of Parliament *(p9)*
Lord Mayor's Show, Guildhall, City *(p9)*
Remembrance Sunday Ceremony, Whitehall, SW1 *(p9)*

DECEMBER
International Show Jumping, Olympia W14

Contrast: Soho celebrates Chinese New Year, Chelsea the English Garden

WHAT TO SEE IN LONDON

Lord Mayor of Westminster's New Year's Day Parade

The Parade starts at *1pm* from Piccadilly, through Regent Street and Oxford Street and finishes in Hyde Park, where marching bands of the US, Europe and the UK perform. Throughout the day there are floats, dancers, many colourful characters and a variety of acts, culminating in a fireworks display.

Chinese New Year

This day is based on cycles of the moon and occasionally falls in late January. Taking place *from 11.40am on the Sunday nearest to the New Year,* it is celebrated in the Soho area around Newport Place, Gerrard Street and Lisle Street, with decorations adorning streets and balconies. Men in colourful costume perform the Lion Dances while the 'Lion' receives gifts of money and food from residents and restaurants around.

Clown's Service

Held on the *first Sunday in February* at Holy Trinity Church, Beechwood Road, Dalston E8 which is the church of the Clowns' International Club. Many clowns in full costume and traditional make-up attend the service at *4pm.* A wreath is laid to Grimaldi who originated the clown character. Afterwards there is a free clown show.

What to See in London

Head of the River Race

This takes place on the Thames, starting from Mortlake and finishing about one and a half hours later at Putney. Starting times vary from year to year according to the tides. This is a professional race for eights and up to 420 crews starting one behind the other at 10-second intervals. The winner is the boat with the fastest time.

Easter Parade

The Easter Parade sometimes falls in March according to the date of Easter. The Parade takes place in Battersea Park SW11 and *starts at 3pm*. Before that, *starting at 12.30pm,* coloured floats and marching bands circle the park and there are entertainments, a funfair and the children's theatre and jazz tent.

Harness Horse Parade

This takes place at The Inner Circle, Regent's Park NW1 and provides an opportunity to see working horses competing for prizes. The competition includes classes such as Heavy Horses, Single Horsed Commercial Vans and Private Turnouts. The parade *ends at 12 noon* with a Grand Parade of winners which continues until about *1pm*.

Beating the Bounds

A traditional Ascension Day ceremony in which choirboys and parishioners walk around the parish boundaries. One of the most colourful (every three years, 1990, 1993, 1996, etc) is when the Chief Yeoman Warder leads the choirboys from the Chapel Royal of St Peter ad Vincula at Tower Bridge. The procession *starts at 6.30pm* and the public are welcome to join in.

Chelsea Flower Show

The first event in the gardening season is the Chelsea Flower Show, held at Chelsea Royal Hospital in the *third week in May.* The private view for members of the Royal Horticultural Society starts on the Tuesday, and public days are Wednesday, Thursday and Friday. Flowers of almost every season can be seen, together with gardens, furnishings, gardening aids, flower arrangements and advice.

Beating Retreat – Household Division

A military display of marching and drilling bands of the Household Division takes place at Horse Guards Parade SW1. Mounted bands, trumpeters, massed bands and pipe and drums perform and in the evening, performances are given by floodlight.

Trooping the Colour

Trooping the Colour

On the *second Saturday in June,* the Sovereign's official birthday is celebrated by the Trooping the Colour. The Colours (flags) of one of the five Foot Guards' regiments are trooped before the Sovereign. Years ago this was necessary so that the regiments could recognise their own colours in battle. At the end of the ceremony, the Sovereign rides to Buckingham Palace ahead of her Guards.

Royal Ascot

Royal Ascot Races take place in the *third week of June.* They are attended by the Queen and members of the Royal Family. Thursday is Ladies' Day – famed for the stylish hats worn by the ladies. A great racing, fashion and social event.

Derby Day

Derby Day takes place at the Epsom Racecourse, Surrey, just outside London. It forms part of a festival of racing and is one of the greatest horse races for three-year-old colts and fillies. A funfair is also set up on Epsom Downs for the week.

What to See in London

Henley Royal Regatta

The *first week in July* heralds Henley Royal Regatta at Henley-on-Thames in Oxfordshire. Though outside London, this annual international rowing regatta can be considered part of the London social season.

The Royal Tournament

The Royal Tournament is held in *July* at Earls Court Stadium. First held in 1880, it is a unique display by representatives of all Britain's armed forces and visiting armed services from abroad. The spectacular show includes feats of daring and training, simulated live battles and musical numbers. The Tournament is always visited by members of the Royal Family.

Swan Upping

The Dyers and the Vintners have the right to own swans on the Thames. At the Swan Upping, in the *third week of July,* families of swans on the Thames are rounded up by the Companies' swanherds who travel up-river in skiffs (small boats) decorated with banners, together with the Queen's Keeper of Swans. Participants are dressed in garments of red, blue, green, white and gold. They mark the beaks of the new cygnets with one nick for the Dyers and two nicks for the Vintners. The Queen's birds remain unmarked. The event closes with a traditional banquet at a riverside inn, which includes a dish of swan meat.

Notting Hill Carnival is the high spot of the year for London's West Indian community

Doggett's Coat and Badge Race

Another summer pageant associated with the City of London, the Doggett's Coat and Badge Race, attracts people to the banks of the Thames *towards the end of July.* The oldest annually contested event in the British sporting calendar, it celebrates the accession of George I to the English throne. In 1715 Thomas Doggett, comedian and manager of London's oldest theatre, the *Drury Lane,* bequeathed a badge of silver and money to pay for a livery coat for the winner of a race for single sculls, starting at London Bridge and ending at Cadogan Pier in Chelsea – a total of 4½ miles.

London Riding Horse Parade

Starting at 1pm at Rotten Row, Hyde Park W2, the competition selects the best turned out horse and rider and the winner is awarded the Astral Sports Perpetual Challenge Cup.

Notting Hill Carnival

This is the largest street festival in Europe and is now 25 years old. Held over the August Bank Holiday weekend, carnival-goers dance to steel and brass bands and dress up in spectacular costumes. The Children's Carnival is the main attraction on Sunday and includes a competition for the best costume.

Thamesday

A carnival of festivities held on the South Bank and including boat races, fireworks and events for children. Many of the events are held in the Jubilee Gardens near the Festival Hall.

Horseman's Sunday

Horses assemble from 11.30am at the Church of St John and St Michael, Hyde Park Crescent W2 and the service *starts at 12 noon,* taken by a vicar on horseback. It lasts about 25 minutes and afterwards there is a procession of horses who, singly or in pairs, receive commemorative rosettes. After the *parade at about 1pm* all the horses continue on into Hyde Park to ride the 2½ miles of riding tracks. *At 1.30pm* there is a Horse Show in Kensington Paddock (the western end of Kensington Gardens) which includes showing classes, showjumping and gymkhana events.

A 1902 Wolsey ready for the Veteran Car Run

Pearly Harvest Festival Service

A service at *1pm* is held at St Martin-in-the-Fields WC2 in which the traditional cockney costermongers, Pearly Kings and Queens, are seen at the service and one reads the lesson. The altar and pulpit are covered with harvest produce and the congregation sings thanksgiving hymns.

Judges' Service

The opening of the legal year on the first weekday in October with judges in full ceremonial robes. *Starts 11am* at Westminster Abbey and arrives at Houses of Parliament at *11.45am*.

Trafalgar Day Parade

Trafalgar Square WC2 *at 11am*. The Parade commemorates the anniversary of Nelson's great sea victory at the Battle of Trafalgar. Five hundred Sea Cadets from all over Great Britain take part and music is played by the Cadet Bands. A national dignatory reviews the whole parade and there is a short service with hymns and a reading of Nelson's Prayer by a young Cadet.

Guy Fawkes Night

The anniversary of Guy Fawkes's death, who took part in the Gunpowder Plot to blow up King James I and his Parliament in 1605, is marked by nationwide fireworks displays. London has many, some in the capital's parks.

London to Brighton Veteran Car Run

Leaving from Hyde Park Corner *between 8am and 9am on the first Sunday in November,* these veteran cars set out for Brighton where they should arrive in Madeira Drive *from approximately 10.45am.* Over 400 entrants participate.

State Opening of Parliament

After a general election, and before each new session of Parliament in *mid-November* the Sovereign attends the State Opening of Parliament, a ceremony dating from the mid-16th century. The Royal procession moves from Buckingham Palace to the Palace of Westminster, where the ceremony takes place at the House of Lords.

In addition to these major ceremonies, on special occasions (like certain royal birthdays) 41-gun salutes are fired in Hyde Park by the King's Troop of the Royal Horse Artillery, and at the Tower of London by the Honourable Artillery Company.

What to See in London

Lord Mayor's Show

The most famous City of London pageant is the Lord Mayor's Show, which takes place on the *second Saturday of November*. The Lord Mayor, elected annually, is head of the Corporation of London, the City's administrative body, and is host to visiting Heads of State and celebrities. This important office makes him or her the first citizen of the City, taking precedence over everyone except the Sovereign. The procession dates from the 14th century and the Lord Mayor rides in the state coach in order to be 'shown' to the citizens and to make the final declaration of office at the Law Courts. The coach is accompanied by floats and military bands.

Remembrance Sunday

A memorial day for members of the three Services and Allied Forces who were killed in action in the two World Wars and other conflicts. The service is held at the Cenotaph Memorial, Whitehall SW1. The Queen arrives at 10.59am when a minute's silence is observed before the firing of a gun from Horse Guards Parade. The ceremony continues with the Queen laying a wreath at the Cenotaph.

The Cenotaph, Whitehall

Daily Events

Daily Events

The Changing of the Guard

From early times, the duty of guarding the Sovereign has been the responsibility of the bodyguard of the Yeomen of the Guard. During the Civil War, Charles I was guarded by troops loyal to his cause. At the Restoration, the responsibility of protecting the Sovereign became the daily task of the Life Guards and the three regiments of foot guards known as the Household Division.

This tradition continues today, for the Queen and her many homes are guarded by the Household Division. The most popular mounting of the Guard is the one that takes place *daily (during the summer)* at Buckingham Palace. Do arrive early if you want to see this ceremony.

The Queen's Guard change takes place inside the Palace railings and starts at approximately 11.25am daily May 1–mid Aug, then alternate days. Tel 071-370 3488 to confirm.

Ceremony of the Keys

At the Tower of London, the Ceremony of the Keys has taken place every night for the last 700 years. The Tower is still officially owned by the Queen as a palace and fortress and is therefore closely guarded and securely locked at night. The Ceremony of the Keys occurs *a few minutes before 10pm nightly*.

Applications for a pass to attend this ceremony, which lasts for about 20 minutes from start to finish, should be made in writing to the Resident Governor.

Handing over the Keys of the Tower of London

Mounting Guard at Whitehall

A detachment of the Household Cavalry guards the old entrance to the demolished Whitehall Palace, a handsome 18th-century building whose east front faces onto Whitehall. Mounting Guard at Whitehall is a colourful spectacle, which takes place at *11am every weekday and 10am on Sundays*. Tel 071-730 3488 to confirm.

The Thames Barrier

WITHOUT THIS ATTRACTION, YOU MIGHT NOT SEE THE OTHERS. THE THAMES BARRIER, THE LARGEST MOVABLE FLOOD BARRIER IN THE WORLD, PROTECTS LONDON FROM FLOODS.

The Thames Barrier Visitors Centre illustrates, through videos, a working model and a spectacular new audio-visual presentation, the important and historic role of London's River Thames and the construction and function of the Thames Barrier. Visit Hallett's Panorama of Bath as seen from a hot air balloon. Browse round our souvenir shop. Enjoy views of this spectacular feat of engineering from the Riverside Walkway and cafeteria, or take a cruise around the Barrier itself.

Function Room and Evening Carvery for groups, telephone: 081-316 4438.
Ample car parking. FREE coach park. A206 Woolwich Road. Arrive in style by boat from Westminster, Tower or Greenwich Piers.
WE ARE OPEN 7 DAYS A WEEK: 10.30-5 (5.30 weekends): TEL: 081-854 1373.
Admission £2 — concessions for children, OAP's, families and groups.

London: **Street atlas and key**

STREET ATLAS AND KEY MAP

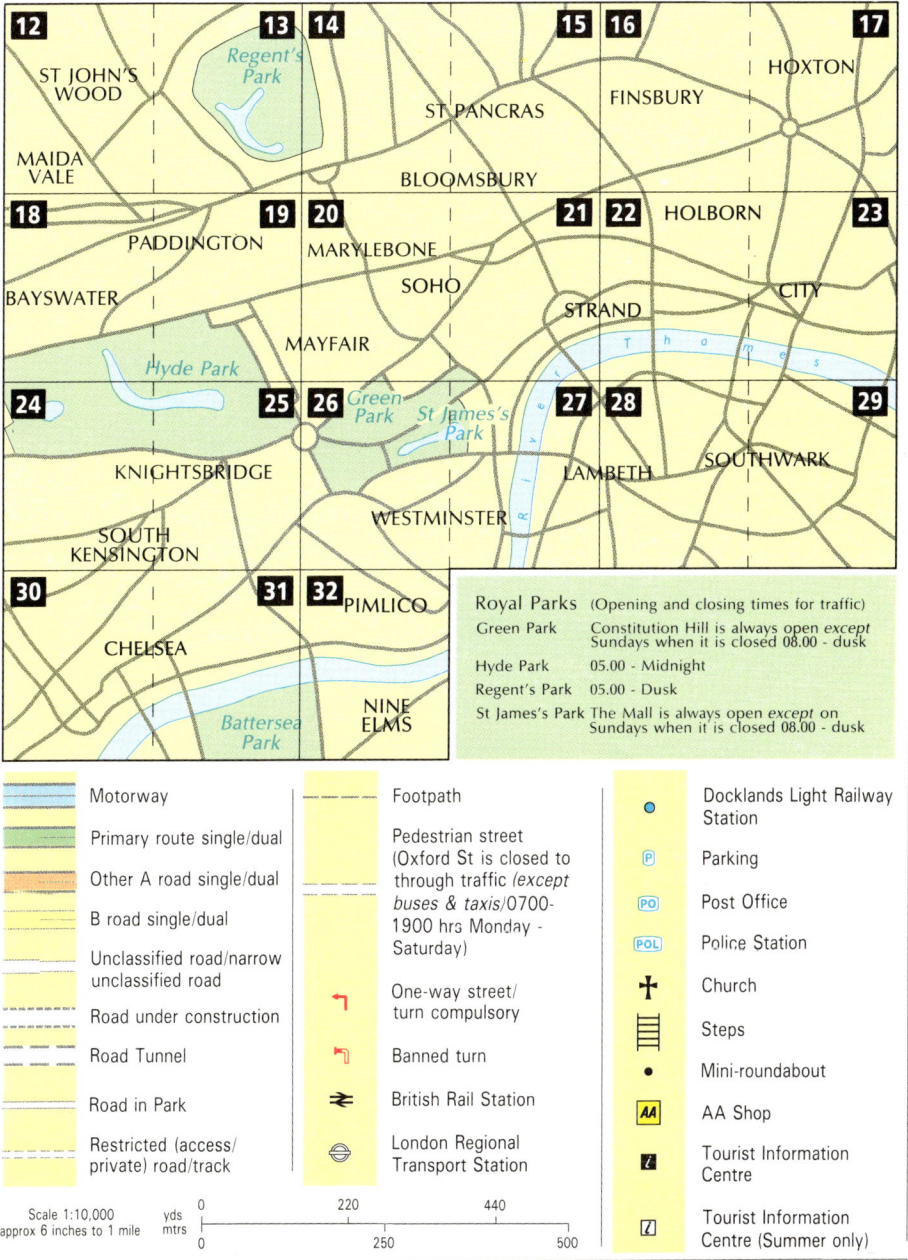

11

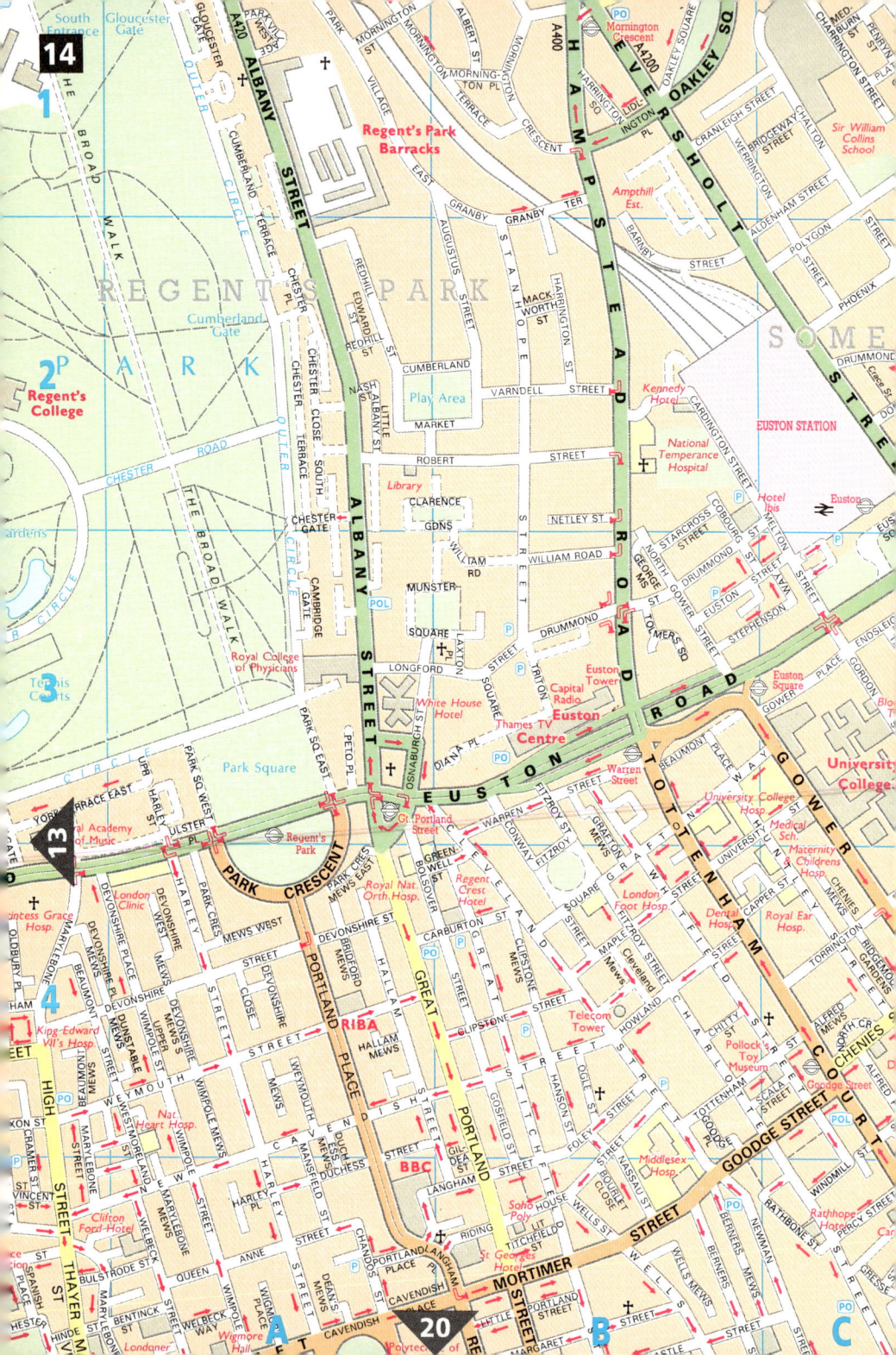

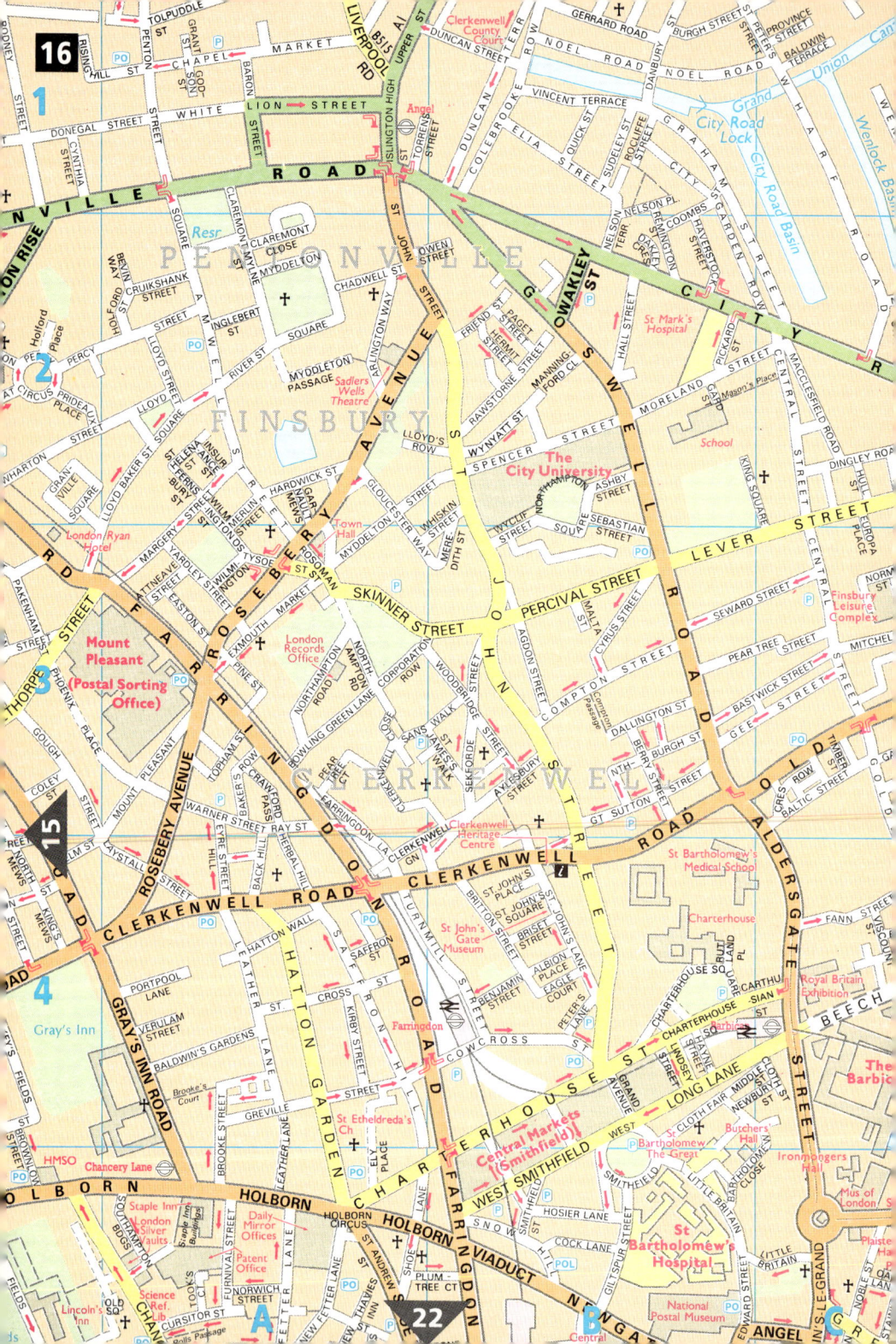

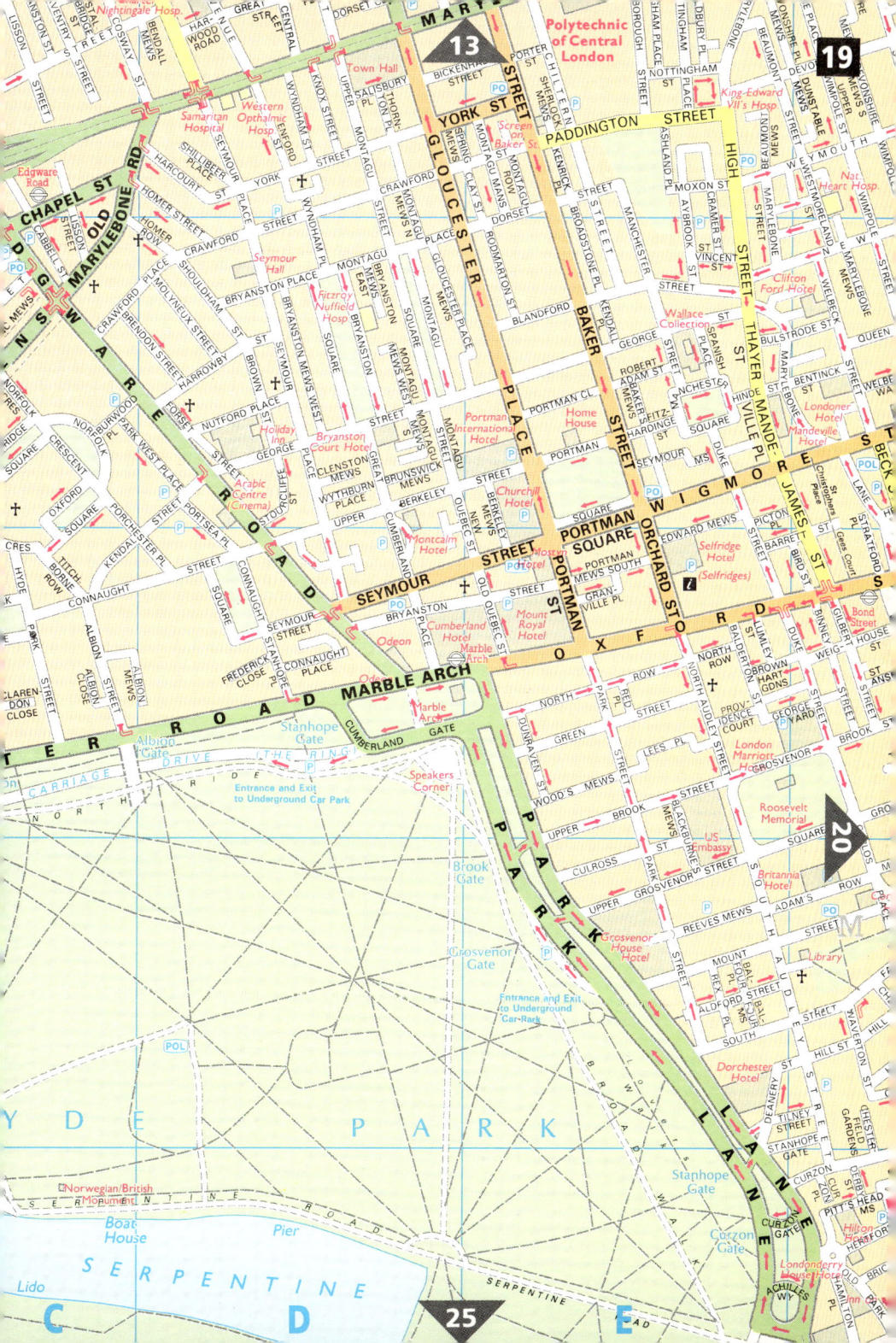

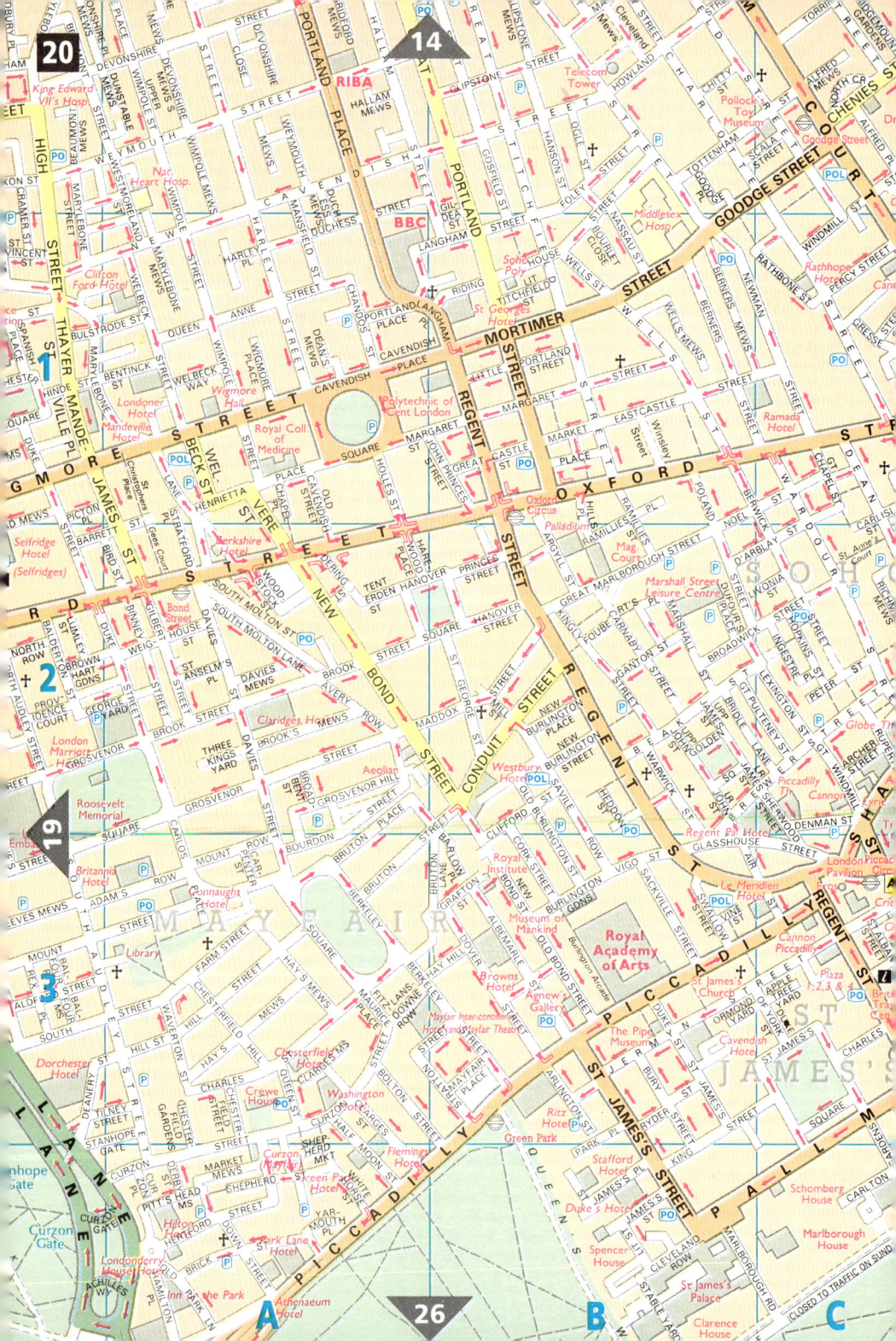

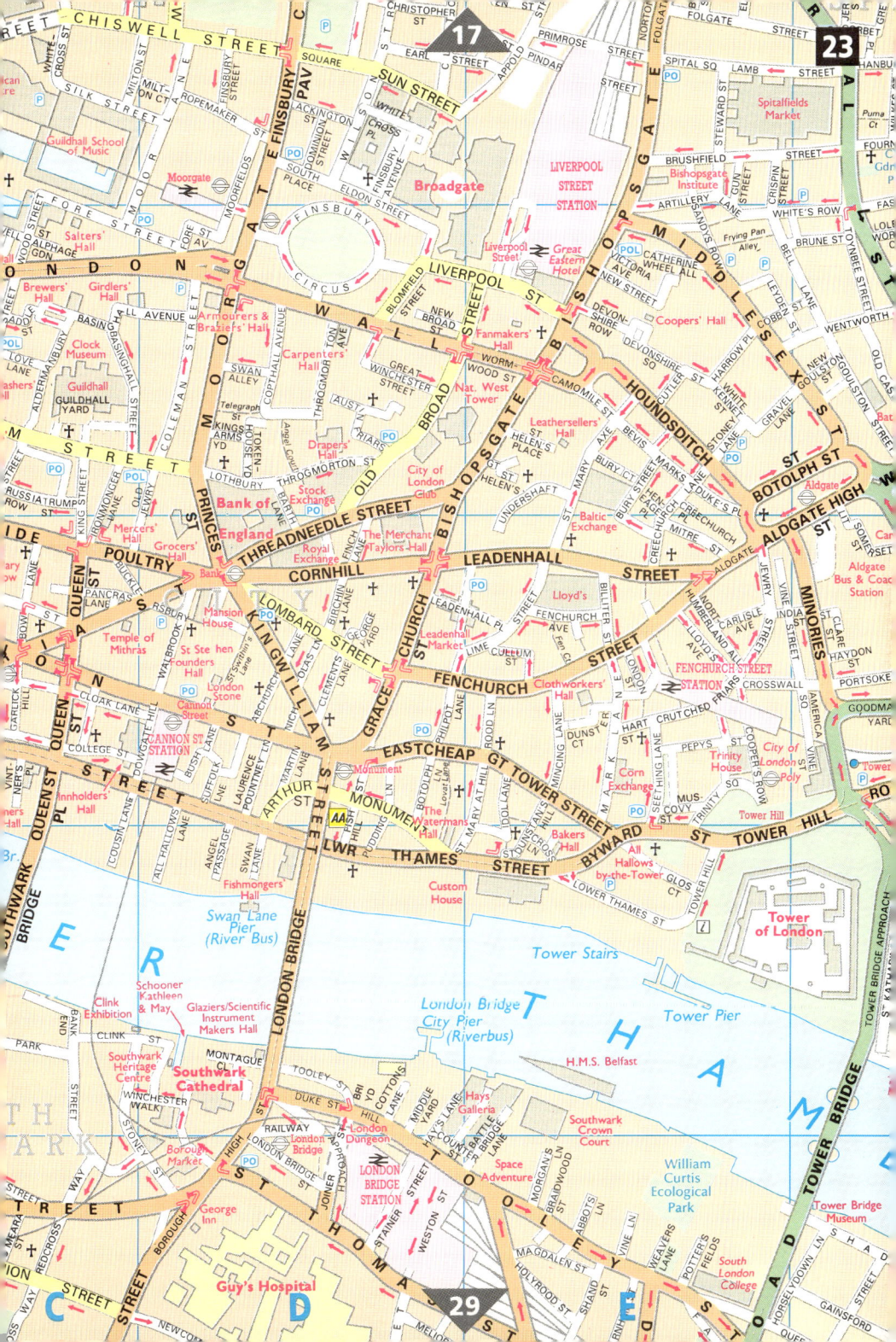

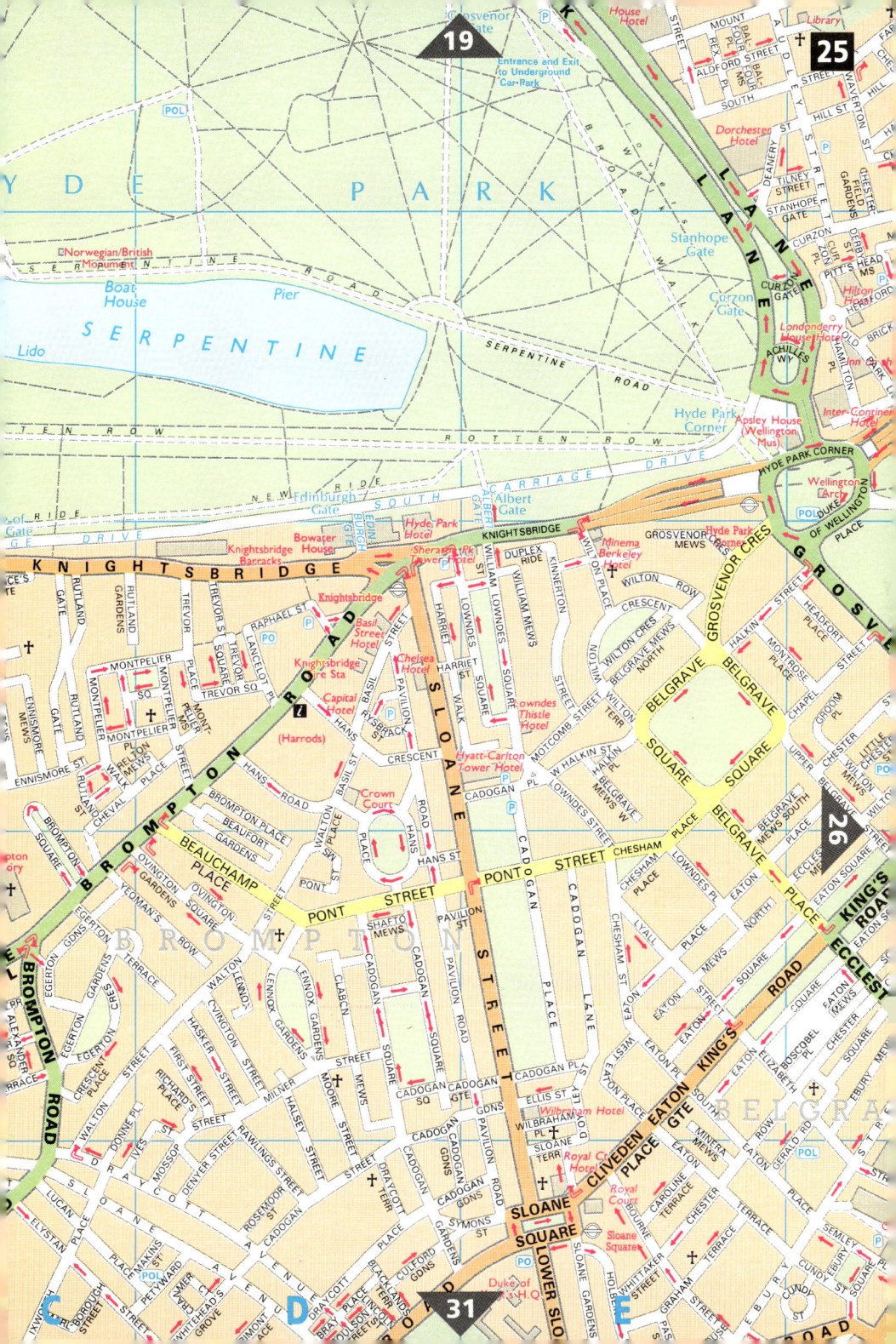

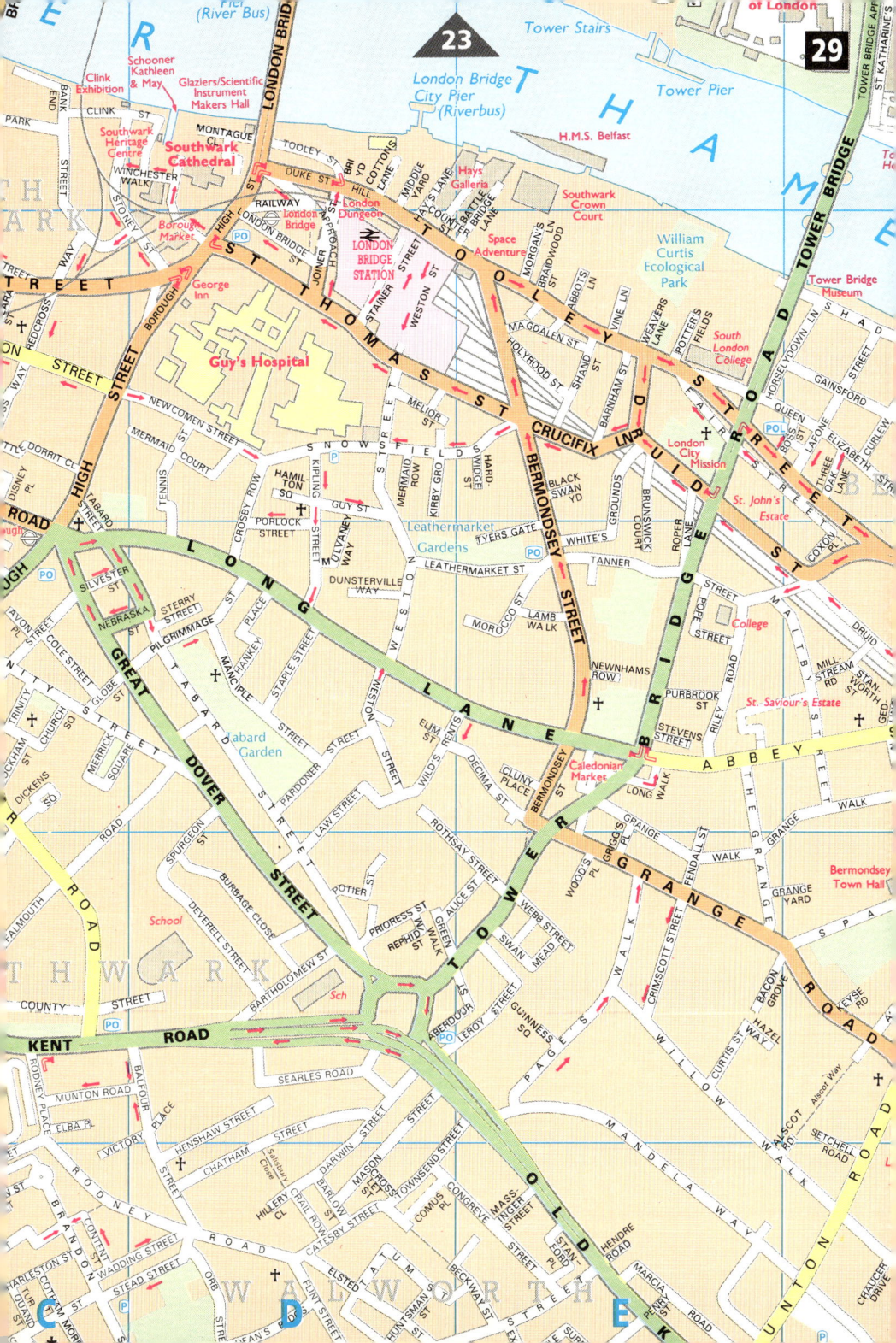

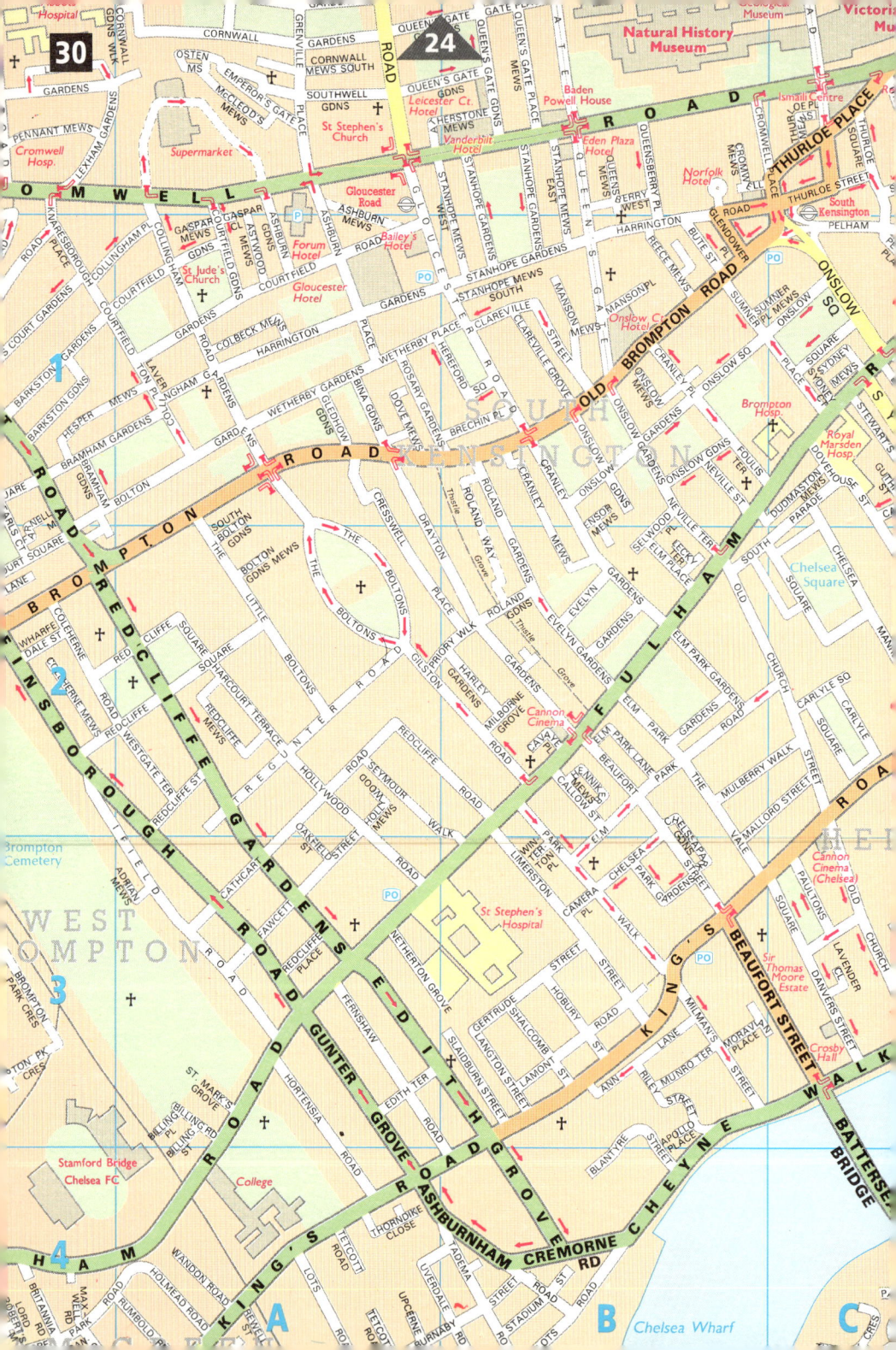

Finding your feet

Finding Your Feet

TOURIST INFORMATION
ACCOMMODATION
Charges
Disabled visitors
AIRPORTS
Heathrow Airport
Gatwick Airport
London City Airport
Stansted Airport
BRITISH RAIL
LONDON'S TRANSPORT
The Underground
Buses
Coaches
River Bus
Concessionary fares
Rush hour
Taxis
SIGHTSEEING TOURS
DOCKLANDS

WATER TRANSPORT
SEEING LONDON BY BICYCLE
LONDON ON FOOT
PEDESTRIANS
BANKS
POST OFFICES
TELEPHONES
EMERGENCY SERVICES
LOST PROPERTY
BLUE PLAQUES
TIPPING
PUBLIC CONVENIENCES
DRIVING A CAR IN LONDON
Parking
Public car parks

The London Tourist Board information offices deal with tens of thousands of visitors to the capital

TOURIST INFORMATION

The London Tourist Board is London's official information centre; all approved members – shops, hotels, tour agencies and operators – display its sign. Whatever information you need about London – what to do, where to go, how to get there, including instant hotel bookings, theatre and tour reservations – can be obtained at the LTB's six central locations:

Victoria Station forecourt, SW1
open April-October 8am–6pm. Bookshop and Britain Desk Mon-Sat 8am–7.30pm (Sun 8am–5.30pm) ▶ 36

London: **District map**

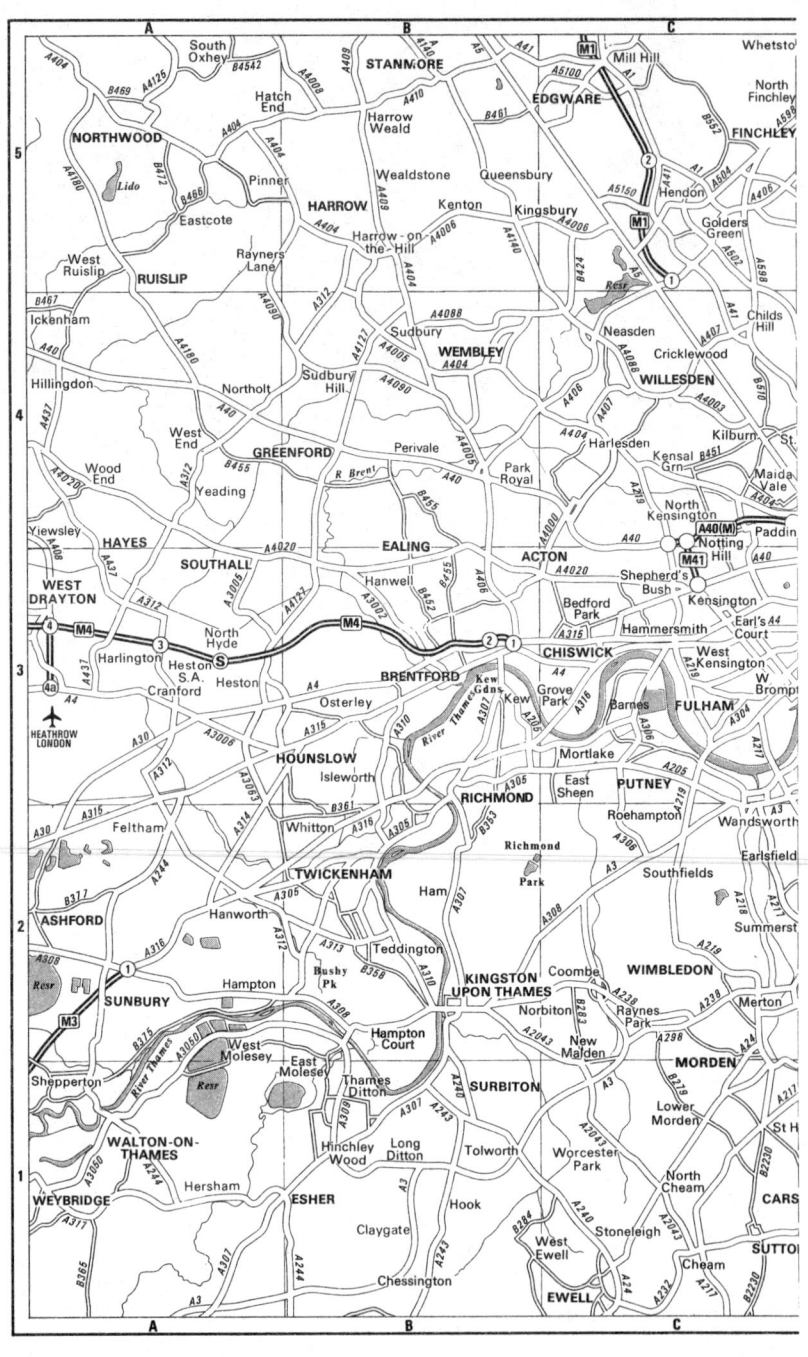

London: **District map**

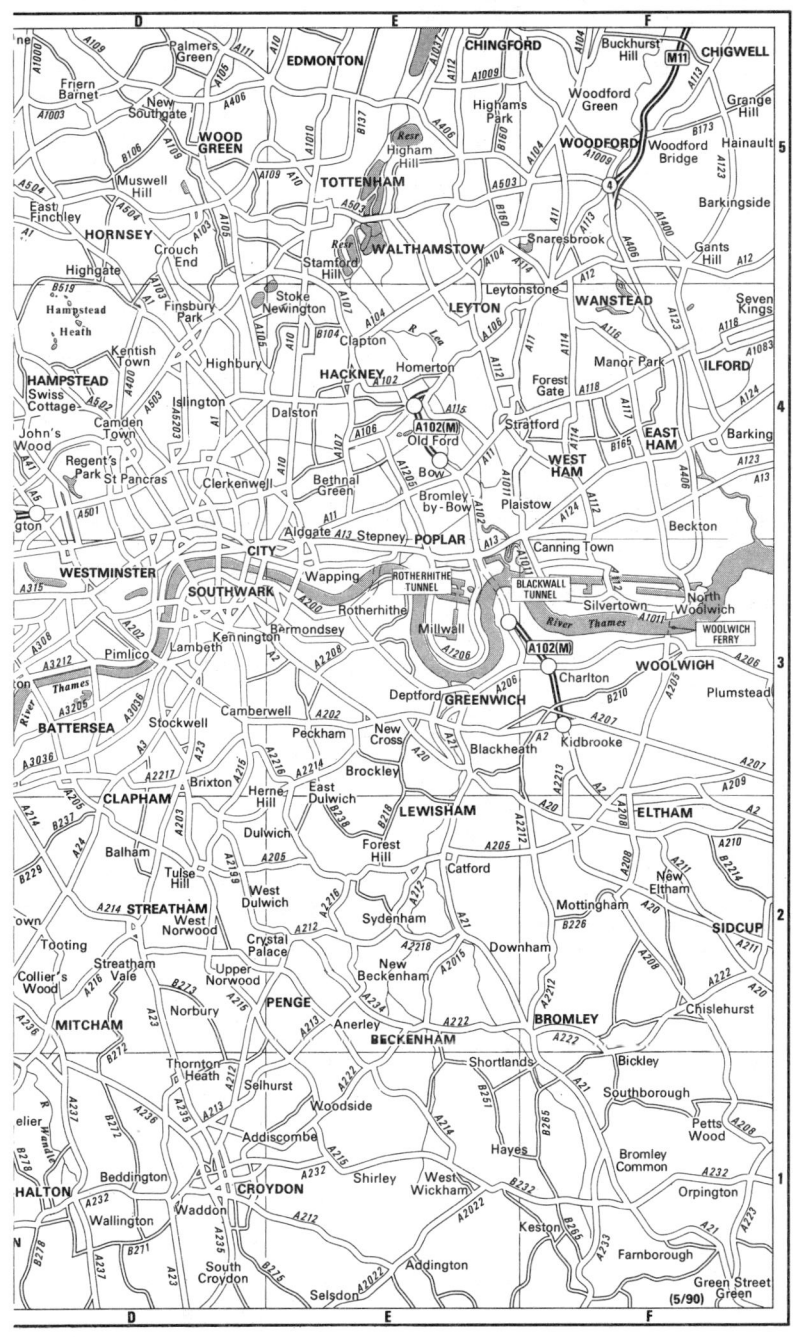

Finding your feet

Selfridges Store, Oxford Street, W1 (basement services arcade)
open store hours
Harrods Store, Knightsbridge, SW1 (basement banking hall)
open store hours
Heathrow Airport, Heathrow Underground Station Concourse
open daily 8am–6.30pm
Liverpool Street Station
open Mon-Sat 9.30am–6.30pm, Sun 8.30am–3.30pm
Tower of London, EC3 (West Gate)
open daily April-October 10am–6pm and telephone enquiries can be made on 071–730 3488, Mon-Fri 9am–5.30pm

In addition, there are several local Tourist Information Centres around the capital.

ACCOMMODATION

London is renowned for some of the best and most famous hotels in the world. There are also lots of smaller establishments with lower prices, and an enormous number of privately run bed-and-breakfast guesthouses. See page 132 for a list of AA-recommended places to stay.

It can all be very confusing, but help is on hand to assist you sort things out. If you wish to make advance reservations before leaving home, your local travel agent will know about special 'package' arrangements. For advance bookings of two nights or more, you can write to the London Tourist Board at 26 Grosvenor Gardens, London SW1W 0DU *at least six weeks* before you intend to travel. They will act as an agency and make provisional reservations for you. For reservations on your arrival in London, you should go in person to one of the LTB's five central Information Centres – at Victoria and Heathrow Stations, Harrods, Selfridges, and The Tower – or to the British Travel Centre in Regent Street (see page 37); you will find all the help you need at these centres. A returnable deposit must be paid when making a reservation there, and this is deducted from your final bill; in addition, a small non-returnable booking fee is charged.

If you think you will be arriving late at your hotel, you should mention this at the time of booking; similarly, if you are delayed for any reason, it is advisable to telephone the management to warn them of your late arrival.

It is also possible to book accommodation by telephoning the LTB on 071–824 8844 (credit card holders only).

Charges

It is usual for breakfast to be included in the cost of a night's accommodation. Many hotels and guesthouses offer special all-in prices for full-board (bed, breakfast, lunch and dinner) and half-board stays (bed, breakfast, and lunch or dinner).

All establishments with four or more bedrooms are required by law to display in their entrance halls notices showing the minimum and maximum overnight charges. All displayed prices must include service charges (if any), and it must be clear whether they include meals and Value Added Tax (currently 15 per cent).

You may find the following hotel booking agencies of help: Concordia, 52 Grosvenor Gardens, SW1 (Tel 071–730 3467) kiosk Victoria Station (Tel 071–828 3467)
Gatwick Airport (Tel (0293) 34851)
GB Hotel Reserves, Sydney Hall, Pond Place, SW3 (Tel 071–581 0161/2)
HBI/HOTAC, Kingsgate House, Kingsgate Place, NW6 (Tel 071–625 8631)
Hotel Booking Service, 13–14 Golden Square, W1 (Tel 071–437 5052)
Hotel Finders, 20 Bell Lane, NW4 (Tel 081–202 7000)
British Hotel Reservation Centre personal callers: Victoria Station, outside Platform 8 (Tel 071–828 1027/1849) Liverpool Street Station, outside Platform 9 (Tel 071–621 1842)

Disabled Visitors

For information and advice on accommodation for physically handicapped people contact the **Holiday Care Service**, 2 Old Bank Chambers, Station Road, Horley, Surrey RH6 9HW (Tel (0293) 774535) or the London Tourist Board Central Accommodation Unit (071–730 3450).

AIRPORTS

London is well served by its airports, to which it is connected by excellent road and rail links. The main London airports are Heathrow and Gatwick.

Heathrow Airport

Travellers arriving at Heathrow pass through one of the busiest airports in the world. Handling millions of passengers a year, it is situated some 15 miles to the west of central London, to which it is directly connected by the M4 motorway. Heathrow Information Desk – Tel 081–759 4321.

The following public transport serves Heathrow.

Underground

The extension of the Piccadilly

Accommodation, airports, trains

line tube, opened in 1977, provides a direct link from all Heathrow terminals to the West End of London. Departures from the airport start at about 5am on Monday to Saturday and at about 7am on Sunday; the last train leaves at just before midnight, Monday-Saturday, and just before 11pm on Sunday. The first train to Heathrow leaves King's Cross station at about 6am on Monday to Saturday and at about 7.30am on Sunday; the last train leaves just after midnight, Monday-Saturday, and at about 11.30pm on Sunday.

Airbus

This London Regional Transport Airbus A1 leaves Victoria Station (Grosvenor Gardens) every 20–30 minutes from 6.35am to 9pm, with a journey time of 55–70 minutes. Airbus A2 leaves Euston Station (Russell Square) every 20–30 minutes from 6.45am to 10.15pm, with a journey time of 65–90 minutes. Airbuses stop at major hotels en route.

Although airbuses and tubes do not operate during the night, there is an all-night bus service – No 97 – which runs at regular intervals from midnight to 5am between central London and Heathrow.

Gatwick Airport

Twenty-eight miles south of London, Gatwick is the second most important airport in Britain. One of the most convenient ways of travelling to Gatwick is by rail, as the station forms an integral part of the airport terminal building. Trains leave from Victoria Station in London every 15 minutes between 5.30am and 10pm, and every hour throughout the night; the journey takes about 30 minutes. Driving to Gatwick takes about an hour, depending on traffic conditions, via the A23 and the M23 motorway. Although there are no tubes, there is a good coach service to Gatwick from Victoria Coach Station.

Gatwick Information Desk – Tel (0293) 31299.

London City Airport

This airport is located six miles from the Bank of England in the Royal Docks area of Beckton, close to the A13 and A117. London City Airport is mainly intended for use by businessmen, but offers the general public a regular and convenient service to UK and European destinations.

London Transport bus route 276 serves the airport terminal building itself; routes 69 and 101 pass Connaught Road, where a turning off a mini-roundabout leads to the terminal (about 500 yards).

By rail, the nearest station is Silvertown and City Airport on North London Link. This connects to the underground at West Ham (District Line) and Stratford (Central Line).

There is also a Riverbus service from Charing Cross Pier and Swan Lane Pier (in the City of London).

Stansted Airport
Rail

To get to the airport from London, take the train from Liverpool Street to Bishops Stortford, then bus or taxi.

Coach

Cambridge Coach Services service 38 operates from Eccleston Bridge, Victoria, and National Express operates from Victoria Coach Station. Both take about one and a half hours. Information from Cambridge Coach Services on (0223) 440640; for National Express on 071-730 0202.

Stansted Airport – Tel (0279) 502380.

BRITISH RAIL

Britain's extensive rail network links all major cities in the country with London. British Rail offer a full range of travel facilities at **The British Travel Centre**, 12 Regent Street, SW1 (Tel 071-730 3400). Here you can buy rail tickets and make reservations, book tickets for theatres and sightseeing tours, arrange accommodation, and change foreign money. The Centre is open from 9am to 6.30pm, Monday to Saturday, and on Sundays from 10am to 4pm. In addition, BR Travel Centres can be found at:

14 Kingsgate Parade, Victoria Street, SW1
87 King William Street, EC4
170b Strand, WC2
(Open 9am–5pm, Mon-Fri)
and at these main London terminals:
Cannon Street, Charing Cross, Euston, King's Cross, London Bridge, Liverpool Street, Paddington, St Pancras, Victoria, and Waterloo.

Almost all the main-line London stations are worth a visit in themselves, if only for their architectural grandeur or Victorian pretensions. Each one serves a particular region of the country. The main ones are:

King's Cross Station

(Tel 071-278 2477)
The main London terminal of the Eastern Region, serving east and north-east England, and Scotland via the east coast. It is connected to the Northern, Piccadilly, Circle, Metropolitan, and Victoria lines of the Underground.

Liverpool Street Station

(Tel 071-928 5100)
The terminus for East Anglia, it is connected to the Central, Circle, and Metropolitan lines of the Underground.

Euston Station

(Tel 071-387 7070)
Serves east and west Midlands,

37

Finding your feet

north-west England, Scotland via the west coast, and north Wales. A modern station of concrete and glass with direct escalators to the Northern and Victoria lines of the London Underground.

St Pancras Station
(Tel 071–387 7070)
This famous Gothic-style station serving the east Midlands is close to King's Cross and connects with the same tube lines.

Victoria Station
(Tel 071–928 5100)
The main Southern Region terminus serving the south coast and connected to the Circle, District, and Victoria lines of the Underground. For a hundred years, Victoria has been the rail gateway to the Continent, and the Orient Express – though now privately run – still starts from platform 8.

Waterloo Station
(Tel 071–928 5100)
This Southern Region terminus is the biggest and busiest station in London, thanks to the enormous amount of commuter trains which pour in each day. It connects to the Underground's Bakerloo and Northern lines.

Charing Cross Station
(Tel 071–928 5100)
Designed by the great railway engineer, Brunel, Charing Cross serves the Southern Region and connects with the Jubilee, Bakerloo, and Northern lines of the Underground.

Paddington Station
(Tel 071–262 6767)
Another Brunel station, this terminus of the Western Region serves the west Midlands, the west of England, and south Wales with 125mph high-speed trains, the fastest scheduled diesels in the world.

St Pancras is the East Midlands terminus

London's transport

The station is connected to the Bakerloo, District, Circle, and Metropolitan lines of the Underground.

Full details of scheduled rail services are shown in local timetables. Free copies are available from British Rail stations and Travel Centres.

British Rail fares are calculated on the distance travelled. It is generally cheaper to travel after the morning rush hour (9.30 Monday to Friday), and at any time over the weekend. Buy a Cheap Day Return or, for longer journeys, a Saver Return ticket. You must buy a ticket before travelling, and surrender it either to the guard on the train or to the ticket-collector on the platform at your destination. Children under five travel free; under 16, half-price.

LONDON'S TRANSPORT

The visitor arriving in London will need to know first of all how to get about the capital. Fortunately, though Greater London is over 610 square miles in size, twice as large as New York or Paris, it is served by one of the finest transport systems in the world.

You have a choice of three means of public transport: the familiar red London bus, the Underground railway – or 'tube' - network, and the London taxi.

The buses and Underground are controlled by London Regional Transport whose headquarters is at 55 Broadway, Westminster, SW1. This authority maintains Travel Information Centres at the following Underground stations in Central London: Victoria, Piccadilly Circus, King's Cross, Oxford Circus, Euston, St James's Park and Heathrow. They answer all queries about travel in London,

Victoria Station is London's 'Gateway to the Continent'

as well as issue tickets, book tours and sell publications. Or you can telephone 071–222 1234 any time, day or night.

The Underground

Please refer to the map of the London Underground at the back of this book.

As with many capital cities, the quickest and most efficient means of public transport in London is the Underground railway – known as 'the tube'. With 273 stations, the Underground covers a wide area reaching out from central London to the suburbs where it rises above ground as an ordinary surface railway. There is almost always a tube station close at hand throughout London, and trains run frequently between 5.30am and 0.15am (until 11.30pm on Sundays). There are no all-night services, however, and it is important to note that certain stations are closed at weekends.

There are large Underground maps posted at all stations, in the booking halls and on all platforms, and each car displays a map of that train's route. Each line has a name and is clearly indicated in a separate colour; it is usually easier to follow the colours than go by the names of the lines.

Bakerloo line	– brown
Central line	– red
Circle line	– yellow
District line	– green
East London	– orange
Jubilee line	– grey
Metropolitan line	– purple
Northern line	– black
Piccadilly line	– dark blue
Victoria line	– light blue

The Docklands Light Railway has been extended to Bank Underground station. It runs to Tower Gateway and Island Gardens (opposite Greenwich), with another section from Stratford to Island Gardens.

Signs throughout the tube stations show the way to the line required, but make sure you wait on the correct platform and board the right

Finding your feet

train by checking the direction indicators on the platform and on the front of the train.

A list of fares is displayed in ticket halls; you must buy a ticket before you begin your journey, either from the booking office or from automatic machines (some of them give change), and keep it to show or surrender at your destination.

Under–14s travel at a reduced fare, as do 14- and 15-year-olds with a Child Rate Photocard – these are available free from Post Offices in the London area. Under-fives travel free.

Buses

One of the best ways of seeing London is to take a seat on the top deck of one of its famous double-decker buses. The fact that the traffic may be slow on occasions is no great handicap, but offers a wonderful opportunity for leisurely sightseeing. Buses operate from about 6am to midnight on most routes, including those connecting the main-line railway stations, and offer a comprehensive service in central London and the suburbs. A network of special All Night buses runs through central London serving Piccadilly Circus, Leicester Square, Victoria, Trafalgar Square, Hyde Park Corner, Marble Arch, and many other parts convenient for theatres, cinemas, and restaurants. However, do check times before using these buses; their stops have distinctive blue and yellow route numbers.

You should pick up a free, detailed bus map from any Travel Enquiry Office or Underground station. Each bus route is identified by a number

The best way to see London is by bus (right); the most relaxing is by taxi (far right)

which appears on the front, sides, and back of each bus. The final destination also appears on the front and back, and a short list of major ports of call on the sides. Bus-stop signs, which generally list the numbers of the buses which stop there, are displayed on a red or white background. Red backgrounds denote 'Request Stops', where the bus will only stop if hailed in good time; the white background signs are compulsory stops. You should always take your turn in the queue at a bus-stop – if there is one.

On double-decker buses, there are usually conductors who control the number of passengers allowed on and collect fares; on single-decker buses you give your fare to the driver as you get on. Always try and have a lot of change with you when you use buses, so that you can tender the right money. Smoking is not allowed on the ground floor of double-decker buses.

Under–14s pay a reduced flat fare until 10pm, as do 14- and 15-year-olds with a Child Rate Photocard, and up to two under-fives per person travel free. Remember to keep your ticket until you leave the bus.

Coaches

National Express operate to all Britain. Most coaches leave from Victoria Coach Station, telephone 071–730 0202. Green Line operate to many interesting places around London, such as Windsor and Hampton Court. Enquiries: 081–668 7261.

River Bus

The River Bus operates every 20–30 minutes from Charing Cross to Greenwich, stopping at nine intermediate piers with a sheltered waiting area and a River Bus attendant. The journey from Charing Cross to Greenwich takes about 30 minutes. A separate service links Charing Cross Pier to London City Airport, stopping at Swan Lane Pier (in the City). This is an hourly service, and a 'Hoppa Bus' operates from the pier to the airport terminal. For further information on the River Bus (Tel 071–512 0555).

London's transport

Concessionary fares

If you intend to use public transport in London extensively for just one day, it is best to buy a one-day Travelcard. This will give you unlimited travel on London Underground, British Rail Network Southeast, Docklands Light Railway, and most London buses. Travelcard holders will not have to queue for separate tickets, or search for change at Underground ticket machines or on buses. One-day Travelcards can be used any time after 9.30am Monday to Friday, and all day at weekends and on public holidays. They can be bought from any London Transport or LTB Information Centre, or any Underground station.

Travelcards are available for travel in London for periods longer than one day. For these you will need to obtain a photocard, available free from Underground stations, selected London newsagents, and Network Southeast stations – just take along a passport-type photograph. (There are instant-photo booths at the major railway and tube stations.) For the purposes of the Travelcard, London is divided into five concentric zones radiating from the centre of London, and the price of the Travelcard will depend upon the number of zones in which you will need to travel. Travelcards for periods of more than one day can be used in the specified zones for unlimited travel any time during their validity.

Period Travelcards can be purchased for any number of days, but you will need to give at least 12 hours notice if you want to buy a ticket for anything other than seven days or one month.

As Travelcards are available from all Network Southeast stations, they can offer a great saving if you are not actually staying within the capital.

Rush hour

From Monday to Friday the buses and trains of London Regional Transport carry a daily average of over 6,000,000 passengers. In Central London all forms of public transport become extremely crowded between 8am–9.30am and 4pm–6.30pm when most of London is travelling to and from work. London's rush hour is really most uncomfortable, and if travel can be arranged outside these times, the visit will be considerably more enjoyable. Buses and tubes also get quite busy at lunchtime, but not as bad as during the rush hour.

Taxis

The London taxi is one of the friendliest sights a visitor will see. The traditional colour is still black, though in recent years red, blue and yellow vehicles have added a splash of colour to London's fleet. Taxis are a salvation for those who get lost; after midnight they are a godsend and the only way to get about. Taxi drivers are also a useful source of information as they know London inside-out – they have to, in order to get their licence.

London taxis can be hailed in the street if the yellow 'For Hire' or 'Taxi' sign above the windscreen is lit, hired from

Finding your feet

taxi-ranks, or called by telephone: for numbers, see 'Taxi' in the Business and Services section of the London Telephone Directory. Charges vary according to the distance covered and are recorded on the meter; additional charges are made for extra people, luggage, and night journeys. It is customary to tip about 10–15 per cent of the fare, or perhaps a little more if the driver has been particularly helpful. For journeys over six miles – for example, from Heathrow Airport to Central London – you should negotiate a fare in advance.

SIGHTSEEING TOURS

An excellent way to get to know London – particularly if this is your first visit – is to join one of the many sightseeing bus or coach tours.

London Transport's **Official Sightseeing Tours** on double-decker red buses start from Piccadilly Circus (Haymarket), Marble Arch (Speakers Corner), Baker Street Station, and Victoria Station. The 18-mile route (lasting about 1 ½ hours) passes most of London's landmarks including St Paul's, Westminster Abbey, and The Tower. These guided tours leave every half-hour from each point from 10am to 5pm daily (except Christmas Day). Buy your tickets in advance from any London Transport or LTB Information Centre at a special low rate; or just pay as you board the bus. A special tour includes direct entrance (no boring queuing) to Madame Tussaud's Waxworks. The buses may be open-top in summer. Details from London Transport, 55 Broadway, SW1 (Tel 071–222 1234).

Sightseeing bus/coach tours are run by: Evan Evans Tours Ltd (071–930 2377); Rickards (071–837 3111); Golden Tours (071–937 8863); London Tour Company (071–734 3502); London Cityrama (071–720 5971); Travellers Check-In (071–580 8284); Harrods Sightseeing (071–581 3603); London Crusader (071–437 0124); and Thomas Cook Ltd (071–499 4000).

DOCKLANDS

London's newest and most dramatic development is taking place in eight-and-a-half square miles of what was once a forgotten and largely derelict backwater – an area on both sides of the Thames stretching from London Bridge to North Woolwich. Transport is provided by the new and highly automated Docklands Light Railway, operating from Tower Gateway east through Limehouse and Poplar to Island Gardens on the southern tip of the Isle of Dogs, with a branch going north from Poplar to Stratford.

Development is still very much in progress, but new and innovative projects include leisure facilities and residential, office and shopping developments. At the same time great effort is being made to preserve the wealth of historic and beautiful buildings that make up the heritage of the area, and, not least, the immense dock system – dating from the 17th century and still largely intact. Many Georgian and Victorian warehouses have undergone imaginative conversion, attractive churches are being rediscovered, and some of the oldest and best pubs and taverns in London are enjoying a new popularity – some dating back to the 16th and 17th centuries.

In this area of such new development, finding your way about can be bewildering, but an excellent first stop is the London Docklands Visitor Centre, which offers first-time visitors comprehensive information, as well as an exhibition area and tours (Tel 071–515 3000; alight at Crossharbour on the Docklands Light Railway, see page 97).

WATER TRANSPORT

A holiday in London cannot be complete without the unique views offered by a boat trip on the Thames. Passenger boat services operate a full programme during the summer months and a restricted one in the winter. From Westminster Pier (071- 930 4097), Charing Cross Pier (071–839 3572), and Tower Pier (071–488 0344), services operate downstream to Greenwich, and from Westminster and Charing Cross Piers downstream to the Tower. Upstream services operate from Westminster Pier to Kew, Richmond, and Hampton Court, and from Tower Pier to Westminster. Check departure times with the enquiry numbers given with each pier, or telephone the River Boat Information Service on 071–730 4812 (weekdays, 9am–6pm).

London also has two canals – the Grand Union and the Regent's Canal. Boat trips operate mainly on the Regent's Canal: the Regent's Canal Waterbus goes from Camden Lock to Little Venice, via London Zoo (071–482 2550); Jason's Canal Cruises (071–286 3428) run luncheon and evening trips along the picturesque part of Regent's Canal using a pair of traditional narrow-boats; there are cruises on the *Jenny Wren* through the zoo and Regent's Park, and on the *My Fair Lady*, a luxury cruising restaurant (071–485 4433), for a meal with a difference.

Sightseeing, banking, post & telephone

SEEING LONDON BY BICYCLE

A different way to get about London is to use a bicycle. Traffic, especially in Central London, is often congested and the cyclist has a freedom denied the motorist. There are many firms in London who offer a cycle hire service and who are able to meet the needs of both the casual and experienced cyclist, whether it be for a three-speed or a ten-speed bike. Most firms can also supply items of cycling equipment and can provide information on sights to see. *On Your Bike*, 52–54 Tooley Street SE1 (Tel 071–378 6669) provides bicycles for hire. They are open from 9am–6pm Monday to Friday, 9.30am–5.30pm Saturday, and they also have a shop within Lilywhites, Piccadilly, open normal shop hours. *Airport Skis* also have bicycles for hire at 18 Gillingham Street SW1 (Tel 071–834 8011), open 10am–5pm Monday to Friday, 10am–4pm Saturday.

LONDON ON FOOT

If you want to discover London by foot – one of the best ways to get to know any city – several firms organise guided walking tours. Information from:
City Walks 071–937 4281
Citisights 081–806 4325 (archaeological walks)
Cockney Walks 081–504 9159
Footloose in London 071–435 0259
Footsteps 0622 682072
London Walks 081–441 8906
SJ Harris 071–624 9981
Historical Tours 081–668 4019
Tour Guides Ltd 071–839 2498

If you want to explore London on your own, the Silver Jubilee Walkway covers ten miles of historic London. This walkway was created in 1977 to commemorate the 25th anniversary of the Queen's accession to the throne. The entire route is signposted by silver plaques in the shape of a crown set into the pavement. Parliament Square is a good place to start.

PEDESTRIANS

At a Zebra street-crossing (one with flashing orange beacons and black-and-white stripes on the road) you have absolute right-of-way when you have stepped off the kerb – but do use this sensibly and make sure drivers have seen you before you cross.

At Pelican crossings (two lines of studs with traffic lights to halt the traffic), you have to push a button to make the signals stop the traffic for you. When the signal shows a green man, cross. If this signal starts to flash while you are crossing, carry on, you will have plenty of time to reach the other side; do not start to cross when this is flashing nor, of course, when the red man is showing.

Be aware of the bus lanes where buses may travel in the opposite direction to the main flow of traffic.

BANKS

All banks are open between 9.30am and 3.30pm Monday to Friday (3pm in the City), and some now open on Saturday mornings. They are closed on Sundays and Public Holidays. There are 24-hour banks at Heathrow and Gatwick airports. Most banks now operate a queuing system. When changing foreign currency, banks usually give the best rates at the lowest commission charges – look out for their special foreign exchange counters. Bureaux de Change are located throughout the capital and are usually open longer hours than banks, in the evenings and at weekends, but do check the rates of commission they charge – they can be very high, cancelling out the advantage of a seemingly generous exchange rate. Wherever you change money or cash cheques, exchange rates and charges should be clearly displayed.

POST OFFICES

In the UK you can buy stamps at Post Offices and some newsagents; letters and cards can be posted at Post Offices and in the hundreds of distinctive red pillar-boxes in the capital. Parcels must be posted at Post Offices.

Each district in London has its own chief Post Office, and there are also many smaller sub offices. The London Chief Office is in King Edward Street, EC1; it is open for all kinds of postal business on Monday to Friday from 8.30am to 6pm, except on public holidays. The Trafalgar Square Post Office, 22–28 William IV Street, WC2 (Tel 071–930 9580) is open for all kinds of business, Monday-Saturday 8am–8pm. It has the longest post office counter in Britain (56 metres long, with 33 positions), but it is also always full of queues. So try to find one of the smaller offices in which to transact your business; these are often combined with a general shop or newsagent, and are normally open from 9am to 5.30pm, Monday to Friday, and on Saturday mornings.

TELEPHONES

There are hundreds of public payphones throughout the capital, many still found in the distinctive and easily recognisable red phone boxes. Additionally, many pubs, restaurants, hotels, post offices, and other places open to the public have payphones which you may use. There are four types of payphones:

43

Finding your feet

Coin-operated payphones: dial direct to anywhere in the UK and to all countries to which International Direct Dialling is available. They take 10p, 20p, 50p, and £1 coins.

Phonecard phones are quickly becoming more widely available. To use these phones you must first buy one of the special cards which are available from post offices and shops displaying the 'Phonecard' sign. You may then make any number of calls up to the value of the card without the need for cash but only from the special Phonecard phones.

Creditcall Payphones. Phones that accept Visa, Mastercard, Diners Club, and American Express credit cards are now installed in the London area and at airports.

In all cases, instructions for use are clearly displayed.

Remember when dialling an Inner London number from Outer London you will need the 071 prefix (081 for the reverse operation).

EMERGENCY SERVICES

If you are involved in any serious accident, or if you need the police in an emergency, you should always dial 999 in any telephone box (these calls are free), and ask for Fire, Police, or Ambulance.

London Transport Police (for reporting thefts and other crimes which take place on London Transport): telephone 071-222 5600.

If you are injured and require medical attention in Central London, University College Hospital (Gower Street, WC1), St Thomas's Hospital (Lambeth Palace Road, SE1), and the Westminster Hospital (Horseferry Road, SW1), all have 24-hour casualty departments. Several chemists have extended opening hours; these include Boots, Piccadilly Circus, W1 (Monday-Friday 8.30am-8pm, Saturday 9am-8pm), HD Bliss, 5 Marble Arch, W1 (9am-midnight daily), Boots 75 Queensway, W2 (9am-10pm daily). All foreign visitors to Britain can take advantage of the accident and emergency services of the National Health Service without charge.

Emergency dental treatment can be obtained, at a charge, from the Emergency Dental Service: telephone 081-677 6363.

LOST PROPERTY

(a) if you lose anything while travelling on buses or the underground, you should write or go to the London Transport Lost Property Office at 200 Baker Street, NW1, adjoining Baker Street underground station. This office is open Monday to Friday, 9.30am-2pm (closed Saturdays and Sundays). **(b)** for property lost in London taxis or in the street, report any loss to the nearest police station. **(c)** taxis only: write to the Metropolitan Police Lost Property Office, 15 Penton Street, N1. It would be helpful to quote the plate number of the taxi in which you travelled. **(d)** if you lose anything in a store, hotel, airport, etc., contact the premises in question. Should property be lost on a train or at a railway station, contact the arrival/departure station of your journey.

BLUE PLAQUES

Scattered throughout London are the homes of the famous and houses where history was made. Such buildings are marked with a blue plaque recording the event. This scheme was started in 1866 and there are now more than 600 plaques commemorating important events and lives of soldiers, scientists, architects, artists, writers, composers, and politicians. You will see them as you stroll around London's streets.

TIPPING

It is customary to tip for the following services: taxi-drivers; porters, doormen, bell-boys, and room-service waiters; tour guides; barbers and hairdressers; cloakroom attendants; and in restaurants, except where the menu specifically says that service is included.

Never tip bartenders in pubs.

PUBLIC CONVENIENCES

London has a large range of well-signposted public loos, but unfortunately their opening times are sometimes erratic. New individual coin-in-the-slot, French-style conveniences are being erected in central London – for example, in Leicester Square, Soho, and Victoria Street, SW1; these cost 10p. There are conveniences in hotels, large stores, pubs, and at stations – but be sure you have plenty of change in advance; charges vary.

DRIVING A CAR IN LONDON

The best advice for the visitor wanting a worry-free and enjoyable time in the capital must be – don't take your car into central London. Traffic congestion is a problem and parking can be difficult. Many one-way street systems have been introduced which do create difficulties for the visitor. Those unfamiliar with the complexities of London traffic can take advantage of the services offered by larger car-hire agencies, which will provide a driver to meet the

Emergencies, driving & parking

client and drive or guide him in his own car into or across central London. Information on car hire and chauffeur-driven cars is available from London Tourist Information Centres. Those who still wish to drive themselves and are unfamiliar with conditions in the capital should avoid the rush-hour traffic, which is at its height around 8–9.30am and 4–6.30pm. Particular areas to avoid are Buckingham Palace and The Mall between 11am and noon when the Changing of the Guard at the Palace causes traffic delays. Also, no cars are allowed to use Oxford Street between 7am and 7pm, Monday to Saturday.

Parking

Street parking in central London is controlled by a parking policy of meter zones known as the Inner London Parking Area. There are also parking zones in outer London, most of which include meters. The controlled zones are indicated by signs at their boundary points, giving the hours of operation. Special regulations may also apply in areas near to the wholesale markets and where Sunday street markets are held. Street parking other than at officially designated places is prohibited during the specified hours. In many zones, some parking places may be reserved exclusively for residents or other classes of users specified on nearby plates. Temporary restrictions may be found locally, particularly for special events. The usual system of yellow lines indicates waiting restrictions.

Parking meters may take 10p, 20p, 50p or £1 coins but there are differences in charges and variations in the length of time for which parking is allowed. The car must be parked within the limits of the parking bay, indicated by the white lines on the roads. It must also face in the same direction as the traffic flow, unless angle parking is indicated by road marking. Payment must be made on arrival, although unexpired meter time paid for by a previous occupant of the space may be used. After the initial payment has been made, additional parking time may not be bought by making any further payments. Infringement of these rules results in penalties in the form of expensive 'parking tickets', which you will find stuck to the windscreen of the car, and (in extreme cases of misdemeanour) clamps affixed to the front wheel which render the car completely immobile.

Cars may usually be parked at night without lights.

There is some free parking available on the roads in Hyde Park and Regent's Park. The times may be unusual, but are shown by the normal yellow lines and nearby plates.

Public car parks

There are many public car parks in Inner London, which include the multi-storey blocks and underground car parks constucted in recent years to ease traffic congestion. Most are operated by National Car Parks Ltd (Tel 071–499 7050) and are easily spotted by their large yellow NCP signs. Most of these car parks are open during normal business hours, or for a slightly longer period at each end of the working day, depending on local arrangements. It is advisable to ascertain closing arrangements from the car park at the time of entering. In most cases it is not possible to make advance reservations. Charges vary a good deal, but as a general guide, the rates in the West End or the City of London usually start at around £1.80 for the first two hours, rising to approximately £13 for a 24-hour period. Cheaper night rates are available between 6pm and 9am. In outer areas the charges are usually considerably lower.

When parking your car, always remember to secure it against theft and not to leave any valuable property inside.

Information about traffic conditions, parking, and motoring in general can always be obtained from the many AA Centres in London – or phone their central number 081–954 7373.

A good compromise is to park your car at a railway or underground station on the outskirts of London and continue your journey by train or tube to the centre. On, or near, the main approach routes into London, it is always possible to leave a car close to public transport facilities which provide a frequent service into the capital.

The opening hours of British Rail station car parks vary according to the opening and closing hours of the station, which are subject to the current time-table. Underground (tube) car parks are open from the time of the first to the time of the last train. Some run by other bodies may be open 24 hours.

You will find charges displayed at all train and Underground car parks. Some car parks operated by the London Borough under whose jurisdiction they come are free of charge, but this policy could be varied at short notice. There is no standard rate of charges; some are raised during the morning peak hours to discourage commuter parking. However, on Saturdays some car parks double the weekday charges.

45

CAR PARKS

For people who have to bring their cars into the capital, the following selection of London's major public car parks may help you to ease the strain of searching for those elusive unoccupied parking meters, particularly in the West End.

Abbreviations used in text/type of car park

C, Ch and L	Cars, coaches and lorries
M/S	Multi-storey
S	Surface
U/C	Under cover
U/G	Underground
P	Petrol facilities
*	Open 24 hours
Mdnt	Open until midnight

	POSTAL AREA	TYPE	CAP.
Abingdon Street *(entrance Gt College Street)*	SW1	U/G*	250
Acacia Garage, Kingsmill Terrace	NW8	M/S*	250
Adams Row, Britannia Hotel	W1	U/G*	175
Aldersgate	EC1	M/S	740
Arlington Street, Arlington House	SW1	U/G*	108
Audley Square, South Audley Street	W1	M/S*	310
Barbican Centre	EC2	U/G	500
Baynard House, Queen Victoria Street	EC4	U/G*	300
Bayswater Road, Kensington Gardens	W2	SC & CH	100
Bedfordbury	WC2	U/G	62
Bell Street	NW1	M/S*	205
Bishop's Bridge Road, Colonnades, Porchester Terrace North	W2	U/G*	152
Bloomsbury	WC1	S 08.00-22.00 Mon-Sat	45
Bloomsbury Square	WC1	U/G*	450
Bowling Green Lane	EC1	S	150
Brewer Street, Piccadilly Circus	W1	M/S*	450
Britannia Walk *(off City Road)*	N1	S	100
Brunswick Square	WC1	U/G*	524
Bryanston Street *(Marble Arch)*	W1	M/S*	310
Business Design Centre, Upper Street	N1	M/S 07.30-22.00	270
Butlers Wharf, Gainsford Street	SE1	S 07.00-20.00	110
Cadogan Place *(off Sloane Street)*	SW1	U/G*	349
Cambridge Circus *(Newport Place)*	W1	U/G*	365
Carburton Street, Regent Crest Hotel	W1	U/G*	65
Carrington Street, Shepherd Market	W1	M/S	310
Cavendish Square	W1	U/G Mon-Sat 07.00-23.00	545
Chandos Street, Queen Anne Mews	W1	U/G*	390
Charterhouse Square	EC1	S	100
Chesterfield House, Chesterfield Gardens	W1	U/G	50
Chiltern Street, Paddington Street	W1	M/S*	395
Church Street, Penfold Street	NW8	U/G	150
Clere Street	EC2	S	60
Cleveland Street	W1	U/G	84
Clipstone Street	W1	U/G*	347
The Concorde Centre, The Green	W12	Rooftop part U/C	300
Cowcross Street, Caxton House	EC1	U/G	63
Cramer Street	W1	S	200
Crawford Street	W1	S & U/C	90
Cromwell Road, The London Forum Hotel	SW7	U/G*	95
Cromwell Road, Swallow International Hotel	SW5	S U/C	40
Denman Street	W1	U/G*	143
Distaff Lane *(off Cannon Street)*	EC4	U/G	100
Dolphin Square Garage, Grosvenor Road	SW1	U/G* P Servicing	355
Doon Street *(entrance in Upper Ground)*	SE1	S C 08.00-Mdnt	300
Drury Lane,	WC2	U/G	450

Car Parks

Name	Area	Type	Spaces
Parker Street		06.00-Mdnt	
Dufours Place, Broadwick Garage	W1	U/C	75
Earls Court Exhibition *(operator: Sterling Guards)*, Seagrave Road	SW5	S	1,300
Edgware Road, Burwood Place *(Water Gardens; Flats)*	W2	U/G*	300
Edgware Road *(Marks and Spencer)*	W2	U/G open during store hours	55
Edith Yard, Worlds End Estate	SW10	U/C	50
Elephant and Castle	SE1	U/G	150
70/71 Ennismore Gardens *(Kingston House Garage Tel 071–589 6726)*	SW7	U/G Mon-Fri 07.30-23.00, Sat, Sun 08.00-23.00)	60
Euston Station	NW1	U/G*	235
Fieldgate Street *(off Whitechapel Road; south side) (entrance in Fieldgate Street via Plumber's Row)*	E1	S*	120
Finsbury Square	EC2	U/G P*	285
Gloucester Place, Portman Square Garage	W1	M/S*	443
Gt Cumberland Place, Bilton Towers	W1	U/G*	160
Great Sutton Street	EC1	U/C	30
Grosvenor Hill, Bourdon Street	W1	M/S	216
Hammersmith Broadway *(Queen Caroline Street)*	W6	S Mon-Sat 08.00-22.00	300
Harrington Road	SW7	S	45
Harrow Road, London Metropole Hotel	W2	M/S*	80
Hayward Gallery, Belvedere Road	SE1	S 08.00-Mdnt	120
Holland Road, Royal Kensington Hotel *(380 Kensington High Street)*	W14	U/G	70
Hornton Street, Kensington Town Hall	W8	U/G*	410
Houndsditch, Ambassador House	EC3	M/S	196
Hungerford Bridge	SE1	S 08.00-Mdnt	120
Jubilee Gardens	SE1	S 08.00-Mdnt	100
Kendal Street South	W2	U/G*	75
Kilburn Square *(off Kilburn High Road)*	NW6	U/G	120
King's Cross Station	NW1	S	70
King's Mail, Glenthorne Road *(eastern end)*	W6	M/S Mon-Sat 08.00-18.30	960
Knightsbridge, Park Tower Hotel	SW1	U/G*	90
Knightsbridge Green, Raphael Street	SW1	U/G	65
47/67 Lillie Road, Ramada West Hotel	SW6	U/G*	140
Lisson Grove, Bell Street	NW1	S 07.30-20.00	86
London Wall	EC2	U/G	229
Lots Road	SW10	S	80
Maclise Road *(Olympia) (Sterling Guards)*	W14	M/S*	750
Marriot Hotel *(off Duke Street)*	W1	U/G	85
Marylebone Road, Gloucester Place	NW1	U/G*	180
Minories	EC3	M/S	417
Museum Street	WC1	M/S*	250
National Theatre, South Bank	SE1	U/G 08.00-02.00	410
Old Burlington Street, Burlington Garage	W1	M/S	477
Old Park Lane, Brick Street	W1	U/G	65
Olympia Way	W14	S	400
Orchard Street *(enter from Duke Street) (Selfridge Garage Tel 071–493 5181)*	W1	M/S P Mon-Sat 07.00-Mdnt	700
Paddington Station	W2	S U/C	60
Park Lane	W1	U/G*	1,000
Park Lane, Hilton Hotel	W1	U/G*	235
Park Road, Regent's Park	NW1	S	113
Park Walk Garages	SW10	S	44
Park West	W2	U/G	100
Paternoster Row, Ave Maria Lane	EC4	U/G*	260
Pavilion Road	SW1	M/S*	311

Finding your feet

Location	Zone	Type	Spaces
Poland Street	W1	M/S Mon-Sat 06.00-Mdnt Sun & Bank Hols closed	150
Portland Place, Weymouth Mews	W1	U/G	35
Portman Square, Churchill Hotel	W1	U/G	51
Provost Street	N1	S Mon-Fri 07.00-18.30	100
Queensway	W2	U/G*	300
Queensway, Arthur Court (north end of Queensway)	W2	U/C*	85
Ridgmount Place	WC1	S	85
Rivington Street	EC2	S	40
Rochester Row	SW1	M/S*	299
Rodwell House, Middlesex Street	E1	U/G*	180
Royal Garden Hotel, Kensington	W8	U/G*	160
Russell Court, Woburn Place	WC1	U/G*	110
Russell Road	W14	S	250
Russell Square, Imperial Hotel	WC1	U/G	140
Saffron Hill, St Cross Street	EC1	M/S	355
St Georges Circus	SE1	S	150
St Pancras Station	NW1	S	50
Savoy Place, Victoria Embankment (Adelphi Garage Tel 071–836 4838)	WC2	U/G*	70
Seacoal Lane, Hillgate House	EC4	U/G*	120
Semley Place, Ebury Street	SW1	M/S*	422
Shoe Lane, International Press Centre	EC4	U/G	70
Shoreditch High Street (one-way, north/south direction), near junction Commercial Street	E1	S* C&L	300
Skinner Street	EC1	U/G	250
Smithfield Central Market	EC1	U/G C	450
Smithfield Street	EC1	S	100
Smithfield Surface, Hosier Lane	EC1	S	45
Snowhill (off Farringdon Street)	EC1	U/G	126
Snowsfield, Kipling Street	SE1	M/S	493
Spitalfields, Whites Row	E1	M/S*	450
Swan Lane	EC4	M/S	450
Swiss Centre, Leicester Square	WC2	U/G	90
Torrens Street	N1	S	60
Tottenham Court Road, Adeline Place YMCA	WC1	M/S*	450
Tower Hill,	EC3	U/G C & Ch	195
Lower Thames Street			
Trafalgar Square, Spring Gardens	SW1	U/G*	340
Upper St Martin's Lane	WC2	M/S	165
Upper Tooting Road, Castle Hotel	SW17	S	75
Vauxhall Bridge Foot, Vauxhall Station	SW8	S C, Ch & L*	200
Wandsworth (Arndale Centre), Buckhold Road	SW8	M/S	1,060
Wardour Street	W1	M/S*	236
Warwick Road (west side)	W14	S* C, Ch & L	350
Warwick Road, Fenelon Place	W14	S 08.00–18.00	170
Note: All Warwick Road car parks are on the west side, and north of junction West Cromwell Road and are listed in squence of approach.			
Waterloo Station Approach (British Rail SR) (Note - due to work on Channel Tunnel, terminal is likely to have capacity drastically reduced or eliminated.)	SE1	S*	157
Welbeck Street	W1	M/S	392
Westminster Bridge Road	SE1	S	80
Whitcomb Street	WC2	M/S*	300
Wilton Place, Berkeley Hotel	SW1	U/G 06.30-23.00	80
Woburn Place, Royal National Hotel	WC1	U/G 07.00-20.00	150
Young Street	W8	M/S*	250

Shops and markets

SHOPS AND MARKETS

London is one of the best cities in the world for shopping, and whatever your tastes or requirements, you will find what you want somewhere in the capital.

On the following pages are introductions to London's main shopping areas, its specialist shops, and its street and trade markets, all of which make it a uniquely exciting place to shop.

Opening times vary a good deal, especially among the smaller shops, but in general the majority of establishments – including the large stores – open from 9am to 5.30pm Monday to Saturday, and close on Sundays. The Oxford Street and Kensington High Street shops remain open every Thursday until 8pm for late-night shopping: those in Knightsbridge every Wednesday until 8pm. Many of the shops in the Covent Garden area stay open late on Fridays and Saturdays, while some of the fashionable Bond Street shops close on Saturday afternoons.

Selfridges, Oxford Street, London's second largest department store, especially popular for its large food hall, restaurants, kitchenware and cosmetic departments

Shops and markets

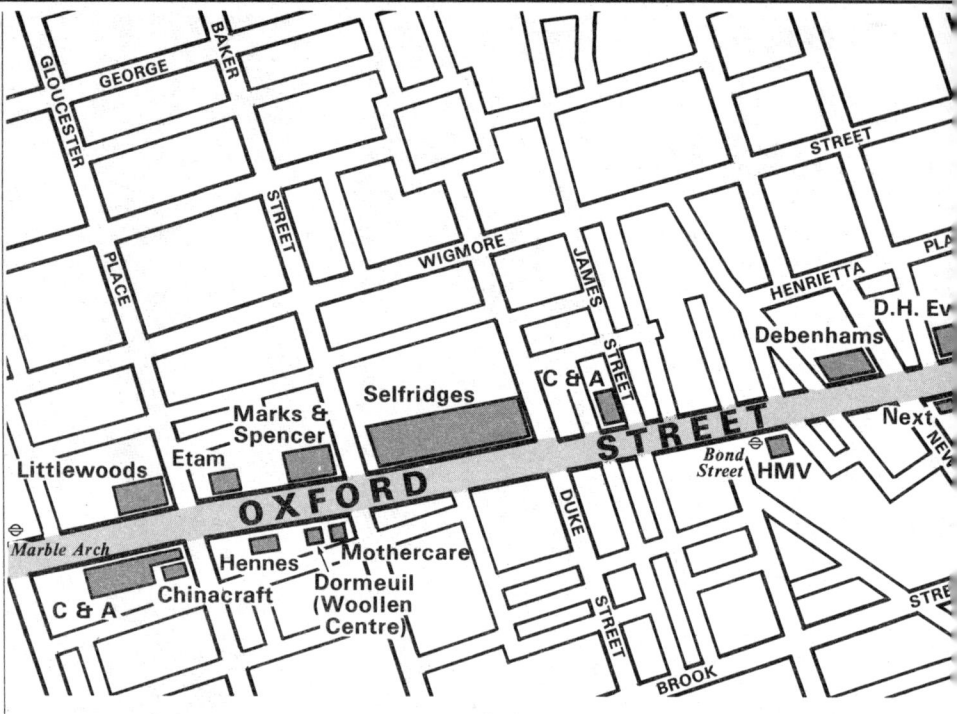

Oxford Street
MAP REF 19, 2E–21, 1C
Justifiably famous, Oxford Street is the backbone of London's shopping areas. There are no particular specialities, but it is the home of many of London's big department stores and nearly every fashion and shoe shop chain has at least one branch in the street.

The busiest stretch is between Marble Arch and Oxford Circus. Here you will find branches of *Dolcis, Russell & Bromley, Bally,* and *Saxone* (shoes); *Dorothy Perkins* and *Etam* (ladies' fashions); *Next, Hennes* and *Benetton* (fashions for both sexes); and *Littlewoods* and *C&A*, both large chain stores selling good value clothing for all the family. Also near the Marble Arch end is the largest branch of *Marks & Spencer*, a favourite with shoppers from all over the world. This open-plan store specialises in reasonably priced, well-made clothes plus high-quality food and household goods. Almost opposite you'll find everything for the pregnant mother, baby, and young child at a large branch of *Mothercare*.

Nearby is *Selfridges*, London's second-largest department store, which is especially popular for its large food hall, restaurants, kitchenware, and cosmetic departments. Other department stores along Oxford Street are *Debenhams, D H Evans,* and *John Lewis*, which is excellent for household equipment and fabrics. It has a slogan 'never knowingly undersold': if you buy something here and subsequently find it cheaper elsewhere, the store will refund the difference.

Next to the entrance to Bond Street station is the *HMV* shop; with its four floors of records and tapes, it is the largest of its kind in Europe. Just past John Lewis towards Oxford Circus is a large branch of *British Home Stores*, another chain specialising in inexpensive clothing for men, women, and children, plus food and household requirements, particularly lighting. Beside the entrance to Oxford Circus station is the *Wedgwood Shop*, displaying fine pottery, porcelain, glass, and gifts; and opposite is *Top Shop/Top Man*, with its wide range of fashions for the young.

Oxford Street continues past Oxford Street station towards Tottenham Court Road, and along this stretch are yet further branches of most of the shops already mentioned, including *Marks & Spencer* and a new huge *HMV* shop.

Shops and markets

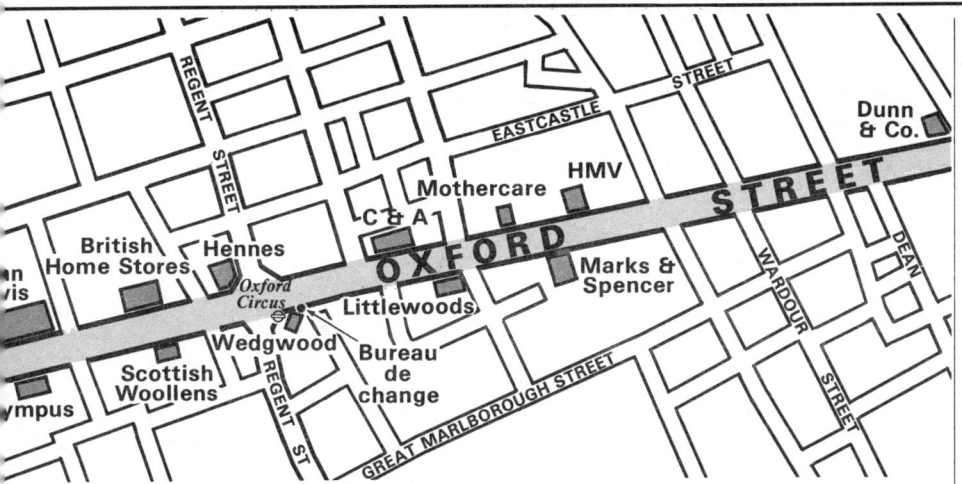

Top Shop/Top Man at Oxford Circus, fashions for the young

Shops and markets

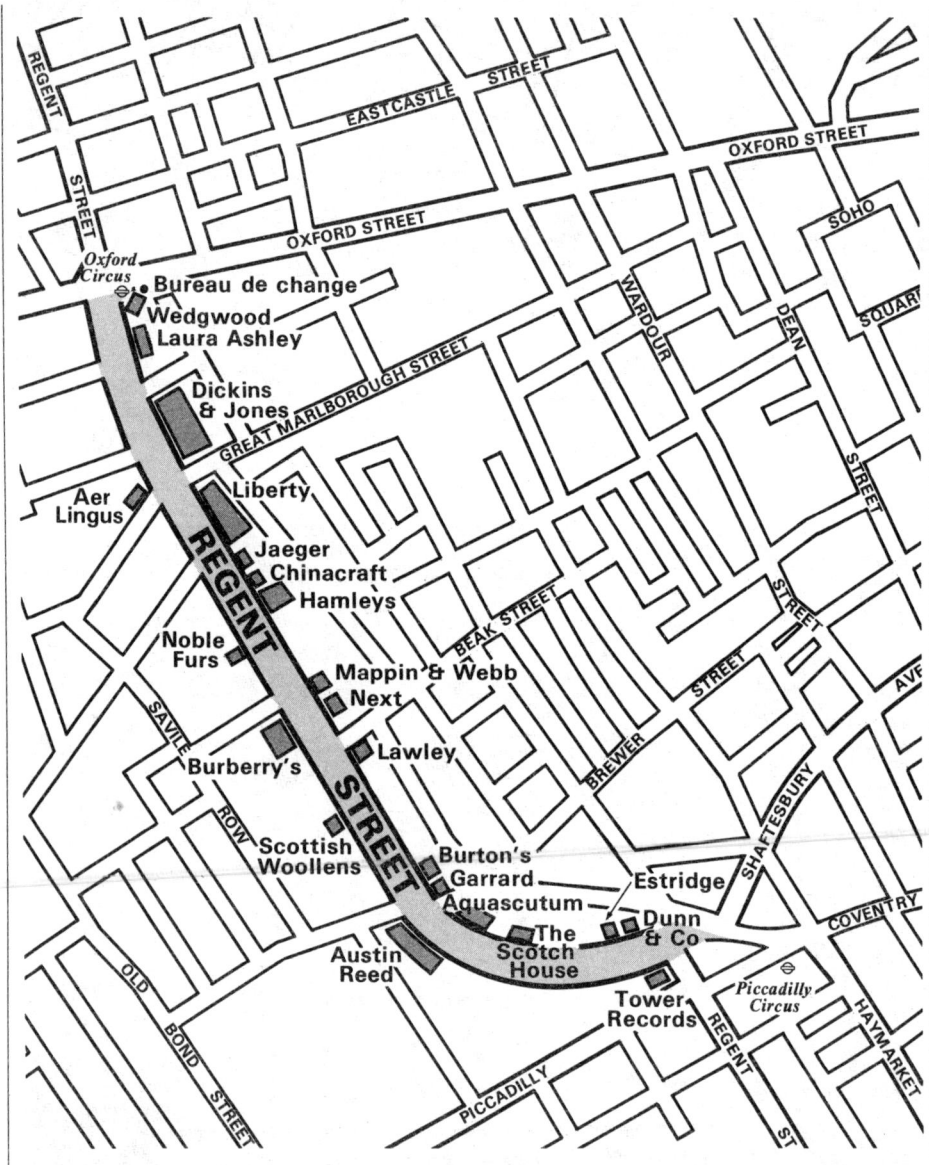

Regent Street

MAP REF 20, 1B–3C

Laid out in 1813–20 by John Nash, though totally rebuilt after 1900, Regent Street crosses Oxford Street at Oxford Circus, and is renowned for its high-class fashion shops, including some of the best-known in British fashion.

Starting at Oxford Circus and heading towards Piccadilly Circus, you soon come to Regent Street's two department stores *Dickins & Jones*, which concentrates on fashions and jewellery, and *Liberty & Co*, the landmark of the street and a most unusual building. Its neo-classical frontage is linked to a reproduction Tudor building at the rear; the half-timbering is structural, not decorative, the timbers coming from genuine men-of-war. Liberty's is world

Shops and markets

famous for its fine fabrics, silks, antiques, and fashion.

There is a branch of *Laura Ashley*, whose fabrics and fashions are now instantly recognisable the world over. *Hamleys*, the largest toy shop in the world, has several floors packed with models, toys, dolls, and games of every description. Classic British-style clothes will be found in such shops as *Jaeger*; *Austin Reed*, purveyor of high-quality men's clothing; *Aquascutum*; the *Scotch House*, notable for woollens, cashmere, and tartans; and *Burberrys*, particularly famous for its raincoats. Among the top-quality jewellers are *Mappin & Webb*, and *Garrard*, the Queen's jeweller, which is responsible for the upkeep of the Crown Jewels.

On the other side of Piccadilly Circus, in Lower Regent Street, is *Lillywhites*, an enormous sports shop, where you can find everything from wet suits to golf balls.

Below: Hamleys, the largest toy shop in the world with models, toys, dolls and games of every description.

Bond Street

MAP REF 20, 2A–2B
New Bond Street runs down from Oxford Street to Burlington Gardens, where it becomes Old Bond Street, and continues to Piccadilly. This is one of London's most expensive streets, where leading names in fashion, jewellery, and beauty salons alternate with the premises of famous art dealers.

At the Oxford Street end there are branches of all the top-quality shoe shops. The street's one department store is *Fenwick*'s, which sells mainly women's fashions. Fashion shops such as *Saint Laurent Rive Gauche, Cerruti 1881, Hermès, Gucci* – the outstanding place in London to buy handbags and beautifully-designed leather goods – *Kurt Geiger* and *Magli* are sprinkled along Bond Street and are the sort of establishments where anyone who has to ask the price can't afford it. You must stop at the breathtaking window displays of *Asprey & Co*, a treasure-house of all that is fine and rare in leather, gold, silver, jewellery, and antiques.

Aspreys, breathtaking window displays

Shops and markets

Above: Fortnum & Mason's clock, try to be there when the figurines strike the hour. Right: Burlington Arcade, a delightful covered walk with bow-fronted shops

Farther along, more beautiful goods are to be found in *Cartier*, and, opposite, *Georg Jensen*, noted for its silver and porcelain. There are a number of photographic shops in New Bond Street, notably *Dixons* and *Wallace Heaton*.

If you have the time, a stop at *Sotheby*'s (34 New Bond Street), the world-famous fine art auctioneers, is really worthwhile. Even if you don't want to buy anything or have nothing you want valued by the experts, it is great fun to wander around the previews (usually 9am to 4.30pm).

Across Burlington Gardens, into Old Bond Street, there are more fine art dealers, jewellers, oriental rug shops, and the exclusive cosmetics and perfumes of *Chanel*.

Piccadilly

MAP REF 26, 1A & 20, 3B–C
There seem to be more airlines and tourist boards represented in Piccadilly than shops, but those that are here are some of the most important names in London. Piccadilly itself was a fashionable area in the 19th century, and the shops here reflect it.

Starting from Piccadilly Circus, you come to *Simpson*, a first-class tailor and outfitter, *Hatchards*, an excellent general bookshop, and the famous name of *Fortnum & Mason*, particularly renowned for its food hall and the assistants wearing full morning dress. Try and be there when the figurines on the mechanical clock strike the hour. *Swaine & Adeney* is the classy place to go for high-quality leather goods, umbrellas and riding equipment.

Off Piccadilly, beyond Fortnums and on the opposite side of the street, you can step back in time by entering *Burlington Arcade*. This delightful covered walk is lined with bow-fronted shops selling antiques, jewellery, and knitwear. The arcade is still patrolled by a beadle in traditional dress who also closes the gates at either end each night.

The well-heeled gentleman can buy his clothes in the streets off either side of Piccadilly. He can have his shirts hand-made in *Jermyn Street*, and his suits supplied from a *Savile Row* or *Sackville Street* tailor.

Kensington High Street

DISTRICT MAP, 3C
At the western end of Hyde Park, the two roads of Kensington High Street and Kensington Church Street make up this lively and fashionable off-centre shopping area.

Kensington High Street tube station is at the heart of things and its entrance is now a new shopping arcade with a branch of *Marks & Spencer* outstanding. From the station

Shops and markets

Top: the well-heeled gentleman can have his shirts hand-made in Jermyn Street. Bottom: Covent Garden, one of the most popular shopping areas and tourist attractions in London

The King's Road
MAP REF 30, 4A–31, 1E
Once a quiet country footpath, this bustling thoroughfare became world-famous as the trendy fashion centre of the 1960s and today it is still lined with boutiques, antique shops, pubs and bistros.

Covent Garden
MAP REF 21, 2D
Since the old Flower Market closed in 1974, Covent Garden has blossomed in another way – as one of the most popular shopping areas and tourist attractions in London.

The Piazza now holds dozens of different stalls six days a week, mostly specialising in antiques, hand-made clothes, jewellery, pottery, and glass. There are shops selling an amazing array of speciality goods of individual and excellent quality – some most unusual and ultra-modern. The atmosphere of the place is enhanced by musicians and other street entertainers who seem to be performing all the time. The restored Market building is Central London's only permanent late-night shopping facility, open until 8pm six days a week. Dozens of restaurants and wine bars cater for every taste and in the adjoining streets are many fashion shops offering all kinds of up-to-the-minute designer-label gear, from knitwear, jeans and evening gowns to braces and sunglasses. Covent Garden is a definite must for every visitor to the capital.

and heading towards Kensington Gardens, you pass a branch of another clothing chain store, *British Home Stores*, before arriving at *Barker*'s. This large department store offers a wide range of international goods from fashions to food, but specialising in household ware. Near by is *Kensington Market*, a massive covered labyrinth containing over 40 up-to-date fashion boutiques and 150 stalls selling mostly antiques. Opposite is *Hyper Hyper*, one of the world's largest antique hypermarkets; make sure you have a full wallet when you visit it, as most of the goods are top collectors' items; there are also clothes and jewellery.

If you turn the other way out of the underground station, you will pass many shoe shops, more fashion chain stores, chemists, individual fashion shops such as *Jigsaw* and *Next*, branches of *Mothercare* and the big bookshop, *Waterstones*, all mingling with exotic restaurants to create a most individual atmosphere.

Kensington Church Street is a haven for antique collectors at its eastern end all the way to Notting Hill Gate, and at its western, Kensington High Street end, for those looking out for the most up-to-date in clothing.

55

Shops and markets

Knightsbridge
MAP REF 25, 2C–E
Though the Knightsbridge, Brompton Road, and Sloane Street area has some of the most luxurious fashion boutiques, antique shops and department stores in London, they all tend to be overshadowed by the magnificence of *Harrods*, the largest department store in Europe. The legend of Harrods is that it sells everything – from fresh octopus to travelling rowing machines, from alabaster bathtubs to gold-plated xylophones.

The stretch of the Brompton Road between Harrods and Sloane Street is chock-a-block with shoe shops – *St Laurent, Charles Jourdan, Rayne, Bally, Russell & Bromley* – and fashion shops, particularly *The Scotch House*, which specialises in woollens, knitwear and woven tartans. On the corner of Knightsbridge and Sloane Street is *Harvey Nichols*, a luxurious department store particularly noted for women's and children's wear as well as all kinds of furniture and furnishings.

Beauchamp Place
MAP REF 25, 3D
Not far from Harrods, you can turn off the Brompton Road into the delightful Regency Beauchamp Place, a street full of highly fashionable boutiques, top-class restaurants, and unusual antique shops, each with its own speciality.

Sloane Street
MAP REF 25, 2D–3E
This fashionable, long, straight road runs from Sloane Street station to Sloane Square; here you can buy some of the finest antique and modern furniture, and gifts, in the country. Here too you can look at top Japanese designer fashion in *Issey Miyake, Kenzo* and *Yohji Yamamota*. Definitely worth a visit at the Sloane Square end is the *General Trading Company* with its marvellous range of smart furniture and household goods. In Sloane Square is the large department store *Peter Jones*, a branch of the John Lewis Partnership.

Harrods, the largest department store in Europe.

Whiteleys, Queensway
MAP REF 18, 2A
Just off the Bayswater Road, Queensway, with its own selection of high street shops, leads to what used to be Whiteleys department store. The old store has been given a new lease of life by being completely redeveloped into a modern spacious shopping precinct, with a big *Marks &*

Shops and markets

Spencer on two floors covering one whole side. The rest of the development consists of bright speciality shops selling clothes, shoes, gifts, novelties, books, etc. The whole of the top floor is devoted to food and drink, with a good variety of restaurants and snack bars, confectioners and off-licences.

SPECIALITY STREETS

Charing Cross Road
MAP REF 21, 1C–3D
At the southern end of Tottenham Court Road, running down to Trafalgar Square, Charing Cross Road is a magnet for scholars and musicians. There is a great variety of new and second-hand bookshops, many of the latter specialising in antique and out-of-print volumes. *Foyles*, the largest bookshop in London, has a stock of over four million volumes; here you can find any new book you like, provided you are prepared to search for it. Almost next door is a large branch of *Waterstones*, and further down the road *Books Etc*, with a permanent bargain basement. *Zwemmer*'s carry the most extensive stock of English and foreign books on art and architecture in London. There are several narrow pedestrian precincts linking Charing Cross Road with St Martin's Lane: *Cecil Court*, in particular, is lined with antiquarian and second-hand bookshops. Of the many shops selling music and musical instruments along and around the street, *Macari*'s is particularly notable.

Neal's Yard
WC2
MAP REF 21, 2D
A most unusual, small area sandwiched between Neal Street and Monmouth Street, where you will find a number of co-operatively run shops, stalls and eating places specialising in wholefoods and organically-grown foods. *Neal's Yard Dairy* sells many varieties of British cheeses, and there is even a wine shop. It is a particularly delicious place to visit at lunchtimes.

Old Compton Street
MAP REF 20–21, 2C
This street is famous for its exotic provision shops, the legacy of the 19th-century flood of immigrants – particularly French, Italians and Greeks – into the area.

Tottenham Court Road
MAP REF 14, 3–4C & 20–21, 1C
Running up from New Oxford Street to the Euston Road, Tottenham Court Road is now renowned for its shops selling hi-fi, electrical, and computer equipment. You can find everything from spare parts to the very latest systems. *Laskys* has an extensive range of computer stock, and *Hi-Fi Care* specialises in accessories of every kind.

Tottenham Court Road was once regarded as the furniture centre of London, and there are still a number of high-quality stores specialising in this field: *Maples* and *Heal's* are the largest, where you will find everything you need for equipping the home. There is also a branch of the *Habitat* chain, whose modern furniture, fabrics, and accessories are internationally popular. Other interesting shops are *Paperchase*, a lovely place in which to wander among unique ranges of wrapping paper, cards, posters, and other paper items, and *The Reject Shop* which stocks a wide range of seconds in pottery and all kinds of household goods.

Cecil Court, lined with antiquarian and second-hand bookshops

SPECIALIST SHOPS

Following is a selection of the establishments which specialise in a certain field. It excludes those shops already mentioned in previous pages.

ANCIENT AND OLD-ESTABLISHED SHOPS

There are a number of small, old-fashioned shops dotted around London's streets which typify the Victorian 'gaslight' image of the capital. Those mentioned below have retained their essential character and many still retain their original façades and fittings.

R Allen and Co
117 Mount Street, W1
MAP REF 19, 3E
This traditional English butcher's shop has a dark sculptured exterior and has served the residents of Mayfair for almost 200 years. It retains the mosaic wall tiles and threshold for which butchers' shops were once famous.

57

Shops and markets

Arthur Beale
194 Shaftesbury Avenue, WC2
MAP REF 21, 2C
Rope has been made by this company for something approaching 400 years. The premises were originally located on the old Fleet River. Arthur Beale is now a general chandlers selling wire, rope, rigging and charts.

J Floris
89 Jermyn Street, SW1
MAP REF 20, 3B–3C
Established in 1739, J Floris continues to sell perfume from its small but impressive premises, which are presided over by descendants of the original founder. It is considered by many to be London's leading perfumer.

Fulham Pottery
8–10 Ingate Place, SW8
DISTRICT MAP, 3D
Founded in 1671, this is said to be the oldest pottery in the country. Nowadays clay, tools and other equipment are on sale and complete beginners kits are also available for the novice.

Gieves and Hawkes
1 Savile Row, W1
MAP REF 20, 3B
A good English gentleman's suit is generally agreed to be the best in the world, and Savile Row has long been the home of England's best tailors. Gieves and Hawkes was founded in 1771 and has been making fine clothes for discerning, and frequently very eminent, clients ever since.

Inderwick's
45 Carnaby Street, W1
MAP REF 20, 2B
Inderwick's are the country's oldest pipe-makers. Their extensive stock includes all styles of pipes, from the familiar briars to more unusual hookahs, and meerschaums.

James Lock
6 St James's Street, SW1
MAP REF 26, 1B
Established as hatters for over 200 years. Lock's made the first bowler hat, known as the *Coke* after its inventor. At first glance, the shop seems little changed since Regency times.

The Old Curiosity Shop
Portsmouth Street, WC2
MAP REF 21, 1E
This venerable antique shop, which may date from the latter part of the 16th century, is said to have been the model for Charles Dickens' *Old Curiosity Shop*.

Paxton and Whitfield
93 Jermyn Street, SW1
MAP REF 20, 3B–3C
An old-established cheese shop, crammed with cheeses of every variety and of the highest standard from all over the world. An unmistakable aroma guides patrons to its portals.

Purdey
57 South Audley Street, W1
MAP REF 19, 3E
For more than 100 years, Purdey's have been the foremost makers of sporting guns. Each weapon is hand-made and today an order takes around four years to be completed.

G Smith & Sons
74 Charing Cross Road, WC2
MAP REF 21, 1C–3D
An old-fashioned tobacconists, specialising in snuff.

James Smith
53 New Oxford Street, WC1
MAP REF 21, 1D
Umbrellas and sticks of all kinds have been made and sold here since 1830. Smith's is notable for its old-fashioned signs and for the variety of its stock, which includes custom-made sword sticks and ceremonial maces for African chiefs. They also undertake repairs.

Smythson
44 New Bond Street, W1
MAP REF 20, 2A
Top-quality stationers for over a century, they are particularly noted for their own watermarked paper.

ANTIQUE SHOPS

Halcyon Days
15 Brook Street, W1
MAP REF 20, 2A
Beautiful enamel boxes are one of the specialities of this shop.

Howard Phillips
11A Henrietta Place, W1
MAP REF 20, 1A
The owner is a specialist in glass from ancient times up to 1830. The stock in this shop includes decanters, paperweights and medieval stained glass.

Spink
5 King Street, SW1
MAP REF 20, 3B
Famous as coin and medal dealers since the mid-17th century, this shop has a fascinating selection of ancient and modern coins and decorations from all parts of the world.

Strike One
51 Camden Passage, N1
DISTRICT MAP, 4D
These specialists in English 18th- and 19th-century clocks also offer a repair and restoration service.

Through the Looking Glass
563 King's Road, SW6
MAP REF 30, 4A
Specialists in 19th-century mirrors which come in an amazingly wide range of shapes and sizes.

Shops and markets

ART AND HANDICRAFT SHOPS

Candle Makers Supplies
28 Blythe Road, W14
DISTRICT MAP, 3C
Candle-making kits are sold here together with moulds and all necessary materials associated with the craft.

Craftsmen Potters Association
William Blake House
Marshall Street, W1
MAP REF 20, 2B
Work by some of the best contemporary British potters is displayed and sold here.

Handweavers Studio and Gallery
29 Haroldstone Road, Walthamstow, E17
DISTRICT MAP, 5E
This shop sells and hires looms, spinning wheels, and weaving materials. Instruction for weavers is also available.

London Diamond Centre
10 Hanover Street, W1
MAP REF 20, 2B
Diamond cutters and polishers can be seen at work here; exhibitions and displays.

London Glass Blowers Workshop
109 Rotherhithe Street, SE16
DISTRICT MAP, 3E
Glassware by Peter Layton and a small group of studio artists is for sale at the workshop and nearby gallery.

Alec Tiranti
21 Goodge Place, W1
MAP REF 14, 4B
All materials required for sculpting and wood-carving may be obtained here, including casting equipment.

Edgar Udny
83–85 Bondway, SW8
MAP REF 33, 2D
Specialises in all kinds of mosaic tiles, together with laying and cutting tools.

BUTTON AND BEAD SHOPS

The Bead Shop
43 Neal Street, WC2
MAP REF 21, 2D
All kinds of beads, from the exotic to the plain, for stringing and decorating; also kits.

The Button Queen
19 Marylebone Lane, W1
MAP REF 20, 1A
Buttons of all kinds, both modern and antique, are the speciality here.

Eaton Shell Shop
30 Neal Street, WC2
MAP REF 21, 2D
All kinds of sea shells are on sale here, together with fossils, polished and natural stones and other objects.

A Taylor
1 Silver Place, W1
MAP REF 20, 2C (*Ingestre Pl*)
Leather, horn and plastic are among the materials used to make the buttons for sale here. Buttons are also made and dyed on the premises.

BOOKS, MUSIC AND RECORDS

Children's Book Centre
237 Kensington High Street, W8
DISTRICT MAP, 3C
This shop is devoted to books for children up to the age of thirteen. Talks by authors and artists are often given and a quarterly newsletter dealing with new children's books is also available.

Cinema Bookshop
13 Great Russell Street, WC1
MAP REF 21, 1D
As the name implies, this shop is filled with books and magazines covering all aspects of the world of cinema, including biographies of stars and directors and theoretical textbooks.

Dillons
82 Gower Street, WC1
MAP REF 14, 4C (*Goodge St*)
A huge bookshop, with more than 50 specialist departments, on four floors. The University of London's bookshop.

 The London Diamond Centre
10 Hanover Street, London, W1R 9HF. Tel. 071-629 5511

At The London Diamond Centre you will see our exhibition which shows a diamond from its mining, through to cutting, sawing, shaping and final faceting and polishing.

You also have the **unique** opportunity to purchase a stone from our collection of diamonds, precious and semi-precious stones – the largest **anywhere in London** – and have it set in a ring of your choice and all at **factory prices**.

£1.00 OFF
normal admission fee of £3.45 per head, including a FREE brilliant cut stone (not a diamond) for each visitor.

10% DISCOUNT on all purchases.

Opening hours: Monday-Friday – 9.30 am-5.30 pm   Saturday – 9.30 am-1.30 pm

Shops and markets

Dobell's Jazz and Folk Record Shop
21 Tower Street, WC2
MAP REF 21, 2D
A treasure-house for all lovers of jazz, folk, and the blues, Dobell's has a huge collection of new and secondhand records. Tapes and CDs are also available. British musicians are represented as strongly as the American greats.

Dress Circle
57–59 Monmouth Street, WC2
MAP REF 21, 2D
This shop specialises in rare, deleted and currently available records, cassettes and CDs of soundtracks, stage musicals and recordings of nostalgic interest as well as of personalities. The catalogues which the shop issues reveal the astonishing amount and variety of their stock.

The Folk Shop
Cecil Sharp House, 2 Regents Park Road, NW1
DISTRICT MAP, 4D
Folk music books and records are available together with a variety of traditional folk instruments such as dulcimers, tabors, and melodeons.

A Moroni and Son
68 Old Compton Street, W1
MAP REF 21, 2C
Newspapers and magazines from all over the world are sold here.

Motor Books
33 St Martin's Court, WC2
MAP REF 21, 2D
Literature on all aspects of the motor car is available here, together with volumes dealing with motorcycles and aircraft.

Stanford's
12 Long Acre, WC2
MAP REF 21, 2D
Maps and guides are the speciality here. The guide book section is one of London's most extensive, and there are not only maps of Britain (including very large-scale Ordnance Survey maps) but also of a wide range of foreign cities and countries. General books are also sold.

CLOTHING SHOPS

Berman and Nathan
18 Irving Street, WC2
MAP REF 21, 3C
An old-established theatrical costumiers, with hire service.

Gallery of Antique Costume & Textiles
2 Church Street, NW8
MAP REF 12, 4B–4C
Specialists in period clothing from 1830 to 1930, the Gallery also stocks shawls, bags and other accessories.

John Lobb
9 St James's Street, SW1
MAP REF 20, 3B
Craftsmen can be seen at work in this old-established bespoke shoemakers, which has long been a byword for traditional boots and shoes of the highest quality.

Moss Bros
27 King Street, WC2
MAP REF 21, 2D
This is the most famous clothing hire firm in Britain. At its smart new shop, high-quality suits and women's wear are sold, and here and at other branches clothes for all occasions are available for hire and can be altered to suit individual requirements.

Pineapple Dance Warehouse
7 Langley Street, WC2
MAP REF 21, 2D
A combined studio and shop, where all kinds of dance wear and a large selection of leisure and activity wear, including shoes, can be bought.

Janet Reger
2 Beauchamp Place, SW3
MAP REF 25, 3D
Super-luxury lingerie in silk, satin, crepe-de-chine and lace.

Patricia Roberts
31 James Street (off Long Acre), WC2
MAP REF 21, 2D
Highly individual designer knitwear is available here, along with exotic wools and Patricia Roberts' own knitting patterns.

FOOD SHOPS

Bendicks Chocolates
53 Wigmore Street, W1
MAP REF 20, 1A
Some 32 varieties of handmade chocolates are on sale here including bittermints and mint crisps.

Ceres
269a Portobello Road, W11
DISTRICT MAP, 4C
A health food store with a wide selection of goods, including breads and cakes.

Cranks
Unit 11, Covent Garden Market, WC2
MAP REF 21, 2D
A health and vegetarian shop, with its own wholegrain store.

Curry Shop
37 The Market, Covent Garden, WC2
MAP REF 21, 2D
All the items needed to make curry are available here, including cooking implements, serving dishes, tablewear and a wide variety of herbs, spices, sauces, pulses and the like.

Fratelli Camisa
1a Berwick Street, W1
MAP REF 20, 2C
A delicious, family-run Italian delicatessen, whose specialities are cheeses and home-made sausages.

Shops and markets

H R Higgins
79 Duke Street, W1
MAP REF 19, 1E
This old-established shop sells over 30 types of coffee, plus a range of teas.

Justin de Blank (provisions)
42 Elizabeth Street, SW1
MAP REF 26, 3A
High-quality take-away foods are presented here. All kinds of fresh quiches and pies, plus many kinds of preserved food are available.

Markovitch
371–373 Edgware Road, W2
MAP REF 12, 4B
Specialists in Kosher food – meat, groceries, hot beef sandwiches, etc.

Prestat
14 Princes Arcade, Piccadilly, SW1
MAP REF 20, 3C
A small confectionery shop specialising in their own exclusive chocolate.

Twinings
216 The Strand, WC2
MAP REF 22, 2A
A famous tea merchant in a fascinating shop. Twinings have had premises here since 1716.

MODEL AND TOY SHOPS

Barnums Carnival Novelties Ltd
67 Hammersmith Road, W14
DISTRICT MAP, 3C
Masks, false noses and many varieties of false beards, moustaches and other novelties are on sale here.

Davenport Magic Shop
7 Charing Cross Underground Concourse, Strand, WC2
MAP REF 21, 3D
The sign showing a rabbit emerging from the traditional top hat proclaims an abundance of conjurers' equipment (professionals get their supplies here).

Kay Desmonde
17 Kensington Church Walk, W8
DISTRICT MAP, 3C
A huge collection of English, French and German dolls, mostly dating from the early 19th century.

The Doll's House
Unit 29, The Market, Covent Garden, WC2
MAP REF 21, 2D
Reproduction and some antique doll's houses are displayed here, but it is very much a collectors' shop. Miniature dolls and furnishings are also available.

Just Games
71 Brewer Street, W1
MAP REF 20, 2C
Specialists in adult board games, war games, card games and puzzles.

The Kite Store
69 Neal Street, WC2
MAP REF 21, 2D
Sells ready-made kites, materials for making them and books on the subject. Also available are model hot air balloons.

Steam Age, Mechanical Antiquities
19 Abingdon Road, W8
DISTRICT MAP, 3C
Engines, railways and steam-boats, mostly collectors' items.

Tradition
5A Shepherd Street, W1
MAP REF 26, 1A
All kinds of lead soldiers are sold here. The stock ranges from Greek and Roman to modern soldiers and includes painted and unpainted items. Antique uniforms and swords are also available.

MISCELLANEOUS SHOPS

Anything Left-Handed
65 Beak Street, W1
MAP REF 20, 2B
Just what the name implies. Scissors, tin-openers, pen nibs, gardening, kitchen and needlework aids are all available, along with left-handed playing cards (with the symbols showing on all four corners).

F H Brundle
75 Culford Road, N1
DISTRICT MAP, 4E
Specialists in nails. All kinds available – wire nails, square nails, lath nails, etc, in fact everything for the DIY man.

L Cornelissen and Son
105 Great Russell Street, WC1
MAP REF 21, 1D
Artist's materials are sold here but an interesting speciality are the quill pens and quills from which pens can be made.

Floral Design
1 St Alban Studios, South End Row, W8
MAP REF 24, 2A
Dried and artificial flowers and plants of all kinds, even hand-made silk trees, are available here.

The Glasshouse
65 Long Acre, WC2
MAP REF 21, 2D
Glassblowers may be seen at work on the premises. All kinds of handblown articles are on sale.

Thomas Goode
19 South Audley Street, W1
MAP REF 19, 3E
This company has produced top-quality china for around 150 years, with numerous crowned heads, including Queen Victoria, among its customers. Personal crests or monograms can be provided.

61

Shops and markets

Berwick Street Market running through the heart of Soho

Keith Johnson & Pelling
11 Great Marlborough Street, W1
MAP REF 20, 2B
Specialists in cameras, both new and second-hand, this shop will also do camera repairs and process film.

STREET MARKETS

There is very little that cannot be bought in a London street market. Whether you want to pick up a bargain or buy an antique worth thousands, choose from the best meat and vegetable produce in the country, watch the traders at work, or just soak up the colourful atmosphere, there is a market to suit you.

Berwick Street Market
W1
MAP REF 20, 2C
This cheerful, cluttered market runs through the heart of Soho. The stallholders are noted for their generally good humoured banter as they clamour to attract customers. Fruit and vegetable stalls predominate here, but shellfish, clothing and household goods are also available, and some of the stalls are attached to neighbouring shops. The market is especially crowded at lunchtimes, as shoppers queue up at stalls which are reputed to sell some of the best quality fruit and vegetables in London.

Brixton Market
Electric Avenue, SW9
DISTRICT MAP, 3D
This market has a distinct Caribbean flavour, with much exotic food on display. There are also second-hand clothes and household goods stalls, and the entire market is enlivened by the compulsive rhythms of West Indian music.
  Monday–Saturday (Wednesday am only)

Camden Lock
Chalk Farm Road, NW1
DISTRICT MAP, 4D
The rich cram of stalls here, many presided over by young and enthusiastic traders, spreads inside and outside the buildings around the attractive

Shops and markets

Fruit and vegetable stalls predominate at Berwick Street

canal loch. You will find antiques, bric-à-brac, hand-knitwear, new and second-hand clothes, jewellery, ceramics and food stalls. Cafés, restaurants and chic shops selling pine furniture, trendy clothes and all kinds of oddities are dotted along the opposite side of the road, and further markets stretch towards Camden Town, with more clothes stalls, and a good cheese stall in the small fruit and vegetable market in Inverness Street.

Camden Passage
Off Upper Street, N1
DISTRICT MAP, 4D
A rich and varied mixture of antique shops and stalls. A holiday atmosphere pervades the market, largely because the majority of the traders give the impression of thoroughly enjoying their work. A few of the shopkeepers have been known to carry relaxation to the extreme by conducting their business from the Camden Head, the market's adopted pub, leaving a note on the shop door to direct prospective customers to their temporary premises. The arcades of the market become very crowded on Saturdays, and only those arriving early can hope to find a bargain. Camden Passage is as good a place as any for a wide variety of antiques, with dealers specialising in furniture, jewellery, prints, pottery, books, pub mirrors, period clothing and silverware.
Wednesday and Saturday

Chapel Market
White Conduit Street, N1
DISTRICT MAP, 4D
This rather congested market is very popular with the locals at weekends. Fruit and vegetables are always available, and there are usually stalls selling fish, groceries, and household goods.
*Tuesday–Sunday
Thursday & Sunday am*

Church Street and Bell Street
Lisson Grove, NW8
MAP REF 12–13, 4C
A mixture of stalls is to be found in these adjacent markets. Antiques are well represented, as are clothes, household and food stalls.
Tuesday–Sunday

Columbia Road Market
Shoreditch, E2
MAP REF 17, 2E
An enormous variety of flowers, plants, and shrubs make this market a Mecca for all gardening enthusiasts.
Sunday am

East Street Market
Walworth, SE17
DISTRICT MAP, 3D
This is an old-established general market with some bric-à-brac stalls. Plants and fruit are usually available on Sundays.
*Friday and Saturday;
Tuesday–Thursday and
Sunday am.*

Jubilee Market
Covent Garden, WC2
MAP REF 21, 2D
There are fruit, vegetable, and bric-à-brac stalls, and antiques (Mon), general goods (Tue–Fri), crafts (Sat & Sun).
Monday–Sunday

63

Shops and markets

Leadenhall Market
Gracechurch Street, EC3
MAP REF 23, 2D
There has been a market in the general area of this site since the 14th century. Samuel Pepys recorded in his diary that he purchased a 'leg of beef, a good one, for sixpence' here. While still specialising in meat and poultry, Leadenhall also offers fish, vegetables, and plants. The Victorian arcade, containing cafés and pubs as well as rows of carcasses suspended on tiers of hooks outside the shops, is noted for its old-world market atmosphere, and is a favourite lunch-time haunt for City office workers.
Monday–Friday

Leather Lane
Holborn, EC1
MAP REF 22, 1A
Fruit, groceries, vegetables, clothing, household goods of all descriptions – particularly crockery – are always on display here, and some of the most vociferous and quick-witted stallholders in the capital provide a feast of noisy entertainment for the vast crowds who throng the market which fills this narrow street during the lunch-hour. Bargains abound and the sight of an entire dinner service being expertly tossed in the air is a regular occurence, and one which never fails to impress.
Monday – Friday lunchtimes

Lower Marsh and The Cut
Lambeth, SE1
MAP REF 28, 1A
This busy general market with many clothes stalls nestles in the shadow of Waterloo Station and becomes very popular during the lunch period.
Monday–Friday lunchtimes

Leadenhall Market, specialising in meat and poultry, its Victorian arcade houses cafés and pubs

New Caledonian Market
Bermondsey Square, SE1
DISTRICT MAP, 3E
The Old Caledonian Market moved to this site from Islington after the end of World War II, and its modern offspring is now primarily a dealers' antique market. An enormous selection of articles is on view, set out on closely-packed stalls, but you need to get there early to pick up a bargain; trading begins at 5am. Although something of a closed community, run principally by dealers for dealers, private collectors and casual visitors are made very welcome.
Friday am

Northcote Road
Battersea, SW11
DISTRICT MAP, 3D
A fruit and vegetable market at its busiest on Saturdays.
Monday–Saturday

North End Road
Fulham, SW6
DISTRICT MAP, 3C
This general market specialises in fruit and vegetables, and flowers and plants are on sale during the summer months.
Monday–Saturday

Shops and markets

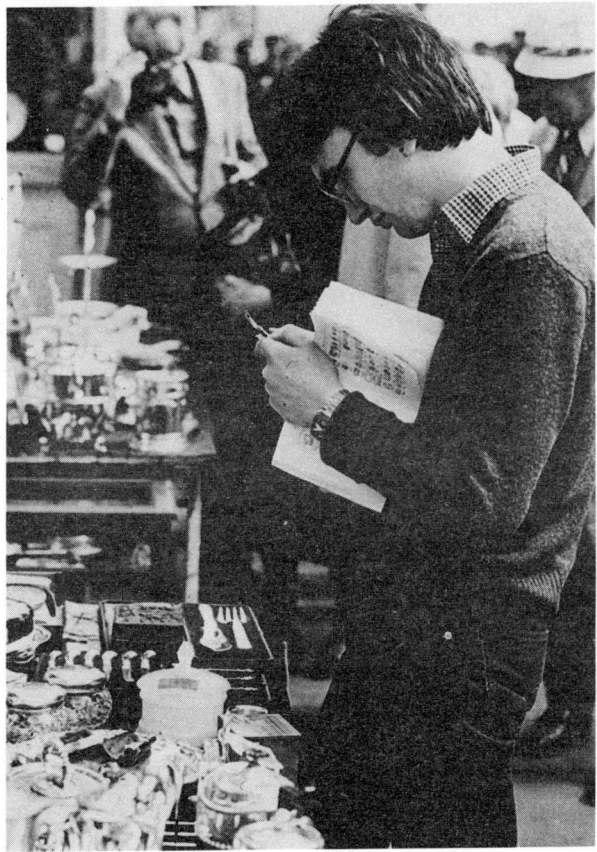

Portobello Road Market, over 2,000 stalls of household items, clothes, jewellery, Victoriana and junk

Petticoat Lane
Middlesex Street, E1
MAP REF 23, 1E
This most famous of all London markets got its name during the 17th century because of the number of old clothes dealers who congregated here. It opens around 9am, but the stallholders begin to set up their premises about 7.30am before an interested audience of sightseers. Despite its present-day cosmopolitan atmosphere, engendered by the Indian, West Indian, and Jewish communities which are prevalent in the area, Petticoat Lane still retains its essential Cockney character. The maze of stalls occupies every available corner, and there is very little in the way of household goods and clothes of every description that cannot be purchased.
Sunday am

Portobello Road
Notting Hill, W11
DISTRICT MAP, 4C
A general market with fruit, vegetable and meat stalls operates all the week, but it is at its best on Saturdays. Then all the stalls and shops open – more than 2,000 of them – containing all kinds of furniture, clothes, jewellery, ancient gramophones and records, books, bottles, coins, medals, toys, a great deal of Victoriana, and an endless selection of junk. Buskers, street singers, photographers (some with monkeys), jostle with the crowds. It is rare to find a genuine bargain in the antique stalls at the lower end of the road these days, since all the traders are experts, but real finds can sometimes be made amongst the piles of junk on the stalls beyond the Westway Flyover. A great cosmopolitan atmosphere.
Monday–Saturday

Ridley Road
Hackney, E8
DISTRICT MAP, 4E
One of the better known of London's East End markets, the stalls here are patronised by the local Jewish and West Indian communities. It is a general market, with many fruit and vegetable stalls, and becomes very crowded on Saturdays.
Monday–Saturday (Thursday am only)

Roman Road
Tower Hamlets, E3
DISTRICT MAP, 4E
A busy market with stalls on either side of the road offering a good variety of fashion and other wares.
Thursday am and Saturday

Shepherd's Bush
W12
DISTRICT MAP, 3C
A general market stretching alongside and under the railway viaduct between Shepherd's Bush and Goldhawk Road.
Monday–Saturday (Thursday am only)

Shops and markets

Walthamstow
The High Street, E17
DISTRICT MAP, 5E
This extensive general market straggles along either side of Walthamstow's main street. It is particularly busy towards the end of the week.
Monday–Saturday (Wednesday am only)

Whitecross Street
EC2
MAP REF 17, 3C
A busy market which caters, to a large extent, for lunch-time shoppers. It is particularly crowded on Wednesdays and Fridays.
Monday–Friday

TRADE MARKETS

Noise, a rich variety of smells, and seeming confusion typify London's wholesale markets. In fact, all the business is carried out with breathtaking efficiency. Although the public is admitted, hordes of visitors are not encouraged; you have to be there early to see the markets in full swing.

Billingsgate
North Quay, West India Docks, Isle of Dogs, E14
DISTRICT MAP, 3E
The first official mention of this historic wholesale fish market was made as long ago as the end of the 13th century, when a royal charter was granted to the Corporation of London for the sale of fish. A market is known to have been held on Billingsgate's old site in Lower Thames Street in the City of London at least 400 years earlier. From about 5am, Tuesday–Sunday, the market becomes a hive of activity and the air is pervaded by a pungent aroma of fish and the uninhibited language of the porters. By 8am most of the business is over and about 300 tons of fish will have changed hands.

Borough Market
Stoney Street, SE3
MAP REF 23, 4D
This fruit and vegetable market claims a direct descent from the market which was held on London Bridge in the 13th century; it was moved to the present site in 1757. It operates from Monday to Saturday, with traders commencing business as early as 3am. Activity builds up in a crescendo of noise and bustle between 6 and 7am, and most of the business has been completed by the middle of the morning.

New Covent Garden
Nine Elms, SW8
MAP REF 32, 4C & 33, 3D
To the sorrow of many people – as the original Covent Garden had a unique and irreplaceable character – this famous fruit, vegetable, and flower market was moved in 1974 to its present purpose-built premises beside the river at Vauxhall. Trading begins about 4am; the flower market is on Saturdays during the summer.

Smithfield
Charterhouse Street, EC1
MAP REF 16, 4B
Smithfield is London's principal wholesale meat market, and its annual turnover of some 200,000 tons of produce makes it one of the largest meat, poultry, and provision markets in the world. The total area covered by all the market buildings is over eight acres. The site has great historical significance as the scene of tournaments and fairs, and has had livestock connections since the 12th century. Trading begins at 5am, Monday to Friday.

Spitalfields
Commercial Street, E1
MAP REF 17, 4E
Named after the priory of St Mary Spital which was founded here in 1197, Spitalfields refers both to the area and to the wholesale market, which trades in fruit, vegetables, and flowers. The market covers five acres to the east of Liverpool Street Station, on a site which was once a Roman burial ground. There are extensive underground chambers, used principally for ripening bananas, beneath the market. Trading begins at 4.30am every weekday and is generally completed by 9am.

Smithfield, London's principal wholesale meat market, one of the largest in the world, covering over eight acres and selling some 200,000 tons of produce a year

Churches and cathedrals

The interior of Brompton Oratory, rich in marble and mosaic decoration

CHURCHES AND CATHEDRALS

London's churches suffered great damage during the Fire of 1666 and, much later, the air raids of World War II. Of those which stand today, most date from the 17th and 18th centuries, but there are some earlier survivors, and a number of superb Victorian examples. A selection of the most interesting is given on the following pages.

All Hallows
London Wall, EC2
MAP REF 22/23, 1C/D
A stretch of the Roman wall which once surrounded the City of London can be seen in the churchyard. The church itself was designed by George Dance the Younger in the 18th century; its elegant and sumptuously decorated interior is by Sir John Soane. Exhibitions of church art are held here.

All Souls'
Langham Place, W1
MAP REF 20, 1B
John Nash designed and built this large church in 1822 to close the northward vista of Regent Street. It has a circular Classical portico surmounted by a slender needle spire.

Brompton Oratory
Brompton Road, SW3
MAP REF 25, 3C/4D
An imposing Roman Catholic church built in Italian Renaissance style at the end of the 19th century. Its interior is rich in marble and mosaic decoration and the nave is a remarkable 51ft wide.

Holy Trinity
Sloane Street, SW1
MAP REF 25, 2D/3E
Magnificent stained-glass windows designed by Edward Burne-Jones and made by William Morris light the interior of this splendid 19th-century church. It was designed by J D Sedding, one of the principal architects of the Arts and Crafts Movement. At present the church is only open on Sundays because of improvement work.

Churches and cathedrals

Left: the 14th-century doorway of St Ethelburga-the-Virgin, Bishopsgate. Right: an interior view of St Bartholomew the Great, which dates from the 12th century

St Alfege

Church Street, Greenwich, SE10
DISTRICT MAP, 3E
Built in 1718 to the designs of Nicholas Hawksmoor, this church houses the tombs of General Wolfe (d.1759) and the 'father of English church music', Thomas Tallis. (Closed Mondays.)

St Anne Limehouse

Commercial Road, E14
DISTRICT MAP, 4E
One of Hawksmoor's spectacular Classical-style East End churches. It was built in 1712 and has recently been designated a Grade II listed building, within The Limehouse conservation area.

St Bartholomew the Great

West Smithfield, EC1
MAP REF 22, 1B
This is one of the few surviving examples of Norman architecture in London. It dates from the 12th century and is the chancel of a great Norman monastery church which once stood here. It contains a fine oriel window, the font where Hogarth was baptised in 1697 and a half-timbered Elizabethan gatehouse above a 13th-century arch.

St Ethelburga-the-Virgin

Bishopsgate, EC2
MAP REF 23, 1E
Entered by a 14th-century doorway, this tiny medieval building is one of the best preserved of the City's pre-Fire churches. Closed temporarily for repairs.

St Etheldreda, or Ely Chapel

Ely Place, EC1
MAP REF 16, 4A
Originally built in the 13th century as the chapel of a palace of the Bishops of Ely, the structure is two-storeyed and has a massive vaulted undercroft dating from 1252. It is the oldest pre-Reformation Roman Catholic church in London.

St George

Bloomsbury Way, WC1
MAP REF 21, 1D
Noted for its striking façade, this 18th-century church was built by Nicholas Hawksmoor.

St Giles-in-the-Field

St Giles High Street, WC2
MAP REF 21, 1D
This church's fine 161ft Baroque steeple makes it a prominent landmark. A church was founded on this site by

Churches and cathedrals

St John, Smith Square, one of the many London churches damaged by air raids in World War II. The fine Baroque-style building is now used as a music and cultural centre

St James Garlickhythe
Upper Thames Street, EC4
MAP REF 23, 2C
Founded as long ago as the 12th century, the present church on this site was built by Wren after the Great Fire, and is one of his more elaborate designs. Its most distinguishing exterior feature is the handsome spire. The interior, which was restored after bomb damage, has excellent woodwork, as well as ironwork hat racks and sword rests. The church reputedly owes its name to the fact that garlic was once sold near by.

St John
Smith Square, SW1
Tel 071-734 4511
MAP REF 27, 3D
This notable Baroque-style church (1713-28) by Thomas Archer was gutted during World War II, and now serves as a musical and cultural centre.

St Lawrence Jewry
Gresham Street, EC2
MAP REF 23, 1C
Rebuilt by Wren on the site of a medieval church, this church stands in the forecourt of the Guildhall. The name Jewry has survived from the period between 1066 and 1290 when the neighbourhood had a large Jewish population. The church was rebuilt after bomb damage, and the present spire incorporates a replica of the incendiary bomb which gutted the interior. It is the guild church of the Corporation of London.

Matilda, the wife of Henry I, in the 12th century, but the present building dates from the 18th century. It was beautifully restored in 1952-53, and has superb interior decorations and fittings.

St Helen Bishopsgate
Great St Helen's, EC3
MAP REF 23, 1E
One of the largest churches in the City, this magnificent structure was built in the 13th century and was originally two churches joined by an arcade of pillars. The church is famous for its beautiful brasses, two fine sword-rests (one dating from 1665 and very rare), and a carved Jacobean pulpit.

St James's
Piccadilly, W1
MAP REF 20, 3B
A Wren church of 1676 with a magnificent galleried interior beneath a barrel-vaulted ceiling. The font, reredos, altarpiece, and organ case are all the work of the master-woodcarver and sculptor, Grinling Gibbons.

Churches and cathedrals

St Martin-in-the-Fields, a shelter for the homeless by night

St Martin-in-the-Fields
Trafalgar Square, WC2
Tel 071–930 1862
MAP REF 21, 3D
The medieval church on this site was extensively rebuilt by James Gibbs in the early 18th century. It has an imposing temple-like portico, and a spacious galleried interior. Buckingham Palace is within the parish boundaries, and there are royal boxes at the east end of the church. The vaulted crypt contains a 16th-century chest and an 18th-century whipping post, but is better known for the fact that it is opened each evening as a shelter for the homeless.

St Mary-le-Bow
Cheapside, EC2
MAP REF 23, 2C
Restored by Wren after the Great Fire, this church was extensively fire-damaged during the Blitz. Wren's steeple survived, however, and still towers over Cheapside. The famous Bow Bells originally rang as a curfew. Those born within their sound are said to be true Cockneys.

St Paul's
Covent Garden, WC2
MAP REF 21, 2D
The first new Anglican church to be built in London after the Reformation, St Paul's was designed by Inigo Jones between 1631 and 1633, and is known as the Actors' Church.

St Paul's Cathedral
Ludgate Hill, EC4
Tel 071–248 2705
MAP REF 22, 2B
Wren's crowning masterpiece, begun in 1675 after the Great Fire. The beautiful central dome rises to a height of 365ft and around its interior is the famous Whispering Gallery, where a message whispered into the wall on one side can clearly be heard 112ft away on the other side. The Gallery is reached through a doorway in the western corner of the South Transept that leads to the stairs, which also give access to the library and the two external galleries of the dome with their panoramic views across London. From the end of the nave there is a superb view along the whole length of the cathedral through the Choir to the High Altar and its ornate canopy, the focal point of the whole building. The altar is a modern replacement of the one which was damaged during World War II, and is an exact copy of Wren's original design. The cathedral contains numerous chapels, many of which include exquisite furniture and decorations. Holy Communion is celebrated on most days in the Chapel of St Dunstan at the western end of the cathedral. The crypt contains the tombs of Wren, Nelson, Wellington, Reynolds and Turner, and among other notable monuments is the 17th-century effigy of John Donne, poet and Dean of the Cathedral, which survived the Great Fire. The wooden choir stalls are by Grinling Gibbons, the Royal master carver.

Top right: interior of St Paul's Cathedral, Wren's crowning masterpiece. Bottom right: St Paul's, where the Prince and Princess of Wales were married in 1981

Churches and cathedrals

Westminster Abbey
Parliament Square, SW1
Tel 071–222 5152
MAP REF 27, 2D
Edward the Confessor was determined to have the abbey at Westminster enlarged and made the crowning-place of English kings; his Norman church was consecrated on 28 December 1065, and every English sovereign since has been crowned here. All that remains of Edward the Confessor's building are the Chamber of Pyx (once the Royal Treasury) and the Norman Undercroft (which now houses a museum). The whole abbey was rebuilt from 1245 to 1269 in honour of Edward, and rebuilding continued throughout the 15th and early 16th centuries. The 225ft-high towers were added in the mid–18th century by Nicholas Hawksmoor. Much 19th-century renovation has marred the external detail, but the abbey's proportions still give a sense of continuity and permanence. The graceful flying buttresses and the delicately shaped walls of the Henry VII Chapel make it one of the most impressive sights

Churches and cathedrals

A medieval roof boss from Southwark Cathedral depicting the devil devouring Judas Iscariot

Westminster Cathedral
Ashley Place, Victoria Street, SW1
MAP REF 26, 3B
The principal Roman Catholic cathedral in Britain was built between 1895 and 1903 in an Italian-Byzantine style by the distinguished architect J F Bentley. It is an imposing building, with a 273ft campanile and the widest nave in England. The most outstanding works of the interior are Eric Gill's early 20th-century Stations of the Cross.

Among the other outstanding Wren City Churches are: *St Andrew*, Holborn Circus, EC1, which contains the organ (given by Handel in 1750), font, and pulpit from the Foundling Hospital; *St Anne and St Agnes*, Gresham Street, EC2, with its fine collection of ecclesiastical antiquities; *St Benet*, Paul's Wharf, off Queen Victoria Street, EC4, the Welsh Metropolitan Church; *St Bride*, Fleet Street, EC4; *St Clement Danes*, Strand, WC2, the memorial church of the RAF; *St Clement Eastcheap*, Clements Lane, EC4; *St Magnus the Martyr*, Lower Thames Street, EC3, containing outstanding woodwork; *St Margaret Pattens*, Rood Lane, Eastcheap, EC3, with two canopied pews, one marked C W; *St Martin-within-Ludgate*, Ludgate Hill, EC4; *St Mary Abchurch*, Abchurch Lane, EC4, containing Grinling Gibbons reredos of 1686 and a notable painted dome; and *St Stephen Walbrook*, Walbrook, EC4.

in the capital, particularly when viewed from Parliament Square or Dean's Yard to the south.

The Abbey presents a stunning array of historical and commemorative monuments and memorials in a setting of outstanding architectural beauty. There are elaborately carved royal tombs, including that of Elizabeth I; memorials to the nation's statesmen, politicians, scientists, servicemen; and the famous Poets' Corner. The Coronation Throne, with the historic Stone of Scone, and the Tomb of the Unknown Warrior, brought from Flanders in 1920, attract particular attention.

Southwark Cathedral
Borough High Street, SE1
Tel 071–407 3708
MAP REF 23, 3D
A church has stood on this site since the 7th century, but it was not until 1905 that the basically 16th-century parish church of St Saviour was elevated to cathedral status. Despite rebuilding, particularly during the 19th century, its medieval Gothic style has remained largely intact, and parts of the church date back to at least the 13th century. It is, after Westminster Abbey, the most important Gothic building in London.

The new extension has a restaurant and Chapter House.

Palaces

PALACES

Buckingham Palace
The Mall, SW1
MAP REF 26, 2B
This most famous of royal homes was built in 1703 by the Duke of Buckingham, and subsequently bought by George III in 1762. Nash altered and remodelled it for George IV in 1825, but it was not much used until Victoria came to the throne in 1837. She had its huge gateway, now known as Marble Arch, moved to Tyburn. It has been the London home of the monarch ever since, and the interior is not open to the public. When the sovereign is in residence, the Royal Standard is flown. The Changing of the Guard, a colourful and very popular ceremony, is carried out by the Brigade of Guards in the forecourt most mornings (see page 10).

Royal Mews
Buckingham Palace, SW1
MAP REF 26, 2A
Designed by John Nash, the Royal Mews contain the state coaches, including the Gold State Coach of 1762 which has been used for every coronation since. In the stables are the Windsor Greys and Cleveland Bay carriage horses.
Open Wed and Thu, 2–4. Admission charge.

Greenwich
DISTRICT MAP, 3E
The best way to visit Greenwich, which has one of England's finest riverside vistas and a superb group of royal buildings, is by one of the boats which leave from Charing Cross, Westminster, or Tower Piers.

Buckingham Palace, London residence of the monarch

Royal Naval College
Consists of buildings designed by Webb and Wren, with additions by Hawksmoor, Vanbrugh, and Ripley. Formerly the Naval Hospital, it became a College in 1873. Particularly splendid are the Chapel, rebuilt in the 18th century, and the Painted Hall with its ceiling by Sir James Thornhill.
Painted Hall and Chapel only, open daily 2.30–5 (closed 25 Dec). Admission free.

Queen's House
Built by Inigo Jones for Queen Henrietta Maria as part of the original Greenwich Palace (demolished by Charles II), it now houses part of the National Maritime Museum: a notable collection of paintings, maps, and models. The Nelson collection, Navigation Room, and the Barge House are of considerable interest.
Open Mon-Sat 10–6; Sun 2–6. Weekends only Oct-Mar (closed Good Fri, 23 Dec-2 Feb). Admission charge.

Palaces

Old Royal Observatory
In Greenwich Park – which was laid out to plans by Le Nôtre, famous French gardener of the time of Louis XIV – the Observatory is now part of the National Maritime Museum, exhibiting items of astronomical, horological, and navigational interest.
Open all year, daily, 10–6 (2–6 Sun; Oct-Mar 10–5, Sun 2–5). Closed Good Fri, 23–25 Dec & 1 Jan. Admission charge.

Cutty Sark
Greenwich Pier
This famous tea clipper was the fastest to be built (in 1869). She once sailed 363 miles in a single day, and has been preserved here in dry dock since 1957.
Open Mon-Fri 10.30–5; Sun 2.30–5 (6 in summer) (closed 24–26 Dec & 1 Jan). Admission charge.

Gipsy Moth IV
Greenwich Pier
The yacht in which Sir Francis Chichester sailed single-handed round the world in 1966–67, starting the fashion for round-the-world sailing races.
Last ticket 30 minutes before closing. Open daily Apr-Oct 10–6. Admission charge.

Hampton Court Palace
DISTRICT MAP, 2B
Built by Cardinal Wolsey and passed on to Henry VIII, this magnificent group of buildings played an important part in the lives of the monarchy, and the influence of the individual kings and queens can still be seen: Henry VIII built the stunning hammer-beamed Great Hall; Elizabeth I brought plants from the New World to the gardens; William and Mary commissioned Wren to remodel parts of the palace, and his Fountain Court is particularly fine; William also created the famous maze.

The last monarch to live in Hampton Court was George II, and today it can be seen as a grand palace, filled with paintings, tapestries, and furniture recalling great moments of English history.
Open: Gardens and grounds daily, summer 7–9 (or dusk) winter 9-dusk. Banqueting House and Tudor tennis courts Apr-Sep, Mon-Sat 9.30–6.
State apartments open Apr-Sep, Mon-Sat 9.30–6; Oct-Mar, 9.30–4 (closed Good Fri, 24–26 Dec & 1 Jan). Admission charge.

Houses of Parliament and Westminster Hall
SW1
MAP REF 27, 2D
The Houses of Parliament are also known as the Palace of Westminster because from the time of Edward the Confessor to Henry VIII the site was the main London residence of the monarch.

Most of the original palace was destroyed by fire in 1834, and the present Gothic-style building was designed by Sir Charles Barry and Augustus Pugin. The two chambers of Parliament are set either side of a central hall and corridor – the House of Lords to the south and the House of Commons to the north.

At the north end is the famous Clock Tower known to all as Big Ben. The name actually refers to the huge 13½-ton bell which strikes the hours. The minute hands on the clock's four 23ft-wide dials are each as tall as a double-decker bus. It is well known for keeping perfect time; tiny adjustments are made by adding or removing old pennies to or from the mechanism.

While Parliament is in session the Union Jack flies from the south tower, Victoria Tower, by day and by night a light shines from the Clock Tower.

The House of Commons suffered bomb damage in 1941 and a new chamber was constructed to the design of Sir Giles Gilbert Scott and opened in 1950.

To gain admission to the Strangers' Galleries join the queue at St Stephen's entrance from approx 4.30pm Mon-Thu, approx 9.30am Fri (House of Commons) or from approx 2.30pm Tue & Wed, from 3pm Thu & occasionally 11am Fri (House of Lords) or by arrangement with MP (House of Commons) or Peer (House of Lords). Free, although guides require payment if employed.

Westminster Hall was originally constructed by William Rufus, son of William the Conqueror, as an addition to the Palace of Westminster. It was remodelled at the end of the 14th century: the lower parts of the Norman walls were retained and massive buttresses added to support the 600 tons of roof. An outstanding engineering feat in its day, it meant that supporting piers were no longer needed and it is the earliest surviving example of a hammer-beam roof. The Hall has miraculously survived almost intact.
Open Mon-Thu am, by arrangement with an MP only. Free although guides require payment if employed.

Kensington Palace
W8
MAP REF 24, 1A
Acquired by William III in 1689, remodelled and enlarged by Wren, the Palace is today still a royal residence, that of Princess Margaret and the

Palaces

Left: Kensington Palace Orangery. The palace is still a royal residence but state rooms are open to visitors. Bottom left: Lambeth Palace, the London home of the Archbishop of Canterbury for over 700 years

Prince and Princess of Wales. The state apartments are open to the public and contain pictures and furniture from the royal collection.
The *Court Dress Collection* displays costumes worn at court from 1750 to the present day.
Open Mon-Sat 9–5; Sun 1–5 (Closed Good Fri, 24–26 Dec & 1 Jan). Admission charge.

Kew Palace
Kew
DISTRICT MAP, 3B
Standing in the Royal Botanical Gardens, this Dutch-gabled 17th-to 18th-century house contains souvenirs of George III. Queen Charlotte died here in 1818.
Open daily Apr-Sep, 11–5.30.

Queen Charlotte's Cottage
The interior remains as it was in the 18th century when royalty were in residence.
Open Sat, Sun & Bank Hols, Apr-Sep 11–5.30. Admission charge.

Lambeth Palace
Lambeth Palace Road, SE1
MAP REF 27, 3E
Unlike other palaces, this one has no connection with royalty. It has been the London residence of the Archbishop of Canterbury for 700 years, but much of it was rebuilt during the 19th century. Of the old palace, the most interesting parts are the Lollards Tower and the Gatehouse, both of the 15th century. The palace is not open to the public.

Palaces

St James's Palace, now occupied by servants of the Crown

Lancaster House
Stable Yard, off the Mall, SW1
MAP REF 26, 1B
This massive palace was originally built in the 19th century for the 'grand old' Duke of York. Chopin played here before Queen Victoria in 1848. It is now a government hospitality centre and is not open to the public.

Marlborough House
Pall Mall, SW1
MAP REF 26, 1C
Built by Wren for the Duke of Marlborough. In 1850 it became the official residence of the Prince of Wales. George V was born here; later both Queen Alexandra and Queen Mary lived here. The house is now the Commonwealth Centre and is open by appointment.

St James's Palace
St James's Street, SW1
MAP REF 26, 1B
The original palace was started by Henry VIII in 1531 and, after the destruction of Whitehall Palace, was the sovereign's official London residence. Foreign ambassadors are still appointed to the Court of St James's. The Gatehouse facing St James's Street is the main remnant of the Tudor building, and has the initials of Henry VIII and Anne Boleyn carved over the doors. The Chapel Royal was originally built by Henry VIII but was much altered in 1837. However, the ceiling by Holbein is original.

St James's Palace is now occupied by servants of the Crown, and is not open to the public. However, services may be attended in the Chapel Royal between October and July.

Tower of London
EC3
MAP REF 23, 3E
Begun by William the Conqueror in about 1078 as a symbol of power over rebellious Londoners, the Tower stands today as perhaps the most important castle in England. As well as being used as a royal palace until the 17th century, it has also been a mint, observatory, arsenal, menagerie, public records office and, of course, state prison, mainly reserved for the high and mighty who incurred the displeasure of sovereign or government.

The nucleus of the fortress, from which it gets the name 'Tower' rather than 'Castle', is the original White Tower, which now contains the Royal Armouries – including four of Henry VIII's personal armours. Also notable here is the Chapel of St John, probably London's

Palaces

In the course of its long history (dating from about 1078) the Tower of London has been a royal palace, mint, observatory, arsenal, menagerie, public record office and state prison

most outstanding example of early Norman architecture, little changed since the 11th century.

Forming part of the Tower's inner defences is the Bell Tower, in which many famous prisoners were detained, among them Princess Elizabeth and the Duke of Monmouth.

Originally called the Garden Tower, the Bloody Tower is believed to have been the site of the murder of the little Princes by their uncle Richard III. However, the tower was not called 'Bloody' until 1597. Its most famous prisoner was probably Sir Walter Raleigh, who spent 12 years here in a specially constructed top floor. The gateway under the Bloody Tower opens out on to Tower Green, where Royal prisoners were executed. The less exalted – though equally famous – ended their days on the more public scaffold on nearby Tower Hill. In the days when the Thames was one of London's principal highways, prisoners were brought by boat from Westminster to the Tower, arriving at the infamous Traitors' Gate.

Other royal deaths associated with the Tower include those of Henry VI, who may have been murdered in 1471 in the Wakefield Tower, and the Duke of Clarence, believed to have been drowned in a butt of malmsey wine in the Bowyer Tower in 1478.

The half-timbered Queen's House is the finest example of a Tudor domestic building in London. All state prisoners were taken here on arrival, where they were searched and registered.

The Yeoman Warders – universally known as 'beefeaters' – wear a ceremonial uniform unchanged in style since the reign of Henry VIII; their everyday uniform is similar but less colourful. In the inner ward of the Tower there are tame ravens which may originate from the former king's menagerie at one time kept here. Tradition has it that if the ravens leave, the Tower will fall. Although six is the minimum requirement, eight are kept for safety's sake.

The magnificent Crown Jewels are kept underground in a new Jewel House entered from the Waterloo barracks.

The Tower is locked up each night during the Ceremony of the Keys, which the public may view by appointment only.

Open Mar-Oct, Mon-Sat 9.30–5, Sun 2–5; Nov-Feb, Mon-Sat 9.30–4 (Closed 1 Jan, Good Fri & 24–26 Dec. Jewel House closed Feb). Admission charges.

Homes

HOMES

Carlyle's House
24 Cheyne Row, Chelsea, SW3
MAP REF 31, 3C
Thomas Carlyle, one of the most distinguished essayists in the English language, moved from Scotland to London in 1834; he lived in this house in Chelsea for the rest of his life.

Here he wrote his major historical works, including *The French Revolution*, and he became known as the Sage of Chelsea. The house, now owned by the National Trust, contains much Carlyle memorabilia; his sound-proofed attic study, where he took refuge from 'dogs, cocks, pianofortes and insipid men', is faithfully preserved, as is the kitchen where he often entertained Tennyson.

Open 29 Mar-Oct Wed-Sun & Bank Hol Mons, 11–4.30. Admission charge.

Dickens' House
48 Doughty Street, WC1
MAP REF 15, 3E
Dickens and his family lived here from 1837 to 1839, during which period he completed *The Pickwick Papers*, wrote *Oliver Twist* and *Nicholas Nickleby*, and began *Barnaby Rudge*. There is a reconstruction of Dingly Dell Kitchen, as described in *The Pickwick Papers*, in the basement. The Dotheboys Hall display case proves that Dickens did not exaggerate the horrors of 19th-century school life: Smike was based on a boy called George Taylor whose 'Happy' letter to his mother was followed by the bill for his tombstone.

Open Mon-Sat 10–4.30 (Closed Sun, Bank Hols, Good Fri & Xmas week). Admission charge.

Left: Hogarth's 'little country box by the Thames' at Chiswick, now home to many paintings, prints and mementoes. Right: Dr Johnson's house where he completed his dictionary

Hogarth's House
Hogarth Lane, Great West Road, Chiswick, W4
DISTRICT MAP, 3C
In 1749 Hogarth moved to this 17th-century house in Chiswick which he called 'a little country box by the Thames'. It was his home for 15 years, and now contains many paintings, prints, and personal mementoes.

Open Mon, Wed-Sat 11–6; Sun 2–6 (4pm Oct-Mar). (Closed Tue, Good Fri, 1st 2 weeks Sep, last 3 weeks Dec & 1 Jan). Admission free.

Dr Johnson's House
17 Gough Square, EC4
MAP REF 22, 1A
Samuel Johnson lived in this handsome 18th-century house between 1749 and 1759 and it was here that he completed his *Dictionary*. The house is full of mementoes of the man who is the most frequently quoted Englishman after Shakespeare.

Open Mon-Sat; May-Sep 11–5.30, Oct-Apr 11–5 (Closed Sun, Bank Hols, Good Fri & Xmas). Admission charge.

Homes

Keats's House
Wentworth Place, Keats Grove, Hampstead, NW3
DISTRICT MAP, 4D
From 1818 to 1820 John Keats lived at Wentworth Place with his friend Charles Brown, while next door lived his lover and nurse Fanny Brawne. It was here that Keats produced his greatest poetry, including the famous *Odes*. The two Regency houses occupied by Keats and Fanny have now been made into one. They are furnished in period style and contain manuscripts, letters, and relics. *Ode to a Nightingale* was written in the garden.
Open Mon-Fri 2–6; Sat 10–5, Sun & Bank Hols 2–5 (Closed Good Fri, Etr Sat, May Day, Xmas & 1 Jan). Admission free.

Wellington Museum (Apsley House)
149 Piccadilly, W1
MAP REF 25, 1E
This mansion was designed by Robert Adam in the late 18th century and was the London home of the 1st Duke of Wellington from 1829 until his death in 1852. Apsley House, known during the Iron Duke's time as 'Number One, London', now contains some outstanding paintings; these include Goya's *Wellington on Horseback*, Murillo's *Unknown Man*, Caravaggio's *Agony in the Garden*, and a number by Velazquez. There are busts and statues – including one of Napoleon by Canova which was presented to Wellington by George IV – fine porcelain, banners, uniforms, and a host of other memorabilia.
Open Tue-Sun 11–4.30. Admission charge.

Some famous London homes you can only view from the outside:

Wren's House
49 Bankside, SE1
MAP REF 22, 3C
A plaque on the wall of this 17th-century house marks the building in which Wren lived while supervising the rebuilding of St Paul's.

Pepys's House
12 Buckingham Street, WC2
MAP REF 21, 3D
Samuel Pepys, most famous of all diarists for his descriptive account of life in Charles II's London, lived in this house from 1679 until 1688.

Wesley's House
47 City Road, EC1
MAP REF 17, 3D
John Wesley, founder of Methodism, lived in this house from 1778 until his death in 1791. His study, bedroom, and prayer room are preserved, along with his furniture and many personal items.
Open Mon-Sat 10–4. Admission charge.

Handel's House
25 Brook Street, W1
MAP REF 20, 2A
George Frederick Handel lived in this house for 35 years, until his death in 1759. *The Messiah* was composed here.

Karl Marx's House
Leoni's Quo Vadis, 26 Dean Street, W1
MAP REF 21, 2C
Karl Marx lived in a room above this long-established Italian restaurant from 1851 to 1856.

Oscar Wilde's House
34 Tite Street, SW3
MAP REF 31, 2D
Oscar Wilde, famous dramatist and wit, lived here with his wife from 1884 until his trial in 1895.

John Wesley's house where his study, bedroom and prayer room are preserved

Buildings

The Bank of England, virtually rebuilt between 1925 and 1939; and the Stock Exchange, damaged by a bomb in July 1990

BUILDINGS

Bank of England
Threadneedle Street, EC2
MAP REF 23, 2D
This is the bank of the Government, incorporated in 1694 by Royal Charter. The old 18th-century building was almost entirely rebuilt between 1925 and 1939 by Sir Herbert Baker, who retained only the massive outer walls and columns. In the vaults is stored Britain's gold reserve. Since the 'No Popery' riots of 1780, a nightly 'picket' from the Brigade of Guards keeps watch at the Bank.
The Bank of England Museum, in Bartholomew Lane, is open Mon-Fri, 10–5. Admission charge.

British Telecom Tower
Maple Street, W1
MAP REF 14, 4B
Completed in 1964, this 619ft-high needle of concrete and glass is one of the tallest buildings in London. Now closed to the public.

Caxton Hall
Caxton Street, SW1
MAP REF 26, 2C
The name and look of this registry office were once familiar to all followers of high society doings, as until 1977 it was the most fashionable place for out-of-church weddings.

Central Criminal Courts
Old Bailey, EC4
MAP REF 22, 1B
The notorious Newgate Prison, which stood on this site, was the scene of public executions between 1783 and 1868. It was demolished in 1902 and replaced by the Central Criminal Court, which takes its popular name from the street in which it stands. Most of the major trials of this century have been heard here, including those of Crippen, Christie, Haig, and the Kray brothers. The public may view the proceedings in No 1 Court by queueing for a seat in the Visitors' Gallery (entrance in Newgate Street).
Mon-Fri 10.30–1 and 2–4. Admission free.

Clarence House
Stable Yard, St James's Palace, SW1
MAP REF 26, 1B
Designed by Nash for William IV when he was Duke of Clarence, this house was restored for Princess Elizabeth before her accession in 1952. Princess Anne was born here and it is now the home of Queen Elizabeth, the Queen Mother.

The College of Arms
Queen Victoria Street, EC4
MAP REF 22, 2B
Sometimes called the Heralds' Office, this is the official authority on all heraldic matters. Its officers, who have resounding titles such as Rouge Dragon Pursuivant, also assist the Earl Marshal, an office hereditary to the Duke of Norfolk since 1672, in arranging state ceremonies such as coronations. The imposing 17th-century building itself stands on a site that has been occupied by the College of Arms since 1555.

Commonwealth Institute
Kensington High Street, W8
DISTRICT MAP, 3C
Contains over 40 exhibitions depicting life in the countries of the Commonwealth. There is also a library, art gallery, and arts centre.
Open Mon-Sat 10–5; Sun 2–5 (Closed Good Fri, May Day, 24–26 Dec & 1 Jan). Admission free.

Buildings

The Guildhall
EC2
MAP REF 23, 1C
The building dates from 1411, but only the walls of the medieval great hall, porch, and crypt survive. Restoration work after Blitz damage was completed in 1954 to the designs of Sir Giles Gilbert Scott. Here the Court of Common Council, which administers the City, meets and entertains; the Lord Mayor's Banquet is held in the great hall, at the end of which stand huge wooden figures of Gog and Magog, legendary British giants who are said to have fought against Trojan invaders around 1000 BC.
Open May-Sep, Mon-Sat 10–5; Sun & BH 2–5. Admission free.

Guildhall Library
Founded in 1425, it contains an unrivalled collection of books, manuscripts, and prints on all aspects of London.
Open Mon-Sat 9.30–5 (Closed Bank Hols).

The Guildhall Clock Museum
Contains 700 exhibits illustrating 500 years of timekeeping including spring clocks, chronometers and precision watches.
Open Mon-Fri 9.30–4.45 (Closed Bank Hols).

The House of St Barnabas
Greek Street, W1
MAP REF 21, 1C
One of the finest Georgian houses in London, with richly decorated ceilings, woodcarvings, and ironwork, the House of St Barnabas was founded as a charitable institution in 1846 to help the destitute in London.
Open Wed 2.30–4.15; Thu 11–12.30 (guided tours). Admission free (donations).

Above: The Guildhall, dating from 1411 and, below, Gray's Inn, dating from 1560, both buildings were damaged in the Blitz and subsequently restored

The Inns of Court
There used to be 12 Inns of Court, but only three still exist in their traditional capacity for the education and lodging of lawyers – Gray's Inn, Lincoln's Inn and Temple. The others survive only in the names of streets and buildings, or as premises whose function has changed.

Gray's Inn
Gray's Inn Road, WC1
MAP REF 15, 4E
The Hall dates back to 1560; the Library is 18th-century. Both were restored after being extensively damaged during World War II. The gardens are thought to have been laid out by Francis Bacon, the most notable member of the Inn, who lived here from 1576 to 1626.
Open: gardens May-Sep, Mon-Fri 12–2.30. Buildings by prior arrangement. Admission free.

Buildings

Lincoln's Inn
Chancery Lane, WC2
MAP REF 21, 1E
Rightly recognised for its fine architecture (some, like the Gatehouse with its original oak doors, dating from the early 16th century) it is perhaps best known for its 12 acres of peaceful and beautifully kept gardens – Lincoln's Inn Fields.
Open: gardens and Chapel Mon-Fri 12–2 (Closed Etr, Xmas, 1 Jan); other buildings only by prior arrangement. Admission free, but tour guides are charged for if employed.

The Temple
Fleet Street, EC4
MAP REF 22, 2A
The best way to enjoy this Inn of Court, named after the Knights Templar who occupied the riverside site from about 1160, is to walk through its lanes and alleys. The buildings are very fine and generally very old, and the sense of space is well married to that indefinable air of peace peculiar to all the Inns.
The Temple Church, whose nave and porch date from the 12th century, is one of only four round churches surviving in England.
Temple Church: open daily 10–4 (except for services) Middle Temple Hall: open Mon-Fri 10–11.30, 3–4. (Closed Xmas, week after Etr, Aug-mid Sep) Inner Temple Hall: open Mon-Fri 10–11, 1.45–4. Admission free.

The Jewel Tower
Abingdon Street, SW1
MAP REF 27, 2D
This inconspicuous moated tower is in fact a survival of the medieval Palace of Westminster. It was built in 1365 to house the monarch's personal treasure, and this remained its function until the death of Henry VIII. It now houses a collection of pottery and other items found during excavations in the area.
Open Apr-Sep, Mon-Sat 9.30–1 & 2–6.30; Oct-Mar, Mon-Sat 9.30–1 & 2–4. Admission free.

Lloyd's of London
Lime Street, EC3
MAP REF 23, 2E
The world's leading insurance market in the controversial building designed by Richard Rogers. An exhibition explains the workings of Lloyds, and there is a viewing gallery.
Open Mon-Fri 10–2.30 (Closed 24 Dec–1 Jan & Bank Hols). Parties must book in advance. Admission free.

The Royal Exchange
Cornhill, EC4
MAP REF 23, 2D
Dating from 1568 as a meeting place for City merchants,

The controversial Lloyd's of London building

Buildings

Queen Victoria opened the present building in 1844. No business has been transacted here for over 40 years, but important announcements such as the proclamation of new sovereigns and declarations of war are traditionally made from the broad flight of steps at its entrance.

The Royal Hospital
Royal Hospital Road, Chelsea, SW3
MAP REF 31, 2E
Built by Wren in 1682 as an asylum for aged and invalid soldiers, it is considered one of the finest examples of his work. Alterations and additions were made by Robert Adam and Sir John Soane. The Hospital now houses 500 army pensioners, unmistakable in their scarlet frock-coats. The famous Chelsea Flower Show is held annually in the grounds during the early summer.
   Open: grounds Mon-Sat 10-dusk; Sun 2-dusk (Ranelagh Gardens closed 12.45–2); buildings Mon-Sat 10–12 & 2–4; Sun 2–4. Admission free.

The Royal Exchange, traditional site of important proclamations

Stock Exchange
Throgmorton Street, EC2
MAP REF 23, 1D
The centre of industrial finance, where stocks and shares in individual companies are bought and sold. The public gallery, from which the trading floor could be viewed, was extensively damaged by a bomb in July 1990 and the visitor facilities have been closed for repair.

The Temple of Mithras
Temple Court, EC4
MAP REF 23, 2C
The excavated foundations of a Mithraic temple, dating from the Roman occupation of London, and reconstructed near to the site where they were discovered in 1954. Viewing platform. Finds from the site are displayed in the Museum of London

US Embassy
Grosvenor Square, W1
MAP REF 19, 3E
The design of this huge modern building, by Eero Saarinen, is one of the most controversial in London. An eagle with a wingspan of 35ft dominates the structure.

Windsor Castle
Windsor, Berkshire
The largest inhabited castle in the world covering 13 acres, Windsor castle is the official residence of H.M. The Queen. Begun in the 11th century it has had many additions. It is in three parts: the Upper Ward, the Middle Ward, and the Lower Ward with St George's Chapel where many sovereigns and notable men and women are buried. From the Round Tower there are good views of the Thames and 12 surrounding counties.

Villages and favourite haunts

VILLAGES AND FAVOURITE HAUNTS

Bloomsbury
MAP REF 15

Bloomsbury is justly noted for its many unspoilt squares – notably Tavistock, Russell, Bedford and Bloomsbury Squares. In 1660 the latter, then known as Southampton Square, became London's first square to be so named. Greater houses were soon built in the area, the most famous of which was Montague House, completed in 1678 and now the home of the British Museum, though greatly expanded.

In the 1920s and 1930s the area became the haunt of influential painters, writers and intellectuals – including John Maynard Keynes, Virginia Woolf and E.M. Forster – who were soon collectively labelled the Bloomsbury Group.

The British Museum and the University of London buildings bring crowds to the area, which also contains many of London's hospitals and medical research facilities. But Bloomsbury is still surprisingly peaceful. A stroll down Woburn Walk off Upper Woburn Place, will provide a feel for its atmosphere. This is a genteel thoroughfare with a double row of early 19th-century houses, all with picturesque shop fronts.

Bloomsbury is still a surprisingly peaceful area and has many unspoilt squares such as Tavistock Square, pictured above, showing the Gandhi Memorial to the Indian religious and political leader

Villages and favourite haunts

Cheyne Walk, Chelsea

Chelsea
MAP REF 30/31

Although it was known as a 'Village of Palaces' in the 16th century, Chelsea's traditional image is one of bohemianism – an image that began when it was the home of Swift and Addison and reached its most extreme in the 1960s when the King's Road became a parade-ground for the fashionable young. The cafés and boutiques in this street seem rather worn out now and more 'street life' seems to take place along Fulham Road. But the 'swinging' image has always been a veneer, with the heart of the area remaining quietly sedate and respectable in its long streets of lovely townhouses, converted mews houses and many squares. The area's most well-loved treasure is the Royal Hospital, begun by Christopher Wren in 1682, and still a home for retired soldiers and the site of the annual Chelsea Flower Show.

One of the most elegant streets of the area is Cheyne Walk, a beautiful, unspoilt row of 18th-century houses by the river. No. 24 was Carlyle's home from 1834 (*see page 78*), and a few years later Rossetti attracted his wide circle of artistic friends to the street.

The Docklands
DISTRICT MAP, 3E

After World War I, London's docks started to decline and the Port of London soon seemed abandoned. A few years ago developers began to turn the enormous riverbank warehouses into flats and restaurants. The Docklands Light Railway runs through the area and also to the Thames Flood Barrier, designed to look like a fleet of ships. Many make the visit to see the Design Museum in Butler's Wharf, or to wander along Seething Lane, site of the Navy Office in which the diarist Samuel Pepys worked. St Olave's Church opposite is where Pepys and his wife were buried. Another attraction in the area is St Katharine's Dock, designed by Thomas Telford, one of the greatest engineers of the 19th century, which was forced to close after World War II. The dock basins have

The Docklands Light Railway running through the dockland area and to the Thames Flood Barrier.

been restored and there is a path around the dock which will take you past the tastefully modernised warehouses. You can have a drink at the Dickens Inn while gazing at the yachts in the marina.

The City
MAP REF 22, 2B/C

Londinium, the original Roman city, occupied a square mile north of the Thames. The Tower of London was originally a Roman fort designed to protect Londinium from sea attacks. The present Tower was begun in the Middle Ages and embellished through the centuries. Often crowded, the Tower still remains one of London's major sightseeing venues. Especially popular are Henry VIII's armour and the Crown Jewels.

Villages and favourite haunts

St Paul's Cathedral (above left) and the tomb-like Bank of England (above right) in the heart of the City; the original Roman Londinium occupying a square mile north of the Thames

Further west stands Christopher Wren's intimidating St Paul's Cathedral. The nearby streets are the heart of the City today, with its sense of quiet but urgent activity surrounding the Stock Exchange and the tomb-like Bank of England. Nestled beneath the modern insurance and bank buildings are countless well-preserved churches, many of which continue their long tradition of holding lunchtime concerts.

The Barbican, an impressive new development, was built around the remaining portion of the old Roman wall as an ambitious scheme to promote the City as a residential area rather than a place to be visited only for the purpose of daily work. It contains high-rise blocks of flats, shops, offices, pubs, the new City of London School for Girls, the 16th-century church of St Giles Cripplegate, and the new Guildhall School of Music. The centrepiece of the scheme is the Barbican Arts Centre (see page 119), which contains the permanent London homes of the Royal Shakespeare Company (the Barbican Theatre) and the London Symphony Orchestra (the Barbican Hall). The Museum of London (see page 110) lies on the south-western extremity of the development.

The Centre is open daily. Admission free.
Tel Information: 071 638 4141

Hampstead
DISTRICT MAP, 4D

Hampstead, despite the traffic in its busier areas, still wears the air of a chic village. Narrow streets shelter tiny cottages worth well of over £1 million and grander townhouses edge Hampstead Heath, which borders Hampstead on the north and east. This enormous area of untamed land also includes swimming pools and tennis courts, outdoor cafés and, to the north, Kenwood House, built in 1616 and housing the Iveagh Bequest, a glorious art collection including works by Turner, Rembrandt and Gainsborough. Kenwood also sports a lakeside theatre, the site of annual summer concerts.

In the more bustling part of Hampstead, with its fashionable shops and restaurants, one can visit Flask Walk, which takes its name from the wells which made Hampstead a fashionable spa in the 18th century. The Victorian Flask Walk Baths are here (though now closed) and next to them is an attractive group of restored Georgian artisans' cottages.

Villages and favourite haunts

Keats's charming house (above right) and Admiral's House (below right), both to be found in the 'chic village' of Hampstead

Hampstead has long been known as the home of artists and intellectuals, among the best-known being Keats, whose charming house, now a small museum, is in Keats Grove (see page 79). Other famous names include Leigh Hunt, Lord Byron, John Constable, H.G. Wells, D.H. Lawrence and Sigmund Freud.

Mayfair
MAP REF 20, 2A/3A/B

Traditionally one of London's most sought-after addresses, Mayfair retains its well-bred air, despite being thought of as a playpen for the rich. The bombing of World War II left a shortage of office building in central London, so many of the Georgian mansions here were converted to commercial premises. Modern international hotels took over Park Lane and the American Embassy now looms over Grosvenor Square. Mayfair is also home to London's more traditional prestigious hotels, including Browns in Dover Street, the Connaught in Carlos Place and Claridges in Brook Street. No 25 Brook Street was Handel's home for over thirty years (see page 79). Nearly all his works, including the *Messiah* (1741), were composed here.

Shepherd's Market, in the heart of Mayfair, is one of the most delightful areas in London. Some of the original 18th-century buildings survive, but it is the unique village atmosphere which gives this tiny oasis its special charm. Mayfair also hosts some of London's finer shopping areas: Bond Street, South Molton Street and Savile Row.

Villages and favourite haunts

Piccadilly Circus, with its crowds and illuminations, contrasts with some of the more worthy establishments ranged along Piccadilly itself, such as St James's Church, Fortnum and Mason, The Royal Academy of Art, the Burlington Arcade and the Ritz Hotel

Piccadilly and St James's
MAP REF 20, 3B/C

The locations of St James's Palace and Buckingham Palace have ensured the continuing importance of this area. Piccadilly Circus, with its crowds and illuminations, is somewhat atypical. Along Piccadilly itself are ranged more staid London landmarks: St James's Church designed by Christopher Wren, Fortnum and Mason, the Royal Academy of Art, the Burlington Arcade and the Ritz Hotel. Green Park then spreads, alongside St James's Park, south towards the two Palaces. Jermyn Street is famous for its many old-established shops. Further along is the Cavendish Hotel with its wrought-iron lamps, which, although rebuilt, still carries memories of the eccentric hotelier Rosa Lewis, the original 'Duchess of Duke Street'.

Another approach to Buckingham Palace, Pall Mall takes its name from *paille maille*, a French ball game similar to croquet, introduced into England in the reign of Charles I. Numerous famous, and usually exclusive, clubs are situated in Pall Mall. Outside the entrance to the Athenaeum Club, in Waterloo Place, are two slabs of stone, placed here as a mounting-block at the request of the Duke of Wellington.

The southern half of Waterloo Place was once occupied by Carlton House, sadly demolished by George IV. But in 1827–32 John Nash built two dignified terraces, now known as Carlton House Terrace, as part of his architectural scheme for Regent Street. At No 6 is the Royal Society and No 12 is now the Institute of Contemporary Arts. While in St James's try to see Queen Anne's Gate. A quiet close, built in 1704, it is undoubtedly one of London's most charming streets. No 26 still has the snuffer for extinguishing the linkman's torch after he had lighted its owner's home.

Soho
MAP REF 20, 2B/C

In the mid–18th century, the aristocracy began to desert Soho, as artists and musicians moved in. By the late 19th century John Galsworthy could describe the area as 'untidy ... full of cats, Italians, tomatoes, restaurants, people

Villages and favourite haunts

looking out of upper windows ...'. Although now much more tidy, no one has ever cleaned Soho up to the extent of neighbouring Covent Garden – and it has never quite lost its working population of residents. Today the sleazy areas are confined to a few streets, and it is indeed famed for its excellent restaurants and food shops. Amidst the cacophony of Soho, including the music from Ronnie Scott's long-established jazz club, you can still find quiet passageways, one of which is Meard Street, built in the 18th century, with Nos 1–21 now beautifully preserved. A stroll down Greek Street can also be evocative of things past. The street has associations with many famous people: here Dr Johnson and Sir Joshua Reynolds founded a Literary Club; Sir Thomas Lawrence, the 18th-century painter, lived and worked; Thomas de Quincey indulged his opium addiction; and Josiah Wedgwood had his London showroom to show off his famous china. In more recent times, the street was home to London's satirical magazine *Private Eye*.

The principal thoroughfare of Soho is Shaftesbury Avenue, laid out in 1877–86. The majority of it runs from Cambridge Circus southwards to Piccadilly Circus and is ranked with theatres. At the other edge of Soho is the surprisingly well-maintained Soho Square, today the centre of the British film industry.

Victoria Embankment
MAP REF 21 3D/E
A riverside road running between Westminster and Blackfriars was proposed by Christopher Wren after the Great Fire of London, but it was not built until 1870. Along it are fine iron lamp posts with dolphins twined round their bases, and seats supported by kneeling camels. The river wall is made of granite and is eight feet thick. You can visit Victoria Embankment Gardens, on either side of Hungerford railway bridge, to the west of the Embankment itself. Between Waterloo and Hungerford bridges stands Cleopatra's Needle, a 3,500-year-old monument presented to the British by the Turkish Viceroy in Egypt in 1819.

From the Embankment you can see the back of the Savoy Hotel, which opened in 1889 with 300 lavish bedrooms. Claud Monet painted his well-known Thames series from here. The forecourt is the only place in Britain where driving on the right is mandatory. The hotel faces The Strand, extending only ¾ mile from Charing Cross to the Law Courts and a major artery linking Westminster and the City. In Elizabethan times and long afterwards, the Strand was bordered by noblemen's mansions with gardens running down to the riverside. In the 1890s the Strand contained more theatres than any other London street. Sadly only the Adelphi, the Vaudeville and the Savoy remain. However, two very fine churches, St Mary Le Strand and St Clement Danes, still stand in the middle of the street. Both are well worth visiting.

Whitehall
MAP REF 27, 1D
Most people to whom the name 'Whitehall' is synonymous with Government will be surprised to learn that the road called Whitehall running from Parliament Square with the Houses of Parliament to Trafalgar Square only became the home of most government offices during the early 18th century. In Downing Street, No 10 has been the official residence of the Prime Minister since Robert Walpole first lived there in 1735. No 11 is the residence of the Chancellor of the Exchequer, and the Government Whips' Office is at No 12. Margaret Thatcher has had the street blocked off, but you can still peek through the iron railings. Among the other government buildings still found in Whitehall are the Treasury and the Admiralty, and Horse Guards, behind which is Horse Guards Parade where Trooping the Colour takes place. The Ministry of Defence stands near the surviving relic of the former Palace of Whitehall, the Banqueting House. This was designed by Inigo Jones in a fine Palladian style and erected in 1625.

Open Tue-Sat 10am–5pm; Sun 2–5pm (Closed Good Fri, 24–26 Dec and for Government functions). Admission charge.

Charles I was executed outside the Banqueting House in 1649.

In the middle of Whitehall stands the Cenotaph, a simple pillar of Portland stone designed by Sir Edwin Lutyens to commemorate those who fell during World War I. Now services for the dead of both world wars are held here annually on the second Sunday in November.

At the north end of Whitehall, passing Great Scotland Yard, until 1891 headquarters of the Metropolitan Police, you come to Trafalgar Square. Inhabited by thousands of pigeons, and dominated by Nelson's Column with its four lions designed by the Victorian painter Landseer, the Square was laid out in memory of Nelson and completed in 1841; the fountains were added in 1948.

Parks and gardens

PARKS AND GARDENS

London's ten Royal parks are the survivors of areas enclosed by Henry VIII for hunting, and were first opened to the public by Charles I and Charles II. They are:

Bushy Park
DISTRICT MAP, 2B
The famous ¾-mile Chestnut Avenue, laid out by Wren, runs from Hampton Court to the Teddington Gate. This superb double row of enormous trees is best seen in springtime.

Green Park
MAP REF 26, 1B
Once meadowland where duels were fought, this is the smallest of the parks in Central London, situated in the triangle between teeming Piccadilly, the processional Mall, and Constitutional Hill (which gets its name from where Charles II took his constitutional stroll). There are no flowerbeds, though in springtime the grass is sprinkled with daffodils and crocuses. Tyburn Stream flows just beneath the surface and is the reason for the park's greenness.

Greenwich Park
DISTRICT MAP, 3E
Mostly laid out by Le Nôtre, whose love of symmetry is very noticeable, this park contains the Meridian, a stone-set strip of brass that marks zero degrees longitude, and the Wilderness, 13 acres of woodland and wild flowers inhabited by a herd of fallow deer. On the northern perimeter is the largest children's playground in any Royal park; in the centre is the historic 20ft stump of Queen Elizabeth's Oak.

Bushy Park: Longford River and woodland gardens

Parks and gardens

Hampton Court
DISTRICT MAP, 2B
An outstanding collection of formal gardens – particularly fine is the Privy Garden with its combination of flowers, statues, and fountains. There is the Orangery, the 200-year-old-vine, the modern reproduction Knot Garden, and the geometric perfection of the famous Maze.

Hyde Park
MAP REF 19, 3C/D
A Royal park since 1536, Hyde Park now consists of 340 acres of trees and grass intersected by paths. Main features include the Serpentine – the habitat of wild creatures that cannot find sanctuary elsewhere in the city centre – and Speakers' Corner near Marble Arch, where, every Sunday, anyone can stand up and say just what they please.

Kensington Gardens
MAP REF 18, 3A/B
The boundary between Kensington Gardens and Hyde Park, which were one and the same before William III enclosed his palace garden, runs north to south across the Serpentine Bridge. Noted for its tranquillity and formality, Kensington Gardens includes the Round Pond, Queen Anne's Orangery, and the Sunken Garden and Flower Walk.

Primrose Hill
DISTRICT MAP, 4D
Once part of the same hunting forest as Regent's Park, Primrose Hill retains in its name the rural character and charm that it undoubtedly had in the past. The view from the summit is panoramic and encompasses virtually the whole of central London. In 1842 its 62 acres gained gaslights, a gymnasium, and respectability as a Royal park.

Above: the Sunken Garden, one of the fine formal gardens at Hampton Court. Right: centuries-old oak trees at Richmond Park.

Regent's Park
MAP REF 13, 2D/E
Laid out by John Nash, who also designed the imposing terraces which surround it. It contains the Zoo, a boating lake, the lovely Queen Mary's Rose Garden, and the Regent's Canal. The elegant charm of the park is enhanced by several Victorian garden ornaments; a group of fossil tree trunks are the only surviving reminders that the Royal Botanic Gardens were once situated here.

Richmond Park
DISTRICT MAP, 2B
With its herds of deer, abundant wild life and

centuries-old oaks, Richmond is a favourite haunt for visitors and naturalists. A formal garden can be seen at Pembroke Lodge, and the various plantations show a wealth of exotic shrubs and wild flowers. Model sail boats are allowed on Adam's Pond, where the deer drink, and 18-acre Pen Ponds have been specially made for angling (a fishing permit is required).

Parks and gardens

The attractive wrought iron and glass Palm House at Kew maintaining palms from all over the world

St James's Park
MAP REF 26, 1C
This most delightful of the Royal parks contains walks and paths threading through a mixture of flower borders, shrubs, and trees. Weeping willows drape themselves into the Chinese-style lake, the nucleus of the park. Duck Island in the centre is a haven for water birds, the most famous being the pelicans.

Escape from the crowded streets and hectic bustle of London also lies elsewhere within the capital:

Hampstead Heath
NW3 and NW11
DISTRICT MAP, 4D
The 790 acres of Hampstead Heath include some of the highest ground in the capital, and the views of London that can be enjoyed from the heath are famous. There are extensive tracts of open grassland dotted with majestic old trees, and carefully planned formalised areas that were originally set out during the Regency period. Part of society's interest in Hampstead was due to the springs which rise from its depths. These were claimed to have health-giving properties, and the 18th-century fad for 'taking the waters' ensured its popularity.

Highgate Cemetery
Swains Lane, N6
DISTRICT MAP, 5D
One of the private cemeteries which were created in the 1830s. The western part, decaying and overgrown through years of neglect, provides a marvellous backdrop for the many magnificent Victorian tombs, vaults and monuments, including those of George Eliot, Faraday, and Charles Dickens's family. Most famous, of course, for the enormous grave of Karl Marx.

Open: Eastern cemetery, daily, Apr–Sep 10am–5pm; Oct–Mar 10am–4pm; Western cemetery guided tours Mon–Fri 12 noon, 2pm, 4pm; Sat–Sun on hour every hour 11am–4pm. Tel 081–340 1834 to confirm. Admission charge.

Kew Gardens
DISTRICT MAP, 3B
The 300 acres of the legendary Royal Botanic Gardens now contain over 50,000 different types of plants and flowers. The largest living collection in the gardens is the Arboretum, where many species of trees and shrubs grow harmoniously. The Tropical and Palm Houses are interesting too, while the magnificent flower borders of the Herbaceous Section are a constant delight. Great cushions of alpines grow amongst sandstone outcrops and beside the stream of the Rock Garden, and the woodland garden around The Mound exudes a green coolness.

Gardens open daily, all year Mon–Sat 9.30am–6.30pm; Sun 4–8pm and public holidays; museums & glasshouses from 10am, some buildings close lunchtime (closed 25 Dec & 1 Jan). Admission charge.

The Zoo
Regent's Park, NW1
MAP REF 13, 1E
In 1828, the Zoological Society founded a small collection of animals on a five-acre site in Regent's Park, from which modest beginnings has grown one of the world's foremost zoos – a collection that still receives no aid from the government, and subsists entirely on the proceeds of ticket sales. Today it shows a staggering 6,000 living species of animals, many in environments that are hardly a whisker away from their natural habitats. Some of the creatures could be encountered on a country walk in southern England; others are endangered species that would be difficult to find anywhere.

Among the outstanding buildings are the new Lion

Parks and gardens

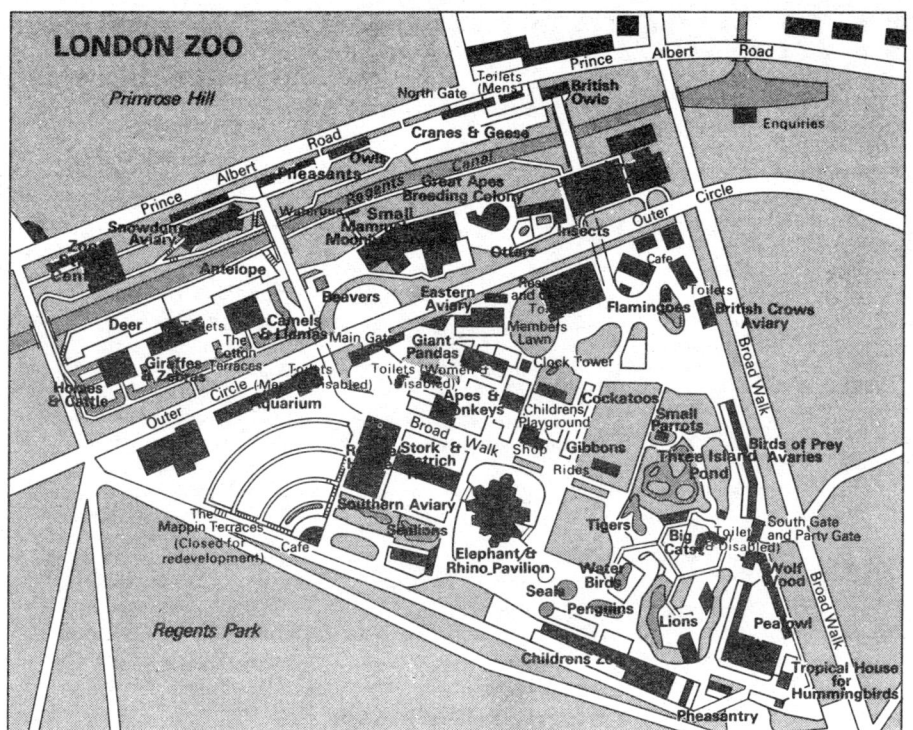

Terraces; the Freshwater, Seawater and Tropical Halls of the Aquarium; the Reptile House; the Elephant and Rhino Pavilion; the Charles Clore Pavilion for small mammals, and Lord Snowdon's famous aviary. Nobody can deny that this is an ideal place to see birds. Inside the enclosure is a cantilevered bridge from which visitors can watch free-flying birds in a number of recreated habitats – nesting, fighting and feeding as they would in the wild. Deer and antelope roam the Cotton Terraces above the Regent's Canal. You can take a canal boat ride from the Zoo landing stage, or to the Zoo from Camden Lock or Little Venice. Elsewhere are camels and llamas, giraffes, and a worldwide selection of cattle. There is a lovely Children's Zoo, where the young are encouraged to mingle with the animals. Keep an eye open for notices of feeding times.

Open daily, all year, Apr–Oct 9am–6pm; Nov–Mar 10am till dusk (closed 25 Dec).
Admission charge.

Among the public parks and other oases of greenery are: **Battersea Park**, SW11, with its sub-tropical and wildflower gardens, and masses of things for children to do; **Chelsea Physic Garden**, Royal Hospital Road, SW3, the second oldest botanic garden in England, set up in 1673; **Holland Park**, W8, a quiet haven in the heart of Kensington, which Macaulay called the 'favourite resort of wits and beauties, painters and poets, scholars, philosophers, and statesmen'; **Lincoln's Inn Fields**, WC2 (see page 82); **Syon Park**, Isleworth – beautifully laid out in the 16th century by Capability Brown, this was the country's first national gardening centre; **Waterlow Park**, Highgate Hill, N6 – pretty terraces, flower gardens, lake, and ponds; **Wimbledon Common**, SW19, with attractive ponds and an ancient earthwork known as Caesar's Camp; **Victoria Embankment Gardens**, WC2, containing numerous statues and memorials; **Victoria Tower Gardens**, SW1, with the Buxton Drinking Fountain commemorating the emancipation of slaves in the British Empire in 1834; and **Vauxhall Bridge Gardens**, SW1, from where convicted prisoners were transported.

WATERSIDE LONDON

THE THAMES

Much of London's past, present and future lie together on the banks of the River Thames. The source of the Thames is in Kemble, Gloucestershire, and it eventually reaches London at approximately Hampton Court in the west before coursing through the capital to the North Sea, the last item of tourist interest to the east being the Thames Barrier (see page 97). There are attractions on both the north bank and the south bank of the river, which is spanned by numerous bridges, the most famous of which is probably Tower Bridge, and the prettiest of which, with its cobweb-like ironwork, is Albert Bridge. River cruises operate between Hampton Court Pier in the west as far as Barrier Garden Pier in the east and a river bus operates in the areas between (see page 40).

Putney Bridge
DISTRICT MAP, 3C
Graceful Putney Bridge is a 19th-century replacement of an earlier wooden toll bridge. It marks the starting point of the Oxford and Cambridge Boat Race, and all along the riverside here there are well-kept boat and clubhouses.

Chelsea Bridge
MAP REF 32, 3A
This handsome suspension bridge was opened in 1937 and replaced a similar structure of 1858. The river here is the widest reach west of London Bridge.

Westminster Bridge
MAP REF 27, 2D
The present bridge was designed by Thomas Page and completed in 1862. It replaced a stone bridge of 1750 on which Wordsworth composed his famous sonnet in 1802. At the western end stands a statue of Queen Boadicea (see page 99). Westminster Pier is situated just north of the bridge and is one of the principal starting places for trips up and down the river.

The Jubilee Walkway
South Bank
MAP REF 27, 1E
The 12-mile Silver Jubilee Walkway (named after Queen Elizabeth's 25th year as Queen) goes from Westminster along the south bank of the Thames, across Tower Bridge and back to the West End through the City of London. The whole route is marked by special paving stones and wall plaques showing the Jubilee symbol of a crown within the dome of St Paul's Cathedral. The starting points at Leicester Square, Parliament Square, Jubilee Gardens (on the south bank, turn left after Westminster Bridge), Southwark Cathedral and Tower Hill are marked by special three-dimensional assembly-point markers.

Waterloo Bridge
MAP REF 21, 3E
John Rennie's beautiful Waterloo Bridge, which had been built in the early part of the 19th century, began to show signs of structural weakness in 1923. In 1934 demolition work began, and the old bridge was replaced by the present structure in 1939. It was designed by Sir Giles Scott and is considered to be the most graceful bridge in London. The buildings of the South Bank Arts Complex (see page 121) are on either side of the southern end of the bridge.

The South Bank Arts Complex
South Bank
MAP REF 21, 3E
This group of buildings near Waterloo has become a major centre for arts in London and includes three concert halls: The Royal Festival Hall, Queen Elizabeth Hall and Purcell Room (see page 121); the National Theatre which has three theatres: The Olivier, the Lyttleton and the Cottisloe (see page 123); the Hayward Gallery, the base for the South Bank Centre's touring exhibitions in this country (see page 106); the National Film Theatre, a film club, and, opened in 1988, the Museum of

Hampton Court Palace

Hampton Court Pier

River Thames

Not to scale

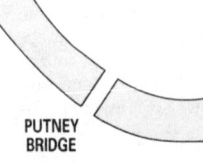

PUTNEY BRIDGE

Waterside London

the Moving Image (see page 110 and advert on inside cover).

Also on the South Bank there are frequently small exhibitions, live music, sometimes in the open air, as well as many very good places in which to eat within the Arts Complex. Proposals are currently afoot to enhance the existing complex by the addition of a new terraced building as well as general improvements in access and facilities.

The Canal System

The history of London's canal network is related to the expansion of the port of London in the early part of the 19th century and it gradually became linked with the existing canal system. In 1820 the Regent's Canal scheme linking Paddington (north London) with the River Thames at Limehouse (Docklands) was completed.

Since 1962 the canals have been under the control of British Waterways.

Work is now going on to revive the many canals that became neglected and many of London's canals now have an important role as a leisure amenity.

There are many interesting walks giving the walker the opportunity to see familiar landmarks from an unfamiliar viewpoint and to discover some of the past industrial sites and machinery. A permit is needed to cycle along the canal towing path and for people with disabilities the going may be difficult.

The Regent's Canal

Little Venice
**DISTRICT MAP &
MAP REF 12, 4A/B**
One of the prettiest stretches of the Regent's Canal is the section between Camden Town and Little Venice. The journey starts at the Camden Lock Centre (nearest underground Chalk Farm on the Northern Line) with its converted craft shops, artists' workshops, discotheque and restaurants. At the weekend a very popular market is held here. Crowds of people flock to this market so that public transport is a *must* as a means of getting there. It takes about two and half hours to walk from Camden Lock to Little Venice. This is approached through an area of great architectural interest with fine Regency houses. Brightly coloured boats are moored and at a canalside cottage called *Junction House* you come to Little Venice. This triangular stretch of water is also known as Browning's Pool and Island after the poet.

The pool of Little Venice with its tree-clad island in the middle marks the junction where the Regent's Canal meets Paddington Basin and the Paddington Arm of the Grand Union Canal leading to the Midlands. Little Venice is a boarding stage of the Waterbus, which also stops at

The Houses of Parliament

The Tate Gallery

Waterside London

London Zoo. The Inland Waterways Association organises walks along the canal on the first Sunday afternoon every month between February and November. Tel 071-586 2510. Canal cruises run from April to October.

London Bridge City
South Bank
MAP REF 23, 3D
This is the largest riverside commercial development in Europe, and is on the South Bank of the Thames. By 1992 a reconstruction of Shakespeare's Globe Theatre is due to open, close to its original site opposite St Paul's. Access is via London Bridge. The nearest underground station is London Bridge.

sculpture, *The Navigators*, is a focal point. One of London's most stylish new attractions, the Galleria is a centre for performing arts, shopping and eating, part of 'London Bridge City', also providing a pier for the ferry and a landscaped walkway by the river.

London Bridge
MAP REF 23, 3D
London Bridge was first built in stone between 1176 and 1209. It became almost a town on its own, having houses,

St Paul's Cathedral

St Katharine Docks
North Bank
DISTRICT MAP, 3E
Built by the famous engineer Thomas Telford in 1826 and designed to handle cargoes such as ivory, tea and silver, it has been transformed into a commercial, residential and recreational area with a modern hotel, luxury apartments and a shopping arcade. There is also a yacht marina, several restaurants and the Dickens Inn pub, an 18th-century brewery warehouse, now a galleried inn. It is close to Tower Hill underground station and is a popular tourist attraction.

The Tower of London

shops, a chapel, fortified gates, and even water mills built upon it. All the buildings were pulled down in 1760, and the bridge itself was replaced in 1832 as it was rapidly being eroded away. The present structure was opened in 1973, at which time its predecessor was reassembled stone by stone in Arizona, USA.

Hay's Galleria
South Bank
MAP REF 23, 3E
This is Hay's Wharf reconstructed. The dock was sealed over and floored and the whole area covered by a spectacular glass and steel vaulted roof. A giant kinetic

HMS Belfast
South Bank
MAP REF 23, 3E
Built in 1938, it was the largest World War II battle cruiser in the Royal Navy. She is now a floating museum moored permanently on the Thames off Symons Wharf, Vine Lane, Tooley Street.
Open Summer 10am–5.20pm; Winter 10am–4pm. Admission charge.

Waterside London

Tower Bridge
DISTRICT MAP, 3E
This fairy-tale structure was built in 1894. Much of the original machinery for raising and lowering the bridge is still in place, though in 1975 electric motors replaced the great steam hydraulic engines. These can be seen in a museum in the main South Tower. Also open to the public is the main North Tower and the 142ft-high glass-covered walkway which provides a unique view of the river.

Open all year Apr–Oct, 10am–6.30pm; Nov–Mar, 10am–4.45pm (last ticket sold 45 minutes before closing). Closed Good Fri, 24–26 Dec and New Year's Day. Toilets for disabled, shop. Admission charge.

London Docklands
North Bank
DISTRICT MAP, 3E
8½ square miles of land including the 17th-century dock system and warehousing are now being renovated and rebuilt. Examples of Georgian and Victorian industrial architecture, churches and ancient pubs, museums and tourist shopping centres, restaurants and even three small farms (open to the public) are intermingled with high-tech modern office and residential buildings. Access to Docklands is by car, by the Docklands Light Railway from Tower Hill underground station, or by river bus.

you can walk along Wapping High Street to St Katharine Docks.

which Sir Christopher Wren, the architect, considered had the best view of Greenwich Palace across the water. There is a subway under the Thames to Greenwich which comes out by the sailing tea clipper ship, the *Cutty Sark* (page 74). The London Light Railway (Island Gardens branch) terminates here (starting from Tower Hill underground station) providing a quick way of getting to Greenwich underneath the Thames.

The Thames Barrier
South Bank
DISTRICT MAP, 3F
A magnificent feat of engineering, justifiably described as the 'Eighth Wonder of the World', the Thames Barrier was opened in 1984. Designed to look like a fleet of ships with ten moving steel gates mounted between

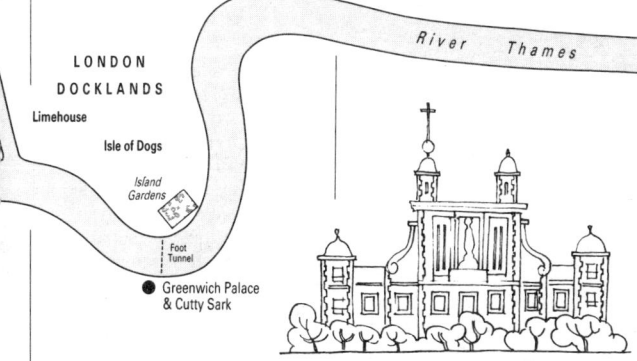

The Old Royal Observatory

Tobacco Dock
North Bank
DISTRICT MAP, 3E
At present one of the best renovated areas of Docklands. This fortress of a warehouse with vaults originally built to store tobacco and wines, has now been attractively transformed into a 'shopping village' – a warren of small shops and restaurants, some of which look onto the quay where two full-size replicas of old sailing ships can be viewed. From Tobacco Dock

Island Gardens
North Bank
DISTRICT MAP, 3E
A small park on the southern-most point of the Isle of Dogs – a loop in the River Thames that encloses a peninsula. The name is thought to come from the days of King Charles II when he lived at Greenwich and kept his hunting dogs across the river. Island Gardens park opened in 1895 to commemorate the spot

nine concrete piers, the barrier spans a third of a mile across the Thames at Woolwich Reach and is the largest movable flood barrier in the world.

Built to save London from disastrous flooding at a cost of some £480 million, the impressive construction is well worth a visit. To enable public viewing of the barrier a visitor centre has been built on the south side, along with a pier for passenger boats. There is also a restaurant, souvenir shop, models, information displays and a video film explaining the development of the project. The barrier gates are raised every month for testing (see advertisement in the colour section, pp 4-10).

Eros, one of London's most famous landmarks

STATUES AND MONUMENTS

The Albert Memorial
Kensington Gore, SW7
MAP REF 24, 2B
This enormous and imposing memorial was commissioned by Queen Victoria in memory of her husband, and was designed by Sir George Gilbert Scott in 1872. The Prince is depicted reading a catalogue of the Great Exhibition of 1851, for which he was largely responsible.

Alfred the Great
Trinity Church Square, off Trinity Street, SE1
MAP REF 29, 2C
Thought to date from 1395, this is the oldest statue in London.

The Burghers of Calais
Victoria Tower Gardens, SW1
MAP REF 27, 3D
Rodin's superb group of figures represents the citizens of Calais who surrendered to Edward III in 1340 to save their town from destruction.

Charles I
Trafalgar Square, WC2
MAP REF 21, 3D
Cast in bronze in 1633, this statue was to have been melted down during the Commonwealth, but was hidden and re-erected in 1660.

Sir Winston Churchill
Parliament Square, SW1
MAP REF 27, 2D
This statue of the great statesman and leader of the Second World War coalition government was unveiled in 1973 and depicts Churchill in a typically pugnacious attitude.

Cleopatra's Needle
Victoria Embankment, SW1
MAP REF 21, 3E
Originally this famous landmark stood in Heliopolis, Egypt, where it was one of a pair erected 3,500 years ago. It was presented to Britain in 1819. Its twin now stands in Central Park, New York, and neither has any connection with Cleopatra.

The 1st Duke of Wellington
Hyde Park Corner, W1
MAP REF 25, 1E
The Duke can be seen on Copenhagen, the horse he rode throughout the Battle of Waterloo. Copenhagen was buried with full military honours at the Duke's country home, Stratfield Saye, Hampshire.

The Duke of York Column
Waterloo Place, SW1
MAP REF 27, 1C
This tall monument commemorates the second son of George III – the 'Grand Old Duke of York' – who marched ten thousand men up and down a hill in the nursery rhyme. The same men paid for the memorial – most of its cost was met by stopping one day's pay from every soldier in the army. The column was designed by Benjamin Wyatt in 1833.

Eros
Piccadilly Circus, W1
MAP REF 20, 3C
One of London's most famous landmarks, this figure of an archer was erected as a memorial to the Victorian reformer and philanthropist, the Earl of Shaftesbury. The statue actually represents the Angel of Christian Charity, not Eros at all. It has recently been completely restored.

Statues and monuments

Left: The Monument, by Wren and Hooke, commemorating the Great Fire of 1666. Right: the Victoria Memorial depicting the Queen attended by Truth, Motherhood and Justice, with other symbols of Peace and Progress overlooked by the Winged Victory

The Fat Boy
Giltspur Street, EC1
MAP REF 22, 1B
This peculiar gilded figure marks the spot, originally known as Pie Corner, where the Great Fire was halted in 1666.

The Griffin
Strand, EC4
MAP REF 22, 2A
The Griffin, the unofficial badge of the City of London, stands at the point where the Strand ends and Fleet Street begins. Originally this was the site of the Old Temple Bar gateway, and the spot traditionally marks the western limit of the City.

Sir Henry Irving
St Martin's Place, WC2
MAP REF 21, 3D
Erected in 1910, this is the only statue in London of an actor.

James II
Trafalgar Square, WC2
MAP REF 21, 3D
Usually regarded as the finest statue in London, this figure of the king was made by Grinling Gibbons.

The London Stone
Cannon Street, EC4
(Overseas – Chinese Banking Corporation)
MAP REF 23, 3C
This is said to be the milestone from which distances were measured on the great military roads radiating outwards from Roman London.

Lord Nelson
Trafalgar Square, WC2
MAP REF 21, 3D
This 17ft 4in statue by E H Bailey stands on the top of the famous column. Together they reach a combined height of almost 185ft. Four identical lions, cast from a single original by Sir Edwin Landseer, guard the base of the column.

The Monument
Monument Street, EC3
MAP REF 23, 2D
Designed by Wren and Hooke to commemorate the Great Fire of 1666, which is reputed to have started in nearby Pudding Lane. Be prepared for a climb of 311 steps to the summit from where there are splendid views over the City.
Open daily Mar–Sep, Mon–Fri 9am–5.40pm, Sat & Sun 2–5.40pm; Oct–Mar, Mon–Sat 9am–4pm, closed Sun. (Closed 25–27 Dec, Good Friday, May Day, Bank Hols.) Admission charge.

Peter Pan
Kensington Gardens, W2
MAP REF 18, 3B
This statue of Sir James Barrie's immortal character has delighted several generations of children. It was made by Sir George Frampton in 1911.

Queen Boadicea
Westminster Bridge, SW1
MAP REF 27, 2D
Thomas Thornycroft made this statue of Queen Boadicea, or Boudicca, in 1902. She is depicted in her war chariot, accompanied by her daughters, and appears to be defiantly waving her spear at the Houses of Parliament.

Queen Victoria
Queen Victoria Memorial, The Mall, SW1
MAP REF 26, 2B
This elegant group of statuary stands in front of Buckingham Palace.

The Whittington Stone
Highgate Hill, N19
DISTRICT MAP, 4D
Dick Whittington is supposed to have sat on this spot and heard the Bow Bells of St Mary-le-Bow chiming: 'Turn again Whittington, Thrice Mayor of London'. Whittington actually was mayor of London three times during the 14th century.

99

Pubs

It can be great fun exploring that most typical of British institutions, the pub. There are thousands in London, each with its own atmosphere and character, some relying on special attractions like music (all sorts), drag shows and plays. Here, as a starting point, is a list of those noted for their historical interest. Opening times vary slightly but are generally 11am to 11pm, Monday to Saturday, and noon to 2 or 3pm and 7 to 10.30 or 11pm Sunday, though some pubs may shut in the afternoons.

Note: the British drink-and-drive laws are most strict, and we do recommend that you use public transport when going pub-hunting.

Jack Straw's Castle, a coaching inn evoking the days of the highwayman

PUBS

The Anchor
34 Park Street, SE1
MAP REF 22, 3C
A historic Bankside pub, the third to stand on this site, very close to where both Shakespeare's Globe Theatre and the old Clink Prison once stood.

The Angel
101 Bermondsey Wall, SE16
DISTRICT MAP, 3E
Naval tavern dating back to the 15th century, patronised in the 17th century by Samuel Pepys and in the 20th century by Laurel and Hardy.

The Antelope
22 Eaton Terrace, SW1
MAP REF 31, 1E
Regency inn of character and charm.

The Audley
41 Mount Street, W1
MAP REF 19, 3E
Large Victorian pub with lots of mirrors, close to the American Embassy.

The Black Friar
174 Queen Victoria Street, EC4
MAP REF 22, 2C
An ancient history and a splendid art-nouveau interior, with gold leaf on the ceiling, gas lighting and open fireplaces.

The Bunch of Grapes
207 Brompton Road, SW3
MAP REF 25, 3C
Victorian gem, with perfectly preserved glass, decorated windows and doors.

Cittie of York
22–23 High Holborn, WC1
MAP REF 22, 1A
One of the longest bars in London, dating back to the 17th century.

The City Barge
27 Strand-on-the-Green, W4
DISTRICT MAP, 3B
Old pub on the bank of the Thames.

Dickens Inn
St Katharine's Way, E1
DISTRICT MAP, 3E
At the heart of the dock redevelopment, an 18th-century brewery warehouse formed into a galleried inn with beams and low ceilings.

The Flask
77 Highgate West Hill, N6
DISTRICT MAP, 4D
Characterful, 17th-century pub where Hogarth painted and drank.

The French House
49 Dean Street, W1
MAP REF 20, 1C
The meeting place for De

Pubs

Jack Straw's Castle
Hampstead Heath, NW3
DISTRICT MAP, 4D
This enormous old coaching inn has associations with highwayman Dick Turpin.

King's Head
115 Upper Street, N1
DISTRICT MAP, 4D
Lovely pub, famous for its theatrical evenings.

King's Head & Eight Bells
50 Cheyne Walk, SW3
MAP REF 31, 3C
Atmospheric old pub favoured by artists and writers.

The Lamb
94 Lamb's Conduit Street, WC1
MAP REF 15, 3E
Fine Victorian pub with unusual period features.

Lamb and Flag
33 Rose Street, WC2
MAP REF 21, 2D
400-year-old ale tavern in a back alley, reputed to be the scene of the attempted assassination of the poet Dryden in 1679.

The Mayflower
117 Rotherhithe Street, SE16
DISTRICT MAP, 3E
Very old pub which changed its name in the 17th century as a tribute to the original *Mayflower* which sailed for the New World from nearby.

Minogue's
80 Liverpool Road, N1
DISTRICT MAP, 4D
Recreated Dublin pub with a lively Irish atmosphere.

Above: the 400-year-old Lamb and Flag. Below: The Mayflower

Museum Tavern
49 Great Russell Street, WC1
MAP REF 21, 1D
Lots of Victoriana and Edwardiana in this popular pub opposite the British Museum whose famous patrons have included Karl Marx and Virginia Woolf.

Gaulle's Free French during World War II and a drinking haunt of Brendan Behan and Dylan Thomas.

The George Inn
77 Borough High Street, SE1
MAP REF 29, 1D
The last remaining galleried coaching inn in London. Actors play scenes from Shakespeare and Dickens in the inn's courtyard during the summer months.

The Grenadier
18 Wilton Row, SW1
MAP REF 25, 2E
Old-world mews pub, said to be haunted.

Pubs

Nell of Old Drury
29 Catherine Street, WC2
MAP REF 21, 2E
Charming theatrical pub with bow-fronted windows, named after Nell Gwynn.

Olde Bull and Bush
North End Way, NW3
DISTRICT MAP, 4D
'Come and have a drink or two down at the Olde Bull and Bush' sang Florrie Ford in her still-popular Music Hall song, and down the years people have happily done just that.

Old Wine Shades
6 Martin Lane, EC4
MAP REF 23, 2D
This old tavern and wine shop, built in 1663, was the only city of London hostelry to survive the Great Fire.

Paxton's Head
153 Knightsbridge, SW1
MAP REF 25, 2D
Victorian-style pub named after Joseph Paxton, designer of the Crystal Palace.

Prospect of Whitby
57 Wapping Wall, E1
DISTRICT MAP, 3E
Very old and famous pub, on the river and near the docks. Among past habitués were Pepys, Whistler, Turner, Dickens, and Judge Jeffreys.

St Stephen's Tavern
10 Bridge Street, SW1
MAP REF 27, 2D
Frequented by MPs and journalists. The House of Commons division bell rings in the bar.

The Salisbury
90 St Martin's Lane WC2
MAP REF 21, 2D
Very large, plush Victorian pub in the heart of theatreland.

Sherlock Holmes
10 Northumberland Street, WC2
MAP REF 21, 3D
Lively pub with outside tables, full of Holmes memorabilia including Conan Doyle's recreated study.

The Ship
10 Thames Bank, SW14
DISTRICT MAP, 3C
Old riverside pub featuring rowing mementoes and viewing terrace for the Oxford-Cambridge boat race.

The Spaniards Inn
Spaniards End, NW3
DISTRICT MAP, 4D
Famous 16th-century inn with beams and low ceilings, and a garden; always crowded.

The Swan
66 Bayswater Road, W2
MAP REF 18, 2C
Old coaching-house with a popular terrace.

Victoria
10a Strathearn Place, W2
MAP REF 18, 2C
Splendidly ornate Victorian pub full of Queen Victoria memorabilia.

The Waterman's Arms
1 Glengarnock Avenue, Isle of Dogs, E14
DISTRICT MAP, 3E
Victorian pub with an authentic Cockney atmosphere.

The Windsor Castle
114 Campden Hill Road, W8
DISTRICT MAP, 3C
Fashionable, unspoilt west London pub with a popular walled beer garden.

Ye Olde Cheshire Cheese
145 Fleet Street, EC4
MAP REF 22, 2A
17th-century tavern of architectural, historical, and literary interest.

Ye Old Watling
29 Watling Street, EC4
MAP REF 22, 2C
Historic early 17th-century inn which housed the builders of St Paul's Cathedral.
The Olde Bull and Bush of music hall fame

Art galleries and museums

Art Galleries and Museums

Of the many hundreds of museums and art galleries open to the public in the capital, a selection of the more notable ones is described on the following pages. Many, in addition to their permanent collections, mount special exhibitions from time to time, and details of these can be obtained from newspapers and periodicals.

Agnew's Galleries
43 Old Bond Street, W1
Tel 071–629 6176
MAP REF 20, 3B
If you happen to be shopping for Old Masters, then Thomas Agnew & Sons Ltd is the place to visit. They have a worldwide reputation for exhibiting some of the finest Old Master paintings and drawings, and many works pass through their hands on the way to famous art galleries and museums. Some contemporary English works are also displayed.

Open Mon–Fri, 9.30–5.30, 6.30 on Thu during major exhibitions. (Closed Bank Hols). Admission free.

The Imperial War Museum houses vast collections recording all aspects of the two World Wars and other military operations since 1914

Bear Gardens Museum
Bear Gardens, SE1
Tel 071–928 6342
MAP REF 22, 3C
This museum stands on the site of the last bear-baiting ring on Bankside, close to the site of the Hope Theatre and Shakespeare's Globe. It occupies a 19th-century warehouse and consists of a permanent exhibition relating to Elizabethan theatre.

Open Mon–Fri 10–5, Sat 10.30–5.30, Sun 1.30–5.30. Admission charge.

Art galleries and museums

HMS Belfast
Morgans Lane, Tooley Street, SE1
Tel 071-407 6436
MAP REF 23, 3E
At 11,000 tons, this is the largest cruiser ever built for the Royal Navy. She was saved from the breaker's yard to be opened to the public in 1971 as a permanent floating naval museum.

Sights and smells of life at sea during World War II are recreated aboard.

Open all year, daily 20 Mar–31 Oct, 10–6, Nov–19 Mar, 10–4.30 (Closed 24–26 Dec & 1 Jan). Admission charge.

Bethnal Green Museum of Childhood
Cambridge Heath Road, E2
Tel 081-980 4315
DISTRICT MAP, 4E
A branch of the Victoria and Albert Museum. Its chief exhibits are toys, dolls and dolls-houses, model soldiers, puppets, games, model theatres, wedding dresses, children's costumes, all housed in an attractive Victorian building.

From Sep 1990 there will be a new schools programme.

Open Mon–Thu & Sat 10–6, Sun 2.30–6 (Closed Fri, spring Bank Hol Mon, 24–26 Dec & 1 Jan). Admission free.

The British Museum
Great Russell Street, WC1
Tel 071-636 1555
MAP REF 15, 4D
One of the greatest museums of the world, founded in 1753, the British Museum shows the works of man from all over the world, from prehistoric times.

Among the vast array of treasures not to be missed are the **Elgin Marbles** in the Duveen Gallery: the **Rosetta Stone**, dating from 195BC; the **Mildenhall Treasure**, a collection of 4th-century silver; the famous display of Egyptian mummies: and the exquisite 12th-century **Lewis Chessmen**.

WELCOME ABOARD   HMS BELFAST

Europe's largest preserved World War II warship *** Explore all seven decks, inside and out. Defend the ship against a simulated air attack! *** Exhibitions · Art Gallery · Cinema · Shop · Walkman tours now available

***

Open seven days a week   Group discount rates

***

Nearest underground stations: London Bridge, Monument, Tower Hill
HMS Belfast, Morgans Lane, Tooley Street, London SE1 2JH   Tel: 071-407 6434

Art galleries and museums

The new Japanese galleries, built as a whole floor over the King Edward VII building, house Japanese paintings, prints, sculpture and lacquer. Original documents are on show in the British Library, a separate institution within the British Museum building.

There is a regular programme of gallery talks, lectures and films, and young visitors can enjoy a special children's trail.

The ethnography collection is in the Museum of Mankind in Burlington Gardens.

Open all year Mon–Sat 10–5, Sun 2.30–6 (Closed Good Fri, May Day, 24–26 Dec & 1 Jan). Admission free. Toilets for disabled, shop.

Cabinet War Rooms

Clive Steps, King Charles Street, SW1
Tel 071–930 6961
MAP REF 27, 1D
The most important surviving part of the underground emergency accommodation provided to protect the Prime Minister and his Cabinet against air attacks during World War II. Some rooms

HMS Belfast: recalling life at sea during the Second World War

have been left intact; others are restored to their wartime appearance. New 'Walkman' tours take you through the War Rooms; 45 minutes. A special Young Adventurer tour is available for children.

Open all year, daily 10–6 (last admission 5.25) (Closed 24–26 Dec & 1 Jan). Admission charge. Toilets for disabled, shop.

Contemporary Applied Arts

43 Earlham Street, Covent Garden, WC2
Tel 071–836 6993
MAP REF 21, 2D
Current arts and crafts are to be found in this centre which runs a programme of special exhibitions and retail displays including wallhangings, furniture, ceramics, pottery and jewellery. There are also books and magazines on craft and design for sale.

Open all year Mon–Sat 10–5.30 (Closed Sun & Bank Hol Mon). Admission free.

Courtauld Institute Galleries

North Block, Somerset House, Strand, WC2
MAP REF 21, 2E
Recently moved from premises in Gordon Square, the galleries reopened in early summer 1990. They contain the superb collection of paintings begun by Samuel Courtauld in the 1930s and presented to the University of London in memory of his wife. This is the most important collection of Impressionist and post-Impressionist works in Britain and includes paintings by Monet, Renoir, Degas, Cezanne, Van Gogh and Gauguin. There are also works by Michelangelo, Rubens,

Goya, and other notable masters, as well as early Italian paintings. British and French 20th-century works given to the University by Roger Fry are also displayed here. Exhibitions are changed regularly.

Open all year, Mon–Sat 10–6, Sun 2–6. Admission charge. Toilets for disabled, shop.

Cricket Memorial Gallery

Lord's Ground, St Johns Wood, NW8
Tel 071–289 1611
MAP REF 12, 2B
Located in the best known cricket ground in the country, this gallery was founded in 1865. It contains a collection of cricket memorabilia, including the first urn to contain the 'Ashes', and 18th-century paintings of the sport. There is also a fine library of cricketing literature, and a new 'Gestetner Tour of Lords' in which visitors are taken on a tour of Lords and its exhibits. Advance booking required.

Open, Match days Mon–Sat 10.30–5. Other times by prior appointment. Admission charge. Toilets for disabled, shop.

Cuming Museum

155 Walworth Road, SE17
Tel 071–703 3324 ext 212
DISTRICT MAP, 3D
The museum is mainly devoted to the history of Southwark and items found in the area, and includes displays on Chaucer, Shakespeare and Dickens, demonstrating in lively fashion their associations with Southwark. It also houses a fascinating collection of exhibits relating to London's superstitions.

Open all year, Thu–Sat 10–5. School & adult parties daily by appointment. Admission free.

Art galleries and museums

Design Museum
Butlers Wharf, Shad Thames, SE1
Tel 071-403 6933
DISTRICT MAP, 3E
Exhibitions of design and graphics in a modern white building converted from a 1930s warehouse. The exhibition includes the design of everyday items – everything from tea kettles and radios to Porsches.
Open all year, Tue–Sun 11.30–6.30 (Closed Mon ex Bank Hols.) Admission charge. Toilets for disabled.

Dulwich College Picture Gallery
College Road, SE21
Tel 081-693 5254
DISTRICT MAP, 2E
The oldest public picture gallery in England, this is also one of the most beautiful galleries in London, containing a notable collection of Old Masters, including works by Gainsborough, Raphael, Rembrandt and Rubens.
Open all year, Tue–Sat 11–5, Sun 2–5 (Closed Mon). Guided tours Sat & Sun 3pm. Admission charge.

Earth Galleries, The (Natural History Museum)
Cromwell Road, SW7
Tel 071-938 9388
MAP REF 24, 3C
These galleries, formerly known as the Geological Museum, form part of the Natural History Museum. Here you can experience a simulated earthquake, and see the many fascinating exhibits including a piece of the moon and the largest exhibition on basic earth science in the world. There is also a notable collection of fine gemstones. These are shown in their parent rock, in their natural crystal form, and in their final cut stage. The regional geology of Great Britain and ore deposits of the world are also displayed. 'British Fossils' and 'Treasures of the Earth' are just two more of the interesting permanent exhibitions.
Open Mon–Sat 10–6, Sun 1–6 (Closed Good Fri, May Day, 24–26 Dec & 1 Jan). Admission charge. Toilets for disabled, shop.

Geffrye Museum
Kingsland Road, E2
Tel 071-739 8368/9893
DISTRICT MAP, 4F
Occupying the former almshouses of the Ironmongers' Company, this museum consists of a series of period room settings from the Elizabethan age to 1939.
Open all year, Tue–Sat 10–5; Sun 2–5; Bank Hol Mons 10–5 (Closed Mon, Good Fri, 24–26 Dec & 1 Jan). Admission free. Toilets for disabled, shop.

Guinness World of Records Exhibition
Trocadero Centre, Coventry Street, Piccadilly Circus, W1
Tel 071-439 7331
MAP REF 20, 3C
With the use of life-size models, tableaux, videos and the latest audio technology, this exhibition illustrates many of the feats and records contained in the Guinness Book of Records on the subject of the Human World, the Animal World, Our Planet Earth, Structures and Machines, the Sports World, the World of Entertainment and British Innovation and Achievement.
Open all year, daily 10am–10pm (last admission). (Closed Xmas Day). Admission charge. Toilets for disabled, shop.

Hayward Gallery
The South Bank Complex, SE1
Tel 071-921 0876
MAP REF 27, 1E
Opened in 1968, this purpose-built, ultra-modern building is an international venue for major art exhibitions and is also the base for the South Bank Centre's touring exhibitions.
Open daily 10–6 (Tue and Wed until 8). Details of current exhibitions can be obtained from the national press. Admission charge.

Rembrandt   RVBENS   D. Teniers. F
J Reynolds   A. VAN·DYCK   N Poussin

The quiet genius of the past

DULWICH PICTURE GALLERY
College Road, London SE21 7AD   Recorded Information 081-693 8000   Open Tuesdays-Sundays

Art galleries and museums

Horniman Museum
London Road, SE23
Tel 081–699 2339
DISTRICT MAP, 2E
Displays from different cultures, natural history collections – including living creatures – and musical instruments from all parts of the world can be seen.
   Open all year, Mon–Sat 10.30–5.50, Sun 2–5.50 (Closed 24–26 Dec). Admission free. Toilets for disabled, shop.

Imperial War Museum
Lambeth Road, SE1
Tel 071–416 5000
MAP REF 28, 3A
Founded in 1917 and established in 1920 by an Act of Parliament, this museum illustrates and records all aspects of the two World Wars and other military operations involving Britain and the Commonwealth since 1914. It has recently undergone major renovations and although the vast collections are still housed within the imposing walls of the original building in Lambeth Road, it is now a thoroughly modern museum employing all the latest technology to make its exhibitions more vital and atmospheric for the visitor, such as the 'Blitz Experience' and the 'walk-through trench'. Improvements include a new, large exhibition hall, art galleries and a shop and licensed restaurant. There are always special exhibitions and the programme of events includes film shows and lectures. The Imperial War Museum has a wealth of military reference material, although some reference departments are open to the public by appointment only.
   Open all year, daily 10–6. (Closed 24–26 Dec & 1 Jan). Admission charge (free day Fri). Toilets for disabled, shop.

Recently renovated, The Imperial War Museum now employs all the latest technology to bring its exhibits to life

---

EXPLORE THE HORNIMAN MUSEUM AND GARDENS
100 LONDON ROAD, FOREST HILL, SE23

Experience the world's living heritage in the unique Horniman Museum — arts & crafts, musical instruments and the natural environment — it's all here for all ages to enjoy. Enjoy one of the best views of London from the famous Horniman Gardens with live animals, nature trails, concerts, events and a picnic area.

Open MON-SAT 10.30am to 5.50pm, SUN 2pm to 5.50pm   GARDENS OPEN TO SUNSET. BOTH FREE.

Tel: 081-699 2339

BR Forest Hill, Buses P4, 312, 78, 176, 185.   Free Parking in Sydenham Rise

Art galleries and museums

Jewish Museum
Woburn House, Tavistock Square, WC1
Tel 071-388 4525
MAP REF 15, 3C
A fascinating exhibition displaying a collection of ceremonial art, portraits and antiques illustrating Jewish life, history and religion. Two audio-visual programmes explain Jewish festivals and ceremonies.
Open Tue–Thu & Sun 10–4 (Fri: Apr–Sep 10–4, Oct–Mar 10–12.45). (Closed Sat, Mon, Public & Jewish Hols). Admission free (donations). Toilets for disabled, shop.

Kenwood House (The Iveagh Bequest)
Hampstead Lane, NW3
Tel 081-348 1286
DISTRICT MAP, 5D
The House at Kenwood was enlarged for Lord Mansfield in 1767 by the great architect Robert Adam. It was bequeathed to the nation in 1927 by the first Earl of Iveagh, and it makes a magnificent setting for his collection of English and Dutch masterpieces; they include works by Frans Hals, Vermeer, Rembrandt, Reynolds and Turner.
The 200-acre grounds of Kenwood House contain a lakeside platform where open-air concerts are held during the summer.
Open daily, Apr–Sep 10–6; Oct–Mar 10–4. Admission free (charges for special exhibitions and concerts). Toilets for disabled, shop.

London Diamond Centre
10 Hanover Street, W1
Tel 071-629 5511
MAP REF 20, 2B
Everything you ever needed to know about diamonds and their related craft is displayed at the London Diamond Centre. Visitors can watch diamond cutters and polishers at work; a goldsmith creating settings; walk into a reconstructed diamond mine and see a collection of replicas of some of the world's most famous and historic stones. A video explains other interesting aspects of the industry.
Open all year, Mon–Fri 9.30–5.30, Sat 9.30–1.30. Admission charge, toilets for disabled.

London Dungeon
28–34 Tooley Street, SE1
Tel 071-403 0606
MAP REF 23, 3D
The London Dungeon has won the British Tourist Authority's Award for Outstanding Tourist Enterprise. Its modest entrance off a street near London Bridge station will lead the visitor through to a series of slimy vaults where the seamy side of life in past centuries is convincingly re-created. Methods of torture and death, the tools of witchcraft and black magic and some of the more grisly medicinal practices are well represented. Viewing takes about an hour; this museum is not recommended for the faint-hearted.
Open all year, daily. Apr–Sep 10–5.30; Oct–Mar 10–4.30. Admission charge. Toilets for disabled, shop.

London Planetarium
Marylebone Road, NW1
Tel 071-486 1121
MAP REF 13, 4E
The beauty of the night skies is majestically represented and explained by means of a projection onto the inside of the London Planetarium's dome. This is done with a two-ton Zeiss instrument and accompanied by a fascinating and informative commentary. Music adds to the atmosphere. On the way into the dome, visitors pass through an exhibition called 'The Astronomers', which includes wax figures of scientific luminaries such as Einstein and Galileo and three-dimensional representations of their theories and discoveries. There are fantastic laser light rock shows most evenings, employing all the latest laser technology to give a visual and musical spectacle.
Open all year, daily (ex 25 Dec), star shows 10.20–5, every 40 mins. (From 12.20–5 wkdys during school holidays). Admission charge. Shop.

London Silver Vaults
Chancery Lane, WC2
Tel 071-242 3488
MAP REF 22, 1A
A fine collection of antiques and modern silverware in an underground location. Visitors can browse and traders are happy to talk about their wares, look up hallmarks and explain histories.
Open Mon–Fri 9–5.30; Sat 9–12.30. Admission free.

London Toy and Model Museum
October House, 21–23 Craven Hill, W2
Tel 071-262 9450
MAP REF 18, 2A
Victorian building housing one of the finest collections of commercially made toys and models with an emphasis on trains, cars and boats. Extensive garden railway.
Open Tue–Sat 10–5.30, Sun 11–5.30 (Closed ex Bank Hol Mons, Mon, Xmas Day & New Years Day). Admission charge.

The activity garden of The London Toy and Model Museum, with carousel, trainrides and picnic area

Art galleries and museums

London Transport Museum
The Piazza, Covent Garden, WC2
Tel 071–379 6344
MAP REF 21, 2D
A unique collection of vehicles associated with 150 years of public transport in London. It includes trams, trolley-buses, horse-drawn and motor buses, steam locomotives and railway coaches; and a selection of signs, tickets, posters and models.
Open daily, 10–6 (last admission 5.15) (Closed Xmas). Admission charge. Toilets for disabled, shop.

Madame Tussaud's
Marylebone Road, NW1
Tel 071–935 6861
MAP REF 13, 4E
Founded in Paris, Mme Tussaud's Wax Exhibition settled in London in the early 19th century. It contains a large collection of famous historical and contemporary figures, new versions of the tableaux, and the grim Chamber of Horrors. It is always very popular, so be prepared to queue.
Open all year, 10–5.30 (9.30am wknds, 9am summer) (Closed 25 Dec). Admission charge.

Museum of London
150 London Wall, EC2
Tel 071–600 3699 ext 240 or 280
MAP REF 22, 1C
Early December 1976 saw the official opening of the Museum of London. The collections of the former London and Guildhall museums were brought together under one specially designed roof, located in the Barbican development. The site adjoins a stretch of the original Roman wall which surrounded the city.

Devoted to and detailing all aspects of London life from pre-history to contemporary times, the museum offers a fascinating display presented in chronological order. The exhibits and tableaux are arranged to give the visitor a realistic view of life in the capital through the ages; archaeological levels are illustrated by a relief model of the Thames Valley which provides an apt starting point for the story. Features of special interest include the superb models of William the Conqueror's White Tower and old St Pauls; the audio-visual reconstruction of the Great Fire of London in 1666 (superbly atmospheric) and the exhibition of ceremonial London with the Lord Mayor's State Coach as its centrepiece. It is also worth looking out for the medieval hen's egg, a lift from Selfridges department

109

Art galleries and museums

Museum of Mankind, Worldwide art and cultural exhibits

store and a 1930s Ford motor car.

Open all year, Tue–Sat 10–6, Sun 2–6 (Closed 25–26 every Mon ex Bank Hols). Parties by arrangement. Admission charge. Toilets for disabled, shop.

Museum of Mankind

6 Burlington Gardens, W1
Tel 071-636 1555 ext 8043
MAP REF 20, 3B
The ethnographical department of the British Museum was re-housed in 1970 at Burlington Gardens to form the Museum of Mankind. Its vast collections embrace the art and material culture of tribal, village and pre-industrial societies from most areas of the world other than Western Europe. It also houses archaeological collections from the Americas and Africa. The museum's policy is to mount a number of fascinating temporary exhibitions (usually lasting for at least a year) rather than have permanent displays, although there are a number of outstanding permanent exhibits. The reserve collection is stored in Shoreditch and can be made available for serious study. Film shows and educational services are provided.

Open all year, Mon–Sat 10–5, Sun 2.30–6. (Closed Good Fri, May Day, Xmas & 1 Jan). Admission free. Shop.

Museum of the Moving Image

National Film Theatre, South Bank, SE1
Tel 071-401 2636
MAP REF 21, 3E
A journey through cinematic history, from the earliest experiments to all the technical wizardry of modern animation, is what this museum offers the visitor. There are artefacts to handle, buttons to press and films to watch as well as a detailed explanation of the operations of a television studio. A fascinating insight into the world of films and television with each chapter as exciting as the last.

Open all year, Oct–May, Tue–Sat 10–8, Sun & Bank Hols 10–6; Jun–Sep, Sun & Bank Hols 10–8 (Closed Mon & 24–26 Dec). Admission charge. Toilets for disabled, shop.
See advertisement on inside front cover

Museum of the Order of St John

St John's Gate, EC1
Tel 071-253 6644 ext 35
MAP REF 16, 4B
One of London's more obscure museums shows a collection of paintings, silver and furniture belonging to the Order of St John. The medieval gatehouse also houses items relating to the history of the St John Ambulance.

Open all year, Mon–Fri 10–5, Sat 10–4 (Closed Etr, Xmas wk & Bank Hols). Guided tours 11 & 2.30 Tue, Fri & Sat. Donations. Shop.

National Army Museum

Royal Hospital Road, SW3
Tel 071-730 0717
MAP REF 31, 2D
The history of the British, Indian and Colonial forces from 1485 onwards unfolds in this museum. Displayed, in chronological order, are uniforms, weapons, prints, photographs, relics and mementos together with a special display of the orders and decorations of the Duke of Windsor and those five great Field Marshals – Lord Roberts, Gough, Kitchener, Wolseley and Sir George White VC. The picture gallery includes portraits by Gainsborough and Reynolds as well as battle scenes and pictures of the Indian regiments.

Open daily, Mon–Sat 10–5.30, Sun 2–5.30. (Closed Good Fri, May Day, Xmas & 1 Jan). Admission free. Toilets for disabled, shop.

Art galleries and museums

National Gallery
Trafalgar Square, WC2
Tel 071-839 3321, recorded information 071-839 3526
MAP REF 21, 3D
In 1824 the government bought the collection of pictures accumulated by John Julius Angerstein, a London underwriter, and exhibited them at his former residence in Pall Mall. These formed the major part of the collections of the National Gallery. Further bequests and purchases were made and by 1831 space had become limited, so plans were made for a special building to house the works of art. The present classical-style building in Trafalgar Square was opened in 1838. All the great periods of European painting are represented here although only a limited selection of British works is displayed, as most of the national collection is housed at the Tate. The gallery's particular treasures include Van Eyck's *Arnolfini Marriage*, Velazquez's *Toilet of Venus*, Leonardo da Vinci's cartoon (the Virgin and Child with saints Anne and John the Baptist), Rembrandt's *Belshazzar's Feast* and *Bacchus and Ariadne*. The British paintings include Gainsborough's *Mr and Mrs Andrews* and Constable's *Haywain*. There are many more captivating masterpieces to be seen at the National Gallery which houses one of the finest and most extensive collections in the world. Lectures, guided tours, children's worksheets and quizzes are available.

Open all year, Mon–Sat 10–6, Sun 2–6; Jun–Aug, Wed 10–8. (Closed Good Fri, May Day, 24–26 Dec & 1 Jan). Admission free. Toilets for disabled, shop.

National Maritime Museum
DISTRICT MAP 3E
See pages 73/74.

National Portrait Gallery
2 St Matthews Place, WC2
Tel 071-930 1552
MAP REF 21, 3D
With the aim of illustrating British history by means of a collection of portraits of famous, and infamous, men and women, the gallery's first home was established in George Street, Westminster. After several moves the collection was finally housed in its present accommodation in 1896. Located behind the National Gallery, the building was designed in the style of an Italian palazzo. A further wing was added in 1933, and the annexe in nearby Carlton House Terrace contains part of the reserve collection and houses temporary exhibits. The portraits, arranged in chronological order, are displayed among furnishings, maps, weapons and other items to set them in their historical context. As well as paintings, there are sculptures, miniatures, engravings, photographs and cartoons among the displays. With the exception of the royal family, portraits of living persons are not usually shown in this gallery. Special exhibitions are mounted several times a year.

Open all year, 10–5, Sat 10–6 & Sun 2–6. (Closed Good Fri, May Day, 24–26 Dec & 1 Jan). Admission free. Shop.

National Postal Museum
King Edward Street, EC1
Tel 071-239 5420
MAP REF 22, 1B
This museum is a philatelist's paradise; it contains the most comprehensive collection of postage stamps in the world. Established in 1965, the National Postage Museum has obtained a vast collection of material charting the history of the postal system since its inception. Exhibits include a collection of virtually every stamp issued worldwide since 1878; the R M Phillips collection of 19th-century British stamps, including the

N**P**G
NATIONAL PORTRAIT GALLERY

St Martin's Place, London WC2H 0HE
Telephone 071-306 0055

Admission Free

Open Daily.
Closed 24–26 December, 1 January,
Good Friday and May Day Bank Holiday.

Nearest ⊖ Leicester Square or Charing Cross

111

Art galleries and museums

celebrated 'Penny Black', and the correspondence archives of Thomas de la Rue and Co, a company which furnished stamps to over 150 countries for nearly 100 years. Visitors can also view the original drawings for many of the stamps that have been issued since 1840, and thousands of unique proof sheets.
Mon–Thu (ex Bank Hols) 9.30–4.30, Fri 9.30–4. Admission free. Shop.

Natural History Museum

Cromwell Road, SW1
Tel 071–938 9123
MAP REF 24, 3B
The museum's collections were built up around the specimens collected by Sir Hans Sloane and which formed a part of the nucleus of the British Museum. By 1860 the continued expansion of the collections meant that a separate natural history museum was required; it was not until 1881 though that the new museum – officially called the British Museum (Natural History) – was opened. The vast and elaborate Romanesque-style building, with its terracotta facing showing relief mouldings of animals, birds and fishes, covers an area of four acres. The collections are divided into five departments covering botany, entomology, mineralogy, palaeontology and zoology. Over 2,000 native plants and animals are displayed; in the bird pavilion many of Britain's bird songs are recorded; in the Whale Hall a life-size model of the enormous blue whale can be seen, and in the Hall of Human Biology visitors can learn about the way their bodies work (including how it feels to be in the womb). Leaflets regarding public lectures and films are available on request.
Open Mon–Sat 10–6, Sun 1–6. (Closed Good Fri, May Day, 24–26 Dec & 1 Jan). Admission charge. Toilets for disabled, shop.

North Woolwich Old Station Museum

Pier Road, E16
Tel 071–474 7244
DISTRICT MAP, 3F
Imposing restored station building with three galleries of photographs, models, and an original turntable pit. Each Sunday a locomotive is in steam.
Open Mon–Sat 10–5; Sun & Bank Hols 2–5 (Closed Xmas). Admission free.

The vast and elaborate Romanesque-style building of the Natural History Museum

Art galleries and museums

The Photographers' Gallery
5/8 Great Newport Street, WC2
Tel 071–831 1772
MAP REF 21, 2D
As well as monthly exhibitions, the gallery aims to show the best of the many types of professional photography – from reportage and advertising to the purely creative.
Open Tue–Sat 11–7. Admission free.

Pollock's Toy Museum
1 Scala Street, W1
Tel 071–636 3452
MAP REF 14, 4B
In two charming interconnected houses are displayed dolls, teddy bears, board games, toy theatres and mechanical toys from all over the world. There is also a shop.
Open all year, Mon–Sat 10–5 (Closed Sun & Bank Hols).

The Public Records Office
Chancery Lane, WC2
Tel 071–636 3452
MAP REF 22, 1A
This is the chief repository for the national archives. The Search Rooms contain records from the Norman Conquest to the present day. Among the famous documents on display are the *Domesday Book*, letters from Cardinal Wolsey and Guy Fawkes, and Shakespeare's will.
Open all year, Mon–Fri 10–5. Admission free.

Queen's Gallery Buckingham Palace
Buckingham Palace Road, SW1
Tel 071–799 2331
MAP REF 26, 2B
Items from the Royal Collection are housed in a building originally designed as a conservatory by John Nash.
Open Tue–Sat & Bank Hol Mons 10.30–5; Sun 2–5 (ex for short periods between exhibitions). Admission charge.

Royal Academy of Arts
Burlington House, Piccadilly, W1
Tel 071–439 7438
MAP REF 20, 3B
An annual Summer Exhibition of works of living artists has been held here since 1769. Other exhibitions of international importance take place as announced in the press.
Open all year, daily 10–6. Admission charge. Shop.

Royal Air Force Museum
Grahame Park Way, NW9
Tel 081–205 2266
DISTRICT MAP, 5C
Over 60 aircraft are included in these galleries devoted to military aviation history.
Open Apr–Oct Mon–Sat 10–6, Sun 2–6 (Closed Good Fri, May Day). Admission charge.

Royal College of Music Museum of Instruments
Prince Consort Road, SW7
Tel 071–589 3643
MAP REF 27, 2B
Among the 500 musical instruments housed here are the Donaldson collection of rare keyboard pieces, some dating from the 15th century; the Ridley woodwind collection; and the Tagore collection from South-east Asia.
Open Wed 2–4.30 and by appointment. Admission charge.

St Bride's Crypt Museum
Fleet Street, EC4
MAP REF 22, 2B
A wealth of history and relics can be seen on permanent display in the crypt museum beneath this 'parish church of the press'.
Open Mon–Sat 9–5, Sun 9–8. Admission free.

Schooner Kathleen & May
St Mary Overy Dock, SE1
Tel 071–403 3965
MAP REF 23, 3D
The last British, wooden, three-masted topsail schooner is in a berth at St Mary Overy Dock, on the South Bank of the River Thames. There are exhibitions on board, and film and audio-visual displays.
Open all year, daily 10–5 (4 at wknds); Nov–Mar 11–4. (Closed Xmas & New Year & wknds Nov–Feb). Admission charge. Shop.

Science Museum
Exhibition Road, SW7
Tel 071–938 8000
MAP REF 24, 3C
The extensive collections illustrate the development of engineering and industry throughout the ages. Of all London museums, this is the one most loved by children. There are plenty of opportunities for hands-on experiences with knobs to press, handles to turn, and all sorts of exhibits that light up, rotate and make noises.

There are galleries dealing with astronomy, printing, chemistry, nuclear physics, navigation, photography, electricity, communications. The exhibits include a superb collection of model ships, and forming part of the Exploration of Space Gallery, the *Apollo 10 Space Capsule*.

In the huge new wing of the ground floor devoted to road and rail transport may be seen *Puffing Billy*, the world's oldest steam locomotive, and George Stephenson's *Rocket*. The Wellcome collections of medicine and medical history are on the 5th and 6th floors.
Open all year, Mon–Sat 10–6, Sun 11–6 (Closed Good Fri, May Day, 24–26 Dec & 1 Jan). Admission charge.

Art galleries and museums

Sir John Soane's Museum housing the collection of pictures, sculptures and antiquities founded by the original architect of the Bank of England

Sir John Soane's Museum

13 Lincoln's Inn Fields, WC2
Tel 071–405 2107
MAP REF 21, 1E
A fine 1813 house contains the collection of pictures, sculptures and antiquities founded by the original architect of the Bank of England building. There are paintings by Hogarth, notably his *Rake's Progress*, and the sarcophagus of Seti 1, dating from 129 BC. More than 20,000 architectural drawings can be viewed by appointment only.
Open all year, Tue-Sat 10–5 (Closed Bank Hols). Admission free. Shop.

Space Adventure

64–66 Tooley Street, SE1
Tel 071–378 1405
MAP REF 23, 3D
In the same street as the London Dungeon, but light years away from its murky glimpse into the past, is Space Adventure: an entirely new concept in leisure entertainment. Instead of medieval horrors, the sights, sounds and sensations of space travel are cleverly recreated to take the visitor on an incredible journey through the solar system to Mars, via the moon. Video presentations and computer-controlled technology achieve impressive realism. Space Adventure is also the home for a *Dr Who* exhibition featuring animated figures of many of the Time Lord's adversaries.
Open all year, Mar-Oct, daily 10–6; Nov-Apr, daily 10.30–5. Admission charge. Shop.

The Tate Gallery

Millbank, SW1
Tel 071–821 1313
MAP REF 33, 1D
Opened in 1897, the gallery houses the national collections of British painting of all periods, modern foreign painting and modern sculpture. There is also a large collection of contemporary prints. Hogarth, Blake, Turner, Constable and the Pre-Raphaelites are particularly well represented, and the English mastery of landscape painting is superbly illustrated. All schools of painting and sculpture are represented in the modern and foreign

Art galleries and museums

The Tate, showing national collections of British painting and modern foreign works

collections which trace the development of art from Impressionism to the present day. The Tate is especially renowned for its modern works of art, buying some almost before they are finished, so reflecting the constantly changing emphasis of contemporary art.

A new display of the collection, 'Past, Present, Future', is the first rearrangement in 20 years.

Open Mon-Sat 10–5.50; Sun 2–5.50 (Closed 8–19 Jan, Good Fri, May Day, 24–26 Dec & 1 Jan). Admission free; admission charge to special exhibitions.

Telecom Technology Showcase
135 Queen Victoria Street, EC4
Tel 071-248 7444
MAP REF 22, 2B

A fascinating exhibition featuring the past, present and future of Britain's telecommunications. The many working exhibits chart 200 years of progress from the earliest telegraphs to the satellites and optical fibres which have revolutionised mass communications across the world. Examples of the different styles of domestic telephones through the decades are displayed among the collection of interesting exhibits.

Open all year, Mon-Fri 10–5. (Closed Bank Hols). Admission free. Shop.

The Thomas Coram Foundation for Children
40 Brunswick Square, WC1
Tel 071-278 2424
MAP REF 15, 3D

The Foundation was formed in 1739 with the granting of a royal charter to Captain Thomas Coram to open a Foundling Hospital for destitute children. At the instigation of William Hogarth, various works of art were presented to the Foundation to attract the public and raise funds. The building now houses the vast number of exhibits which have been presented to the Foundation over the years.

Open Mon-Fri, 10–4 (Closed Bank Hols). (Advisable to check). Admission charge.

Art galleries and museums

The Victoria and Albert Museum

Victoria and Albert Museum

Cromwell Road, SW7
Tel 071-938 8500
MAP REF 24, 3C

Covering art and design, from all countries and from all periods and styles, this museum has over seven miles of galleries. It is impossible to take it all in on one visit, so it is advisable to buy a guide book and plan a route in advance. The collection was founded at Marlborough House after the Great Exhibition, and was known as the Museum of Manufactures. In 1857 it moved to its present site and was called the South Kensington Museum. Enlarged and redesigned by Sir Aston Webb at the end of the 19th century it was re-opened in 1909 by Edward VII as the Victoria and Albert Museum. There are two types of galleries: the primary ones which give a comprehensive picture of a period or civilisation; and subject galleries which contain the specialised collections. Features include a series of rooms decorated and equipped with the paintings, furniture and household accessories of particular periods in British history including the enormous 16th-century Great Bed of Ware. The Toshiba Gallery of Japanese Art and Design, the Constable Paintings, Raphael Cartoons and the costume exhibition displayed in the Octagon Court

Open all year, Mon-Sat 10–5.50, Sun 2.30–5.50. (Closed Good Fri, May Day, 24–26 Dec & 1 Jan). Admission charge. Toilets for disabled, shop.

Art galleries and museums

Wallace Collection
Manchester Square, W1
Tel 071-935 0687
MAP REF 19, 1E
An elegant 18th-century town house makes an appropriate gallery for this outstanding collection of art. Founded by the 1st Marquis of Hertford and brought to England from Paris in the late 19th century by Richard Wallace (son of the 4th Marquis) it was bequeathed to the nation in 1897 and came on public display three years later. As well as an unrivalled representation of 18th-century French art with paintings by Boucher Watteau and Fragonard, Hertford House displays a wealth of furniture, porcelain and beautiful works of art. It is the home of Frans Hals' 'Laughing Cavalier' and of paintings by Gainsborough, Reubens, Delacroix and Titian.
Open all year, Mon-Sat 10–5, Sun 2–5. (Closed Good Fri, May Day, 24–26 Dec & 1 Jan). Admission free.

The Wellington Museum
149 Piccadilly, W1
Tel 071-499 5676
MAP REF 26, 1A
Known as Number One London, Apsley House was the property of the first Duke of Wellington, Arthur Wellesley, from 1817 until his death in 1852. During the time that he was Prime Minister the windows of Apsley House were broken so frequently that they had to be covered with iron shutters (despite his distinguished military career he was extremely unpopular as Prime Minister). The mansion was designed by Robert Adam, built in 1771–8 and enlarged, under the Duke's direction, by Benjamin Wyatt in the late 1820s. The 7th Duke of Wellington presented it to the nation in 1947 and it opened to the public a few years later. Canova's colossal marble figure of Napoleon dominates the exhibits which also include paintings, silver, porcelain and personal relics of the first Duke.
Open all year, Tue-Sun 11–5. (Closed Mon, 24–26 Dec & 1 Jan). Admission charge. Shop.

William Morris Gallery
Lloyd Park, Forest Road, E17
Tel 081-527 5544 ext 4390, 081-527 3782
DISTRICT MAP, 5E
William Morris was a great Victorian artist, craftsman, poet and free thinker. This house, his home from 1848 to 1856 and then known as the Water House, has been devoted to the life and work of Morris, his followers, contemporaries and the Morris Company. Exhibits include fabrics, wallpaper and furniture, much of which is still fashionable today. To complete the picture of this innovative period in the history of art and philosophy there are also Pre-Raphaelite paintings, sculpture by Rodin, ceramics and a collection of pictures by Frank Brangwyn, who worked for Morris for many years. A varied programme of events is run by the museum throughout the year.
Open all year, Tue-Sat 10–1 & 2–5, and 1st Sun in each month 10–12 & 2–5. (Closed Mon & Bank Hols.). Admission free. Shop.

Wimbledon Lawn Tennis Museum
Church Road, SW19
Tel 081-946 6131
DISTRICT MAP, 2C
The only one of its kind in the world, this museum, situated within the internationally renowned grounds of the All England Lawn Tennis and Croquet Club (see page 129), traces the development of the game over the last century. There is a library and audio-visual theatre.
Open all year, Tue-Sat 11–5, Sun 2–5 (closed Mon & Bank Hols and Fri-Sun before championships). Admission charge. Toilets for disabled, shop.

The Wimbledon Lawn Tennis Museum
ALL ENGLAND CLUB, CHURCH ROAD, WIMBLEDON, SW19 5AE
Telephone: 081-946 6131

Fashion, trophies, replicas and memorabilia are on display representing the history of lawn tennis. An audio-visual theatre shows films of great matches and the opportunity is now given to observe the famous Centre Court from the Museum. The Museum shop offers a wide range of attractive souvenirs.
Open Tuesday — Saturday 11am—5pm, Sunday 2pm-5pm. **Closed** Mondays, Public & Bank Holidays and on the Friday, Saturday and Sunday prior to The Championships.
During The Championships Admission to the Museum is restricted to those attending the tournament. **Admission** Adults £1.50, Students £1.00, Children & OAP's 75p. Limited facilities are available for disabled visitors who are most welcome.

Entertainment

ENTERTAINMENT

However you like to be entertained, you will find something to suit your taste in London. There is always a wide variety of plays and musicals to choose from in the theatres; a host of cinemas show the latest releases, classic oldies, and the more obscure movies which you missed the first time round; and there is music everywhere, from jazz in cafés and folk music in church crypts, to the usual concert venues. Full details of all current and forthcoming concerts, together with theatre and cinema programmes, can be found in the entertainments section of London's evening newspaper, *The Standard*, and in specialist London magazines such as *Time Out*, *What's On*, and *City Limits* – on sale at bookstalls and newsagents.

Over 400 years after live theatre first appeared in London there are now about 40 commercial theatres in the West End

BOOKING

Tickets can be booked, of course, at the box offices of the individual theatres and concert halls. Many now accept credit card booking, which means you can telephone the box office to reserve your seats, quote your credit card number, and then collect the tickets half-an-hour before the performance begins. Some places have special phone numbers for credit card bookings, and these are prefixed *cc* in the listings which follow. Or you can use the services of ticket agencies such as Keith Prowse (Tel 081–741 9999); or try First Call (Tel 071–240 7200), a new

Entertainment

telephone booking service mainly for credit card holders wanting theatre and concert tickets. It is open 24 hours a day, seven days a week.

ARTS CENTRES

Amongst the most exciting venues in London, these centres offer several different types of entertainment under one roof. Even if you only go once, you cannot but be aware of the creativity generated by the other activities; they are, anyway, pleasant places to go for an evening meal, snack, or drink, as they all offer refreshments of one sort or another.

Barbican Centre
Barbican, EC2
MAP REF 16/17, 4C
Tel Box Office 071–628 8795; recorded information on events 071–628 9760; cc 071–638 8891
It is best to allow plenty of time to find where you want to go within this massive complex; the free guide *Welcome to the Barbican Centre* will help get you to your seats on time. The **Barbican Theatre** (levels 3–6), London home of the Royal Shakespeare Company, presents modern drama and classic revivals as well as regular productions of Shakespeare's plays. Beneath, on level 1, more experimental works, as well as the classics, are presented in the Studio theatre called the Pit.
In the **Barbican Hall** on levels 5 and 6, the London Symphony Orchestra – whose home this is – offers over 80 concerts a year. It is also used by visiting orchestras and for jazz and light musical concerts. **Cinema 1**, on level 1, shows current general releases, and **Cinema 2**, level 9, shows occasional series of international films.

Whenever you go to the Barbican, even on Sunday mornings, you will find frequent free entertainment – mostly of a musical nature – in the foyers on most levels. Refreshments of one sort or another can also be found on all levels. Particularly pleasant is the Waterside Café on level 5, where you can sit outside overlooking the artificial lake.

Broadgate Arena
(Cnr Liverpool Street & Eldon Street) 3 Broadgate, EC2
MAP REF 17, 4D
Tel 071–588 6565
Broadgate Arena is located next to Liverpool Street Station. It is an open-air amphitheatre where entertainment takes place throughout the year. There are shops, wine bars, and restaurants surrounding the Arena which are open from 8am till late Mon–Fri; plus shops and a Travellers Fare close by which are also open at weekends.
During the summer season – May to October – a full programme of weekday events takes place from *12.30 to 2pm*. The events are free to the public, and range from all types of music, theatre and dance to exhibitions, poetry and circus. Information on the monthly programme of events is displayed around the arena.
During the winter season – November to April – the Arena becomes an open-air ice rink – Britain's first. For a programme of summer events and further details on the ice rink contact the Arena Office on 071–588 6565.
Nearest underground station: Liverpool Street.
Facilities for the Disabled
The Arena can be accessed from street level by a ramp leading from the corner of Liverpool Street and Eldon Street to the lower level where

you pass under a small bridge to the Arena. There is also a lift to all levels of the Arena as well as a toilet located in the Arena Office.
Guided Tours of Broadgate
To book contact 071–588 6565.

Institute of Contemporary Arts (ICA)
12 Carlton House Terrace, SW1
MAP REF 27, 1C
Tel 071–930 0493; recorded information 071–930 6393
You must be a member – if only for a day – in order to enjoy the ICA's facilities. The cinema shows foreign, avant-garde, and unusual films in the evenings and at weekend matinees, and there is a Children's Cinema Club at weekends. The theatre stage often changes shape in order to suit its different productions, which are mostly of a new and experimental nature. There are regular lunchtime debates between artists, writers, critics and the public, and evening lectures on cultural issues.
The Centre is open from noon to 11pm, Tue to Sun.

Riverside Studios
Crisp Road, W6
DISTRICT MAP, 3C
Tel Box Office 081–748 3354; cc 081–563 0331
This rewarding centre for the arts in Hammersmith was formerly a BBC studio. It now houses two theatre studios, a luxury 200 – seater cinema and an art gallery where an exciting mixture of drama, dance and music can be enjoyed. Occasionally there is a one-off concert or show on Sundays. The studios' huge, welcoming foyer houses a bar and a café where a wide range of hot food is available.
Open 10am–11pm, Mon–Sat; 10.30am–10.30pm Sun.

Entertainment

MUSIC

London is one of the most exciting music centres in the world. International stars of ballet, opera, and classical music have long been drawn to the footlights of London's theatres. Jazz, folk, and pop enthusiasts are similarly well catered for.

CONCERT HALLS

The Barbican Hall
(see page 119)

Royal Albert Hall
Kensington Gore, SW7
MAP REF 24, 2B
Tel 071-589 8212 (Ticket Shop)
This famous Victorian building on the edge of South Kensington is perhaps best known for the Sir Henry Wood Promenade Concerts ('The Proms') – performed daily from mid-July to mid-September – whose last night is traditionally full of patriotic fervour. It is also the venue for *The Royal Albert Hall*, renowned for 'The Proms' performed daily from mid-July to mid-September concerts ranging from classical to pop throughout the rest of the year, and for a varied mixture of other events.

St John's
Smith Square, SW1
MAP REF 27, 3D
Tel 071-222 1061
This 18th-century church holds regular lunchtime and evening concerts: from solo recitals to choral works. Become a Friend for advance booking and discounts. Lunchtime concerts are at 1pm on Mondays and at 1.15pm on alternate Thursdays. Evening concerts run from September to July, at 7.30pm. Details can be obtained by phoning the box office.

Other churches, in the City, hold regular lunchtime concerts or recitals; they include the following. Tel 071-606 3030 for full details of venues and programmes, and to check times.

All Hallows-by-the-Tower, Byward Street, EC3
1pm Mondays; 12.15pm and 1.15pm Thursdays
Holy Sepulchre, Holborn Viaduct, EC1
1.15pm Tuesdays, Wednesdays, Fridays; 1.20pm Thursdays
St Bride, Fleet Street, EC4
1.15pm Wednesdays
St Lawrence Jewry, Gresham Street, EC2
1pm Mondays & Tuesdays
St Martin-in-the-Fields, Trafalgar Square, WC2
1.05pm Mondays & Tuesdays
St Mary-le-Bow, Cheapside, EC2
1.05pm Thursdays
St Mary Woolnoth, Lombard Street, EC3
1.05pm Fridays

Entertainment

St Michael-upon-Cornhill,
Cornhill, EC3
1pm Mondays
St Olave, Hart Street, EC3
1.05pm Wednesdays &
Thursdays
St Paul's Cathedral, EC4
12.30pm Fridays
Southwark Cathedral,
Borough High Street, SE1
1.10pm Mondays

The South Bank Arts Complex
SE1
MAP REF 21, 3E
This includes three concert halls (central phone number 071-928 3191; cc 071-928 8800).
 The Royal Festival Hall, built in 1951 as part of the Festival of Britain, is a 3,000-seat concert hall staging orchestral and choral programmes. The foyers, which are open from noon every day, hold exhibitions as well as bars, a café, and a restaurant. These facilities are shared with the *Queen Elizabeth Hall*, which stages symphony and orchestral concerts as well as other cultural events such as Poetry International, and the *Purcell Room*, whose smaller concert hall is ideal for chamber music and solo performances. The complex has a prime position overlooking the Thames.

Wigmore Hall
36 Wigmore Street, London W1
MAP REF 20, 1A
Tel 071-935 2141
The Wigmore Hall, opened in 1901, is one of the oldest concert halls in London. With its intimate atmosphere and renowned acoustics, it is a popular recital and chamber music venue. In each 11-month season there are eight concerts per week (including Sunday Morning Coffee Concerts) featuring a wide variety of new and established artists in many different fields of music.

OPERA AND BALLET
The London Coliseum
St Martin's Lane, WC2
MAP REF 21, 3D
Tel 071-836 3161; cc 071-240 5258
The Coliseum was built in 1904, and was at first used primarily as a music hall. It is easily identified by the giant electrical globe on the roof which twinkles into the sky each evening. The largest theatre in London, it was the first to install a revolving stage, and Sarah Bernhardt, Lillie Langtry, and Ellen Terry have all trodden its boards. Since 1968 the Coliseum has been the home of the English National Opera Company, who always sing in English. Their varied season lasts from August to May; visiting ballet companies fill in while the ENO go off on their summer tours. There is a bookstall in the foyer which is open all day.

The Royal Opera House, Covent Garden

Royal Opera House
Covent Garden, WC2
MAP REF 21, 2D
Tel 071-240 1066; Box Office 071-240 1911
The present building is the third theatre of its name on the site, and opera has flourished here since 1847. It is the home of the Royal Opera Company; in 1911 Thomas Beecham brought ballet to the theatre and it became the headquarters of the Royal Ballet Company in 1956. The very best names in the world of ballet and opera can be seen here in suitably lavish settings and productions. It is advisable to book well in advance, although you can queue on the day for a limited number of cheaper amphitheatre tickets.
 The elegant Crush Room is the largest reception room in a London Theatre; a unique setting for a product launch, press conference, seminar, buffet lunch, or any other special function during the daytime or after curtain down.

Entertainment

Sadler's Wells
Rosebery Avenue, EC1
MAP REF 16, 2A
Tel 071–278 8916; recorded information 071–278 5450
The well or natural spring, discovered by Richard Sadler in 1683 and developed as a spa, is still preserved within the theatre. Famous for the performances of the clown Joe Grimaldi in the early 19th century, and for its Shakespearean productions a few years later, the building was renovated by Lilian Baylis and re-opened in 1931. Sadler's Wells then acquired fame as a ballet and operatic centre and it was here that the Royal Ballet first achieved world-wide status under the guidance of its artistic director Ninette de Valois.

OPEN-AIR MUSIC
During the summer, military bands offer free lunchtime entertainment in the Royal Parks, and in certain City parks and squares.
Royal Parks:
Military and brass bands play free most lunchtimes and/or afternoons in Hyde Park, St James's Park, Regent's Park and Greenwich Park.
City sites:
Phone the City Information Centre on 071–606 3030 for details.
Finsbury Circus Gardens, Moorgate, EC2: lunchtime band concerts, usually Wednesdays.
Lincoln's Inn Fields, WC2: military bands, usually Tuesday and Thursday lunchtimes.
Paternoster Square, EC4: military bands, daily, lunchtimes.
St Paul's Steps, EC4: sit in full view of St Paul's and listen to a full military band concert; usually Thursdays.
Tower Place, EC3: military bands, usually Fridays.

Victoria Embankment Gardens, SW1: riverside setting for military bands, massed bands, and light orchestras, most lunchtimes of the week.
Other sites:
Holland Park Court Theatre, W8 Tel 071–602 7856. A small open-air theatre with a canopy which offers a programme of opera, dance and classical theatre from mid June to mid August.
Kenwood, Hampstead Lane, NW3 Tel 081–348 1286. Leading orchestras give symphony concerts in this beautiful setting by the lake on Saturday evenings during June, July and August. To be seen to be 'in', take a picnic.
Parliament Hill, NW3 Tel 071–485 4491. Massed bands play beside the lake on Saturday evenings during the summer.

ROCK AND JAZZ
As well as frequent – and sometimes huge – rock concerts (Wembley Arena is a notable venue), and internationally recognised jazz clubs, many pubs in London hold informal, often free, sessions. Information about these can be found in the London magazines – see page 118. Here is a small selection of regular venues.

Dingwall's
Camden Lock, Chalk Farm Road, NW1
DISTRICT MAP, 4D
Tel 071–267 4967
There is dancing and live rock groups here most nights of the week, plus live jazz Sunday lunchtimes.

Dominion Theatre
Tottenham Court Road, W1
MAP REF 21, 1D
Tel 071–580 9562
This is one of the largest theatres, having 2,007 seats. A wide programme of events is presented, from opera to rock, with limited seasons of pantomime. Opened in 1929, it has been used for many years as a cinema.

Half Moon
93 Lower Richmond Road, SW15
DISTRICT MAP, 3B
Tel 081–788 2387
Big-name bands play rock, pop, or jazz in this pub every night and at lunchtime on Sundays.

Hammersmith Odeon
Hammersmith Broadway, W6
DISTRICT MAP, 3C
Tel 081–748 4081
This huge cinema is given over entirely to concerts with internationally known stars.

The Marquee
90 Wardour Street, W1
MAP REF 20, 2C
Tel 071–437 6603
One of the first of the London rock clubs, you can hear music here every evening from 7pm.

100 Club
100 Oxford Street, W1
MAP REF 20, 1C
Tel 071–636 0933
Jazz and dancing every evening from 7.30 to midnight or 1am.

Rock Garden
The Piazza, Covent Garden, WC2
MAP REF 21, 2D
Tel 071–240 3961
Live rock in the basement of this hamburger joint every night.

Ronnie Scott's
47 Frith Street, W1
MAP REF 21, 2C
Tel 071–439 0747
International jazz at its best; open 8.30pm to 3am Monday to Saturday.

Entertainment

THEATRE

More than 400 years after live theatre was first presented in London, there are now about 40 commercial theatres open in the West End of London and two major subsidised companies, the National Theatre and the Royal Shakespeare Company, all combining to give entertainment of unrivalled quality and variety.

BOOKING

The Half-Price Ticket Booth in Leicester Square, a chalet-type building opposite the Swiss Centre, is open to personal callers only and sells tickets from 12 noon–2pm for matinee performances and from 2.30–6.30pm for evening shows. Tickets are for that day only; a booking fee is charged. See also page 118.

A SELECTION OF FAMOUS THEATRES

Her Majesty's
Haymarket, SW1
MAP REF 21, 3C
Tel 071–839 2244; cc 071–379 4444
Founded by Sir Herbert Beerbohm Tree in 1897, this pavilioned theatre is crowned by a Baroque copper dome.

Lyric Hammersmith
King Street, W6
DISTRICT MAP, 3C
Tel 081–741 2311
This is almost an arts centre in itself. The theatre, with its lavish recreation of a Victorian auditorium, is on the second and third floors, and stages classic, modern, and fringe productions.

The National Theatre
South Bank, SE1
MAP REF 21, 3E
Tel 071–928 2033
Part of the South Bank Arts complex, the National was opened in 1976 and in the few years since has won for itself a world-wide reputation for the quality of its productions of new, classic, foreign, and experimental plays. The building in fact houses three theatres which share the same facilities: the open-staged Olivier, the Lyttleton, with its proscenium arch, and the small Cottesloe studio. A few seats are held back for sale to personal callers from 10am on the day of the performance. Even if you are not going to a play, the National is a lovely place to browse among the bookstalls and exhibitions, listen to live music in the Lyttleton foyer every evening, or have a drink in the various bars on every floor. You can even enjoy a guided tour of the whole building, including backstage: phone 071–633 0880 to book.

The Old Vic
Waterloo Road, SE1
MAP REF 28, 1A
Tel 071–928 7616
Also known as the Royal Victoria Theatre, this building was erected in 1818. It was noted for lurid melodramas until 1880 when Emma Cons acquired the premises and made them the home of classical plays and opera – a tradition which was carried on by her niece, Lilian Baylis. For many years famous for its Shakespearean productions, the Old Vic was the headquarters of the National Theatre Company until it transferred to the South Bank in 1976. The building was closed between 1981 and 1983 for extensive refurbishment.

Open Air Theatre
Regent's Park, NW1
MAP REF 13, 2E
Tel 071–486 2431; cc 071–486 1933
This theatre has been in operation from 1932; since 1962, the New Shakespeare Company has presented summer seasons of classical plays (mainly Shakespeare), and in 1975 the new amphitheatre-style auditorium was built. The beautiful wooded surroundings, combined with an excellent range of food and drink and a relaxed atmosphere, provide the ideal setting for a summer evening out.

The season runs from the end of May to the beginning of September.

Palladium
8 Argyll Street, W1
MAP REF 20, 2B
Tel 071–437 7373
This famous music hall opened in 1910. Spectacular revues took over in the 1920s, and the famous Crazy Gang Shows enjoyed permanent residency until after the War. In 1946 the Palladium returned to a policy of top-name variety shows. In the 1960s it was famous for television's *Sunday Night at the London Palladium*.

Today it is a well-known concert venue, and host to the Royal Variety Performance and the Prince's Trust Concert.

Royal Court
Sloane Square, SW1
MAP REF 31, 1E
Tel 071–730 1745
Ever since its opening in 1870, the Royal Court has specialised in innovative plays. The farces of Arthur Pinero were performed here in the 1890s, followed by premiere productions of some of Shaw's plays at the beginning of the century. Probably the most famous and controversial of modern avant-garde plays, the English Stage Company's production of John Osborne's *Look Back in Anger*, ran here in 1956. Since 1969 the small Theatre Upstairs has

Entertainment

The Palladium (see page 123) of 1960s TV fame, now a well-known concert venue and host to the Royal Variety Performance

specialised in particularly new and experimental work.

Savoy
Strand, WC2
MAP REF 21, 3E
Tel 071–836 8888; *cc* 071–379 6219
This theatre, now incorporated in the famous Savoy Hotel, was commissioned by the great D'Oyly Carte and it was here that his productions of Gilbert and Sullivan's comic operas were staged between 1881 and 1889. It was the first public building in the world to be lit by electricity, and now presents a variety of plays and musicals.

Shaftesbury
Shaftesbury Avenue, WC2
MAP REF 21, 1D
Tel 071–379 5399
This theatre was acquired in 1983 by a company of some of the best of British comedy actors, and is now a Theatre of Comedy, showing works of all sorts from classical to modern, farcical to sophisticated.

Theatre Royal Drury Lane
Catherine Street, WC2
MAP REF 21, 2E
Tel 071–836 8108
The Theatre Royal is situated on one of the oldest theatre sites in London. The first building, dating from 1663, was destroyed by fire and replaced by one designed by Wren. A third building opened in 1794 under the management of Richard Sheridan, but this too burnt down. The present theatre, which was opened in 1812, is the largest in London, with sumptuous furnishings and surroundings, a portico and Ionic colonnade at the side, and numerous monuments to former exponents of the dramatic art. Many famous and spectacular musicals are presented, including *My Fair Lady* and *42nd Street*.

Theatre Royal
Haymarket, SW1
MAP REF 21, 3C
Tel 071–930 8800
Quality plays are presented at this theatre, designed by John Nash and opened in 1821, as befits its grand exterior.

Young Vic
66 The Cut, SE1
MAP REF 28, 1A
Tel 071–928 6363
This is basically a young people's repertory company where the emphasis is put on classics and established plays.

OTHER WEST END THEATRES

Adelphi, Strand, WC2 Tel 071–836 7611
Albery, St Martin's Lane, WC2 Tel 071–867 1115; *cc* 071–867 1111
Aldwych, Aldwych, WC2 Tel 071–836 6404
Ambassadors, West Street, WC2 Tel 071–836 6111; *cc* 081–741 1171
Apollo, Shaftesbury Avenue, W1 Tel 071–437 2663 *cc* 071–379 4444
Apollo, Victoria, 17 Wilton Road, SW1 Tel 071–828 8665; *cc* 071–630 6262
Astoria, Charing Cross Road, WC2 Tel 071–434 0403
Barbican, Barbican, EC2 Tel 071–638 4941; *cc* 071–638 8891
Comedy, Panton Street, SW1 Tel 071–867 1045; *cc* 071–079 4444

Entertainment

Donmar Warehouse, Earlham Street, WC2 Tel 071-240 2766
Duchess, Catherine Street, WC2 Tel 071-836 8243; *cc* 081-741 9999
Duke of York's, St Martin's Lane, WC2 Tel 071-836 5122; *cc* 071-836 9837
Fortune, Russell Street, WC2 Tel 071-836 2238; *cc* 071-497 9977
Garrick, Charing Cross Road, WC2 Tel 071-379 6107; *cc* 071-379 6433
Globe, Shaftesbury Avenue, W1 Tel 071-437 3667
ICA Theatre, Carlton House Terrace, SW1 Tel 071-930 0493; *cc* 071-930 3647
Jeanetta Cochrane, Theobalds Road, WC1 Tel 071-242 7040
King's Head, Upper Street, N1 Tel 071-226 1916
Lyric, Shaftesbury Avenue, W1 Tel 071-437 3686; *cc* 071-497 9977
Mayfair, Stratton Street, W1 Tel 071-629 3036
Mermaid, Puddle Dock, EC4 Tel 071-410 0000; *cc* 071-836 3464
New London, Drury Lane, WC2 Tel 071-405 0072; *cc* 071-404 4079
Palace, Shaftesbury Avenue, W1 Tel 071-434 0909
Phoenix, Charing Cross Road, WC2 Tel 071-867 1044; *cc* 071-497 9977
Piccadilly, Denman Street, W1 Tel 071-867 1118; *cc* 071-867 1111
Prince Edward, Old Compton Street, W1 Tel 071-734 8951
Prince of Wales, Coventry Street, W1 Tel 071-839 5972; *cc* 071-836 3464
Queen's, Shaftesbury Avenue, W1 Tel 071-734 1166
St Martin's, West Street, WC2 Tel 071-836 1443
Strand, Aldwych, WC2 Tel 071-240 0300; *cc* 071-497 9977
Vaudeville, Strand, WC2 Tel 071-836 9987

Victoria Palace, Victoria Street, SW1 Tel 071-834 1317; *cc* 071-379 4444
Westminster, Palace Street, SW1 Tel 071-834 0283; *cc* Tel 071-834 0048
Wyndhams, Charing Cross Road, WC2 Tel 071-867 1116; *cc* 071-867 1111

CINEMAS

ABC 1 & 2, Shaftesbury Avenue, WC2 Tel 071-836 8861
Cannon (Baker Street), Marylebone Road, NW1 Tel 071-224 0312; *recorded information* 071 935 9772
Cannon, Haymarket, SW1 Tel 071-839 1527; *cc* 071-839 1528
Cannon, Oxford Street, W1 Tel 071-636 3851
Cannon, Panton Street, SW1 Tel 071-930 0631
Cannon (Piccadilly Circus), Piccadilly, W1 Tel 071-437 3561
Cannon Premier, Swiss Centre, Leicester Square, WC2 Tel 071-437 2096
Cannon, Tottenham Court Road, W1 Tel 071-636 6749
Curzon (Mayfair), Curzon Street, W1 Tel 071-499 3737
Curzon (West End), Shaftesbury Avenue, WC2 Tel 071-439 4805
Dominion, Tottenham Court Road, W1 Tel 071-580 9562

Empire, Leicester Square, WC2 Tel 071-437 1234
Lumiere, St Martin's Lane, WC2 Tel 071-836 0691
Metro, Rupert Street, W1 Tel 071-437 0757
Minema, 145 Knightsbridge, SW1 Tel 071-235 4225
National Film Theatre, South Bank, SE1 Tel 071-928 3232
Odeon, Haymarket, SW1 Tel 071-839 7697
Odeon, Leicester Square, WC2 Tel 071-930 6111
Odeon, Marble Arch, W2 Tel 071-723 2011
Plaza 1, 2, 3 & 4, Regent Street, W1 Tel 071-437 1234; *cc* 071-240 7200
Prince Charles, Leicester Place, WC2 Tel 071-437 7003; *recorded information* 071-437 8181; *cc* 071-494 4687
Renoir, Brunswick Square, WC1 Tel 071-837 8402
Screen on Baker Street, Baker Street, W1 Tel 071-935 2772
Warner West End 1, 2, 3 & 4, Cranbourn Street, WC2 Tel 071-439 0791

St Martin's Theatre, West Street, showing Agatha Christie's play 'The Mousetrap', the world's longest ever theatrical run

Sport

Wembley Stadium

Empire Way, Wembley
DISTRICT MAP, 4B
Built in 1923 as part of the British Empire Exhibition, this 100,000-capacity stadium is most famous as the staging ground of *the* football match of the year – the FA Cup Final (held in May). Also used for the football Littlewood's Cup Final and international matches, it is every footballer's dream to 'go to Wembley'.

A host of other events take place here each year, including the Rugby League Challenge Cup Final, women's hockey internationals, schoolboy internationals, the Gaelic Games, pop festivals, speedway championships, and regular twice-weekly greyhound racing. In 1934 an indoor sports building, the Empire Pool and Sports Arena, was built, and though no longer used for swimming, the arena is frequently adapted to stage ice shows and ice hockey, boxing (the ABA Championships are held here in May), badminton (All England Championships in March), tennis (the Benson & Hedges World Doubles Championship in November), gymnastics, basketball, cycling, and horse shows (the Horse of the Year Show in October). For most of these events, it is almost impossible to get in unless you have tickets in advance: apply in the first instance to the Wembley Stadium Box Office, Tel 081–902 1234.

ASSOCIATION FOOTBALL

As football is the national game it is not surprising that London itself boasts several first division football clubs. In a season lasting from August to May there is a top League fixture in the capital on almost every Saturday afternoon, plus mid-week League and Cup games. Many more London-based clubs play in the lower divisions of the Football League and in the leading competitions of non-League football.

LONDON'S FOOTBALL CLUBS

Arsenal

Arsenal Stadium, Highbury, N5
DISTRICT MAP, 4D
Arsenal have won the FA Cup five times, the most recent being in 1979. They have achieved a total of nine League Championships, including four between 1931 and 1935. In 1971 they were the second team this century to win the League and Cup double.

London boasts several first division football clubs

Sport

Brentford
Griffin Park, Braemar Road, Brentford
DISTRICT MAP, 3B
Brentford is in the Third Division under former 'Spurs' star Steve Perryman. It has a large family following.

Charlton Athletic
Selhurst Park,
Whitehorse Lane, SE25
DISTRICT MAP, 1D
Charlton Athletic played in the first post-war Cup Final in 1946. Their player Bert Turner scored for each side in Derby County's 4–1 victory and the ball burst. Charlton redeemed themselves the following year, beating Burnley 1–0. The ball burst again.

Chelsea
Stamford Bridge,
Fulham Road, SW6
DISTRICT MAP, 3C
Chelsea, perhaps London's most fashionable club, won the League Championship in 1955 and the FA Cup in 1970. This was the first Wembley final to require a replay. The following year they beat Real Madrid in the European Cup-Winners Cup Final, again in a replay. They are now in the First Division. They recently won the Zenith Cup.

Crystal Palace
Selhurst Park,
Whitehorse Lane, SE25
DISTRICT MAP, 1D
Formed in 1905, Crystal Palace is now establishing itself as one of the leading clubs in the land. A return to the First Division in 1989 was rapidly followed by their first Wembley Cup Final appearance twelve months later. With a fine Stadium at Selhurst Park the Club is well-equipped to face the future with high expectations.

Fulham
Craven Cottage,
Stevenage Road, SW6
DISTRICT MAP, 3C
Fulham, a Third Division club, went to Wembley in 1975 for an all-London FA Cup Final against West Ham, but found their First Division opponents too much for them, losing 2–0.

Millwall
The Den, Cold Blow Lane, New Cross, SE14
DISTRICT MAP, 3E
Millwall were in the First Division for two seasons but are now in the Second Division.

Orient
Leyton Stadium,
Brisbane Road, E10
DISTRICT MAP, 4E
Orient's fine Cup form in 1954, when they reached the 6th round as a Third Division side, was surpassed in 1978 when they reached the semi-final – only to lose to Arsenal.

Queen's Park Rangers
South Africa Road, W12
DISTRICT MAP, 3C
Queen's Park Rangers' supreme moment came in 1967 when they appeared in the first Wembley League Cup Final – a Third Division club facing First Division opponents, West Bromwich Albion. Rangers were losing 0–2 but staged a dramatic fight-back to win 3–2. They are now in the First Division.

Tottenham Hotspur
748 High Road, N17
DISTRICT MAP, 5E
Tottenham Hotspur, currently in the First Division, have consistently been the most successful London club over the last two decades, their total of seven FA Cup triumphs including wins in 1961, 1962, 1967, 1981 and 1982. In 1961 they were the first team this century to achieve the League and Cup double in the same year. Spurs, as they are popularly known, became the first English club to win a European trophy when they defeated Athletico Madrid 5–1 in the 1962–63 European Cup-Winners Cup Final. Since then they have added two League Cup Final victories (1971 and 1973) as well as winning the UEFA Cup in 1972 and 1984. In 1987 they made it to the FA Cup Final but lost to Coventry City.

West Ham United
Boleyn Ground, Green Street, Upton Park, E13
DISTRICT MAP, 4F
West Ham United have never been League Champions but they won the FA Cup in 1964, 1975 and 1980, and defeated Munich 1860 in the European Cup-Winners Cup Final at Wembley in 1965. They are now in the Second Division.

Wimbledon
Plough Lane Ground,
45 Durnsford Road, SW19
DISTRICT MAP, 2C
Wimbledon were elected to the Football League in 1977 after three consecutive Southern League Championships. Earlier that year they had a splendid FA Cup run. Thirteen years on they are in their fifth consecutive year in the First Division, and along the way they collected the FA Cup in 1988.

ATHLETICS

Crystal Palace National Sports Centre
Crystal Palace Park,
Sydenham, SE19
DISTRICT MAP, 2E

New River Sports Centre
White Hart Lane, Wood Green, N22
DISTRICT MAP, 5E

Sport

Parliament Hill Fields
Gospel Oak, NW3
DISTRICT MAP, 4D

Victoria Park
Victoria Park, E9
DISTRICT MAP, 4E

White City Stadium
Wormwood Scrubs, W12
DISTRICT MAP, 4C

London has witnessed many great moments in athletics history, including the staging of the 14th Olympic Games at Wembley in 1948. Built at the beginning of this century, the White City Stadium was the venue for the 4th Modern Olympic Games and was London's principal athletics stadium for more than half a century.

In 1964 the Crystal Palace National Sports Centre opened and the White City finally ended its long and honourable association with athletics. The purpose-built Sports Centre at Crystal Palace has an all-weather track and covered accommodation for spectators, and stages all manner of athletics ranging from major international matches to country championships.

THE BOAT RACE

The Boat Race, a contest between two crews of eight rowers and one coxswain representing the universities of Oxford and Cambridge, is one of the most famous sporting events in the world. The first Boat Race took place at Henley-on-Thames in 1829, but in 1845 the event was moved to its present location in London. The course runs on the Thames from Putney to Mortlake, a distance of over 4 miles, and it takes place annually on a Saturday shortly before Easter. Thousands of people watch from the towpath along the course; no tickets are required, though many pay for the privileged positions near the finish at Duke's Meadows, Chiswick, or on floating barges.

The Boat Race between the universities of Oxford and Cambridge, one of the most famous sporting events in the world

CRICKET

Lord's Ground
St John's Wood Road, NW8
MAP REF 12, 2C

The Foster's Oval
Kennington, SE11
MAP REF 33, 3E

Cricket, first played in Tudor times, is still one of the most widely played games in England. Even the smallest village will probably have its team and its own ground where the quiet of a Sunday afternoon is broken only by the slap of leather on willow and a gentle ripple of applause.

The game of cricket accompanied the British to the colonies and it became equally popular in Australia, New Zealand, the West Indies, India, and Pakistan. It is these countries who play England in the Test Matches, which are played here and in their own countries. The first ever Test Match was played at the Oval. A Test Match is usually five days long and there can be as many as six in a series. Nowadays England will also play one-day Tests against visiting international sides.

Cricket is widely played in London, on commons and playing fields, but the two major venues are Lord's Cricket Ground and the Foster's Oval at Kennington. Lord's is probably the most famous cricket ground in the world and is home to two clubs – Middlesex County CC who play their county matches here, and the famous Marylebone Cricket Club, perhaps even better known by its initials, MCC. Lord's is a traditional venue for Test Matches, and the first-ever Test was played here in 1880. Many other matches are played at Lord's, including the finals of the NatWest Cup and

Sport

the Benson & Hedges Cup, and the annual match between Eton and Harrow.

The Foster's Oval is the home ground of Surrey County CC, and is usually the site of the final Test in a series.

The cricket season runs from April to September.

TENNIS

All England Lawn Tennis and Croquet Club

Church Road, Wimbledon, SW19 5AE
DISTRICT MAP, 2C
'Wimbledon' – for tennis fans the world over, the name resounds with the excitement and magic of that summer fortnight when top players from across the globe converge on London to compete for the most coveted prizes in lawn tennis. In the last week of June and the first week in July. The All England Lawn Tennis and Croquet Club hosts, in effect, the world tennis championships on grass. Over 2,000 members of staff cater for the 300,000-plus spectators who attend throughout the fortnight, and almost as coveted as the prizes and trophies is a ticket to the Centre Court for one of the final matches. Near-continuous TV coverage of the Wimbledon fortnight sweeps the whole country with tennis-madness, and 'Wimbledon' has become one of those great British institutions which everybody loves – or simply learns to live with. It is best to apply for tickets – which are allocated by a ballot system – in about October, or queue on the day.

There are also various other tournaments held in the London area; those which are held immediately before Wimbledon fortnight – for example, at Queen's Club, Palliser Road, W14 – include top international players.

For tickets to Wimbledon, the public should write, *enclosing a S.A.E.*, to:

All England Club,
PO Box 98
Church Road
Wimbledon
SW19 5AE
Recorded ticket information
Tel 081–946 2244

Ticket application forms are available between September and December.

THE LONDON MARATHON

Since its first running in 1981, the London Marathon has grown into the biggest in the world and attracts thousands of overseas runners as well as entries from all over Britain. In 1990, 24,953 entrants completed the course and it is now a major fund-raising event – and the runners annually raise over £4 million to help a wide range of charities. Top

Wimbledon fortnight, when top players from across the world compete for the most coveted prizes in lawn tennis

Sport

international marathon runners regularly take part, as was proved when Ingrid Kristiansen set a new women's world record time for the 1985 race. The course, which is over the traditional marathon distance of 26.2 miles, starts at Greenwich, winds its way through London's dockland, the Isle of Dogs, along the embankments of the Thames, through the City, and finishes at Westminster Bridge in Central London. The 1991 race is scheduled to take place on Sunday 21 April and will be known as the IAAF/ADT World Marathon Cup with international champions taking part. Four separate categories will start between 8.45 and 9.30am. Thousands of people turn out to watch, lining the route all along the way. There are special spectator areas at the most popular places to watch: along Charlton Way and Shooters Hill Road in Greenwich for the start, and all along The Mall and Birdcage Walk in St James's Park for the finish on Westminster Bridge. Each year on marathon day it seems as if the whole of London turns out in festive and carnival mood, and great fun is had by competitors and spectators alike. *Application forms (£2) are available from Trustee Savings Bank offices. Entry costs £8–£12. Tel 081-948 7935 for further information.*

GREYHOUND RACING

Catford
Greyhound Stadium, SE6
DISTRICT MAP, 2E

Hackney Wick
Waterden Road, E15
DISTRICT MAP, 4E

Walthamstow
Chingford Road, E4
DISTRICT MAP, 5E

Wembley
Stadium Way
DISTRICT MAP, 4B

Wimbledon
Plough Lane SW19
DISTRICT MAP, 2C

'Going to the dogs' has always been a popular pastime, especially with East End Londoners. Pure-bred greyhounds chase after an artificial hare on an electrified rail at speeds of up to 40mph. Races, either on the flat or over hurdles, are over varying distances and attract a good deal of betting and prize money. The most successful tracks are Wimbledon (where the Greyhound Derby is staged in June) and Walthamstow. Several of the tracks have restaurants overlooking the races. Most greyhound racing takes place in the evening.

HORSE RACING

Racecourses near London include: ***Ascot***, Berkshire – famous for its Royal meeting in June; ***Epsom***, Surrey – stages the world-famous *Derby* in June; ***Kempton Park***, Sunbury-on-Thames, Middlesex; ***Lingfield Park***, Surrey; ***Sandown Park***, Esher, Surrey – famous for the *Whitbread Gold Cup*; ***Windsor***, Berkshire.

Sport

Epsom Racecourse stages the world famous Derby in June

The flat-racing season extends from March to November, steeplechasing from August to June.

RUGBY UNION FOOTBALL

Rugby Football may have been born when, in 1823, W W Ellis picked up a soccer ball and ran with it – but there is no doubt it was nursed to maturity in London. Guy's Hospital claims to have the world's oldest Rugby Club, formed in 1843. Blackheath Club, the first group to come together specifically for the purpose of playing Rugby (in 1858), Richmond (founded 1861) and Harlequins (founded 1866) played important roles in shaping the game as it is now played.

The Twickenham ground (Whitton Road, Twickenham, Middlesex), is the HQ of the Rugby Football Union, controlling body of the sport. Fixtures to look out for at Twickenham are internationals (which are well publicised), the Oxford v Cambridge match in early December, the RFU Pilkington Cup Competition final in April, and the Inter-Services Championships played during March and April.

The major clubs in London which play matches every week during the season (September–April) include:

Blackheath RFC
Rectory Field, Charlton Road, SE3
DISTRICT MAP, 3F

Harlequin FC
Stoop Memorial Ground, Craneford Way, Twickenham TW2 7SQ
DISTRICT MAP, 2B

London Irish RFC
Pavilion, The Avenue, Sunbury-on-Thames
DISTRICT MAP, 2A

London Scottish RFC
Richmond Athletic Ground, Richmond, Surrey
DISTRICT MAP, 3B

London Welsh RFC
Old Deer Park, Kew Road, Richmond, Surrey
DISTRICT MAP, 3B

Metropolitan Police RFC
Police Sports Club, Ember Court, Embercourt Road, East Molesey, Surrey
DISTRICT MAP, 1B

Richmond RFC
Richmond Athletic Ground, Richmond, Surrey
DISTRICT MAP, 3B

Rosslyn Park RFC
Priory Lane, Upper Richmond Road, Roehampton, SW15
Clubhouse Tel 081–876 1879
DISTRICT MAP, 3C

Saracens RFC
The Pavilion, Bramley Sports Ground, Green Road, N14
DISTRICT MAP, 5D

Wasps RFC
Repton Avenue, Sudbury, Wembley
DISTRICT MAP, 4B

SPEEDWAY

Hackney Wick
Waterden Road, E15
(Fridays, 7.30pm)
DISTRICT MAP, 4E

Wimbledon
Plough Lane, SW19
(Wednesdays, 7.45pm)
DISTRICT MAP, 2C

Introduced to Britain in the 1920s, speedway has grown to be one of the most popular of all spectator sports. It is a highly specialised form of motorcycling. Speedway bikes are a powerful 500cc and are run on pure methanol. They have no brakes, so a great deal of skill and daring is demanded of the rider to execute the long, broadside drifts on the sweeping curves at each end of the track, sending showers of the loose shale surface into the air. Speedway events are usually held within large football grounds or greyhound stadiums. With thrills, spills, and the roar of machines under brilliant floodlighting, speedway racing is very exciting entertainment.

Where to Stay: Hotels, Guesthouses

Key to Where to Stay

Hotels and guesthouses (fictional example)

Establishment name

Classification and merit award

★ **73% Lydford House** AB13 2AZ
(Guest accom)
☎ (071-911 4444) 239 Telex no 67737
FAX 071-911 1932
Closed 25-26 Dec
Warm, friendly private hotels tastefully decorated and offering good standard of accommodation.
13rm (9 ⇌ 1 ⋔) Annexe: 15rm (11 ⇌ 4 ⋔)
® CTV in all bedrooms ⚹ T sB&B £25.50
sB&B ⇌ ⋔ £16 dB&B £40 dB&B ⇌ ⋔
£32 OR
CTV 30P NC ✿ 15nc 5yrs
TC Lunch £8.50 Dinner £16.50 &alc
Wine £5.00 Last dinner 8pm
Credit cards [1][2][5]

Annexes
If annexe rooms are shown, this indicates that their standard is acceptable. They may, however, lack some of the facilities available in the main building. If you are offered an annexe room, check facilities and charges before booking.

Credit cards The numbered boxes indicate the credit cards which the establishment will accept.

[1] Access/Eurocard/Mastercard
[2] American Express
[3] Barclays/VISA/
[4] Carte Blanche
[5] Diners

Specific details
To interpret details of opening times, prices, facilities etc consult 'Symbols and Abbreviations' below.

Star classifications and subjective awards
The majority of hotels are indicated by **black stars** and offer traditional hospitality and service in traditional accommodation.
★ Hotels and inns generally of small scale with good facilities and furnishings adequate bath and lavatory arrangements. Meals are provided for residents, but their availability to non residents may be limited.
★★ Hotels offering a higher standard of accommodation with 20% of the bedrooms containing a private bathroom or shower with lavatory.
★★★ Well appointed hotels with more spacious accommodation with two thirds of the bedrooms containing a private bathroom/shower with lavatory. Fuller meal facilities are provided.
★★★★ Exceptionally well appointed hotels offering a high standard of comfort and service with all bedrooms providing a private bathroom/shower with lavatory.
★★★★★ Luxury hotels offering the highest international standards

Red Star Hotels
These hotels are considered by the AA to be of outstanding merit within their classification. The award is reviewed annually.

Rosette Award for Food
This award highlights those hotels where it is judged that food can be specially recommended.
✿ Indicates that the food is a higher standard than is expected for its classification.
✿✿ Indicates excellent food and service irrespective of its classification.
✿✿✿ Outstanding food and service irrespective of its classification.

Guesthouses
For our purposes, we include small and private hotels in this category when they cannot offer all the services required for our star classification system. London

Where to Stay: Hotels, Guesthouses

prices tend to be higher than those in the provinces, but those that we list offer cost-conscious accommodation, although normally only bed and breakfast is provided. To allow for all eventualities, we have also included a few which provide a full meal service and the charges for these will naturally be higher. Guesthouses are indicated by the letter 'Q' (see Merit Awards below).

Merit Awards

The Percentage award
This is a system of quality assessment awarding a percentage rating to all hotels.

Quality assessment for guesthouses
We make quality assessment for all the guesthouses listed in the gazetteer. This is made on a subjective basis, following each inspection, to indicate the overall quality of the facilities and services provided by each establishment.

Each establishment receives from one to four symbols in ascending order of merit, denoting: **Q** A simple establishment with clean, modest accommodation and adequate bathroom facilities. **QQ** A sound establishment offering a higher standard of accommodation in terms of furnishing, décor and comfort; likely to have some en suite facilities. **QQQ** A well-appointed establishment offering superior accommodation with comfortable public areas. En suite facilities may be provided. **QQQQ SELECTED** The very best of AA-listed establishments, offering excellent standards of accommodation, a high degree of comfort, good food and hospitable, caring hosts. Many provide a high proportion of en suite facilities.

Opening dates
Unless otherwise stated, the establishments are open all year. Hotels show inclusive dates when they are closed (i.e. closed Xmas) whereas guesthouses, farmhouses and inns give inclusive dates when they are fully open (i.e. Apr–Oct). Although some establishments are open all year, they may at times offer a restricted service during the less busy months, this may mean there is a reduction in meals and/or accommodation.

Disabilities
Members with any form of disability should notify proprietors so that appropriate arrangements can be made to minimise difficulties, particularly in the event of an emergency. The AA *Guide for the Disabled Traveller* is available free to members.

Symbols & Abbreviations

English

★	Hotel classification	♫	entertainment
73%	Percentage award	V	Vegetarian meals offered
ⓢ	See page 132	sB&B	Single room including breakfast per person per night
Ⓠ	Quality assessment See above	sB&B⇌	Single room with private bath and WC and breakfast per person per night
✲	1990 prices		
☏	Telephone	sB&Bⁿ	Single room with private shower and WC and breakfast per person per night
⇌	Private bathroom with own WC		
⋒	Private shower with own WC	dB&B	Double room (2 persons) including breakfast
⊟	Four-poster bed		
®	Tea/coffee-making facilities in bedrooms	dB&B⇌	Double room (2 persons) with private bath and WC and breakfast
✗	No dogs allowed overnight in bedrooms	dB&Bⁿ	Double room (2 persons) with private shower and WC and breakfast
⚹	Bedrooms and/or area set aside for non-smokers	OR	This symbol shows that the hotel offers cheaper off-season weekends
P	Open parking for cars		
⌂	Garage or covered space	TC	Type of cooking. If this symbol is not shown the type of cooking is English, Scottish or Welsh according to the part of Britain in which the hotel is situated
✗	No parking on premises		
NC	No coach parties accepted		
☒	Indoor swimming pool		
⚇	Tennis court(s)	▼	Afternoon tea
alc	*à la carte*	MC	Morning coffee
CFA	Conference facilities available	S%	Service included in price quoted
CTV	Colour television	✿	Garden
fb	Family bedrooms	●	Night porter
fr	from	AC	Air conditioning
hc	Number of bedrooms with hot and cold water	B&B	Bed and breakfast for £13 or under
		wB&B	Weekly term bed & breakfast, per person
Lic	Licensed		
nc	No children, *eg* no children under...years of age	WbD	Weekly terms bed, breakfast and evening meal, per person
rm	Letting bedrooms in main-building	W	Weekly
T	Direct dial telephones in rooms	♨	Full central heating
xmas	Special Christmas programme for residents	① ② ③ ④ ⑤	Credit cards

Where to Stay: Hotels, Guesthouses

Français

★	Classement des hôtels
73%	Voir page 133
❀	Rosettes Voir page 132
Ⓠ	Symbole AA d'évaluation qualitative (voir page 133)
✳	Prix 1990
☏	téléphone
⇥	salle de bain privée avec WC particulier
♌	Douche privée avec WC particulier
🛏	Lits a quatre montant
Ⓡ	Possibilité de faire le thé/le café dans les chambres
🐕	Défense de garder des chiens pendant la nuit dans les chambres
⚭	Chambres et/ou section de restaurant réservée(s) aux non-fumeurs
P	Stationnement pour voitures
⌂	Garages ou espaces couvertes
✈	Pas de stationnement sur place
NC	Les groupes en car ne seront pas admis
☒	Piscine à l'intérieur
⚲	Court(s) de tennis
alc	à la carte
CFA	Installations de conférence
CTV	TV en couleurs
fb	Chambre de famille
fr	à partir de
hc	Nombre de chambres avec eau chaude et froide
Lic	Licence de boissons alcoholiques
nc	Enfants pas admis, par ex, enfants audessous de ... ans pas admis
rm	Location de chambres dans le bâtiment principal
T	Téléphone dans la chambre, direct avec l'extérieur
xmas	Programme spécial de Noel pour les clients
♫	disco, dance etc.
V	Menu Végétarien offert
sB&B	Chambre à un lit et petit déjeuner par personne et par nuit
sB&B⇥	Chambre à un lit avec bain et WC particuliers, et petit déjeuner par personne et par nuit
sB&B♌	Chambre à un lit avec douche privée et WC particulier et le petit déjeuner par personne la nuit
dB&B	Chambre à deux lits (2 personnes) avec petit déjeuner
dB&B⇥	Chambre à deux lits (2 personnes) avec bain et WC particuliers, et petit déjeuner
dB&B♌	Chambre à deux (2 personnes) avec douche privée et WC particulier et le petit déjeuner
OR	Ce symbole indique que l'hôtel offre des weekends à prix réduit hors saison
TC	Categorie de cuisine. Si ce symbole ne figure pas, la cuisine est anglais, écossaise ou galloise, selon la région de la Grande Bretagne ou l'hôtel se trouve
⛾	Thé l'apres-midi
MC	Café le matin
S%	Le service est compris dans le prix
✿	Jardin
☽	Concierge de nuit
AC	Conditionnement d'air intégral
B&B	Chambre et petit déjeuner pour moins £13
wB&B	Prix par semaine et par personne, chambre et petit déjeuner inclus
WbD	Prix par semaine et par personne, chambre et diner inclus
W	par semaine
♨	Chauffage central intégal
①②③④⑤	Cartes de crédit (voir page 132)

Deutsch

★	Hotelklassifikation
73%	Siehe Seite 133
❀	Rosetten
Ⓠ	AA Katagorisierung der Qualität (siehe Seite 133)
✳	1990 Preise
☏	Telefon
⇥	Privatbadezimmer mit eigener WC
♌	Privatdusche mit eigener WC
🛏	Himmelbelt
Ⓡ	Tee/Kaffee möglichkeiten im Zimmer
🐕	Hundeverbot im Zimmer ährend der Nacht
⚭	Zimmer bzw. Restaurant abschnitt für Nichtraucher
P	Parken im Freien
⌂	Garegen bzw, überdachtes Parken
✈	Parken an Ortund Stelle
NC	Reisebusgesellschaften nicht aufgenommen
☒	Hallenbad
⚲	Tennisplatz (Platze)
alc	à la carte
CFA	Tagungseinrichtungen vorhanden
CTV	Farbfernsehen
fb	Familienzimmer
fr	Von
hc	Zimmer mit Warm-und Kaltwasser
Lic	Ausschank alkoholischer Getränke
nc	Kinder nicht aufgenommen z. B. Kinder unter Jahren nicht aufgenommen
rm	Zimmeranzahl im Hauptgebäude
T	Zimmertelefon mit Aussen- verbindung über Telefonzentrale
xmas	Sonderweihnachtsprogramm für Gäste
♫	Disco, Tanzen usw
V	Vegetarische Kost vorhanden
sB&B	Ubernachtung in einem Einzelzimmer mit Frühstück pro Person
sB&B⇥	Einzelzimmer mit Privatbad und WC und Frühstück pro Person pro Nacht
sB&B♌	Einzelzimmer mit Privatdusche und WC und Frühstück pro Person pro Nacht
dB&B	Doppelzimmer (2 Personen) mit Frühstück
dB&B⇥	Doppelzimmer (2 Personen) mit Privatbad und WC mit Frühstück
dB&B♌	Doppelzimmer (2 Personen) mit Privatdusche und Frühstück
OR	Betrieb gibt Wochenendermässigung für Vorund Nachsaison
TC	Küch, Wenn dieses Zeichen nicht aufgeführt wird, ist die Küche englisch, schottish oder Walisisch je nach der Gegend, wo das Hotel sich befindet
⛾	Nachtmittagstee
MC	Kaffee vormittags
S%	Im preis eingeschlossen
✿	Garten
☽	Nachtportier
AC	Klimaanlage durchaus
B&B	Bett mit Frühstück für unter £13
wB&B	Wochenpreis pro Person Ubernachtung mit Frühstück
WbD	Wochenpreis pro Person, Ubernachtung mit Frühstück und Abendessen
W	Wochenpreis
♨	Vollfernheizung
①②③④⑤	Kreditkarten (siehe Seite 132)

Where to Stay: Hotels, Guesthouses

WHERE TO STAY

Places are listed below in postal district order, commencing East, then North, South and West, with a brief indication of the area covered.

Hotels, Guesthouses and Camping and Caravanning

E1
★★★★ **60% Tower Thistle** St Katherine's Way E1 9LD
☎ 071–488 4134 Telex no 885934 FAX 071–488 4106
Overlooking Tower Bridge from the banks of the Thames. This large modern hotel offers a choice of eating options in the comfortable Princes Room and an informal café which doubles as a night club; well-appointed but rather functional bedrooms are shortly to be upgraded, and some of them offer stupendous views. Service is genuinely helpful throughout.
808 ⇌ ↑ (24fb) CTV in all bedrooms ® T ⊁
* sB ⇌ ↑ fr£99 dB ⇌ ↑ fr£112 (room only) OR
Lift ● AC 1360 P (charged) 116 ☎ (charged) CFA ♫
TC International MC ▱ ⊁ Lunch fr£18.75&alc Dinner fr£24.50&alc Last Dinner 10.30pm
Credit cards [1] [2] [3] [4] [5]

E18 South Woodford
🄀🄀 **Grove Hill Hotel** 38 Grove Hill E18 2JG ☎ 081–989 3344 & 081–530 5286
A popular, efficiently managed, small hotel offers compact, well-maintained rooms, each with radio and TV. The generous breakfasts served each day are inclusive.
21rm (10 ⇌ 2 ↑ 9hc) (2fb) CTV in all bedrooms ®
* sB&B £25–£34.20 sB&B ⇌ ↑ fr£34.20 dB&B £42.82–£49.15 dB&B ⇌ ↑ fr£49.15
Lic ⚏ CTV 8 P 4 ☎ (£2.25)
Credit cards [1] [2] [3]

N8 Hornsey
🄀🄀 **Aber Hotel** 89 Crouch Hill N8 9EG ☎ 081–340 2847
Friendly service is provided by this small, family-run hotel which stands in a residential area within easy reach of the city centre.
9hc (4fb) ⊁
sB&B £15–£17 dB&B £26–£28 WB&B £85–£93
⚏ CTV ♪

NW2 Cricklewood
🄀🄀 **Clearview House** 161 Fordwych Rd NW2 3NG ☎ 081–452 9773
This peaceful family-run guesthouse in a quiet residential area offers comfortable accommodation, all bedrooms being well equipped.
6hc (1fb) ↑ CTV in 1 bedroom TV in 5 bedrooms ⊁ (ex guide dogs)
⚏ CTV ⊁ nc5yrs

🄀 **The Garth Hotel** 70–76 Hendon Way NW2 2NL ☎ 081–455 4742 Telex no 914360
A commercial hotel standing beside the busy Hendon Way has nicely appointed bedrooms and functional public areas; current refurbishment will provide additional bedrooms.
61 ⇌ ↑ (10fb) CTV in all bedrooms ® ⊁
Last dinner 10pm
Lic ⚏ CTV 30 P

NW3 Hampstead
★★★★ **65% Holiday Inn Swiss Cottage** 128 King Henry's Rd, Swiss Cottage NW3 3ST ☎ 071–722 7711 Telex no 267396 FAX 071–586 5822
A modern, multi-storey hotel, well placed for central London, provides spacious and well-equipped accommodation which has recently been refurbished. Public areas include a comfortable split-level lounge and cocktail bar, and a pleasant airy restaurant, while the leisure club features sauna, solarium and gymnasium as well as a heated indoor pool.
303 ⇌ ↑ (166fb) ⊁ in 52 bedrooms CTV in all bedrooms ® T
* sB ⇌ ↑ £119–£139 dB ⇌ ↑ £140–£162 (room only) OR
Lift ● AC 50P 100 ☎ [3] (heated) sauna solarium gymnasium xmas
TC International V MC ▱ ⊁ Lunch fr£17.50 High tea fr£7.50 Dinner fr£18 Last dinner 10.30pm
Credit cards [1] [2] [3] [4] [5]

★★★ **59% Charles Bernard** 5–7 Frognal, Hampstead NW3 6AL ☎ 071–794 0101 Telex no 23560 FAX 071–794 0100
Well-appointed, fully equipped bedrooms are available at this commercial hotel within easy reach of central London.
57 ⇌ ↑ CTV in all bedrooms ® T ⊁
* S% sB&B ⇌ ↑ £52–£72 dB&B ⇌ ↑ £64–£87 OR
Lift ● CTV 15P
MC ▱ Lunch £9–£15.75alc High tea £3.50–£5.50alc Dinner £9–£15.75alc Last dinner 9.15pm
Credit cards [1] [2] [3] [5]
(**see advertisement on p136**)

★★★ **58% Post House** Haverstock Hill NW3 4RB ☎ 071–794 8121 Telex no 262494 FAX 071–435 5586
This particularly comfortable hotel offers fine views south-west across the city; the daily roast served in its restaurant is worthy of recommendation, though dishes from the à la carte menu lack the flavour expected from fresh produce.

GROVE HILL HOTEL

FOR EASY ACCESS TO CENTRAL LONDON

Bed and breakfast
Quiet location with every modern comfort
Rooms with or without bathroom
Lockable garaging

Just off A11 and 1 minute from M11, A406, Central line tube, restaurants, shopping centre and cinema.
All rooms with satellite colour television

38 Grove Hill, South Woodford, London E18 2JG

081-989 3344   FAX: 081-530 5286

Where to Stay: Hotels, Guesthouses

140 ⇨ ⋔ ⤴ in 28 bedrooms CTV in all bedrooms ⓡ T
* sB ⇨ ⋔ fr£79 dB ⇨ ⋔ £90–£95 (room only) OR
Lift ◐ 70P xmas
TC English & French V MC ⌒ ⤴
Lunch fr£11.95&alc Dinner fr£11.95&alc Last dinner 10.30pm
Credit cards [1] [2] [3] [4] [5]

Ⓠ Ⓠ **Seaford Lodge** 2 Fellows Rd, Hampstead NW3 3LP ☎ 071–722 5032
Well placed for reaching central London and personally supervised by the proprietors, this guesthouse offers well-equipped modern bedrooms with en suite facilities, some of which are ideal for family use.

NW4 Hendon
Ⓠ Ⓠ Ⓠ **Peacehaven Hotel** 94 Audley Rd NW4 3HB ☎ 081–202 9758 & 081–202 1225
A bright yellow breakfast room overlooking the landscaped garden of this guesthouse reflects the cheerful disposition of the proprietor; all the modern bedrooms are equipped with colour television and many also have en suite facilities.
13rm (7 ⇨ 2 ⋔ 4hc) CTV in all bedrooms ⓡ ⤴ (ex guide dogs)
* sB&B sB&B ⇨ ⋔ £45–£50 dB&B £55 dB&B ⇨ ⋔ £65 ⊟ 2P
Credit cards [1] [2] [3] [5]

NW7 Mill Hill
★★ **62% Welcome Lodge** M1 Scratchwood Service Area, Mill Hill NW7 3HB (access from motorway only) ☎ 081–906 0611
FAX 081–906 3654
100 ⇨ (12fb) CTV in all bedrooms ⓡ T (prices given on application)
◐ 100P CFA
V MC ⌒ ⤴
Credit cards [1] [2] [3] [5]

SE3 Blackheath
SELECTED RECOMMENDED
Ⓠ Ⓠ Ⓠ **Bardon Lodge Hotel** 15 Stratheden Rd SE3 7TH ☎ 081–853 4051
This warm, friendly and tastefully decorated private hotel provides a good standard of accommodation.
40 ⋔ (4fb) CTV in 38 bedrooms ⓡ ⤴
* sB&B ⋔ £44 dB&B ⋔ £64 Last dinner 9.30pm
Lic ⊟ CTV 16P
Credit cards [1] [2] [3]

Ⓠ Ⓠ **Stonehall House** 35–37 Westcombe Park Rd SE3 7RE ☎ 081–858 8706
Old-fashioned and comfortable, the guesthouse features a pleasant television lounge and garden.
27rm (1 ⇨ 3 ⋔ 23hc) (10fb) CTV in all bedrooms
* sB&B fr£23 sB&B ⇨ ⋔ fr£27 dB&B £32–£36 dB&B ⇨ ⋔ fr£36

⊟ CTV ⤴
Credit cards [1] [3]
(see advertisement on p137)

Ⓠ Ⓠ Ⓠ **Vanbrugh Hotel** 21/23 St Johns Park, Blackheath SE3 7TD ☎ 081–853 5505
30 ⇨ ⋔ CTV in all bedrooms ⓡ ⤴ (ex guide dogs)
* sB&B ⇨ ⋔ £58 dB&B ⇨ ⋔ £78–£110 16P

SE9 Eltham
Ⓠ Ⓠ Ⓠ **Yardley Court Private Hotel** 18 Court Rd SE9 ☎ 081–850 1850
Small and privately managed, the hotel offers comfortable bedrooms with showers and modern furnishings; generous English breakfasts are freshly cooked.
9 ⋔ (1fb) CTV in all bedrooms ⤴ (ex guide dogs)
* sB&B ⋔ fr£33.35 dB&B ⋔ fr£44.85
⊟ 8P
Credit cards [1] [3]

SE10 Greenwich
Ibis Greenwich 30 Stockwell St, Greenwich SE10 9JN ☎ 081–305 1177 Telex no 929647 FAX 081–858 7139
82 ⇨ CTV in all bedrooms T
* sB ⇨ fr£44 dB ⇨ fr£49 (room only)
Lift ◐ AC 35P
TC International MC ⌒ Lunch £4–£10&alc Dinner £8.75&alc Last dinner 10.30pm
Credit cards [1] [2] [3] [5]

Charles Bernard Hotel Ltd
5 Frognal, Hampstead, London NW3
Telephone: 071-794 0101
Fax: 071-794 0100 ★★★ Telex: 23560
The Charles Bernard Hotel is purpose built, privately owned, and situated near to Hampstead Heath. Completely refurbished in 1989, all 57 rooms have private facilities, colour TV plus satellite, telephone, tea and coffee facilities, trouser press and hair dryer.
Pleasant efficient staff ensure that your stay is comfortable and enjoyable.

PEACEHAVEN HOTEL
94 Audley Road, Hendon Central, London NW4 3HB
Telephone: 081-202 9758 & 081-202 1225
Small friendly immaculate good value hotel. Modern bright rooms – colour TV, central heating etc, several en suite plus many excellent public bathrooms. Modern breakfast room overlooks landscaped gardens. Easy parking. 5 minutes walk to tube – 15 minutes to West End. Main line station and Brent Cross Shopping Centre within easy reach. 2 minutes by car M1, A1, A41 & RAF Museum.
Access Visa Amex

Where to Stay: Hotels, Guesthouses

SE19 Norwood
◐ ◐ **Crystal Palace Tower Hotel**
114 Church Rd, SE19 2UB ☎ 081-653 0176
A large Victorian house, close to all amenities and within easy reach of central London, provides spaciously comfortable bedrooms, a compact lounge and a basement dining room; car parking is available on the hotel forecourt.
11rm (2 ⇨ 3 ↑ 6hc) (4fb) TV in all bedrooms ®
* sB&B £18–£21 sB&B ⇨ ↑ £21–£25 dB&B £28–£30 dB&B ⇨ ↑ £32–£35
📺 CTV 10P
Credit cards ① ③

SW1 Westminster
(red) ★★★★★ **The Berkeley** Wilton Place, Knightsbridge SW1X 7RL
☎ 071-235 6000 Telex no 919252 FAX 071-235 4330
Considerable refurbishment carried out here over recent years has included the provision of a more attractive restaurant, 'softening' of the corridors, and redecoration of drawing room and bedrooms. Sauna, minigym and heated pool are situated on the top floor. French cuisine of a commendable standard is offered in the restaurant, a wide range of good-value dishes also being available in the popular Le Perroquet Bar and adjacent Buttery. Service throughout is extensive, traditional and formal, marked by a certain aloofness which is part of the establishment's distinctive style, and discretion is total.
160 ⇨ ↑ CTV in all bedrooms ✻ S15% sB ⇨ ↑ £150–£215 dB ⇨ ↑ £215–£265 (room only) OR
Lift ◐ AC 50 ⚘ (£19 per night) NC ③ (heated) sauna solarium gymnasium cinema ♫ xmas
TC International V MC ⌨ S15% Lunch fr£17.50 Dinner £30–£45alc Last dinner 11pm
Credit cards ① ② ③ ⑤

★★★★★ **72% Hyatt Carlton Tower**
Cadogan Place SW1X 9PY
☎ 071-235 5411 Telex no 21944 FAX 071-235 9129

Though somewhat regimented, this modern hotel offers some good facilities, including the refurbished Rib Room and attractive Chelsea Room restaurants and a new health centre with relaxing lounge. Bedrooms are modestly furnished and prices comparatively high.
224 ⇨ ↑ ✻ in 23 bedrooms CTV in all bedrooms T ✻ (ex guide dogs)
* sB ⇨ ↑ £170–£190 dB ⇨ ↑ £170–£190 (room only) OR
Lift ◐ AC 40 ⚘ (£2 per hour) NC CFA ❧ (hard) sauna solarium gymnasium beauty treatment hair salon ♫
TC International V MC ⌨
Lunch £23.50&alc High tea £15–£20alc Dinner £22–£35 Last dinner 11.15pm
Credit cards ① ② ③ ④ ⑤

★★★★★ **77% The Hyde Park**
Knightsbridge SW1Y 7LA
☎ 071-235 2000 Telex no 262057 FAX 071-235 4552
This elegant, dignified hotel, overlooking Hyde Park from the centre of fashionable Knightsbridge, features a stately entrance leading to a reception area ornate with marble, high gilded ceilings and huge displays of fresh flowers. Lounge and bar provide a popular rendezvous which leads into the Park Room Restaurant, with its piano, while the oak-panelled Grill Room downstairs offers English roasts and French specialities. Bedrooms and suites, individually decorated by leading designers, are superbly equipped.
186 ⇨ ↑ ✻ in 6 bedrooms CTV in all bedrooms T S%
sB ⇨ ↑ £199–£225 dB ⇨ ↑ £250–£265 (room only) OR
Lift ◐ AC ✈ NC CFA ♫ xmas
TC English & French V MC ⌨ ✻ S%
Lunch £20–£24alc Dinner £25&alc Last dinner 11pm
Credit cards ① ② ③ ④ ⑤

★★★★★ **63% Sheraton Park Tower** 101 Knightsbridge SW1X 7RN
☎ 071-235 8050 Telex no 917222 FAX 071-235 8231
Bedrooms here are distinguished by their excellent views, elegant furnishings and modern facilities – the upper floor executive rooms, equipped with TV/videos, individual air-conditioning and mini bars being ideally suited to the needs of business travellers. The Edwardian-style restaurant and conservatory provide guests with an inviting setting in which to choose from a tempting range of dishes, while the Champagne Bar serves light meals and snacks throughout the day.
295 ⇨ ↑ ✻ in 20 bedrooms CTV in all bedrooms T ✻
* sB ⇨ ↑ £180–£230 dB ⇨ ↑ £200–£230 (room only) OR
Lift ◐ AC 70 ⚘ (£9 per day) NC ♫ xmas
TC International V MC ⌨ Lunch £16.75–£17.50&alc High tea £5–£8.25alc Dinner £23–£33alc Last dinner 11.30pm
Credit cards ① ② ③ ④ ⑤

★★★★ **63% The Cavendish** Jermyn St SW1Y 6JF ☎ 071-930 2111 Telex no 263187 FAX 071-839 2125
Some of the best bedrooms of this hotel have balconies affording superb views over London, and all accommodation is currently undergoing refurbishment designed to improve its comfort. Meals are served by friendly and attentive staff in the well-supervised restaurant and there is also a gallery lounge where drinks and snacks (including a traditional tea in the afternoon) can be obtained throughout the day.
253 ⇨ ↑ ✻ in 63 bedrooms CTV in all bedrooms T
* sB ⇨ ↑ £120–£135 dB ⇨ ↑ £150–£170 (room only) OR
Lift ◐ 80 ⚘ (fr£16) NC CFA xmas
TC French V MC ⌨ ✻ Lunch £18.50–£23.50 Dinner £20&alc Last dinner 11pm
Credit cards ① ② ③ ④ ⑤

★★★★ **72% Duke's** 35 St James's Place SW1A 1NY ☎ 071-491 4840 Telex no 28283 FAX 071-493 1264
The highly professional staff of this charming Edwardian hotel in a peaceful setting create a relaxed, friendly atmosphere. Superbly

---

Stonehall House Hotel
Open all year round   London Tourist Board   English Tourist Board

**37 WESTCOMBE PARK ROAD
BLACKHEATH, LONDON SE3
Telephone: 081-858 8706**
27 BEDROOM HOTEL NEAR
GREENWICH PARK
BR STATION: MAZE HILL
Tariff from £16 per person

Where to Stay: Hotels, Guesthouses

furnished bedroom accommodation includes some well-appointed suites, while comfortable public areas feature an intimate little restaurant offering a short but interesting menu of skilfully prepared French and English cuisine.
58 ⇌ (22fb) 1 🖃 CTV in all bedrooms ⚑ (ex guide dogs)
(prices given on application)
Lift ◐ ⚑ NC nc5yrs
MC ⌑ Last dinner 10pm
Credit cards 1 2 3 4 5

(red) ★★★★ **Goring** Beeston Place, Grosvenor Gardens SW1W 0JW ☎ 071–834 8211 Telex no 919166 FAX 071–834 4393
Outstanding hospitality and exceptionally good service are the hallmarks of this well-established, family-run hotel; reception area and public rooms are very carefully decorated and furnished to create a cheerful, welcoming atmosphere which is reflected in even the smaller of the well-planned, fully equipped bedrooms. An elegantly attractive restaurant's interesting set-price and à la carte menus feature some particularly noteworthy fish dishes and are accompanied by a carefully balanced, reasonably priced wine list.
90 ⇌ ₨ CTV in all bedrooms T ⚑ S10% sB ⇌ ₨ £105–£115 dB ⇌ ₨ £155–£165 (room only)
Lift ◐ 10P (£7.50) 4 ⚞ (£7.50) NC ♪
TC English & French V MC ⌑ ⚐ Lunch fr£20&alc Dinner fr£24&alc Last dinner 10pm
Credit cards 1 2 3 5

★★★★ **67% Royal Westminster Thistle** 40 Buckingham Palace Rd SW1W 0QT ☎ 071–834 1821 Telex no 916821 FAX 071–931 7542
Spacious, well-appointed bedrooms are complemented by public areas comprising an impressive entrance lobby, comfortable lounge and choice of restaurants – the St Germain Brasserie and the more casual Café St Germain – service being equally helpful and friendly in either.
134 ⇌ ₨ (69fb) ⚐ in 67 bedrooms CTV in all bedrooms T ⚑
* sB ⇌ ₨ fr£105 dB ⇌ ₨ fr£130 (room only) OR
Lift ◐ AC ⚑ ♪
TC English & French MC ⌑ ⚐ Lunch fr£15.95&alc Dinner fr£15.95&alc Last dinner 11.30pm
Credit cards 1 2 3 4 5

★★★★ **72% Stafford** 16–18 St James's Place SW1A 1NJ ☎ 071–493 0111 Telex no 28602 FAX 071–493 7121
An oasis of calm at the heart of the West End's bustle, this hotel is known for its fine wines and good food – traditional afternoon tea being a treat not to be missed. Though some bedrooms are rather compact, all are

individually furnished in soft, elegant fabrics.
62 ⇌ 1 🖃 CTV in all bedrooms ⚑
*sB ⇌ £150–£155 dB ⇌ £186–£385 (room only)
Lift ◐ 5 ⚞ (£12 per night) NC
TC French MC ⌑ ⚐ Last dinner 10pm
Credit cards 1 2 3 4 5

★★★ **63% Royal Horseguards Thistle** Whitehall Court SW1A 2EJ ☎ 071–839 3400 Telex no 917096 FAX 071–925 2263
Guests of many nationalities frequent this large, imposing and conveniently located hotel whose public areas include a majestically appointed lounge next to the elegant reception area, a choice of restaurants and a cosy bar. All bedrooms have modern facilities, though accommodation in the new wing is superior to the more compact rooms of the original building.
376 ⇌ ₨ (98fb) ⚐ in 95 bedrooms CTV in all bedrooms ® T ⚑
* sB ⇌ ₨ fr£93 dB ⇌ ₨ fr£99 (room only) OR
Lift ◐ ⚑ CFA ♪
TC International MC ⌑ ⚐ Lunch fr£15.75&alc Dinner fr£15.75&alc Last dinner 10.30pm
Credit cards 1 2 3 4 5

★★★ **68% Rubens** Buckingham Palace Rd SW1W 0PS ☎ 071–834 6600 Telex no 916577 FAX 071–828 5401
A hotel delightfully located facing the mews to Buckingham Palace and the Royal Parks has been tastefully refurbished and now has air conditioning in the Masters Restaurant; bedrooms are well appointed and staff pleasantly polite.
191 ⇌ ₨ (3fb) ⚐ in 44 bedrooms CTV in all bedrooms ® T ⚑ (ex guide dogs)
* sB ⇌ ₨ £85–£95 dB ⇌ ₨ fr£105 (room only) OR
Lift ◐ ⚑ xmas
TC International V MC ⌑ ⚐ S10% Lunch fr£14.95 Dinner fr£15.50 Last dinner 10pm
Credit cards 1 2 3 5

(red) ★ **Ebury Court** 26 Ebury St SW1 0LU ☎ 071–730 8147 FAX 071–823 5966 Closed 21 Dec–4 Jan
Any lack of space or amenities at this hotel is more than compensated for by its unique and delightful atmosphere. The care and thoroughness of Mrs Topham, in charge here for over fifty years, set the standard for a loyal staff who provide unfailingly good-natured and helpful service, while attractive fabrics, cushions and china bring charm to compact but spotless rooms with particularly comfortable beds. Guests requiring a television set in the bedroom must order it in advance, but one is provided in the lounge, and another small sitting room contains a writing desk; a restaurant decked

in pink and navy stripes serves simple but good British food, with soda bread freshly baked on the premises each day.
43rm (19 ⇌ ₨) (3fb) 4 🖃 CTV in all bedrooms ® T
* sB&B fr£50 dB&B £75 dB&B ⇌ ₨ £95
Lift ◐ ⚑ NC
TC English & Continental V MC ⌑
Credit cards 1 3

Q Q **Belgrave House** 28–32 Belgrave Rd, Victoria SW1V 1RG ☎ 071–828 1563 & 071–834 8620
This imposing four-storey terraced house, ideally situated for Victoria, offers reasonably priced accommodation in recently refurbished bedrooms.
46rm ⇌ ₨ (8fb) ⚐ in 25 bedrooms ⚑ 🖃 CTV ⚑
(see advertisement on p139)

Q Q **Chesham House** 64–66 Ebury St SW1N 9QD ☎ 071–730 8513 Telex no 946797
23hc (3fb) CTV in all bedrooms ⚑
* sB&B £28–£30 dB&B £43–£45
🖃 ⚑
Credit cards 1 2 3 5

Q Q **Winchester Hotel** 17 Belgrave Rd SW1 1RB ☎ 071–828 2972 Telex no 269674 Closed 23–29 Dec
A high standard of accommodation is provided here, all the well-appointed rooms having en suite shower facilities. Breakfast is served in a pleasant lower-ground-floor dining room.
18 ⇌ ₨ (2fb) CTV in all bedrooms ⚑ 🖃 ⚑ nc10yrs

Q Q **Windermere Hotel** 142 Warwick Way SW1V 4JE ☎ 071–834 5163 & 071–834 5480 Telex no 94017182 FAX 071–630 8831
A friendly hotel within easy reach of central London offers pleasant accommodation in nicely equipped rooms.
9 ₨ (4fb) CTV in all bedrooms ⚑ (ex guide dogs)
🖃 ⚑
Credit cards 1 3
(see advertisement on p139)

SW3 Chelsea
(red) ★ ★★★★ **Capital** Basil St, Knightsbridge SW3 1AT ☎ 071–589 5171 Telex no 91904 FAX 071–225 0011
A modern, continually improving, character hotel, now refurbished in fin de siècle style, features an attractively decorated restaurant where skilfully prepared dishes – accompanied by a very good wine list – can be enjoyed in welcoming surroundings. Bedrooms vary in size, but all are furnished to a high standard of comfort and provided with air-conditioning, modern facilities and such luxurious extras as fresh fruit and bathrobes. Valet

Where to Stay: Hotels, Guesthouses

room service is pleasantly polite, and efficiency prevails in all departments, the pleasant atmosphere more than compensating for any lack of space. Quietly located for a London hotel it stands near another of its assets – the excellent Le Metro wine bar.
48 ➼ CTV in all bedrooms T
* sB ➼ £135–£160 dB ➼ £160–£185
Lift ◐ AC 12 ☎ (£8) NC
TC French V MC ⌨
Credit cards ① ② ③ ④ ⑤

★★★ **62% Basil Street** Basil St, Knightsbridge SW3 1AH ☏ 071–581 3311 Telex no 28379 FAX 071–581 3693
The lounge, wine bar, Punch Restaurant and Ladies' Club are particularly attractive and popular areas of a well-established hotel which is comfortably and stylishly furnished throughout.
92rm (72 ➼) CTV in all bedrooms
sB fr£45 sB ➼ fr£85 dB fr£69 dB ➼ fr£110 (room only)
Lift ◐ ✎ NC xmas
TC International V MC ⌨ Lunch £13.75–£15.75 Dinner £20–£24alc Last dinner 9.45pm
Credit cards ① ② ③ ④ ⑤

◉◉◉ **Claverley House** 13–14 Beaufort Gardens SW3 1PS ☏ 071–589 8541

This delightful, elegant hotel has a warm atmosphere and comfortable rooms. The pretty breakfast room is located on the lower ground floor, and guests can relax in a reading room furnished with leather Chesterfield sofas.
36 ➼ (2fb) CTV in all bedrooms
Lift ⌨ ✎
Credit cards ③

◉◉◉ **Knightsbridge Hotel** 18 Beaufort Gardens SW3 1PT ☏ 071–589 9271
An attractive terraced house whose architecture reflects the charm and elegance of the Victorian era is conveniently located in central London. Accommodation is equipped with modern conveniences, and there is a pleasant breakfast room on the lower ground floor.
20 ➼ ♪ (4fb) CTV in 4 bedrooms
Last dinner 9.30pm
Lic ⌨ CTV ✎
Credit cards ① ② ③

SW5
★★★ **67% Swallow International** Cromwell Rd SW5 0TH ☏ 071–973 1000 Telex no 27260 FAX 071–244 8194
This large, friendly hotel offers accommodation in well-equipped bedrooms.

417 ➼ ♪ (36fb) ✗ in 39 bedrooms CTV in all bedrooms ® T S%
sB&B ➼ ♪ £95–£103 dB&B ➼ ♪ £115–£123 Continental breakfast OR
Lift ◐ 45P (£12.50 per day) 30 ☎ ③ (heated) sauna solarium gymnasium whirlpool spa turkish steamroom ♫ xmas
TC International V MC ⌨ Lunch £11.50&alc Dinner £15&alc Last dinner mdnt
Credit cards ① ② ③ ⑤

SW7
★★★★ **65% Gloucester** 4–18 Harrington Gardens SW7 4LH ☏ 071–373 6030 Telex no 917505 FAX 071–373 0409
This pleasant, modern hotel features an open-plan foyer/lounge and two restaurants, one offering a traditional à la carte menu and the other providing an all-day light meal and snack service; real ale pub and wine cellar complement the cocktail lounge. Bedrooms are spacious and well equipped, with 24-hour room service from pleasant, cheerful staff.
550 ➼ ♪ (2fb) ✗ in 51 bedrooms CTV in all bedrooms ® T
* sB ➼ ♪ £122–£142 dB ➼ ♪ £142–£172 (room only) OR
Lift ◐ AC 100 ☎ (fr£6.50) CFA xmas
TC English & Continental V MC ⌨ ✗
Credit cards ① ② ③ ④ ⑤

Belgrave House Hotel
28-32 Belgrave Road, London SW1V 1RG
Telephone: 071-828 1563

Centrally situated near to British Airways Terminal, Victoria coach & rail stations, Buckingham Palace, Houses of Parliament, the West End, Theatreland and the City. All 46 bedrooms have hot & cold, shaving point and central heating, some have private facilities. Colour television lounge with hot and cold drink vending machines available.

WINDERMERE HOTEL
142/144 Warwick Way, Victoria, London SW1V 4JE
Tel: 071-834 5163/5480
Telex: 94017182 WIRE G   Fax: 071-630 8831

A small, friendly hotel of enormous charm and character, strategically placed for Victoria Coach and Railway Stations, Buckingham Palace and Westminster. A public car park is situated to the rear of the hotel.
Well appointed single, double/twin and family rooms most with en suite shower and toilet. For the discerning traveller we have the more luxurious and spacious Superior rooms.
Our aim remains simply to make your stay with us a most comfortable and enjoyable one.

E.T.B. ♛♛♛   VISA/MC   AMEX

Where to Stay: Hotels, Guesthouses

★★★ **56% Rembrandt** Thurloe Place SW7 2RS ☎ 071–589 8100 Telex no 295828 FAX 071–225 3263
A hotel dating back to the beginning of the century, well located for access to the West End, offers well-equipped bedrooms which vary in size and comfort. Fully air-conditioned conference facilities can cater for up to 250, and guests can make use of the Aquilla Health Club for a nominal fee.
200 ↔ (25fb) ⚥ in 28 bedrooms CTV in all bedrooms ® ✈ (ex guide dogs)
* sB ↔ £85 dB ↔ £105 (room only)
Lift ◐ ♨ ③ (heated) sauna solarium gymnasium beauty parlour massage spa bath
V MC ⌒ S10% Lunch £14.95 Dinner £14.95 Last dinner order 9.30pm
Credit cards ① ② ③ ④ ⑤

QQ Number Eight Hotel 8 Emperors Gate SW7 4HH ☎ 071–370 7516 Telex no 263849 FAX 071–373 3163
A small friendly hotel in a quiet terrace, conveniently placed for access to the West End, provides pleasant bedrooms and limited public areas.
14 ↔ ® (2fb) CTV in all bedrooms ®
Lic ⌂ ♨
Credit cards ① ② ③ ⑤

SW19

★★★★ **68% Cannizaro House** West Side, Wimbledon Common SW19 4UF ☎ 081–879 1464 Telex no 9413837 FAX 081–879 7338
A historic Georgian mansion set in its own beautiful parkland provides guests with a rural peace and tranquillity. Attractively furnished bedrooms have marble-tiled bathrooms, cuisine is reliable and service highly professional.
48 ↔ 4 ⊟ CTV in all bedrooms T
* sB ↔ ® fr£85 dB ↔ ® fr£99 (room only) OR
◐ 60P ✿ ♫
TC International MC ⌒ Lunch fr£16.50&alc Dinner fr£16.50&alc Last dinner 10.30pm
Credit cards ① ② ③ ④ ⑤

QQ Kings Lodge 5 Kings Road, Wimbledon SW19 8PL ☎ 081–545 0191 FAX 081–545 0381 Closed xmas
7 ↔ ® (2fb) CTV in all bedrooms ® ✈ (ex guide dogs)
⌂ CTV 2P 2 ♨
Credit cards ① ② ③ ⑤

QQ Trochee Hotel 21 Malcolm Rd SW19 4AS ☎ 081–946 1579 & 3924
Situated in a quiet residential area and ideally placed both for all amenities and for easy access to either city or countryside, this hotel offers a warm, comfortable atmosphere.
17hc (2fb) CTV in all bedrooms ® ✈ (ex guide dogs)
* sB&B fr£28.50 dB&B fr£40
⌂ CTV 3P
Credit cards ① ③

QQQ Wimbledon Hotel 78 Worple Rd SW19 4HZ ☎ 081–946 9265
A small, family-run hotel with a friendly and cosy atmosphere offers an ideal situation, being only a 10-minute walk from main street and station.
14rm (4 ↔ 4 ® 6hc) (6fb) ⚥ in 8 bedrooms CTV in all bedrooms ® ✈
* sB&B £38 sB&B ↔ ® £42 dB&B £48 dB&B ↔ ® £54
⌂ CTV 10P
Credit cards ① ③

QQQ Worcester House 38 Alwyne Rd SW19 7AE ☎ 081–946 1300
This guesthouse, set only a few minutes' walk from the village centre, provides a pleasant atmosphere and en suite bedrooms equipped with radio, colour TV, direct dial telephones, hairdryer and beverage facilities.
9 ® (1fb) CTV in all bedrooms ® ✈
* sB&B ® £46–£50 dB&B ® £58.50–£65
⌂ ♨
Credit cards ① ③ ⑤

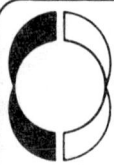

number eight hotel

8 emperors gate, south kensington, london sw7 4hh.
telephone 071 370 7516 fax 071 373 3163 telex 925975 gate G

A late Victorian building situated in elegant South Kensington and a short distance to the famous shops and museums. The bedrooms are designed to a notably high standard most are en suite with no two rooms alike, each room is named after a well known English town. A sumptuous buffet breakfast is served each day complementing your stay in this comfortable hotel.

a small friendly hotel in londons west end   - excellence in comfort and service-

---

TROCHEE HOTEL

21 Malcolm Road, Wimbledon, London SW19 4AS
Telephone: 081-946 3924 & 081-946 1579

Five minutes' walk Wimbledon station · Bed & English breakfast ·
All rooms have hot & cold water, hair dryer, tea and coffee making facilities, shaver point and TV · Rooms with bath also available · Lounge with colour TV · Parking

Where to Stay: Hotels, Guesthouses

W1

★★★★★ **66% The Churchill** 13 Portman Sq W1A 4ZX ☎ 071–486 5800 Telex no 264831 FAX 071–486 1255
A hotel in a pleasant setting overlooking Portman Square Gardens delights guests with a flower-filled lobby, an attractive arcade of shops, a sunken lounge where afternoon tea is served to the accompaniment of harp music, and the choice of bar, coffee shop or restaurant for other meals.
452 ⇌ ⋔ ⊱ in 66 bedrooms CTV in all bedrooms T S%
sB ⇌ ⋔ £212.75–£258.75 dB ⇌ ⋔ £235.75–£281.75 (room only) OR
Lift ◐ AC 60 ☎ (£2.50 per 2hrs) NC ✿ CFA ⋎ (hard) ♪
TC International V MC ▭ ⊱ S% Lunch fr£25&alc Dinner fr£30&alc Last dinner 11pm
Credit cards [1][2][3][4][5]

(red) ★★★★★ **Claridge's** Brook St W1A 2JQ ☎ 071–629 8860 Telex no 21872 FAX 071–449 2210
This Grande Dame of hotels, set at the heart of Mayfair and favourite of royalty and celebrities, continues to maintain its excellent reputation (the majority of bedrooms and nearly all the superb suites having been refurbished, while work continues on the rest) and to incorporate such welcome new features as air-conditioning. The traditional values of exclusiveness, discretion and professional service contribute much to the establishment's individual style and ambience.
190 ⇌ ⋔ CTV in all bedrooms T ⊁ (ex guide dogs) S15%
sB ⇌ ⋔ £190–£220 dB ⇌ ⋔ £245–£285 (room only) OR
Lift ◐ ✗ NC ♪ xmas
TC International V MC ▭ S15% Lunch £29–£48alc High tea £8 Dinner £31–£54alc Last dinner 11.15pm
Credit cards [1][2][3][5]

(red) ✿✿ ★★★★★ **Connaught** Carlos Place W1Y 6AL ☎ 071–499 7070
One of the last bastions of immaculate, traditional hotel-keeping, judged Europe's best in the AA's 1988 survey, an establishment carefully shielded from the glare of publicity provides accommodation in a range of bedrooms and suites which are all elegantly appointed and well equipped though they vary in size and style – those newly decorated tending to have lighter, fresher designs while the others are more restrained and masculine. Antiques and flower arrangements are set against gleaming old wood panelling in the public areas, and guests are assured of charming, highly attentive service whether they are taking afternoon tea in the Regency drawing room or cocktails in the 'clubby' bar; a handsome restaurant and grill room offers fine cuisine – roasts from the trolley always being outstanding – accompanied by a sensible wine list.
90 ⇌ ⋔ CTV in all bedrooms ⊁
Lift ◐ ✗ NC
TC English & French ▭
Credit cards [1]

★★★★ **72% Grosvenor House** Park Ln W1A 3AA ☎ 071–499 6363 Telex no 24871 FAX 071–493 3342
Several years of refurbishment have restored this hotel to its rightful position as one of the leading five-star establishments in the country, featuring a number of shops and a large lounge where afternoon tea is particularly popular as well as its renowned banqueting suites. Guests have a choice of three restaurants – 90 Park Lane, the Pavilion (which represents particularly good value at lunchtime) and the attractive Pasa Vino e Fantasia serving Italian cuisine.
454 ⇌ ⋔ ⊱ in 47 bedrooms CTV in all bedrooms ® T ⊁
* S% sB ⇌ ⋔ £185–£215 dB ⇌ ⋔ £205–£235 (room only) OR
Lift ◐ 20P 100 ☎ (charged) CFA [3] (heated) sauna solarium gymnasium health-&-fitness centre ♪ xmas
TC English French & Italian V MC ▭ ⊱ S% Lunch fr£19 Dinner fr£22.50 Last dinner 10.45pm
Credit cards [1][2][3][4][5]

★★★★ **78% Inn on the Park** Hamilton Place, Park Ln W1A 1AZ ☎ 071–499 0888 Telex no 22771 FAX 071–493 1895/6629
This modern hotel, possibly the best in London, combines elegantly attractive surroundings with every attention to guests' comfort and convenience. An entrance lobby containing a variety of quality shops leads to a foyer lounge where drinks and snacks are available throughout the day, and afternoon tea can be enjoyed against a background of harp and piano music; the first floor houses a further sitting area, the Four Seasons Restaurant with cocktail lounge, and the Lanes Restaurant where a pianist plays each evening. Spacious, well-appointed and air conditioned bedrooms are individually decorated with tasteful soft furnishings; valet room service is professionally polite, and the efficient service throughout the hotel reflects the manager's commitment, expertise and attention to detail.
228 ⇌ ⋔ ⊱ in 48 bedrooms CTV in all bedrooms T ⊁
* S% sB ⇌ ⋔ £201.25–£224.25 dB ⇌ ⋔ fr£247.25 OR
Lift ◐ AC 65 ☎ (£9) NC ♪ xmas
TC International V MC ▭ ⊱ Lunch £20.50–£27 High tea fr£10&alc Dinner £24.50–£38.50&alc Last dinner mdnt
Credit cards [1][2][3][4][5]

✿ ★★★★★ **Inter-Continental** 1 Hamilton Place, Hyde Park Corner W1V 0QY ☎ 071–409 3131 Telex no 25853 FAX 071–493 3476
Still the holder of a rosette award for its Le Soufflé restaurant, where soufflés predictably remain the highlight of the meal though accompanied by an enjoyable range of heartier dishes, this huge cosmopolitan hotel offers exceptionally good service throughout.
467 ⇌ ⋔ ⊱ in 58 bedrooms CTV in all bedrooms T ⊁ (ex guide dogs)
* S% sB ⇌ ⋔ £195.50–£212.75 dB ⇌ ⋔ £207–£253 (room only) OR
Lift ◐ AC 100 ☎ (£21.50 24 hours) NC CFA sauna gymnasium health centre ♪ xmas
TC English French Italian & Oriental V MC ▭ ⊱ Lunch £24&alc Dinner £40&alc Last dinner 11.30pm
Credit cards [1][2][3][4][5]

★★★★★ **59% London Hilton** 22 Park Lane W1A 2HH ☎ 071–493 8000 Telex no 24873 FAX 071–493 4957
A prime position at the heart of Mayfair gives the Hilton's rooms superb views over Hyde Park, Green Park and St James's Park. Well-equipped bedrooms offer cable and satellite TV as well as the usual facilities, while the lively, popular Polynesian restaurant beneath the hotel is complemented by a roof restaurant and a discothèque; cosmopolitan, well-trained and helpful staff contribute much to the establishment's character.
446 ⇌ ⋔ ⊱ in all bedrooms CTV in all bedrooms T
* sB ⇌ ⋔ £178.25–£253 dB ⇌ ⋔ £247.25–£287.50 (room only) OR
Lift ◐ AC ☎ sauna solarium ♪ xmas
TC International V MC ▭ ⊱ S15% Lunch £23.50–£29 Dinner £45&alc Last dinner 1am
Credit cards [1][2][3][4][5]

★★★★★ **56% MayFair Inter-Continental** Stratton St W1A 2AN ☎ 071–629 7777 Telex no 262526 FAX 071–629 1459
The facilities of this long-established hotel – now under new management – include an elegant restaurant, popular coffee house and the new Starlight leisure club; a multi-million pound programme to develop most public areas is under review.
322 ⇌ ⋔ (14fb) CTV in all bedrooms ⊁ (ex guide dogs)
(prices given on application)
Lift ◐ AC ✗ NC
TC English & French V MC ▭ Last dinner 10.30pm
Credit cards [1][2][3][4][5]

✿ ★★★★★ **Le Meridien London** 21 Piccadilly W1V 0BH ☎ 071–734 8000 Telex no 25795 FAX 071–437 3574
The attractions of this visually stunning, luxury hotel include a

141

Where to Stay: Hotels, Guesthouses

superb leisure and health club with swimming pool, jacuzzi, sauna, billiard tables, library, restaurant and bar. A number of other restaurants and bars, together with an elegant lounge, cater for most tastes – bedrooms and bathrooms being the only disappointment in an otherwise excellent establishment.
284 ⇌ ⋒ 1 ⊞ CTV in all bedrooms T ✶ (ex guide dogs)
* S% sB ⇌ ⋒ £184–£201.25 dB ⇌ ⋒ £201.25–£224.25 (room only) OR
Lift ❶ AC ✱ NC ③ (heated) squash snooker sauna solarium gymnasium health & leisure club ♪
TC International V MC ⊡ ✕ Lunch fr£14.50&alc Dinner £16.95–£37.50alc Last dinner 11.30pm
Credit cards ①②③④⑤

★★★★ **71% Ritz** Piccadilly W1V 9DG ☎ 071–493 8181 Telex no 267200 FAX 071–493 2687
The most attractive and elegant hotel in London, with its glittering gold leaf and chandeliers, the Ritz provides accommodation in recently refurbished bedrooms which include some quite outstanding suites. A magnificent restaurant with trompe l'oeil ceiling offers inventive British cuisine, while the Palm Court lounge remains a popular place to take afternoon tea.
130 ⇌ ⋒ CTV in all bedrooms T ✶ S15%
sB ⇌ ⋒ fr£185 dB ⇌ ⋒ fr£215 (room only) OR
Lift ❶ ✱ NC ♪ xmas
TC International V MC ⊡ S15% Lunch fr£25&alc Dinner fr£39.50&alc Last dinner 10.45pm
Credit cards ①②③④⑤

(red) ★★★★ **Athenaeum** Piccadilly W1V 0BJ ☎ 071–499 3464 Telex no 261589 FAX 071–493 1860
Enjoying a conveniently central West End location with views over Green Park and one of the few group-owned hotels to be awarded Red Stars, the Athenaeum maintains a distinctive, understated style and undiminished standards of service, staff combining professional discretion with a pleasant, welcoming manner. All the well-appointed bedrooms have recently been refurbished, while the lounge has been revamped in warmer, more colourful style. The small, almost club-like bar is notable for serving over fifty types of single malt whisky, and an elegant restaurant continues to present unusual combinations of ingredients and flavours.
112 ⇌ ⋒ ✕ in 27 bedrooms CTV in all bedrooms T ✶ (ex guide dogs)
* sB ⇌ ⋒ fr£160 dB ⇌ ⋒ £173–£188 (room only) OR
Lift ❶ AC 300 ☎ (£20.50) NC CFA xmas
TC International V MC ⊡
Credit cards ①②③④⑤

★★★★ **75% Britannia Inter-Continental** Grosvenor Square W1X 3AN ☎ 071–629 9400 Telex no 23941 FAX 071–629 7736
High standards are maintained at this friendly and popular hotel where a helpful staff provides professional service; bedrooms range from small singles to spacious de luxe, but all are individually decorated and well equipped, while the imaginative dishes served in the Adams Restaurant (including some delightful puddings) are skilfully and freshly prepared.
353 ⇌ ⋒ ✕ in 5 bedrooms CTV in all bedrooms T ✶ (ex guide dogs)
sB ⇌ ⋒ £120.75–£184 dB ⇌ ⋒ £149.50–£184 (room only) OR
Lift ❶ AC 15P CFA Satellite TV ♪
TC English, American & Japanese V MC ⊡ ✕ Last dinner 10.30pm
Credit cards ①②③④⑤

(red) ★★★★ **Brown's** Dover St, Albermarle St W1A 4SW ☎ 071–493 6020 Telex no 28686 FAX 071–493 9381
One of the oldest hotels in London, spanning twelve houses among the fine antique shops and art galleries of Mayfair, this is a place of oak panelling, stained glass and deep calm not unlike the nearby gentlemen's clubs. Open fires burn on colder days in a lounge with chintz-covered armchairs and a grandfather clock, and in the intimate St George's Bar where leather sofas stand beneath oil paintings, while the elegant, panelled l'Apéritif dining room offers a range of English and French specialities that includes home-made puddings. Bedrooms individually decorated in Victorian style contain such present day amenities as direct-dial telephones and mini-bars, and service is good-humoured and attentive throughout.
133 ⇌ ⋒ (14fb) ✕ in 12 bedrooms CTV in all bedrooms T ✶ (ex guide dogs) S%
sB ⇌ ⋒ £145–£155 dB ⇌ ⋒ £185–£225 (room only) OR
Lift ❶ ✱ NC CFA gents hairdresser xmas
TC English & French V MC ⊡ ✕ Lunch £25.75–£26.75&alc Dinner £29.95–£30.95&alc Last dinner 9.30pm
Credit cards ①②③④⑤

★★★★ **58% The Cumberland** Marble Arch W1A 4RF ☎ 071–262 1234 Telex no 22215 FAX 071–724 4621
This popular commercial and tourist hotel continues to upgrade its accommodation, the reception area, lounges and most bedrooms now being both comfortable and well equipped. Its range of eating options complements the main restaurant with one in Japanese style which will appeal to guests with exotic tastes and also includes a carvery and

coffee shop.
894 ⇌ ⋒ ✕ in 117 bedrooms CTV in all bedrooms ® T ✶ (ex guide dogs) S15%
sB ⇌ £118 dB ⇌ £149 (room only) OR
Lift ❶ ✱ CFA ♪ xmas
V MC ⊡ ✕ Lunch £15–£18 High tea £3.50–£12 Dinner £19–£35 Last dinner 10.45pm
Credit cards ①②③④⑤

★★★★ **58% Holiday Inn – Marble Arch** 134 George St W1H 6DN ☎ 071–723 1277 Telex no 27983 FAX 071–402 0666
Good management and willing, helpful service contribute much to the appeal of a modern, high-rise hotel which attracts a varied international clientèle, and free parking for residents must be regarded as a useful bonus. Well-equipped bedrooms are particularly spacious and, as we went to print, a new European Restaurant was being introduced to augment the services provided by the existing Coffee Shop.
241 ⇌ ⋒ (135fb) ✕ in 32 bedrooms CTV in all bedrooms
* S15% sB ⇌ ⋒ £119–£132 dB ⇌ ⋒ £132–£152 (room only) OR
Lift ❶ AC 5P 60 ☎ CFA ③ (heated) sauna solarium gymnasium
TC European V MC ⊡ ✕ Last dinner 11pm
Credit cards ①②③④⑤

★★★★ **75% London Marriott** Grosvenor Square W1A 4AW ☎ 071–493 1232 Telex no 268101 FAX 071–491 3201
A tastefully furnished hotel overlooking Grosvenor Square offers particularly well-equipped bedrooms, a choice of eating options and good business and function facilities.
223 ⇌ ⋒ (26fb) CTV in all bedrooms T ✶ (ex guide dogs)
* sB ⇌ ⋒ £184–£207 dB ⇌ ⋒ £207–£224.25 (room only) OR
Lift ❶ AC ✱ NC CFA ♪ xmas
TC International V MC ⊡ ✕ Lunch £16.50–£25alc Dinner £16.50–£25alc Last dinner 12.30am
Credit cards ①②③④⑤

★★★★ **73% Montcalm** Great Cumberland Place W1A 2LF ☎ 071–402 4288 Telex no 28710 FAX 071–724 9180
A terraced Georgian building has been tastefully modernised to provide fully equipped bedrooms and comfortable public areas which include the Celebrities Restaurant with its interesting range of well-prepared dishes; service throughout combines friendliness and professionalism.
115 ⇌ ⋒ (9fb) CTV in all bedrooms T ✶ (ex guide dogs)
* S15% sB ⇌ ⋒ £152–£162 dB ⇌ ⋒ £169–£195 (room only) OR
Lift ❶ ✱ NC ♪

Where to Stay: Hotels, Guesthouses

TC French V MC ⚆ ✕ Lunch £14–£15.95 Dinner £21.95&alc Last dinner 10pm
Credit cards ① ② ③ ④ ⑤

★★★★ **73% Park Lane** Piccadilly W1Y 8BX ☎ 071–499 6321 Telex no 21533 FAX 071–499 1965
Good management and an old-fashioned atmosphere based on traditional levels of service and hospitality are the secrets of this hotel's success, creating the pleasant ambience that pervades the Palm Court lounge, Bracewells Restaurant and the Brasserie. Leisure facilities are also available.
321 ⇌ ℟ (32fb) ✕ in 44 bedrooms CTV in all bedrooms
sB ⇌ ℟ £133–£154 dB ⇌ ℟ £154–£176 (room only) OR
Lift ◉ 180 ☏ (charged) CFA gymnasium
TC International V MC ⚆ Last dinner 10.30pm
Credit cards ① ② ③ ⑤

★★★★ **74% Portman Inter-Continental** 22 Portman Square W1H 9FL ☎ 071–486 5844 Telex no 261526 FAX 071–935 0537
The attractions of this hotel include an inviting lobby with groups of comfortable armchairs, Truffles Restaurant, a popular bakery and pub, superb function facilities and a choice of modern bedrooms or penthouse suites.
272 ⇌ ℟ ✕ in 14 bedrooms CTV in all bedrooms T ⚠ (ex guide dogs)
sB&B ⇌ ℟ £145–£149 dB&B ⇌ ℟ £174–£194 OR
Lift ◉ AC ✱ CFA ⚸ (hard) tennis court available ♪ xmas
TC French V MC ⚆ ✕ S% Lunch £19.50–£20.50&alc Dinner £29.50&alc Last dinner 11.30pm
Credit cards ① ② ③ ④ ⑤

★★★★ **55% Ramada** 10 Berners St W1A 3BA ☎ 071–636 1629 Telex no 25759 FAX 071–580 3972
A magnificent lounge and dining room are key features of this impressive hotel, conveniently located just off Oxford Street; a successful carvery lunch operation is supplemented by an à la carte menu, and afternoon teas are also very popular. Bedrooms satisfy modern commercial requirements, and refurbishment should now be complete.
235 ⇌ ℟ (10fb) ✕ in 105 bedrooms CTV in all bedrooms T ⚠
* S10% sB ⇌ ℟ £92–£130 dB ⇌ ℟ £150–£230 (room only) OR
Lift ◉ ✱ ♪ xmas
TC English and French V MC ⚆ ✕ S10%
Credit cards ① ② ③ ④ ⑤

★★★★ **50% St George's** Langham Place W1N 8QS ☎ 071–580 0111 Telex no 27274 FAX 071–436 7997

Panoramic views over London are available from the Summit Restaurant, bar and lounge of a hotel that shares a building just north of Oxford Circus with the BBC; bedrooms – all of which are above the ninth floor – have recently been refurbished and upgraded.
86 ⇌ ℟ (8fb) ✕ in 10 bedrooms CTV in all bedrooms ® T ⚠ (ex guide dogs)
S% sB ⇌ ℟ fr£105 dB ⇌ ℟ fr£130 (room only) OR
Lift ◉ AC 2P NC ♪ xmas
V MC ⚆ ✕ S% Lunch £18.50&alc High tea £6.75 Dinner £18.50&alc Last dinner 10pm
Credit cards ① ② ③ ④ ⑤

★★★★ **68% Selfridge** Orchard St W1H 0JS ☎ 071–408 2080 Telex no 22361 FAX 071–629 8849
The fine public rooms of this modern hotel include a panelled lounge, a cocktail bar in country pub style and two restaurants – an extremely comfortable formal one, and another which is much more casual; bedrooms tend to be small but are very well equipped.
296 ⇌ ℟ (25fb) ✕ in 110 bedrooms CTV in all bedrooms T ⚠
* sB ⇌ ℟ fr£125 dB ⇌ ℟ fr£145 (room only) OR
Lift ◉ AC ✱
TC International MC ⚆ ✕ Lunch fr£16.95&alc Dinner fr£16.95&alc Last dinner 10.30pm
Credit cards ① ② ③ ④ ⑤

★★★★ **63% The Westbury** Bond St, Conduit St W1A 4UH ☎ 071–629 7755 Telex no 24378 FAX 071–495 1163
The marble foyer of an attractive hotel ideally set in Mayfair welcomes winter guests with a glowing fire; the compact Polo Bar, with its murals, leads into the gracious, pine-panelled Polo Lounge which serves refreshments twenty-four hours a day supplementing the range of interesting menus offered by a cosy, tastefully appointed restaurant. Individually decorated bedrooms – some designated non-smoking – are pleasant and comfortable, though en suite facilities can be on the small side, and the valet room service is polite and efficient.
243 ⇌ ℟ ✕ in 40 bedrooms CTV in all bedrooms T
* s15% sB ⇌ ℟ £160–£175 dB ⇌ ℟ £190–£210 (room only) OR
Lift ◉ AC 15P NC CFA ♪ xmas
TC French V MC ⚆ ✕ S15% Lunch £18.50–£20.50&alc Dinner £20.50–£22.50&alc Last dinner 10.30pm
Credit cards ① ② ③ ④ ⑤

★★★ **70% Chesterfield** 35 Charles St W1X 8LX ☎ 071–491 2622 Telex no 269374 FAX 071–491 4793
A traditional hotel at the centre of Mayfair now features the new Butlers Restaurant, which offers an

outstanding buffet lunch as an alternative to its à la carte selection. Flowers and antiques create a warm atmosphere in ground-floor public areas that include a wood-panelled library, while colourful bedrooms are furnished to a high standard.
113 ⇌ ℟ 1 🛦 CTV in all bedrooms ⚠ (ex guide dogs)
(prices given on application)
Lift ◉ ✱ NC
MC ⚆ Last dinner 10.30pm
Credit cards ① ② ③ ⑤

★★★ **73% Clifton-Ford** 47 Welbeck St W1M 8DN ☎ 071–486 6600 Telex no 22569 FAX 071–486 7492
A hotel of a quality, elegance and tranquillity not often found in the West End harmoniously blends traditional style with modern facilities; the top-floor rooms and suites, with their panoramic views of London, have recently been equipped with every comfort, and accommodation on other floors has also been upgraded.
211 ⇌ ℟ (4fb) CTV in all bedrooms ® T
* S% sB ⇌ ℟ £115–£138 dB ⇌ ℟ £138–£201.25 (room only)
Lift ◉ 10 ☏ (£12) ♪
TC International V MC ⚆ Lunch £11–£21 Dinner £19–£39alc Last dinner 11pm
Credit cards ① ② ③ ⑤

★★★ **66% Mandeville** Mandeville Place W1M 6BE ☎ 071–935 5599 Telex no 269487 FAX 071–935 9588
Well-placed for Oxford Street shopping and the West End, this hotel offers a friendly reception from both management and staff, and accommodation in well-equipped, attractive bedrooms. The Coffee Shop, residents' lounge bar and Boswell's Pub Bar are all popular.
165 ⇌ ℟ CTV in all bedrooms
(prices given on application)
Lift ◉ ✱ NC
V MC
Credit cards ① ② ③ ⑤

★★★ **66% Mostyn** Bryanston St W1H 0DE ☎ 071–935 2361 Telex no 27656 FAX 071–487 2759
122 ⇌ ℟ (24fb) CTV in all bedrooms ® T ⚠ (ex guide dogs)
* S10% sB ⇌ ℟ £86–£94 dB ⇌ ℟ £103–£113 (room only)
Lift ◉
TC English V MC ⚆ ✕ S10% Lunch £12.95&alc High Tea fr£6alc Dinner £12.95&alc Last dinner 11.45pm
Credit cards ① ② ③ ⑤

★★★ **59% Mount Royal** Bryanston St, Marble Arch W1A 4UR ☎ 071–629 8040 Telex no 23355 FAX 071–499 7792
A large commercial and tourist hotel – its location near Marble Arch making it ideal for visitors to the capital – features a choice of eating

143

Where to Stay: Hotels, Guesthouses

options, conference/banqueting facilities and a number of shops and kiosks. Bedrooms are being tastefully refurbished.
701 ↵ ↑ (31fb) ⌀ in 40 bedrooms CTV in all bedrooms ® ✱
(prices given on application)
Lift ● ✱ CFA
TC Mainly grills MC ☐ ⌀ Last dinner 11pm
Credit cards ① ② ③ ④ ⑤

★★ **52% Regent Palace** Glasshouse St, Piccadilly W1A 4BZ ☎ 071–734 7000 Telex no 23740 FAX 071–734 6435
Good accommodation is provided by this outstanding, value-for-money hotel which stands beside Piccadilly Circus.
882rm (34fb) ⌀ in 210 bedrooms CTV in all bedrooms ®
S15% sB&B fr£56 dB&B fr£73 OR
Lift ● ✱ CFA
V MC ☐ ⌀ Lunch fr£13.95 High Tea fr£3 Dinner fr£13.95 Last dinner 9pm
Credit cards ① ② ③ ④ ⑤

Q Q Bryanston Court 60 Great Cumberland Place W1 ☎ 071–262 3141 Telex no 262076
54 ↵ ↑ (3fb) CTV in all bedrooms ✱
Last dinner 10pm
Lic lift ■ ✱
Credit cards ① ② ③ ⑤

Q Hotel Concorde 50 Great Cumberland Place W1H 7FD ☎ 071–402 6169 Telex no 262076
Tastefully decorated and comfortable accommodation with a good lounge is provided by this well-situated central hotel.
28rm (5 ↵ 23 ↑) (1fb) CTV in all bedrooms ✱
sB&B ↵ ↑ fr£62 dB&B ↵ ↑ fr£72
Lic lift ■ CTV ✱
Credit cards ① ② ③ ⑤

Q Edward Lear Hotel 30 Seymour St W1H 5WD ☎ 071–402 5401
30 ↑ (3fb) CTV in all bedrooms ® ✱
CTV ✱
Credit cards ③

Q Q Q Georgian House Hotel 87 Gloucester Place W1H 3PG ☎ 071–936 2211 Telex no 266079 FAX 071–486 7535
This pleasant central London hotel offers well-equipped, modern accommodation of a good standard with a lift to all floors. The breakfast room is situated at the lower ground floor level.
19 ↵ ↑ (3fb) CTV in all bedrooms ®
✱
Lic lift ■ ✱ nc5yrs
Credit cards ② ③ ⑤

Q Hart House Hotel 51 Gloucester Place W1H 3PE ☎ 071–935 2288
An imposing five-storey terrace house provides accommodation in well-appointed bedrooms.

15rm (7 ↵ ↑ 8hc) (4fb) CTV in all bedrooms ® ✱
sB&B £30–£35 dB&B £45–£50 dB&B ↵ ↑ £55–£65
☐ CTV ✱
Credit cards ① ② ③

Q Montagu House 3 Montagu Place W1H 1RG ☎ 071–935 4632
A conveniently situated guesthouse near Marble Arch, under new ownership this year, is currently being upgraded.
18 ↑ (4fb) CTV in all bedrooms ® ✱
C CTV ✱
Credit cards ① ③

W2

★★★★ **67% Royal Lancaster** Lancaster Ter W2 2TY ☎ 071–262 6737 Telex no 24822 FAX 071–724 3191
Many bedrooms and all of the major suites of this hotel have unrivalled views of Hyde Park's Italian Gardens, though some of the executive rooms are smaller and less comfortable than one would expect in such an establishment. The Rosette restaurants provide a choice of menus but guests requiring a less formal meal should try the Pavement Café. Banqueting facilities have been extended.
418 ↵ ↑ (40fb) CTV in all bedrooms T ✱ (ex guide dogs)
* sB ↵ ↑ £140–£215 dB ↵ ↑ £160–£215 (room only) OR
Lift ● AC 50P (£7.50–£10) 50 ✿ (£7.50–£10) NC CFA xmas
TC International V MC ☐ ⌀ Lunch £15–£17&alc High tea fr£4.30alc Dinner £20–£23&alc Last dinner 10.45pm
Credit cards ① ② ③ ④ ⑤

★★★★ **72% White's** Lancaster Gate W2 3NR ☎ 071–262 2711 Telex no 24771 FAX 071–262 2147
Standards of accommodation and cuisine are high at a small hotel with a club-like atmosphere which overlooks Hyde Park; friendly staff provide service which is both correct and helpful.
54 ↵ 1 ☐ ↵ ⌀ in 10 bedrooms CTV in all bedrooms T ✱ (ex guide dogs)
* sB ↵ £130 dB ↵ £170–£210 (room only) OR
Lift ● AC 25P NC ✿ ♬ xmas
TC English & French V MC ☐ Lunch fr£15.50&alc Dinner fr£15.50&alc Last dinner 10.30pm
Credit cards ① ② ③ ④ ⑤

★★★ **60% Central Park** Queensborough Ter W2 3SS ☎ 071–229 2424 Telex no 27342 FAX 071–229 2904
Contemporary and well-managed, the hotel complements adequate standards of comfort by an attractive terrace restaurant and friendly, helpful service.
251rm (210 ↵ 31 ↑) (10fb) CTV in all

bedrooms ® T
S% sB&B ↵ ↑ fr£57 dB&B ↵ ↑ fr£78
Continental breakfast
Lift ● 10P (£1.50) 20 ✿ (£1.50) sauna solarium gymnasium xmas
TC International V MC ☐
Credit cards ① ② ③ ⑤

★★★ **59% Hospitality Inn** 104/105 Bayswater Rd W2 3HL ☎ 071–262 4461 Telex no 22667 FAX 071–706 4560
Some rooms in this Bayswater Road hotel overlook the park, and though these would benefit from refurbishment bedrooms are equipped with every modern convenience, while friendly staff provide willing service throughout.
175 ↵ ↑ CTV in all bedrooms ® T
S% sB ↵ ↑ £78–£86.50 dB ↵ ↑ £94.50–£103 (room only) OR
Lift ● AC 20P 40 ✿ CFA ♬ xmas
TC International V MC ☐ Lunch fr£7.90&alc Dinner £12–£17alc Last dinner 10.30pm
Credit cards ① ② ③ ④ ⑤

★★★ **65% London Embassy** 150 Bayswater Rd W2 4RT ☎ 071–229 1212 Telex no 27727 FAX 071–229 2633
A modern tourist and commercial hotel overlooking Hyde Park supplements the restaurant's short à la carte menu with a fixed price carvery operation and pre-theatre meal; helpful staff provide some lounge and room service.
193 ↵ ↑ ⌀ in 10 bedrooms CTV in all bedrooms ® T ✱ (ex guide dogs)
S% sB ↵ ↑ £95–£108 dB ↵ ↑ £108–£130 (room only) OR
Lift ● 20P 20 ✿ (£2) CFA
TC International V MC ☐ S% Lunch £12&alc Dinner £7.50–£12&alc Last dinner 10.15pm
Credit cards ① ② ③ ④ ⑤

★★★ **62% Park Court** 75 Lancaster Gate, Hyde Park W2 3NN ☎ 071–402 4272 Telex no 23922 FAX 071–706 4156
The well-equipped accommodation provided by this large, busy hotel includes some executive rooms, and there is an informal, bistro-style restaurant.
398 ↵ ↑ (11fb) ⌀ in 227 bedrooms CTV in all bedrooms ® T
sB ↵ ↑ fr£72.50 dB ↵ ↑ fr£91.50 (room only) OR
Lift ● ✱ CFA xmas
V MC ☐ ⌀ Lunch fr£12.50 High tea fr£10 Dinner £7–£14 Last dinner 11pm
Credit cards ① ② ③ ④ ⑤

Q Q Q Byron Hotel 36–38 Queensborough Ter W2 3SH ☎ 071–243 0987
This quietly positioned and immaculately restored hotel offers a variety of tastefully appointed bedrooms, all with en suite facilities; there is a lift to the breakfast room.

Where to Stay: Hotels, Guesthouses

43 ⇌ (2fb) ⊁ in 10 bedrooms CTV in all bedrooms ® ⊁ (ex guide dogs) Last dinner 8pm
Lic Lift ⊜ CTV ⊁
Credit cards [1] [2] [3] [5]

◎◎ **Camelot Hotel** 45–47 Norfolk Square W2 1RX ☎ 071–723 9118 & 071–262 1980 Telex no 268312
Modern facilities are provided throughout this friendly hotel's range of accommodation.
44 ⇌ ⋔ (8fb) CTV in all bedrooms ® ⊁ (ex guide dogs)
Lift ⊜ CTV ⊁
Credit cards [1] [3]

◎◎ **Mitre House Hotel** 178–180 Sussex Gardens W2 1TU ☎ 071–723 8040 Telex no 914113
31 ⇌ ⋔ (3fb) CTV in all bedrooms
Lift CTV 18P
Credit cards [1] [2] [3] [5]

◎◎ **Norfolk Towers Hotel** 34 Norfolk Place W2 1QW ☎ 071–262 3123 Telex no 268583 FAX 071–724 4090
A pleasant, Victorian-style hotel has been tastefully modernised and refurnished to offer well-equipped accommodation with peaceful lounge bar and basement wine bar; hot and cold meals are available.
85 ⇌ (3fb) CTV in all bedrooms ⊁
Last dinner 10pm

Lic Lift ⊜ ⊁
Credit cards [1] [2] [3] [5]

◎◎ **Parkwood Hotel** 4 Stanhope Place W2 2HB ☎ 071–402 2241
An elegant four-storey terraced house standing conveniently close to the West End provides comfortable, well-appointed bedroom accommodation and an informal, friendly atmosphere.
18 ⇌ ⋔ (5fb) ⊁ in 1 bedroom CTV in all bedrooms ® ⊁ (ex guide dogs)
⊜ CTV ⊁
Credit cards [1] [3]

◎◎◎ **Pembridge Court Hotel** 34 Pembridge Gdns W2 4DX ☎ 071–229 9977 Telex no 298363
This hotel features very comfortable bedrooms with modern facilities and a separate restaurant.
17 ⇌ ⋔ annexe 8 ⇌ ⋔ (4fb) CTV in all bedrooms
* sB&B ⇌ ⋔ £74–£97 dB&B ⇌ ⋔ £88.55–£135 Last dinner 11.15pm
Lic Lift ⊜ 2 ⬜
Credit cards [1] [2] [3] [5]

◎◎ **Slavia Hotel** 2 Pembridge Sq W2 4EW ☎ 071–727 1316 & 071–229 0803 Telex no 917458
Simple, reasonably priced accommodation is provided by this hotel.
31 ⋔ (8fb)

Lic Lift ⊜ CTV 1P (£5)
Credit cards [1] [2] [3] [5]

W4 Chiswick
◎◎◎ **Chiswick Hotel** 71 Chiswick High Rd W4 2LS ☎ 081–994 1712 FAX 081–742 2585
A hotel ideally situated for both central London and Heathrow Airport offers attractive accommodation and good service; the standard of cooking is high, and the restaurant has a residents' bar.
30 ⇌ ⋔ (7fb) CTV in all bedrooms ®
Last dinner 8.30pm
Lic ⊜ 15P sauna solarium jacuzzi
Credit cards [1] [2] [3] [5]

W5
★★★ **70% Carnarvon** Ealing Common W5 3HN ☎ 081–992 5399 Telex no 935114 FAX 081–992 7082
A modern hotel on the edge of Ealing Common, convenient for the North Circular Road, belies its severely functional external appearance with a spacious, bright and comfortable interior which includes fully equipped bedrooms. First-class management and a well-organised, personable staff maintain good housekeeping standards, and extensive car parking facilities are a bonus for visitors to London.

MITRE HOUSE HOTEL

Completely refurbished in 1990 · All seventy rooms with en suite bathroom and satellite television, radio and direct dial telephone · Junior suites available

Free car park · Licensed bar · Lift · English Breakfast

Centrally located to all major sights and shopping areas · Close to Paddington Station and A2 Airbus to Heathrow · Reasonable rates

Contact us now for further information and our brochure

TEL: 071-723 8040
FAX: 071-402 0990
TLX: 914113 MITRE G

178-184 SUSSEX GARDENS
HYDE PARK
LONDON W2 1TU

Where to Stay: Hotels, Guesthouses

145 ↠ ⋔ ⊁ in 10 bedrooms CTV in all bedrooms ® T ⋎ (ex guide dogs) sB ↠ ⋔ £79.50 dB ↠ £105.50 (room only) OR
Lift ● 150P CFA
TC English and European MC ⌯ ⊁
Credit cards [1] [2] [3] [5]

W6
★★★ 58% Novotel London
1 Shortlands W6 8DR ☎ 081–741 1555 Telex no 934539 FAX 081–741 2120
A hotel popular both with businessmen and with tourists exploring the capital enjoys a quiet location close to Hammersmith Centre. Accommodation is spacious and staff provide a warm welcome and good standards of hospitality, but facilities can on occasions be stretched by sheer volume of trade. Light snacks are available throughout the day in La Terrace, more substantial meals being served in Le Grill and the à la carte La Perriche restaurant.
640 ⊁ in 20 bedrooms CTV in all bedrooms
Lift AC CTV 230 ⌂ (£6.50)
TC English & French V MC ⌯ ⊁ Last dinner mdnt
Credit cards [1] [2] [3] [5]

🕻🕻 **Hotel West Six** 99 Shepherd Bush Rd, Hammersmith W6 7LP ☎ 071–603 0948
This imposing three-storey terrace house provides accommodation in well-appointed en suite bedrooms. Continental breakfasts are served.
(See advertisement below)

W8
★★★★★ 61% Royal Garden
Kensington High St W8 4PT ☎ 071–937 8000 Telex no 263151 FAX 071–938 4532
The suites, studios and bedrooms of this hotel, tastefully furnished and equipped with five-star facilities, all look out over Kensington Gardens, Hyde Park, or the lively scene of Kensington High Street. The Garden Café, serving meals throughout the day, shares beautiful views of the park with the adjacent Garden Bar where a resident pianist entertains, while the comfortable Gallery Bar offers a club-like atmosphere and the Roof Restaurant provides an ideal rendezvous for dining and dancing.
380 ↠ ⋔ ⊁ in 10 bedrooms CTV in all bedrooms ⋎ (ex guide dogs)
* sB ↠ ⋔ £135–£165 dB ↠ ⋔ £168–£185 (room only) OR
Lift ● AC 142 ⌂ (£2.50–£15) CFA xmas
TC International V MC ⌯ ⊁
Credit cards [1] [2] [3] [4] [5]

★★★★ 68% Kensington Palace Thistle De Vere Gardens W8 5AF ☎ 071–937 8121 Telex no 262422 FAX 071–937 2816
A busy hotel offers rooms upgraded to provide modern amenities, a choice between the interesting, enjoyable dishes served in the restaurant, and lighter coffee shop meals, and attentively efficient service from a friendly, willing staff.
298 ↠ ⋔ (27fb) ⊁ in 32 bedrooms CTV in all bedrooms ® T ⋎
* sB ↠ ⋔ fr£90 dB ↠ ⋔ fr£105 (room only) OR
Lift ● ♪ CFA ♫
TC International MC ⌯ Lunch fr£17.50&alc Dinner fr£17.50&alc Last dinner 10.45pm
Credit cards [1] [2] [3] [4] [5]

★★★★ 55% London Tara Scarsdale Place, off Wrights Ln W8 5SR ☎ 071–937 7211 Telex no 918834 FAX 071–937 7100
Major bedroom and public area improvements are already well advanced in this hotel, which also provides a good range of eating options and efficient check-in facilities.
831 ↠ ⊁ in 96 bedrooms CTV in all bedrooms T ⋎ (ex guide dogs)
* sB ↠ £80–£95 dB ↠ £95–£110 (room only) OR
Lift ● AC 30 P 80⌂ (£8 per 24hours) CFA
TC French V MC ⌯ Last dinner 11pm
Credit cards [1] [2] [3] [4] [5]

★★★ 62% Kensington Close
Wrights Ln W8 5SP ☎ 071–937 8170 Telex no 23914 FAX 071–937 8289

A large, quietly situated hotel complements a range of well-equipped bedrooms with two restaurants – the Grill and the more popular Biancones which is open all day for snacks. Its health and fitness club includes a swimming pool, two squash courts and a gymnasium.
532 ↠ ⋔ ⊁ in 11 bedrooms CTV in all bedrooms ® T
* sB ↠ ⋔ £80 dB ↠ ⋔ £95 (room only) OR
Lift ● 40 P (£3.50 2 hours) 60 ⌂ (charged) CFA [3] (heated) squash sauna solarium gymnasium health & fitness centre xmas
TC Mainly grills V MC ⌯ ⊁ S% Lunch £3.50–£13.95&alc Dinner £3.50–£13.95&alc Last dinner 11pm
Credit cards [1] [2] [3] [4] [5]

★★ 57% Hotel Lexham 32–38 Lexham Gardens W8 5JU ☎ 071–373 6471 Telex no 268141 FAX 071–244 7827 Closed 23 Dec–2 Jan
The accommodation provided by this traditional hotel represents good value, particularly for central London; what it lacks in imagination is made up in the service provided by pleasant, cheerful staff. There is no bar, but two lounges are available.
64rm (40 ↠ ⋔) (13fb) CTV in all bedrooms T ⋎
* S10% sB&B fr£32.50 sB&B ↠ ⋔ fr£44.50 dB&B fr£41.50 dB&B ↠ ⋔ £58.50–£64.50 OR
Lift ● CTV ♪ NC ✿
TC English and Continental MC ⌯ S% Lunch fr£5 Dinner fr£8.25 Last dinner 8pm
Credit cards [1] [3]

🕻🕻 **Apollo Hotel** 18–22 Lexham Gardens W8 5JE ☎ 071–835 1133 Telex no 264189 FAX 071–370 4853 Closed 24 Dec–2 Jan
The proprietor of this hotel continues to offer friendly service, well-appointed bedrooms (many with en suite facilities) and public areas which are to be upgraded this year.
59rm (40 ↠ 10⋔ 9hc) (4fb) CTV in all

HOTEL WEST SIX
99, Shepherds Bush Road, Hammersmith, London W6
Tel: 071-603 0948
Fax: 071-602 8835

Hotel West Six is owned by Seacourt Limited, known for quality and service. Convenient for all amenities including theatres, shops, casinos and amusements and walking distance from Hammersmith tube station (Piccadilly line).

*All rooms ensuite shower, WC and colour TV. *All major credit cards accepted. *All rooms are centrally heated. *Continental breakfast included. Full English breakfast optional.

*Tariff: Single room £25/day; Double £40/day; Triple: £50/day.

Where to Stay: Hotels, Guesthouses

bedrooms ✠ (ex guide dogs)
sB&B £30 sB&B ⇌ ☏ £44 dB&B ⇌ ☏ £54
Lic Lift ▧ CTV ♪
Credit cards ① ② ③ ⑤

ⓆⒶAtlas Hotel 24–30 Lexham Gardens W8 5JE ☎ 071–373 7873 & 071–835 1155 Telex no 264189 FAX 071–370 4853 Closed 24 Dec–2 Jan
Many of the traditionally furnished bedrooms of this well-situated, value-for-money hotel provide en suite facilities, and all are well equipped; there are also a small bar and separate lounge. The establishment's sister hotel, The Apollo, stands next to it.
64rm (15 ⇌ 30 ☏ 19hc) (7fb) CTV in all bedrooms ✠ (ex guide dogs)
sB&B £30 sB&B ⇌ ☏ £44 dB&B ⇌ ☏ £54
Lic Lift ▧ CTV ♪
Credit cards ① ② ③ ⑤

ⓆⒶ Observatory House Hotel 37 Hornton St W8 7NR ☎ 071–937 1577 & 071–937 6353 Telex no 914972
Delightfully situated in a quiet area a stroll away from Kensington High Street, the hotel offers tastefully designed accommodation equipped with private baths/showers, direct dial telephones, colour TV and other modern facilities. Refurbishment is planned this year.
24 ⇌ ☏ (5fb) ⅍ in 2 bedrooms CTV in all bedrooms ® ✠ (ex guide dogs)
▧ ♪
Credit cards ① ② ③ ⑤

W8
★★★ **London Kensington Hilton**
Holland Park Av W11 4UL ☎ 071–603 3355 Telex no 919763 FAX 071–602 9397
A large and exceptionally comfortable hotel with a distinctly international flavour, well placed for the West End and A40, offers three eating places – the à la carte/carvery Market Restaurant, the Hiroko where authentic Japanese cuisine is served,

and a 24-hour drink and snack bar. There are several shops in the foyer, and spaces are reserved for residents in the car park beneath the hotel.
606 ⇌ ⅍ in 100 bedrooms CTV in all bedrooms ® T
sB ⇌ £98–£158 dB ⇌ £118–£188 (room only) OR
Lift ◐ AC 100 ⚓ (£8.50) CFA ♫ xmas
TC International V MC ⌨ S10% Lunch £18–£22&alc Dinner £20–£35&alc Last dinner 10.30pm
Credit cards ① ② ③ ④ ⑤

W14 West Kensington
SELECTED RECOMMENDED
ⓆⓆⓆ **Ashton Court Hotel** 25/27 Matheson Rd, Kensington W14 8SN ☎ 071–602 9954 Telex no 919208 FAX 071–371 1338
29 ⇌ ☏ (3fb) CTV in all bedrooms ®
✠ (ex guide dogs)
Lic Lift ▧ CTV ♪
Credit cards ① ② ③ ⑤

Ⓠ **Centaur Hotel** 21 Avonmore Rd W14 8RP ☎ 071–283 3857 & 071–603 5973
Set in a residential area with street parking, and ideally situated for both Olympia and Earls Court, this small, family-run hotel provides simple accommodation equipped with radio alarms and direct dial telephones.
12hc (4fb) CTV in all bedrooms ✠

WC1
★★★★ 69% **The Marlborough**
Bloomsbury St WC1B 3QD ☎ 071–636 5601 Telex no 298274 FAX 071–636 0532
Comfortable accommodation, an attractive restaurant offering a wide range of dishes, and efficient, friendly service are provided by this hotel.
169 ⇌ ⅍ in 57 bedrooms CTV in all bedrooms ® T
* S% sB ⇌ ☏ fr£128 dB ⇌ ☏ fr£148 (room only)
Lift ◐ ♪ xmas
. TC French V MC ⌨ ⅍ Lunch

£16.50&alc Dinner £16.50&alc Last dinner 11.30pm
Credit cards ① ② ③ ④ ⑤

★★★★ 69% **Hotel Russell** Russell Square WC1B 5BE ☎ 071–837 6470 Telex no 24615 FAX 071–837 3612
Guests enter this sizable commercial hotel through an imposing entrance hall with large marble pillars, chandelier and staircase. Bedrooms are generally comfortable, though compact in some cases, service is good and there are two restaurants – an informal, colourful brasserie and a well-appointed carvery which also serves an à la carte menu.
326 ⇌ (1fb) ⅍ in 20 bedrooms CTV in all bedrooms T
sB ⇌ £107–£115 dB ⇌ £130–£135 (room only) OR
Lift ◐ ♪ CFA ♫ xmas
TC International V MC ⌨ ⅍ S7.5%
Lunch fr£14.50&alc Dinner fr£14.50&alc Last dinner 10.30pm
Credit cards ① ② ③ ④ ⑤

★★★ 69% **Bloomsbury Crest**
Coram St WC1N 1HT ☎ 071–837 1200 Telex no 22113 FAX 071–837 5374
Extensive refurbishment of a hotel situated between the West End and the City has transformed its exterior, the new stone facia being enhanced by a domed glass entrance. The first-floor restaurant complex serves an extensive range of meals, while the Café Shaw offers a more informal eating style.
284 ⇌ (29fb) ⅍ in 67 bedrooms CTV in all bedrooms ® T ✠ (ex guide dogs)
* sB ⇌ £92–£105 dB ⇌ £106–£114 (room only) OR
Lift ◐ T 100 ⚓ (£8.40 per night)
TC International V MC ⌨ ⅍
Credit cards ① ② ③ ④ ⑤

★★★ 60% **Bonnington** 92 Southampton Row WC1B 4BH ☎ 071–242 2828 Telex no 261591 FAX 071–831 9170
This hotel, set in a prime position between the City and the West End, is at present undergoing a programme of upgrading and improvement.

ASTON COURT HOTEL

25/27 Matheson Road, Kensington, Olympia, London W14 8SN
Telephone: 071-602 9954.   Fax: 071-371 1338

Recently refurbished to very high standard. All rooms with private ensuite facilities, TV, mini-bar, telephone, tea making facilities, trouser press and iron and board. Lift access to all floors.

Single room £57.50.   Double room £67.50

All rates include VAT at 15% and breakfast.

Where to Stay: Camping and Caravanning

Accommodation is of a high standard, all bedrooms being well equipped, though some are compact. Food of good quality is featured both on the à la carte and set-price menus of the Bonnington Grill and in the less formal lounge bar, and a polite staff provide helpful service.
215 ⇌ (16fb) ⥉ in 54 bedrooms CVT in all bedrooms ® T
sB&B ⇌ fr£76 dB&B ⇌ fr£100 OR
Lift ●
TC English & French V MC ⇨ Lunch fr£12&alc Dinner fr£12&alc Last dinner 11.30pm
Credit cards [1][2][3][5]

★★★ 55% **London Ryan** Gwynne Place, Kings Cross Rd WC1X 9QN
☎ 071–278 2480 Telex no 27728 FAX 071–837 3776
This Mount Charlotte hotel provides an ideal base from which to reach any part of London, being located within walking distance of Kings Cross. Bedrooms, though simply furnished and a little clinical, are well equipped – some boasting double glazing. The compact restaurant becomes very busy in the evening, so it is advisable to make a table reservation.
210 ⇌ ℞ (73fb) ⥉ in 20 bedrooms CTV in all bedrooms ® T ⩔ (ex guide dogs)
* sB&B ⇌ ℞ £64.50–£74.50 dB&B ⇌ ℞ £74.50–£89 Continental breakfast OR
Lift ● 28 P 8 ♨
TC English & Continental V MC ⇨ Lunch fr£10.75 Dinner fr£12.50 Last dinner 9.30pm
Credit cards [1][2][3][5]

Ⓠ Ⓠ **Mentone Hotel** 54–55 Cartwright Gardens WC1H 9EL
☎ 071–387 3927 & 071–388 4671
Friendly service is provided by a hotel offering comfortable family accommodation with public shower facilities.
27 ℞ (10fb) CTV in all bedrooms ⩔ ⎕ ♪ (hard)

WC2
(red) ⌘ ★★★★★ **The Savoy** Strand WC2R 0EU ☎ 071–836 4343 Telex no 24234 FAX 071–240 6040
(Rosette awarded for Savoy Restaurant)
This world-famous hotel off the Strand can boast a hundred years of exemplary service, and the uniformed staff who preside over its serene atmosphere today keep alive the old traditions – guests' satisfaction being their prime concern. Its most famous restaurant, the Savoy, overlooks the Thames, and the Grill brings its own touch to such humble favourites as Irish Stew or Farmhouse Sausages. The 'Upstairs' champagne and seafood grill, also provides 'healthy' breakfasts during the week, and in the Thames foyer lounge afternoon tea is served. Some bedrooms and suites feature 1920s/30s furniture.
200 ⇌ ℞ ⥉ in 30 bedrooms CTV in all bedrooms T ⩔ (ex guide dogs)
S15% sB ⇌ ℞ fr£170 dB ⇌ £200–£265 (room only) OR
Lift ● 58 ♨ (£7–£19) NC CFA ♪ xmas
TC English & French V MC ⇨ Lunch £24.50–£26.50&alc Dinner £38.50–£42.50&alc Last dinner 11.30pm
Credit cards [1][2][3][5]

★★★★ 69% **The Waldorf** Aldwych WC2B 4DD ☎ 071–836 2400 Telex no 24574 FAX 071–836 7244
Edwardian elegance was the keynote of the hotel when it first opened in 1908, and modern amenities have been introduced without diminishing this. Bedrooms vary considerably in size, but such attractions as the two bars, the Palm Court and the famous Waldorf Restaurant provide more than adequate compensation.
310 ⇌ (11fb) ⥉ in 40 bedrooms CTV in all bedrooms T ⩔ (ex guide dogs)
S10% sB ⇌ £130–£162 dB ⇌ £162–£199 (room only) OR
Lift ● ♪ CFA hairdressing salon ♪ xmas
V MC ⇨ ⥉ Lunch £17.50–£19.50&alc Dinner £22.50–£24.50&alc Last dinner 10pm
Credit cards [1][2][3][4][5]

★★★ 67% **Drury Lane Moat House** 10 Drury Lane WC2B 5RE ☎ 071–836 6666 Telex no 8811395 FAX 071–831 1548
Comfortably appointed accommodation, a chance of à la carte or buffet-type meals and friendly, efficient service are provided by this stylish, purpose-built Covent Garden hotel.
153 ⇌ (15fb) CTV in all bedrooms T sB ⇌ £109–£119 dB ⇌ £139–£153/50 (room only) OR
Lift ● AC 7 ♨ (£8)
TC French V MC ⇨ Lunch fr£14&alc Dinner fr£17.50alc Last dinner 10.30pm
Credit cards [1][2][3][4][5]

★★★ 56% **Royal Trafalgar Thistle** Whitcomb St WC2H 7HG ☎ 071–930 4477 Telex no 298564 FAX 071–925 2149
A hotel at the heart of London features compact, well-equipped accommodation with 24-hour room service, a French-style brasserie offering daily specials, and, by contrast, a pub in whose traditional atmosphere guests can enjoy real ale and a lunchtime snack.
108 ⇌ ℞ ⥉ in 36 bedrooms CTV in all bedrooms ® T
* sB ⇌ ℞ fr£87 dB ⇌ ℞ fr£93 (room only) OR
Lift ● ♪
TC English and French MC ⇨ ⥉ Lunch fr£12.50&alc Dinner fr£12.50&alc Last dinner 11.30pm
Credit cards [1][2][3][4][5]

★★★ 55% **Strand Palace** Strand WC2R 0JJ ☎ 071–836 8080 Telex no 24208 FAX 071–836 2077
This compact, modernised Regency-style hotel stands at the heart of theatreland, midway between the City and the West End. Refurbished bedrooms are complemented by a choice of self-service restaurants which include a popular Coffee Shop, a Pizzeria and a Carvery; the hotel also has its own interesting shop.
777 ⇌ ℞ ⥉ in 80 bedrooms CTV in all bedrooms ® T
* sB ⇌ £85–£95 dB ⇌ £100–£110 (room only) OR
Lift ● ♪ xmas
TC International V MC ⇨ ⥉ Lunch £14.95–£15.95&alc Dinner £14.95–£15.95&alc Last dinner mdnt
Credit cards [1][2][3][4][5]

Camping and Caravanning

Details of sites within the London postal area are listed below.

AA Pennant rating 1–5:
1 pennant = basic amenities
5 pennants = wide range of facilities

E4 Chingford
DISTRICT MAP, E5
▶▶▶
Sewardstone Caravan Park
Sewardstone Road. Signposted. Tel 081–529 5689 April–October, booking advisable Spring Bank Holiday, July and August. Last arrival 22.00hrs. Last departure noon. No single sex groups. No children under 18 years unaccompanied. No commmercial vehicles.
A site overlooking King George's reservoir and close to Epping Forest. 12 acres 242 pitches. Caravans and tents £8.50 per night. Individual pitches. Late arrivals enclosure. Supervised. Iron, cold storage, calor gas, camping gaz, battery charging, telephone, hairdryers, facilities for disabled, shop. Close to: launderette, fishing, riding, cinema, golf, pub.

N9 Edmonton
DISTRICT MAP, E5
▶▶
Picketts Lock Caravan Site
Signposted. Tel 081–803 9922. Ext.40. Open all year. A 4½-acre site with 160 touring pitches. Part of a large sporting complex with use of swimming pool, roller skating and golf driving range. Charges: £3 an adult, £1.25 per child under 16. £1.50 electrical hook up. Deposit of £5.00. Membership of adjacent sports complex. Close to: launderette, fishing, pub.

Eating Out

EATING OUT

Restaurants are listed below by area and, in the case of Central London, also by postal district. The price is given for the average cost per head of a two-course dinner with an inexpensive wine and coffee.

CENTRAL LONDON

W1

Alastair Little 49 Frith Street
Tel 071–734 5183
This unpretentious small restaurant is very popular with an avant garde clientèle, its celebrated chef-owner providing imaginative, eclectic dishes freshly cooked from quality ingredients (notably fresh fish) and carefully chosen and prepared vegetables. £30. Closed Saturday lunch and Sunday.

Arirang 31–2 Poland Street
Tel 071–437 6633
There is an authentic atmosphere in this intimate little Korean restaurant, where the interesting menu of delicately prepared meals is served by friendly, young national waitresses. £18. Closed Sunday.

Au Jardin des Gourmets 5 Greek Street Tel 071–437 1816
This long-established French restaurant in the heart of Soho continues to serve impressive meals. The regularly changing set menus are augmented by an à la carte selection which offers such interesting dishes as noisettes d'agneau au vinaigre de framboises, and the extensive, reasonably priced wine list includes some good vintages. £24. Closed Saturday lunch and Sunday.

Aunties 126 Cleveland Street
Tel 071–387 1548
Edwardian-style restaurant specialising in traditional and modern English dishes of high standard. £22. Closed Saturday lunch and Sunday.

Bahn Thai 21A Frith Street
Tel 071–437 8504
A peaceful upstairs dining room and a pretty downstairs room provide the setting for authentic Thai dishes, pungently or mildly spiced according to your taste. £16.

Café Royal Grill Room 68 Regent Street Tel 071–439 6320
The ornate décor of carved gilt mirrors, moulded ceilings and plush banquettes provides an effective backdrop to the traditionally formal service that complements sound French cuisine at this restaurant. £40. Closed Saturday lunch and Sunday.

Caravan Serai 50 Paddington Street
Tel 071–935 1208
Smart and exotic restaurant with polite staff serving Middle Eastern specialities such as spicy stuffed poussin and pan-fried king prawns. £16.

Chesa (Swiss Centre) 2 New Coventry Street Tel 071–734 1291
Swiss-style restaurant offering a regularly changing menu of top-class Swiss and classical, mainly French, cuisine, and also Swiss wines. £23.

Chez Nico 35 Great Portland Street
Tel 071–436 8846
The brilliant, international award-winning chef Nico Ladenis provides food of superb skill and imagination, inspired by Provence, in his new smoothly run restaurant. £42. Closed Saturday and Sunday.

Chiang Mai 48 Frith Street
Tel 071–437 7444
An attractively light, two-floored Thai restaurant serving traditional cuisine, with some interesting à la carte dishes for aficionados. £10. Closed Sunday.

Chicago Pizza Pie Factory 17 Hanover Square Tel 071–629 2552
Deep-pan pizzas were first introduced to Britain in this fun-style, popular restaurant. £7.

Defune 61 Blandford Street
Tel 071–935 8311
Good-quality Japanese food, especially the fish and sushi, is served in this pleasant restaurant, popular at lunchtimes. £12 lunch, £30 dinner. Closed Sunday.

Desaru 60–2 Old Compton Street
Tel 071–734 4379
Modern Indonesian restaurant in the heart of Soho, with especially good fish dishes and friendly service. £17.

Down Mexico Way 25 Swallow Street Tel 071–437 9895
Old Spanish tiles line the walls and staircase, and a fountain plays amid the greenery in this calming restaurant serving spicy, authentic Mexican specialities. £15. Closed Sunday.

Efes Kebab House 80 Great Titchfield Street Tel 071–636 1953
This large, ever-busy and cheerful restaurant serves Turkish dishes and is noted for its meat. £13. Closed Sunday.

Fakhreldine 85 Piccadilly
Tel 071–493 3424
The opulent décor and views across Green Park make a suitable setting for this upper-crust Middle Eastern restaurant known for the quality and range of its carefully presented food. £20.

Frith's 14 Frith Street
Tel 071–439 3370
Tasteful design in modern style has created a bright and fresh atmosphere in this popular Soho restaurant, which features a set lunch menu, a mix of mainly Italian, French and Oriental influences, augmented by an à la carte selection in the evening. Service is friendly and polite. £25. Closed Saturday lunch and Sunday.

Fuji 36–40 Brewer Street
Tel 071–734 0957
Japanese restaurant with attentive, friendly service to help you through the long menu. £22 lunch, £35 dinner. Closed Saturday and Sunday lunch.

Gallery Rendezvous 53 Beak Street
Tel 071–734 0445
Chinese paintings are permanently exhibited in this Beijing-style restaurant with reasonable value set menus and some more interesting à la carte dishes. £17.

Gay Hussar 2 Greek Street
Tel 071–437 0973
A small, cosy and popular restaurant, the Gay Hussar has long been established as serving some of London's best, most authentic, Hungarian food. The lengthy menu provides a vast choice of dishes, and service is cheerful, if a little muddled at times. £23. Closed Sunday.

Gaylord 79 Mortimer Street
Tel 071–580 3615
Long-established, popular Indian restaurant with some unusual North Indian dishes on its menu. £15.

Genevieve 13 Thayer Street
Tel 071–935 5023
Popular French restaurant with an unpretentious, high-quality menu and a good international wine list. £22. Closed Saturday and Sunday.

Grahame's Seafare 38 Poland Street
Tel 071–437 3788
A restaurant devoted to kosher fish, with a short wine list. £16. Closed Monday evening and Sunday; last dinner 7.30pm Friday and Saturday.

Greenhouse 27A Hay's Mews
Tel 071–499 3331
Modern elegant dining room with a formal but friendly service

149

Eating Out

accompanying English and French cuisine. £22. Closed Saturday lunch and Sunday.

Green Leaves 77 York Street Tel 071–262 8164
Chinese restaurant with a smart décor. £14. Closed Saturday lunch and Sunday.

Guernica 21A Foley Street Tel 071–580 0623
Formal Spanish restaurant serving interesting modern Basque dishes, with a good selection of Spanish wines. £22. Closed Saturday lunch and Sunday.

Hard Rock Café 150 Old Park Lane Tel 071–629 0382
Almost a tourist institution, this large restaurant, redolent of the rock 'n' roll era, always has queues waiting to eat its excellent burgers and steaks. £12.

Ho Ho 29 Maddox Street Tel 071–493 1228
A red-painted, canopied front opens into a restaurant whose simple, modern décor is brightened by old Chinese photographs and prints. The cuisine is mainly Pekinese and Szechuan. £18. Closed Sunday.

Jason's Court Restaurant 76 Wigmore Street Tel 071–224 2992
White-washed walls and modern art set the scene for this restaurant's skilfully modernised classic British dishes, professionally served. £26. Closed Saturday lunch and Sunday.

Kaya Korean 22–5 Dean Street Tel 071–437 6630
Flute music adds to the soothing, luxurious atmosphere in this traditional Korean restaurant where specialities are impeccably served by waitresses in national costume. £30. Closed Sunday lunchtime.

Kerzenstuberl 9 St Christopher's Place Tel 071–486 3196
Here you can relax in a typically Austrian atmosphere to enjoy authentic Austrian food and wine. Personal service is provided by the proprietors, and in the late evenings staff and guests sing along together to the strains of an accordion. £25. Closed Saturday lunch and Sunday.

Kitchen Yakitori 12 Lancashire Court Tel 071–629 9984
Small Japanese restaurant; eel dishes are a speciality. £16. Closed Saturday dinner and Sunday.

La Cucaracha 12–13 Greek Street Tel 071–734 2253
Long-established Mexican restaurant in a maze of small, white, arched rooms that were once the cellars of an 18th-century monastery. £20. Closed Sundays.

Lal Qila 117 Tottenham Court Road Tel 071–387 4570
Attractive Indian restaurant serving mainly North Indian dishes. £17.

Langan's Bistro 26 Devonshire Street Tel 071–935 4531
Characterful bistro serving some good-value, French-inspired dishes. £17. Closed Saturday lunch and Sunday.

Langan's Brasserie Stratton Street Tel 071–491 8822
This popular, French-style brasserie features an extensive menu of well-prepared, authentic dishes at reasonable prices. It is well frequented by London society and by stars of television, stage and films. £23. Closed Saturday lunch and Sunday.

Le Gavroche 43 Upper Brook Street Tel 071–408 0881
Classically based, innovatively interpreted, Albert Roux and his brigade still provide the best food in the country, presented with real artistry. Such standards of quality in ingredients, cooking and service do not come cheaply, but for those who appreciate them it provides value for money, particularly on some special occasion. From start to finish the attention to detail is awe-inspiring; even the canapés to start, and the chocolates and petits fours to finish, manifest the same supreme skill and dedication.
  There is a Menu Exceptionel of six courses and the à la carte menu, while at luncheon there is a good value fixed-price menu (you need to book this several weeks in advance). The wine list of about 500 is superb and features vintages back to 1918. The head waiter and his brigade of immaculately attired young men will attend to you with unfailing attention and skill in a formal mannner. The restaurant is downstairs, with a bar on the ground floor, and is appropriately handsome, its green walls hung with oil paintings. £40+ lunch, £75+ dinner. Closed Saturday and Sunday.

Le Muscadet 25 Paddington Street Tel 071–935 2883
Relaxed and hearty good French bistro. £23. Closed Saturday lunch and Sunday.

Lee Ho Fook 15–16 Gerrard Street Tel 071–734 9578
Authentic Chinatown atmosphere in this intimate restaurant. £15.

Mandeer 21 Hanway Street Tel 071–323 0660
Atmospheric Indian vegetarian restaurant. £10. Closed Sunday.

Masako 6–8 St Christopher's Place Tel 071–935 1579

Authentic Japanese décor with armour, bamboo walls and waitresses in national costume serving beautifully presented specialities. £30. Closed Sunday.

Mayflower 68–70 Shaftesbury Avenue Tel 071–734 9207
Small, busy, ground-floor and basement Cantonese restaurant with alcoves, open 5pm to 4am. £13.

Melati 30–31 Peter Street Tel 071–437 2011
Modern restaurant serving good Malaysian food. £14. Closed Sunday.

Mr Kai of Mayfair 65 South Audley Street Tel 071–493 8988
Sophisticated, elegant restaurant serving both classical and regional Beijing dishes. £24.

Nakamura 31 Marylebone Lane Tel 071–935 2931
Elegant Japanese basement restaurant with a sushi bar above. £26. Closed Sunday lunch and Saturday.

Nanten Restaurant and Yakitori Bar 6–8 Blandford Street Tel 071–935 6319
Small or large orders grilled while you watch at the friendly, informal yakitori bar, and, downstairs, a more formal Japanese restaurant. £15. Closed Saturday lunch and Sunday.

New World 1 Gerrard Place Tel 071–434 2508
This large ground-floor and basement restaurant has the authentic Chinatown ambience and atmosphere. Many of the dishes offered are well-flavoured provincial specialities, and the service is courteously friendly. £14. Closed Sunday.

Odin's 27 Devonshire Street Tel 071–935 7296
Masquerading as an art gallery, this comfortable English restaurant provides consistently good, interesting food served with quiet professionalism. £35. Closed Saturday lunch and Sunday.

The Olive Tree 11 Wardour Street Tel 071–734 0808
Large, inexpensive Middle Eastern restaurant with a separate vegetarian menu. £9.

Pappagalli's Pizza Inc 7–9 Swallow Street Tel 071–734 5182
US-style, professionally run pizza place, good family value. £10. Closed Sunday.

Red Fort 77 Dean Street Tel 071–437 2525
In the elegant atmosphere of a pink palace, you will be served cocktails

Eating Out

and such regional Indian dishes as spiced and marinated quail baked on a charcoal fire. £18.

Reubens 20A Baker Street
Tel 071–486 7079
Interesting Jewish dishes, plus some English and French, are served in the upstairs restaurant, with standard fare at the downstairs bar counters. £20. Closed Friday evening and Saturday.

Rue St Jacques 5 Charlotte Street
Tel 071–637 0222
Highly exclusive restaurant with a downstairs lounge bar and elegant surroundings where the chef produces an haute cuisine menu that bewitches the palate, and is not, of course, cheap.
There is a good value fixed-price lunch menu (£23) and a very good, extensive wine list. Service is well-informed and highly professional. £45. Closed Saturday lunch and Sunday.

Sawasdee 26–8 Whitfield Street
Tel 071–631 0289
Pleasant Thai restaurant in a basement with alcoves. £15. Closed Saturday lunch and Sunday.

Stephen Bull 5–7 Blandford Street
Tel 071–486 9696
Quiet, bright and white modern restaurant offering a carefully presented, interesting modern cuisine of quality. £25. Closed Saturday lunch and Sunday.

Villa Carlotta 39 Charlotte Street
Tel 071–636 6011
Popular, very Italian restaurant with weekend dance evenings. £20. Closed Sunday.

Veeraswamy 99–101 Regent Street
Tel 071–734 1401
Long-established, atmospheric Indian restaurant where you can eat interesting dishes to piano accompaniment. £20.

Yumi 110 George Street
Tel 071–935 8320
Simply styled downstairs Japanese restaurant serving good traditional dishes. £38. Closed Saturday lunch and Sunday.

Yung's 23 Wardour Street
Tel 071–437 4986
This unusual restaurant, simply appointed and situated on three floors, is open from afternoon until the early hours of the morning. Its speciality is Cantonese cuisine of a high standard and the menu includes some interesting dishes. £13.

WC1
Dee's 17 New North Street
Tel 071–831 7973
Intimate, reasonably priced Thai restaurant. £14. Closed Saturday lunch and Sunday.

Gonbei 151 King's Cross Road
Tel 071–278 0619
Cheerful, basic and inexpensive Japanese restaurant. £13. Closed lunchtimes and Sunday.

The Hermitage 19 Leigh Street
Tel 071–387 8034
Casual and friendly French brasserie. £16.

Konaki 5 Coptic Street
Tel 071–580 9730
Popular Greek restaurant close to the British Museum. £16. Closed Saturday lunch and Sunday.

Martin's Bijou 38 Bloomsbury Street
Tel 071–436 9231
French restaurant below a hotel, serving some interesting dishes. £22. Closed Saturday and Sunday.

Mille Pini 33 Boswell Street
Tel 071–242 2434
Simple trattoria for inexpensive, filling Italian standards. £15. Closed Saturday lunch and Sunday.

Poon's 50 Woburn Place Tel 071–580 1188
Modern, spacious and reliable Chinese restaurant (newest of several branches). £16.

Winston's Restaurant 24 Coptic Street Tel 071–580 3422
The name of the restaurant relates to the Winston Churchill theme which

English-style cuisine attract a busy lunchtime trade. £20. Closed Saturday lunch and Sunday.

WC2
Ajimura 51–3 Shelton Street
Tel 071–240 9424
Small, reasonably inexpensive and informal Japanese restaurant. £18. Closed Saturday and Sunday lunch.

Azami 13 West Street
Tel 071–240 0634
Quiet and formal Japanese restaurant in a complex of bars and clubs. £25. Closed Saturday lunch, Sunday and Monday.

Beotys 79 St Martin's Lane
Tel 071–836 8548
Stylish décor and well-served Greek and also French cuisine. £20. Closed Sunday.

Bertorelli's 44A Floral Street
Tel 071–836 1868
Art deco-style, good value, upstairs Italian restaurant. £15. Closed Saturday lunch and Sunday.

Boulestin 1A Henrietta Street
Tel 071–836 3819

Gracious and elegant, the Edwardian-style restaurant exudes comfort and affluence. Smartly dressed French staff provide professional and attentive service, whilst the menu offers a balanced and interesting selection of imaginative and attractively presented classical dishes, well-geared to the seasonal availability of food. The extensive wine list is designed to appeal to a discerning clientèle. £45. Closed Saturday lunch and Sunday.

Café des Amis du Vin 11–14 Hanover Place Tel 071–379 3444
Traditional, ever-busy French street café with an imaginative menu; quiet salon upstairs. £15–£20. Closed Sunday.

Café du Jardin 25 Wellington Street
Tel 071–836 8796
This lively French brasserie offers a limited selection of wholesome dishes, and food is served by aproned French waiters against the background of a suitably Gallic décor. £18. Closed Saturday lunch.

Café Pelican 45 St Martin's Lane
Tel 071–379 0309
A large and lively French brasserie, the Pelican offers wholesome, provincial-style French dishes in an authentic atmosphere. £18–£22.

Calabash 38 King Street
Tel 071–836 1976
Interesting African specialities in this basement restaurant in the Africa Centre. £18. Closed Sunday.

Chez Solange 35 Cranbourne Street
Tel 071–836 0542
There is good-quality classic French food served in this comfortable old-established restaurant. £25. Closed Sunday.

Flounders 19 Tavistock Street
Tel 071–836 3925
Relaxing fish restaurant. £20. Closed Sunday.

Frère Jacques 38 Long Acre
Tel 071–836 7823
Elegant French fish restaurant and brasserie. £15–£25.

Fung Shing 15 Lisle Street
Tel 071–437 1539
Good Cantonese cooking in this popular and helpful Chinatown restaurant. £18.

Garuda 150 Shaftesbury Avenue
Tel 071–836 2644
Popular, modern Indonesian restaurant. £18. Closed Sunday lunch.

Happy Wok 52 Floral Street
Tel 071–836 3696
This cosy, well-run Chinese restaurant stands at the heart of theatreland,

Eating Out

offering a good range of well-prepared and authentic dishes served by charming staff. £22. Closed Saturday lunch and Sunday.

Indian Club 143 Strand
Tel 071–836 0650
Simple, excellent food in simple surroundings. Unlicenced (no charge for corkage). £10.

Joe Allen 13 Exeter Street
Tel 071–836 0651
Cheerful atmosphere in this popular American basement restaurant with a cocktail bar, serving good American standards. £18.

La Coree 56 St Giles High Street
Tel 071–836 7235
This small and friendly restaurant offers an interesting gastronomic experience as competent and pleasant staff serve authentic Korean dishes. £20. Closed Sunday.

Last Days of the Raj 22 Drury Lane
Tel 071–836 5705
Bright, popular co-operative featuring authentic, honest and skilful Indian cuisine. £15. Closed Sunday.

L'Opéra 32 Great Queen Street
Tel 071–405 9020
Splendid, plush Edwardian restaurant in gilt and green occupying two floors in the centre of theatreland. £25. Closed Saturday lunch and Sunday.

Magno's 65A Long Acre
Tel 071–836 6077
Theatreland restaurant serving good French-style dishes. £23. Closed Saturday lunch and Sunday.

Manzi's 1–2 Leicester Square
Tel 071–734 0224
Family-run Italian fish restaurant, in a first-floor hotel dining room, with a good traditional menu. £25. Closed Sunday lunch.

Mélange 59 Endell Street
Tel 071–240 8077
Small and youthfully lively restaurant serving some good eclectic dishes. £20. Closed Saturday lunch and Sunday.

Mon Plaisir 21 Monmouth Street
Tel 071–836 7243
Small and simple ultra-French restaurant serving good, authentic dishes. £28. Closed Saturday lunch and Sunday.

Mr Kong 21 Lisle Street
Tel 071–437 7341
Good Chinese food in this long-established Chinatown restaurant. £16.

Neal Street Restaurant 26 Neal Street Tel 071–836 8268
Modern restaurant with tasteful basement cocktail bar, serving very original cuisine. £40. Closed Saturday and Sunday.

New Diamond 23 Lisle Street
Tel 071–437 2517
Comfortable setting and good Chinese food with Cantonese specialities. £18.

Orso 27 Wellington Street
Tel 071–240 5269
Popular modern Italian restaurant with a regularly changing menu of well-prepared and authentic dishes. £24.

Plummers 33 King Street
Tel 071–240 2534
Busy and lively, this pretty restaurant offers good value for money in its selection of American and English food. £17. Closed Saturday lunch and Sunday.

Porters 17 Henrietta Street
Tel 071–836 6466
Good English pies served in a modern version of the old pie shop. £10.

Rodos 59 St Giles High Street
Tel 071–836 3177
Good Greek food in homely surroundings. £15. Closed Saturday lunch and Sunday.

Rules 35 Maiden Lane
Tel 071–836 2559
Well-established traditional English restaurant with professional, efficient service. £25. Closed Sunday.

Sheekeys 28–32 St Martin's Court
Tel 071–240 2565
One of the oldest fish restaurants in London, specialising in oysters and traditional English dishes, and with a theatre atmosphere. £25. Closed Saturday lunch and Sunday.

Simpson's in the Strand 100 Strand
Tel 071–836 9112
The traditional place for English roast beef, in suitably traditional surroundings. £25. Closed Sunday.

Taste of India 25 Catherine Street
Tel 071–836 2538
This small, elegant Indian restaurant features some very interesting specialities and authentic dishes, all formally served. £17.

Thomas de Quincey's 36 Tavistock Street Tel 071–240 3972
Attractive, luxuriously furnished restaurant where chef Philippe Gavelle produces original, unusual dishes of high quality, hospitably served and matched by an authoritative wine list. £35. Closed Saturday lunch and Sunday.

SW1
Auberge de Provence 41 Buckingham Gate Tel 071–834 6655
A pleasantly cool restaurant with white walls, arches and hanging plants, which specialises in skilfully prepared French regional cooking. Service by the young French staff is good. £45. Closed Saturday lunch and Sunday.

Bumbles 16 Buckingham Palace Road Tel 071–828 2903
Bustling, bistro-like restaurant with booths downstairs, offering good British food and a fair wine list. £23. Closed Saturday lunch and Sunday.

Como Lario 22 Holbein Place
Tel 071–730 2954
Cheerful, busy Italian restaurant down a side street with good fish dishes. £20. Closed Sunday.

Dolphin Brasserie Rodney House Dolphin Square/Chichester Street
Tel 071–828 3207
A large room with pastel décor and piano music where set price and à la carte menus are offered, providing a good standard of modern international dishes and wine. £25.

Gavvers 61–3 Lower Sloane Street
Tel 071–730 5983
A Roux Brothers enterprise, the restaurant offers a very popular, value-for-money, fixed-price menu, the charge covering not only half a bottle of wine but also service and VAT. Surroundings are comfortable and the young French staff charmingly attentive. £26.

L'Amico 44 Horseferry Road
Tel 071–222 4680
Extensive basement Italian restaurant with several separate rooms, patronised by MPs and civil servants from nearby Parliament. £22. Closed Saturday and Sunday.

La Poule au Pot 231 Ebury Street
Tel 071–730 7763
Friendly French restaurant featuring interesting authentic dishes. £25. Closed Saturday lunch and Sunday.

Le Caprice Arlington House Arlington Street Tel 071–629 2239
Modern restaurant with large plants, serving imaginative international dishes, and good weekend brunches. £25.

Memories of China 67–9 Ebury Street Tel 071–730 7734
Kenneth Lo, acclaimed for his books on Chinese cooking, includes both classical and regional dishes on the menu of his elegant restaurant. £30. Closed Sunday.

Mijanou 143 Ebury Street
Tel 071–730 4099
In a smart little restaurant fronted by her husband Neville, Sonia Blech provides enjoyable dishes with a

Eating Out

French influence. £35. Closed Saturday and Sunday.

Mimmo d'Ischia 61 Elizabeth Street Tel 071–730 5406
Smart Italian restaurant serving Neapolitan specialities. £30. Closed Sunday.

Pomegranates 94 Grosvenor Road Tel 071–828 6560
Cuisine from at least 14 countries features in this intimate basement restaurant. £30. Closed Saturday lunch and Sunday.

Salloos 62–4 Kinnerton Street Tel 071–235 4444
An amiable atmosphere prevails in this first-floor, family-run Pakistani restaurant, tucked away in a quiet corner off Knightsbridge. Menus feature authentic, original dishes. £23. Closed Sunday.

Tate Gallery Restaurant Millbank Tel 071–834 6754
Brightly decorated with Rex Whistler murals, this popular restaurant features an interesting menu of English dishes and an excellent wine list. Lunch only. £23. Closed Sunday.

WEST LONDON

The Ark 35 Kensington High Street W8 Tel 071–937 4294
Bustling French bistro-style restaurant serving reasonably priced food. £17. Closed Sunday lunch.

Belvedere Holland House Holland Park W8 Tel 071–602 1238
Beautifully set in converted stables, this spacious restaurant serves fish and international dishes. £30. Closed Saturday lunch and Sunday.

Caps 64 Pembridge Road W11 Tel 071–229 5177
Cheerful little restaurant, with caps everywhere in sight, serving sensibly priced British-based food; dinner only. £18. Closed Sunday.

Casa Santana 44 Golborne Road W10 Tel 071–968 8764
Portuguese café-restaurant with authentic, inexpensive food. £15.

Chez Moi 1 Addison Avenue W11 Tel 071–603 8267
Tucked away off Holland Park Avenue, this well-established but unostentatious restaurant is patronised by the rich and famous. It offers a cosy, intimate atmosphere, quietly efficient service and a menu that is part traditional and part nouvelle in style. £25. Closed Saturday lunch and Sunday.

Clarke's 124 Kensington Church Street W8 Tel 071–221 9225
A short, daily changing menu offers good dishes by California-inspired Sally Clarke, plus an extensive wine list featuring a selection of Californian wines. Also good home-made breads and chocolate truffles. £25. Closed Saturday and Sunday.

Ganges 101 Praed Street W2 Tel 071–723 4096
Modest restaurant serving Bengal and Indian cuisine. £14.

Kensington Place 201–5 Kensington Church Street W8 Tel 071–727 3184
Stylish modern brasserie-restaurant featuring skilful cooking using high-quality ingredients. £20.

Kensington Tandoori 1 Abingdon Road W8 Tel 071–937 6182
Small, engraved-glass screens afford privacy to diners at this Indian restaurant where formal service and a good wine list complement a menu of North Indian and Persian dishes. £15.

La Pomme d'Amour 128 Holland Park Avenue W11 Tel 071–229 8532
Smart French restaurant with an attractive patio, specialising in classical and provincial dishes. £23. Closed Saturday lunch and Sunday.

Le Quai St Pierre 7 Stratford Road W8 Tel 071–937 6388
Provençal atmosphere and good fish dishes in this attractive French restaurant. £28. Closed Monday lunch and Sunday.

Leith's 92 Kensington Park Road W11 Tel 071–229 4481
Well-established and elegant restaurant that continues to offer reliable and unusual food, particularly the varied starters, at a price for quality. £40. Dinner only.

Maggie Jones 6 Old Court Place Kensington Church Street W8 Tel 071–937 6462
Excellent English food is served at this busy, noisy restaurant, which is decorated on a farmhouse theme. £24.

Maxim 153–5 Northfield Avenue W13 081–567 1719
This enormous Chinese restaurant in Ealing features an extensive menu which specialises in Beijing dishes and includes some interesting set meals for those confused by a breadth of choice. Young oriental staff willingly offer advice on dishes and provide cheerful service. £18. Closed Sunday.

Shireen Tandoori 270 Uxbridge Road W12 Tel 081–749 5927
Popular Shepherd's Bush restaurant with modern décor and a short menu of less usual North Indian and tandoori dishes. £15.

Veronica's 3 Hereford Road W2 Tel 071–229 5079
A pretty restaurant with friendly service offering excellent British food. £25. Closed Saturday lunch and Sunday.

Wodka 12 St Albans Grove W8 Tel 071–937 6513
Simple Polish restaurant serving authentic dishes and home-made vodka. £22. Closed Saturday and Sunday lunch.

SOUTH-WEST LONDON

Avoirdupois 334 King's Road SW3 Tel 071–352 6151
Well-prepared, varied menu of international dishes served in a friendly atmosphere with soft, live music. £25.

Bibendum Michelin Building, 81 Fulham Road SW3 Tel 071–581 5817
Luxurious modern surroundings combine with excellent French country cooking in this popular restaurant where advance booking is essential. £45.

Bombay Brasserie Courtfield Close, Courtfield Road SW7 Tel 071–370 4040
Elegant colonial décor and authentic regional Indian dishes. £28.

Brinkley's 47 Hollywood Road SW10 Tel–071–351 1683
An imaginative French cum international menu is offered by this small, stylish Fulham restaurant where meals are served by friendly young staff. £25. Closed Sunday.

Buzkash 4 Chelverton Road SW15 Tel 081–788 0599
This intimate restaurant in Putney, decorated with Afghan weaponry and carpets, serves spiced and creamy authentic Middle Eastern dishes. £20. Closed Sunday.

Crowthers 481 Upper Richmond Road, West East Sheen SW14 Tel 081–876 6372
A small candle-lit restaurant featuring Philip Crowther's inventive, good-quality, modern meals on a set-price menu. £25. Closed Sunday.

Dan's 119 Sydney Street SW3 Tel 071–352 2718
This busy restaurant, painted in delicate pastel shades, decked with hanging baskets and standing in a garden, offers simple dishes of outstanding quality: the atmosphere is cheerful and the service unobtrusive but attentive. £24. Closed Saturday lunch and Sunday.

Eating Out

Daphne's 112 Draycott Avenue SW3 Tel 071–589 4257
Warm cosy restaurant with fine French cooking. £24. Closed Saturday lunch and Sunday.

English Garden 10 Lincoln Street SW3 Tel 071–584 7272
Well-researched Old English recipes, cooked with considerable skill, are featured in a fashionable conservatory, English-garden setting. £38.

English House 3 Milner Street SW3 Tel 071–584 3002
This elegant restaurant decorated in pretty, chintzy English style serves thoroughly researched traditional English dishes with friendly professionalism. £30.

Fifty-one Fifty-one Chelsea Cloisters, Sloane Avenue SW7 Tel 071–730 5151
North American restaurant with good grilled meat and fish dishes and an extensive American wine list. £28.

Good Earth 91 King's Road SW3 Tel 071–352 9231
Small, comfortable and friendly Chinese restaurant serving well-prepared, authentic dishes. £20.

Harveys 2 Bellevue Road SW17 Tel 081–672 0114
Overlooking Wandsworth Common, this modern, highly reputed restaurant features the brilliant cooking of its Italian chef/owner Marco Pierre White. £35. Closed Saturday lunch and Sunday.

Hilaire 68 Old Brompton Road SW7 Tel 071–584 8993
Fashionable, contemporary restaurant featuring imaginative, daily changing, fixed-price menus, well served. £35. Closed Saturday lunch and Sunday.

Jake's 14 Hollywood Road SW10 Tel 071–352 8692
This straightforward but stylish English restaurant has a lively and informal atmosphere which is complemented by thoroughly enjoyable food and unobtrusive, friendly service. £30. Closed Sunday.

La Brasserie 272 Brompton Road SW3 Tel 071–584 1668
Bustling, authentic French brasserie. £20.

La Croisette 168 Ifield Road SW10 Tel 071–373 3694
Popular, basement restaurant with a Provençal atmosphere, specialising in shellfish and with a good, fixed-price menu. £35. Closed Tuesday lunch and Monday.

L'Arlequin 123 Queenstown Road SW8 Tel 071–622 0555
In this quietly elegant little French restaurant, chef/patron Christian Delteil offers beautifully presented dishes, which are simple and balanced, the delicious sauces complementing the perfectly cooked fish and meat. They are served by expert, friendly staff. £40. Closed Saturday and Sunday.

Le Suquet 104 Draycott Avenue SW3 Tel 071–581 1785
Very popular French seafood restaurant with a formidable range of dishes. £35.

L'Hippocampe 131A Munster Road SW6 Tel 071–736 5588
Small and courteous French restaurant devoted to good fish dishes. £25. Closed Saturday lunch and Sunday.

Maharani 117 Clapham High Street SW4 Tel 071–622 2530
Popular, well-established Indian restaurant with good seafood dishes. £16.

Mao Tai 58 New King's Road SW6 Tel 071–731 2520
Pleasant Chinese restaurant serving Szechuan dishes. £20

Ménage à Trois 15 Beauchamp Place SW3 Tel 071–589 4252
The basement restaurant is a 'fun' place to dine in an intimate atmosphere with live piano music and open fires. The menu is restricted to starters and puddings and the success of this original idea owes much to the innovative preparation of quality ingredients. £30. Closed Saturday lunch.

Nikita's 65 Ifield Road SW10 Tel 071–352 6326
Authentic Russian dishes served in a friendly, candle-lit atmosphere complemented by a fine vodka list. Dinner only. £24. Closed Sunday.

Pollyanna's 2 Battersea Rise SW11 Tel 071–228 0316
Homely, bistro-like atmosphere, skilful, reliable cooking and an extensive wine list, all genially overseen by the patron. £24. Closed Sunday dinner.

Pontevecchio 254–60 Old Brompton Road SW5 Tel 071–373 9052
Large and lively, comfortable modern restaurant in a fashionable forecourt setting, serving a range of authentic Italian dishes including home-made pasta. Friendly, attentive service. £22.

St Quentin 243 Brompton Road SW3 Tel 071–589 8005
Stylish brasserie serving adventurous, tempting food. £30.

San Frediano 62 Fulham Road SW3 Tel 071–584 8375
This long-established and popular Italian restaurant provides an authentic atmosphere and traditional cuisine. £24. Closed Sunday dinner.

Tandoori of Chelsea 153 Fulham Road SW3 Tel 071–589 7617
An intimate atmosphere is created by subdued lighting in this cosy basement restaurant. Pleasant waiters serve good-quality curries and tandoori dishes. £20.

Tante Claire 68 Royal Hospital Road SW3 Tel 071–352 6045
This light and airy restaurant painted in pastel shades is the setting for the wonderfully talented creations of Pierre Koffman. The cooking is in the modern French style and the à la carte menu offers an interesting choice of delicious dishes while at luncheon there is a good-value fixed-price menu. Notable dishes include stuffed pigs trotter, roast pigeon, saddle of rabbit or fillet of bass with black olives. Vegetables are always properly cooked, and desserts are ambrosial. Great attention is paid to detail, and the excellent service is attentive and interested. £45. Closed Saturday and Sunday.

Tiger Lee 251 Old Brompton Road SW5 Tel 071–370 2323
This elegantly modern Chinese restaurant specialises in seafood and offers dishes with such evocative names as 'Shadow of a Butterfly'. The service is attentive and professional and there are some fine French wines on the wine list. £40.

Waltons 121 Walton Street SW3 Tel 071–584 0204
Elegant, old-fashioned comfort is enhanced here by discreet management supervision and professionally formal service. Standards of cuisine are reliable but never dull, and beautifully flavoured sauces, often textured with cream, are particularly noteworthy. £40.

Zen Chelsea Cloisters, Sloane Avenue SW3 Tel 071–589 1781
The Chinese Zodiac is the background to an interesting menu including old Buddhist dishes and other delicacies. £30.

THE CITY AND EAST END

Baron of Beef Gutter Lane EC2 Tel 071–606 6961
Spacious, panelled basement restaurant specialising in English cuisine, particularly roast meats. £28. Closed Saturday and Sunday.

Betjeman's Wine Bar & Rotisserie 44 Cloth Fair EC1 Tel 071–796 4981
Good-quality English meat dishes in

Eating Out

the former home of Sir John Betjeman. £23. Closed Saturday and Sunday.

Bloom's 90 Whitechapel High Street E1 Tel 071-247 6001
Busy, friendly, strictly kosher restaurant with a modestly priced menu. £12. Closed Saturday and Friday evening.

Corney & Barrow 118 Moorgate EC2 Tel 071-628 2898
Impressive wines and a short menu of imaginative modern dishes. £40. Closed Saturday and Sunday.

Farringdon's Traditional English Restaurant 41 Farringdon Street EC4 Tel 071-236 3663
Intimate, candle-lit basement restaurant with alcoves, serving traditional English dishes. £25. Closed Saturday lunch and Sunday.

Ginnan 5 Cathedral Place EC4 Tel 071-236 4120
Simple, modern Japanese restaurant. £26. Closed Saturday evening and Sunday.

Good Friends 139-41 Salmon Lane E14 Tel 071-987 5541
Popular, sophisticated Chinese restaurant specialising in well-prepared Beijing and Cantonese cuisine. £18.

La Rocchetta 40 Clerkenwell Green EC1 Tel 071-253 8676
Family-run, homely Italian restaurant. £18. Closed Saturday and Sunday.

Le Café du Marché 22 Charterhouse Square, Charterhouse Mews EC1 071-608 1609
Large French restaurant in a converted warehouse with good-value set-price menus. £23. Closed Saturday lunch and Sunday.

Le Gamin 32 Old Bailey EC4 Tel 071-236 7931
Small tables and chairs in a large, airy basement create a French café-style atmosphere. Half a bottle of wine is included in the fixed-price of the short menu of carefully prepared dishes, representing good value and contributing to the restaurant's popularity. Lunch only. £27. Closed Saturday and Sunday.

Le Poulbot 45 Cheapside EC2 Tel 071-236 4379
Very popular basement restaurant with an intimate, plush atmosphere. There is a short fixed-price menu, which changes daily, and the chef's individuality and flair is most evident, along with excellent presentation and good blending. Service is efficient and unobtrusive. Lunch only. £38. Closed Saturday and Sunday.

Mi Mi 116 Newgate Street EC1 Tel 071-600 1134
Smart modern Korean restaurant with good-value set lunches. £30. Closed Saturday and Sunday.

Mustards Smithfield Brasserie 60 Long Lane EC1 Tel 071-796 4920
Good meat dishes as well as other well-prepared dishes, plus good snacks in the downstairs wine bar. £16. Closed Saturday and Sunday.

Next Door Restaurant & Wine Bar 55 Clerkenwell Close, Clerkenwell Green EC1 Tel 071-253 5304
Classic English dishes are produced in this popular restaurant, serving lunch only. £16. Closed Saturday and Sunday.

Rudland & Stubbs 35-7 Greenhill Rents, Cowcross Street EC1 Tel 071-253 0148
Stylishly bare restaurant specialising in fish dishes. £20. Closed Saturday lunch and Sunday.

Smithfield's Ale & Chop House 334-8 Central Markets, Farringdon Street EC1 Tel 071-236 2690
Wooden tables and candles set the atmosphere while your choice of meats is cooked on the charcoal grill. £23. Closed Saturday and Sunday.

NORTH AND NORTH WEST LONDON

Anna's Place 90 Mildmay Park N1 Tel 071-249 9379
This small, bustling restaurant cum wine bar, simply furnished and prettily decorated, provides a blackboard menu of excellent Swedish fare at reasonable cost. The informal atmosphere is enhanced by cheerful young staff, supervised by Anna herself. £20. Closed Sunday and Monday.

Asuka Berkeley Arcade, 209A Baker Street NW1 Tel 071-486 5026
This small, neat Japanese restaurant features a sushi bar and speciality dishes cooked at the table, with authentic fish cuisine prominent. Attentive, helpful staff. £25. Closed Saturday lunch and Sunday.

Café Delancey 3 Delancey Street NW1 Tel 071-387 1985
Lively casual brasserie serving some interesting dishes. £15.

Café Rouge 19 High Street NW3 Tel 071-433 3404
A thoroughly authentic French brasserie at the chic heart of Hampstead. £16.

Chutneys 124 Drummond Street NW1 Tel 071-388 0604
Good thali in this modern-style, inexpensive Indian vegetarian restaurant, one of several in this characterful street close to Euston Station. £9.

Frederick's Camden Passage N1 Tel 071-359 2888
Dating back to the 18th century, and originally called 'The Gun', this very popular and well-appointed restaurant was renamed in honour of Prince Augustus Frederick who died in 1813. The enterprising menu is changed fortnightly but always includes some delectable puddings and the formal service is very efficient. £30. Closed Sunday.

Green Cottage 9 New College Parade, Finchley Road NW3 Tel 071-794 3833
The modern décor, informal atmosphere and helpful staff set the scene for the well-selected and varied dishes of this Chinese restaurant with an especially good vegetarian menu. £16.

Keats 3 Downshire Hill NW3 Tel 071-435 3544
This intimate French restaurant cultivates a literary air, its walls decked with bookshelves and prints. Cuisine of a high standard is complemented by a very good wine list, and special gastronomique evenings are organised. £35. Closed Saturday lunch and Sunday.

M'sieur Frog 31A Essex Road N1 Tel 071-226 3495
Well-prepared French food in a bistro atmosphere. Dinner only. £27. Closed Sunday.

Mumtaz 4-10 Park Road NW1 Tel 071-723 0549
The colonial-style décor in this large Indian restaurant makes a pleasant setting for the eclectic cuisine. £14.

Odette's 130 Regent's Park Road NW1 Tel 071-586 5486
This attractive, old-established restaurant with a separate basement wine bar has an imaginative daily changing menu of mixed European cuisines, well prepared and discreetly served. £28. Closed Saturday lunch and Sunday.

Peter's 36 Fairfax Road NW6 Tel 071-624 5142
Friendly bistro with background piano music to accompany the eclectic, fair-value dishes. £25. Closed Saturday lunch.

Quincy's 675 Finchley Road NW2 Tel 071-794 8499
Intimate, well-run restaurant serving imaginative, high-quality dishes. Dinner only. £26. Closed Sunday.

Eating Out

Sagarmatha 339 Euston Road NW1
Tel 071–387 6531
Posters and pictures of Nepal set the tone of this compact little restaurant which specialises in Napalese cuisine. A speciality is Nepali thali, a set meal of five dishes. The atmosphere is friendly and informal; the manager is ready to help you in your choice. £12.

San Carlo 2 Highgate High Street N6
Tel 071–340 5823
Large and light, modern Italian restaurant with a varied menu. £22. Closed Monday.

Viceroy of India 3–5 Glentworth Street NW1 Tel 071–486 3401
Modern, well-appointed North Indian restaurant with marble pillars, statues and well-prepared authentic cooking. £14.

Wakaba 122A Finchley Road NW3
Tel 071–586 7960
Cleanly styled, friendly Japanese restaurant serving a good variety of well-prepared and authentic dishes. £25. Closed Sunday.

Let BR do the driving while you and your family enjoy a relaxing and different view of some of Britain's best scenery. 50 railway routes through England, Wales and Scotland are described and illustrated, identifying landmarks to see from the train and places of interest to stop off and visit.

PLUS Route maps • Standard and narrow gauge preserved railways • Suggested walks, cycling routes, etc • All the practical information you need to make your journey easy.

A joint AA/British Rail publication

Index

Adam, Robert   79, 83, 108, 117
Admiralty, The   89
Agnew's Galleries   103
Airbus   37
Albert Bridge   94, 95
Albert Memorial   98
Albert, Prince   98
Alfred the Great   98
All England Lawn Tennis and Croquet Club, Wimbledon   5, 117, 129
All Hallows, London Wall   67
All Hallows-by-the-Tower   120
All Souls', Langham Place   67
Allen, R. & Co.   57
Anchor, The, Bankside   100
Angel, The, SE16   100
Antelope, The, SW1   100
Anything Left-Handed   61
Archer, Thomas   69
Archbishop of Canterbury   75
Arsenal FC   126
Arts centres   119
Ascot Racecourse   5, 7, 130
Asprey & Co.   53
Association Football   126
Athletics   127-128
Audley, The, W1   100

Bank of England   37, 80, 86, 114
Banks   43
Banqueting House, The   4, 89
Barbican, The   86, 109
Barbican Arts Centre   86, 119
Barbican Cinema   119
Barbican Hall   86, 119, 120
Barbican Theatre   86, 119
Barker, John, Kensington High Street   55
Barnums Carnival Novelties   61
Barrier Garden   94, 97
Barry, Sir Charles   74
Battersea Park   7, 93, 95

Bead Shop, The   59
Beale, Arthur   58
Bear Gardens Museum   103
Beauchamp Place   56
Bedford Square   84
Bendicks Chocolates   60
Berman and Nathan   60
Berwick Street Market   62
Bethnal Green Museum of Childhood   104
Big Ben   74
Billingsgate Market   66
Black Friar, The, EC4   100
Blackfriars   89
Blackheath RFC   131
Blank, Justin de   61
Bloomsbury   84
Bloomsbury Square   84
Blue plaques   44
Bond Street   49, 53-54, 87
Booking - concerts   118
Booking - hotels   36
Booking - theatres   118, 123
Borough Market   66
Bow Bells   70, 99
Brentford FC   127
British Home Stores   50, 55
British Museum   84, 104, 108
British Rail   37-39, 41, 44, 45
British Telecom Tower   80
British Travel Centre   36, 37
Brixton Market   62
Broadgate Arena   119
Brompton Oratory   67
Brompton Road   56
Brook Street   87
Brundle, F.H.   61
Buckingham Palace   4, 7, 9, 10, 45, 70, 73, 88
Bunch of Grapes, SW3   100
Bureaux de Change   43
Burghers of Calais, The   98
Burlington Arcade   54, 88
Burlington Gardens   53, 54
Buses   37, 40, 41, 44
Bushy Park   90
Butler's Wharf   85
Button Queen, The   59

C&A, Oxford Street   50
Cabinet War Rooms   105
Cambridge Circus   89
Camden Head, The   63
Camden Lock   42, 62, 93, 95
Camden Passage   63

Canal System, The   42, 91, 93, 95
Candle Maker's Supplies   59
Car Hire   44, 45
Carlos Place   87
Car Parking   45-48
Carlton House Terrace   88, 111
Carlyle, Thomas, House of   78, 85
Catford Stadium   130
Caxton Hall   80
Cecil Court   57
Cenotaph, The   9, 89
Centre Criminal Court (Old Bailey)   80
Ceremony of the Keys   4, 10, 77
Ceres   60
Changing of the Guard   4, 10, 45, 73

Chapel Market   63
Charing Cross   89
Charing Cross Pier   40, 73
Charing Cross Road   57
Charing Cross Station   37, 88
Charles I   10, 88, 89, 90, 98
Charles II   74, 90
Charlton Athletic FC   127
Chelsea   85
Chelsea Bridge   94, 95
Chelsea Flower Show   5, 7, 83, 85
Chelsea FC   127
Chelsea Physic Garden   93
Cheyne Walk   85
Children's Book Centre   59
Chinese New Year   6
Church Street and Bell Street Markets   63
Churchill, Sir Winston   98
Cinema Bookshop   59
Cinemas   118, 119, 125
Cittie of York, WC1   100
City Barge, The   100
City of London   8, 9, 37, 40, 43, 45, 66, 67, 68, 69, 81, 82, 85, 86, 89, 94, 99, 120, 122, 130
Clarence House   80
Cleopatra's Needle   89, 98
Coaches   37, 40
College of Arms   80
Columbia Road Market   63

Commonwealth Centre   76
Commonwealth Institute   80
Constitution Hill   90
Contemporary Applied Arts   105
Coram, Thomas, Foundation for Children   115
Cornelissen, L. & Son   61
Cottesloe Theatre   94, 123
Courtauld Institute Galleries   105
Court Dress Collection   75
Covent Garden   4, 5, 49, 55, 89
Covent Garden Market (New)   66
Craftsmen Potters Association   59
Cranks   60
Cricket   128-129
Cricket Memorial Gallery   105
Crown Jewels   77, 85
Crystal Palace FC   127
Crystal Palace National Sports Centre   127, 128
Cuming Museum   105
Curry Shop   60
Cutty Sark   74, 97

Dance, George   67
Davenport Magic Shop   61
Debenhams   50
Design Museum   85, 105
Desmonde, Kay   61
Dickens & Jones   52
Dickens, Charles   58, 78, 92, 102, 105
Dickens' House   78
Dickens Inn, E1   85, 96, 100
Dillons   59
Dingwall's, Camden Lock   122
Disabled Visitors   36, 119, 133
Dobell's Jazz and Folk Record Shop   60
Docklands Light Railway   39, 41, 42, 85, 97
Doll's House, The   61
Dominion Theatre   122
Dover Street   87
Downing Street   89
Dress Circle   60
Driving a car in London   44-45

157

Index

Dulwich College Picture Gallery 106

Earth Galleries, The (Natural History Museum) 106
East Street Market 63
Eaton Shell Shop 59
Edward the Confessor 71, 74
Elizabeth I 72, 74
Elizabeth II 5, 7, 9, 43, 80, 83, 94
Emergency Services 44
English National Opera 121
Epsom Racecourse 5, 7, 130-131
Eros 98
Euston Station 37-38
Evans, D. H. 50

Fat Boy, The 99
Fenwick's 53
Finsbury Circus Gardens 122
Flask, The, N6 100
Flask Walk 86
Fleet Street 99
Floral Design 61
Floris, J. 58
Folk Shop, The 60
Fortnum & Mason 54, 88
Foyles 57
Fratelli Camisa 60
French House, The, W1 100
Fulham FC 127
Fulham Pottery 58
Fulham Road 85

Gallery of Antique Costume & Textiles 60
Gandhi, Mahatma 84
Gatwick Airport 36, 37, 43
Geffrye Museum 106
General Trading Company 56
George II 74
George III 73, 75, 98
George IV 73, 79, 88
George V 76
George Inn, The, SE1 101
Gibbons, Grinling 69, 70, 72, 99
Gibbs, James 70
Gieves and Hawkes 58
Gipsy Moth IV 74

Glasshouse, The 61
Goode, Thomas 61
Grand Union Canal 42, 95, 96
Gray's Inn 81
Great Fire of London 67, 68, 69, 70, 89, 99, 102, 109
Greek Street 99
Green Park 88, 90
Greenwich 5, 40, 73-74, 97, 130
Greenwich Palace 4, 73, 97
Greenwich Park 74, 90, 122
Grenadier, The, SW1 101
Greyhound Racing 130
Griffin, The 99
Grosvenor Square 87
Guildhall, The 5, 69, 81
Guildhall Clock Museum 81
Guildhall Library 81
Guinness World of Records 106

Hackney Wick Stadium 130, 131
Halcyon Days 58
Half Moon, Lower Richmond Road 122
Hamleys 53
Hammersmith Odeon 122
Hampstead 86, 92
Hampstead Heath 86, 92
Hampton Court 4, 42, 74, 90, 91, 94
Hampton Court Palace 74
Handel 72, 79, 87
Handel's House 79, 87
Handweavers Studio and Gallery 59
Harlequin RFC 131
Harrods 36, 56
Hatchards 54
Hawksmoor, Nicholas 68, 71, 73
Hay's Galleria 96
Hayward Gallery 94, 106
Heal's 57
Heathrow Airport 36, 42, 43
Henley Royal Regatta 5, 8
Henry VIII 74, 76, 77, 82, 85, 90
Her Majesty's Theatre 123
Higgins, H. R. 61
Highgate Cemetery 92
HMS Belfast 96, 104, 105
HMV Shop 50

Hogarth, William 68, 100, 114, 115
Hogarth's House 78
Holland Park 93
Holland Park Court Theatre 122
Holy Sepulchre, Holborn 120
Holy Trinity, Sloane Street 67
Horniman Museum 107
Horse Guards 89
Horse Guards Parade 5, 7, 9, 89
Horse Racing 130-131
House of Commons 74, 102
House of Lords 9, 74
House of St Barnabas 81
Houses of Parliament 4, 9, 74, 89, 95, 99
100 Club 122
Hungerford Railway Bridge 89
Hyde Park 5, 6, 8, 9, 45, 54, 91, 122

Imperial War Museum 103, 107
Inderwick's 58
Inns of Court 81
Institute of Contemporary Arts 88, 119
Island Gardens 97

Jack Straw's Castle 101
James II 99
Jermyn Street 54, 55, 88
Jewel Tower 82
Jewish Museum 108
Johnson, Dr Samuel 78, 89
Johnson's House 78
Johnson, Keith & Pelling 62
Jones, Inigo 70, 73, 89
Jones, Peter, Sloane Square 56
Jubilee Gardens 94, 95
Jubilee Market 63
Jubilee Walkway 94
Just Games 61

Keats Grove 87
Keats, John, House of 79, 87
Kensington Church Street 54, 55

Kensington Gardens 8, 55, 91
Kensington High Street 49, 54-55
Kensington Market 55
Kensington Palace 4, 74-75
Kenwood 122
Kenwood House (Iveagh Bequest) 86, 108
Kew Gardens 42, 75, 92
Kew Palace 4, 75
King's Cross Station 37
King's Head, N1 101
King's Head & Eight Bells, SW3 101
King's Road 55, 85
Kite Store, The 61
Knightsbridge 49, 56

Lamb and Flag, WC2 101
Lamb, The, WC1 101
Lambeth Palace 75
Lancaster House 76
Laskys 57
Law Courts 89
Leadenhall Market 64
Leather Lane 64
Leicester Square 44, 94
Lewis, John, Oxford Street 50
Liberty & Co. 52
Lilywhites 43
Lincoln's Inn 82
Lincoln's Inn Fields 82, 93, 122
Little Venice 93, 95
Liverpool Street Station 36, 37, 66, 119
Lloyd's of London 82
Lobb, John 60
Lock, James 58
London Bridge 8, 42, 66, 96
London Bridge City 4, 96
London-Brighton Rally 9
London by Bicycle 43, 95
London City Airport 37, 40
London Coliseum 121
London Diamond Centre 59, 108
London Docklands 4, 42, 85, 95, 97, 130
London Docklands Visitor Centre 42
London Dungeon 108
London Glass Blowers Workshop 59
London Irish RFC 131

158

Index

London Marathon 5, 129-130
London Planetarium 108
London Regional Transport 39
London Scottish RFC 131
London Silver Vaults 108
London Stone, The 99
London Symphony Orchestra 86, 119
London Tourist Board 33, 36
London Toy and Model Museum 108
London Transport Museum 109
London walks 43, 94, 95, 96
London Welsh RFC 131
Lord Mayor of London 3, 5, 9, 81, 99, 109
Lord Mayor's Show 5, 9
Lord's Cricket Ground 128
Lost Property 44
Lower Marsh and The Cut Markets 64
Lower Regent Street 53
Lunchtime concerts 120, 121
Lyric, The, Hammersmith 123
Lyttleton Theatre 94, 123

Madam Tussaud's 42, 109
Mall, The 45, 90, 130
Marble Arch 42, 50, 91
Marks & Spencer 50, 54
Markovitch 61
Marlborough, Duke of 76
Marlborough House 76, 116
Marquee, The 122
Marx, Karl 79, 92, 101
Marx's House 79
Marylebone CC (MCC) 128
Mayfair 87
Mayflower, The, SE16 101
Meard Street 89
Metropolitan Police RFC 131
Millwall FC 127
Ministry of Defence 89
Minogue's, N1 101
Monmoth Street 57
Monument, The 99
Maroni, A. & Son 60
Morris, William 67
Morris, William, Gallery 117

Moss Bros 60
Mothercare 50, 55
Motor Books 60
Museum of London 83, 109
Museum of Mankind 105, 110
Museum of the Moving Image 94-95, 110
Museum of the Order of St John 110
Museum Tavern, WC1 101
Music 118, 119, 120-122

Nash, John 52, 67, 73, 80, 88, 91, 113, 124
National Army Museum 110
National Film Theatre, The 94
National Gallery 111
National Maritime Museum 73-74, 111
National Portrait Gallery 111
National Postal Museum 111
National Theatre 94, 123
Natural History Museum 112
Neal Street 56
Neal's Yard 56
Nell of Old Drury, WC2 102
Nelson, Lord 70, 73, 99
Nelson's Column 89, 99
New Caledonian Market 64
New River Sports Centre 127
New Shakespeare Company 123
Nichols, Harvey 56
Northcote Road Market 64
North End Road Market 64
North Woolwich Old Station Museum 112
Notting Hill Carnival 5, 8
Notting Hill Gate 55

Old Compton Street 57
Old Curiosity Shop 58
Olde Bull and Bush 102
Old Royal Observatory, Greenwich 74, 97
Old Vic, The 123
Old Wine Shades 102
Olivier Theatre 94, 123
Open-air music 122

Open Air Theatre, The 123
Opera and ballet 121-122
Orient FC 127
Oval Cricket Ground 128
Oxford and Cambridge Boat Race 5, 94, 102, 128
Oxford Circus 50, 51, 52
Oxford Street 6, 45, 49, 50-52, 53, 57

Paddington Station 37, 38
Palladium, The 123
Pall Mall 88, 111
Park Lane 87
Parliament Hill 122
Parliament Hill Fields 128
Parliament Square 43, 72, 89, 94
Paternoster Square 122
Paxton & Whitfield 58
Paxton's Head, SW1 102
Pepys, Samuel 64, 79, 85, 100, 102
Pepy's Corner 79
Peter Pan 99
Petticoat Lane 65
Phillips, Howard 58
Photographers' Gallery 113
Piccadilly 6, 53, 54, 88, 90
Piccadilly Circus 42, 52, 53, 54, 88, 89, 90
Pineapple Dance Warehouse 60
Poets' Corner 72
Police 44
Pollock's Toy Museum 113
Portobello Road 65
Post Offices 43
Prestat 61
Primrose Hill 91
Promenade Concerts, The 5, 120
Prospect of Whitby, E1 102
Public car parks 45-48
Public conveniences 44
Public Records Office 113
Pudding Lane 99
Purcell Room 94, 121
Purdey's 58
Putney Bridge 94

Queen Anne's Gate 88
Queen Boadicea 94, 99
Queen Charlotte's Cottage, Kew 4, 75

Queen Elizabeth Hall 94, 121
Queen's Club 129
Queen's Gallery, Buckingham Palace 113
Queen's House, Greenwich 73
Queen's Park Rangers FC 127

Regent's Canal 42, 92, 93, 95
Regent's Park 5, 7, 42, 45, 91, 92, 95, 122
Regent Street 6, 52-53, 67, 88
Reger, Janet 60
Rent-a-Bike 43
Richmond Park 91
Richmond RFC 131
Ridley Road Market 65
River Bus 37, 40, 94, 95, 97
Riverside Studios 119
Roberts, Patricia 60
Rock Garden, Covent Garden 122
Roman Road Market 65
Rosslyn Partk RFC 131
Royal Academy of Arts 5, 88, 113
Royal Air Force Museum 113
Royal Albert Hall 5, 120
Royal Armouries 76
Royal Ballet Company 121, 122
Royal Botanical Gardens, Kew 42, 75, 92
Royal College of Music Museum of Instruments 113
Royal Court Theatre 123
Royal Docks 37, 40
Royal Exchange 82-83
Royal Festival Hall 94, 121
Royal Hospital, Chelsea 5, 83, 85
Royal Mews, Buckingham Palace 73
Royal Naval College 73
Royal Opera Company 121
Royal Opera House 121
Royal Parks 90-92, 122
Royal Shakespeare Company 86, 119, 123
Royal Society 88
Royal Tournament 5, 8

159

Index

Rugby Union Football   5, 131
Rush hour   41, 45
Russell Square   84

Sadler's Wells   122
St Alfege   68
St Andrew, Holborn Circus   72
St Anne and St Agnes   72
St Anne Limehouse   68
St Bartholomew the Great   68
St Benet, Paul's Wharf   72
St Bride, Fleet Street   72, 120
St Bride's Crypt Museum   113
St Clement Danes   72, 89
St Clement, Eastcheap   72
St Ethelburga-the-Virgin   68
St Ethelreda   68
St George, Bloomsbury   68
St Giles Cripplegate   86
St Giles-in-the-Field   68
St Helen Bishopsgate   69
St James's   88
St James, Piccadilly   69, 88
St James, Garlickhythe   69
St Jame's Palace   76, 88
St Jame's Park   88, 92, 122, 130
St John, Smith Square   69, 120
St Katherine Docks   85, 96, 97
St Lawrence Jewry   69, 120
St Magnus the Martyr, EC3   72
St Margaret Pattens   72
St Martin-in-the-Fields   5, 9, 70, 120
St Martin-within-Ludgate   72
St Martin's Lane   57
St Martin's Theatre   125
St Mary Abchurch   72
St Mary-le-Bow   70, 99, 120
St Mary Woolnoth   120
St Michael-upon-Cornhill   121
St Olave, Hart Street   85, 121
St Pancras Station   37, 38
St Paul's Cathedral   4, 42, 70, 71, 86, 96, 109, 121
St Paul's Covent Garden   70
St Paul's Steps   122

St Stephen Walbrook   72
St Stephen's Tavern, SW1   102
Salisbury, The, WC2   102
Saracens RFC   131
Savile Row   54, 58, 87
Savoy Theatre   89, 124
Schooner Kathleen & May   113
Science Museum   113
Scotch House, Knightsbridge   56
Scotch House, Regent Street   53
Scott, Ronnie   89, 122
Scott, Sir Giles Gilbert   74, 81, 94, 98
Sedding, J. D.   67
Seething Lane   85
Selfridges   36, 49, 50
Shaftesbury Avenue   89
Shaftesbury Theatre   124
Shepherd Market   87
Shepherd's Bush Market   65
Sherlock Holmes, WC2   102
Ship, The, SW14   102
Sightseeing Bus Tours   42
Simpson's   54
Sloane Street   56
Smith, G. & Sons   58
Smith, James   58
Smithfield Market   66
Smythson   58
Soane, Sir John   67, 83, 114
Soane's, Sir John Museum   114
Soho   5, 6, 44, 62, 88-89
Soho Square   89
Sotherby's   54
South Bank Arts Complex   94-95, 121, 123
South Molton Street   87
Southwark Cathedral   72, 94, 121
Space Adventure   114
Spaniards Inn, The   102
Speakers' Corner   91
Speedway   131
Spink   58
Spitafields Market   66
Stanford's   60
Stansted Airport   37
State Opening of Parliament   4, 5
Steam Age, Mechanical Antiquities   61

Stock Exchange   83, 86
Strand, The   89, 99
Street markets   62-66
Strike One   58
Swan, The, W2   102
Syon Park   4, 93

Tate Gallery   95, 114-115
Tavistock Square   84
Taxis   41, 44
Taylor, A.   59
Teddington Gate   90
Telecom Technology Showcase   115
Telephones   43
Telford, Thomas   85, 96
Temple, The   82
Temple of Mithras   83
Tennis   129
Thames Flood Barrier   4, 85, 94, 97
Thames, River   4, 5, 7, 8, 42, 66, 73, 77, 78, 85, 86, 89, 94-97, 102, 109, 113, 128, 130
Theatre of Comedy   124
Theatre Royal, Drury Lane   124
Theatre Royal, Haymarket   124
Theatre Upstairs   123
Theatres   118, 119, 123-125
Through the Looking Glass   58
Tipping   42, 44
Tiranti, Alec   59
Tobacco Dock   97
Tottenham Court Road   50, 57
Tottenham Hotspur FC   127
Tourist Information   33, 36
Tower Bridge   7, 94, 96, 97
Tower Hill   94
Tower of London   4, 9, 10, 36, 42, 76-77, 85, 96
Tower Pier   42, 73
Tower Place   122
Trade markets   66
Tradition   61
Trafalgar Square   9, 43, 57, 89, 111
Treasury, The   89
Trooping of the Colour   4, 5, 7, 89
Twickenham RU Ground   5, 131
Twinings   61

Underground, The   36-41, 44, 45
Udny, Edgar   59
US Embassy   83, 87, 100

Vauxhall Bridge Gardens   93
Victoria, W2   102
Victoria and Albert Museum   104, 116
Victoria Coach Station   37, 40
Victoria Embankment   89
Victoria Embankment Gardens   89, 93, 122
Victoria Park Sports Centre   128
Victoria, Queen   61, 73, 76, 83, 98, 99, 102
Victoria Station   33, 36, 37, 38, 42
Victoria Tower Gardens   93

Wallace Collection   117
Walthamstow Market   66
Walthamstow Stadium   130
Wasps RFC   131
Water transport   40, 42, 94, 95, 96, 97
Waterloo Bridge   89, 94, 95
Waterloo Place   88
Waterloo Station   37, 38, 64
Waterlow Park   93
Waterman's Arms, E14   102
Wellington, 1st Duke of   70, 79, 88, 98, 117
Wellington Museum   79, 117
Wembley Arena   5, 122
Wembley Stadium   5, 126, 130
Wesley's House   79
West Ham United FC   127
Westminster   89
Westminster Abbey   4, 9, 42, 71-72
Westminster Bridge   94, 95, 130
Westminster Cathedral   72
Westminster Hall   74
Westminster, Palace of   9, 74, 82
Westminster Pier   42, 73, 94
White City Stadium   128
Whitecross Street Market   66

Index

Whitehall   4, 5, 9, 10, 89
Whitehall Palace   10, 76, 89
Whiteleys, Queensway   56
Whittington Stone, The   99
Wigmore Hall   121
Wilde, Oscar, House of   79
William the Conqueror   74, 76, 109
Wimbledon Common   93
Wimbledon FC   127
Wimbledon Lawn Tennis Museum   117
Wimbledon Stadium   130, 131
Windsor Castle   4, 83
Windsor Castle, The, W8   102
Woburn Walk   84
Wren, Sir Christopher   69, 70, 72, 73, 74, 76, 83, 85, 86, 88, 89, 90, 97, 99, 124
Wren's House   79

Ye Olde Cheshire Cheese   102
Ye Old Watling, EC4   102
Yeoman Warders   77
Yeoman of the Guard   10
York, Duke of   76, 98
York's, Duke of Column   98
Young Vic   124

Zoo, The   42, 91, 92-93, 95, 96

161

Readers notes

Readers notes

HOTELS AND RESTAURANTS IN BRITAIN 1991

25th anniversary edition containing thousands of AA-inspected hotels and restaurants, with full details of prices, facilities and AA-classification. Interesting features include best new hotels and restaurants, Top Twenty One-Star hotels, and a Readers' Competition. A special 10 per cent discount for holders of this guide is offered at many of the listed hotels.

Available at good bookshops and AA Centres

Another great guide from the AA

London: Street index

STREET INDEX

In the index, the street names are listed in alphabetical order and written in full, but may be abbreviated on the map.

Postal codes are listed where information is available.

Each entry is followed by its map page number in bold type and an arbitrary letter and figure grid reference.

eg Lyons Place NW8   **12**   B3.

Turn to page **12** The letter 'B' refers to the grid square located at the top of the page. The figure '3' refers to the grid square located at the righthand side of the page. Lyons Place is found within the intersecting square. NW8 refers to the postcode.

A proportion of street names and their references are also followed by the name of another street in italics. These entries do not appear on the map due to insufficient space but can be located adjacent to the name of the road in italics.

Street	Page	Grid
Abbey Gardens NW8	12	A1
Abbey Orchard Street SW1	27	C2
Abbey Road NW6 & NW8	12	A1
Abbey Street SE1	29	E2
Abbots Lane SE1	29	E1
Abchurch Lane EC4	23	D2
Abercorn Close NW8	12	A2
Abercorn Place NW8	12	A2
Aberdeen Place NW8	12	B3
Aberdour Street SE1	29	D3
Abingdon Street SW1	27	D2
Achilles Way W1	26	A1
Acton Street WC1	15	E2
Adam And Eve Court W1	20	B1
Oxford Street		
Adam Street WC2	21	D3
Adam's Row W1	20	A3
Addington Street SE1	27	E2
Addle Hill EC4	22	B2
Addle Street EC2	23	C1
Adelaide Street WC2	21	D3
William IV Street		
Adeline Place WC1	21	C1
Adelphi Terrace WC2	21	D3
Adams Street		
Adpar Street W2	12	B4
Adrian Mews SW10	30	A3
Agar Street WC2	21	D3
Agdon Street EC1	16	B3
Air Street W1	20	B3
Alaska Street SE1	28	A1
Albany Street NW1	14	A1
Albemarle Street W1	20	B3
Albemarle Way EC1	16	B4
Clerkenwell Road		
Albert Bridge Road SW11	31	D4
Albert Bridge SW3 & SW11	31	D3
Albert Court SW7	24	B2
Albert Gate SW1	25	E1
Albert Hall Mansions SW7	24	B2
Albert Mews W8	24	A2
Albert Place W8	24	A2
Albert Street NW1	14	B1
Albion Close W2	19	C2
Albion Mews W2	19	D2
Albion Place EC1	16	B4
Albion Street W2	19	C2
Aldenham Street NW1	14	C1
Aldermanbury EC2	23	C1
Aldermanbury Square EC2	23	C1
Aldermanbury		
Alderney Street SW1	32	A1
Aldersgate Street EC1	16	C4
Aldford Street W1	19	E3
Aldgate EC3	23	E2
Aldwych WC2	21	E2
Alexander Place SW7	25	C3
Alexander Square SW3	25	C3
Alfred Mews W1	14	C4
Alfred Place WC1	14	C4
Alice Street SE1	29	D3
All Hallows Lane EC4	23	D3
All Soul's Place W1	20	B1
Langham Street		
Allington Street SW1	26	B3
Allitsen Road NW8	13	C1
Allsop Place NW1	13	E3
Alma Square NW8	12	B2
Alpha Place SW3	31	D2
Ambrosden Avenue SW1	26	B3
Amen Corner EC4	22	B1
Amen Court EC4	22	B1
Ampton Place WC1	15	E2
Ampton Street WC1	15	E2
Amwell Street EC1	16	A2
Anchor Yard EC1	16	C3
Anderson Street SW3	31	D1
Andrew Borde Street WC2	21	C1

Street	Page	Grid
Charing Cross Road		
Angel Court EC2	23	D1
Angel Passage EC4	23	D3
Angel Street EC1	22	B1
Anhalt Road SW11	31	D4
Ann Lane SW10	30	B3
Anning Street EC2	17	E3
Ansdell Street W8	24	A2
Apollo Place SW10	30	B3
Apothecary Street EC4	22	B2
New Bridge Street		
Apple Tree Yard SW1	20	C3
Appold Street EC2	17	E4
Aquila Street NW8	12	C1
Aquinas Street SE1	22	A3
Archer Street W1	20	C2
Argent Street SE1	28	B1
Loman Street		
Argyle Square WC1	15	D2
Argyle Street WC1	15	D2
Argyle Walk WC1	15	D2
Argyll Street W1	20	B2
Arlington Street SW1	20	B3
Arlington Way EC1	16	A2
Arne Street WC2	21	D2
Arneway Street SW1	27	C3
Arthur Street EC4	23	D2
Artillery Lane E1	23	E1
Artillery Passage E1	23	E1
Artillery Lane		
Artillery Row SW1	26	C3
Arundel Street WC2	21	E2
Ascalon Street SW8	32	B4
Ashburn Gardens SW7	30	A1
Ashburn Mews SW7	30	A1
Ashburn Place SW7	30	A1
Ashburnham Road SW10	30	A4
Ashby Street EC1	16	B2
Ashland Place W1	13	E4
Ashley Place SW1	26	B3
Ashmill Street NW1	13	C4
Ashworth Road W9	12	A2
Aske Street N1	17	E2
Astell Street SW3	31	C1
Astwood Mews SW7	30	A1
Atherstone Mews SW7	24	A3
Attneave Street WC1	16	A3
Aubrey Place NW8	3A1	
Augustus Street NW1	14	B2
Austin Friars EC2	23	D1
Austin Friars Square EC2	23	D1
Austin Friars		
Austin Street E2	17	E2
Austral Street SE11	28	B3
Ave Maria Lane EC4	22	B2
Avery Row W1	20	A2
Avon Place SE1	29	C2
Avonmouth Street SE1	28	C2
Aybrook Street W1	19	E1
Aylesbury Street EC1	16	B3
Aylesford Street SW1	32	C2
Ayres Street SE1	28	C1

Street	Page	Grid
Babmaes Street SW1	20	C3
Jermyn Street		
Bacchus Walk N1	17	E1
Bache's Street N1	17	D2
Back Hill EC1	16	A4
Bacon Grove SE1	29	E3
Bainbridge Street WC1	21	C1
Baird Street EC1	17	C3
Baker Street W1 & NW1	13	E4

Street	Page	Grid
Baker's Mews W1	19	E1
Baker's Row EC1	16	A3
Balcombe Street NW1	13	D3
Balderton Street W1	19	E2
Baldwin Street EC1	17	D2
Baldwin Terrace N1	16	C1
Baldwin's Gardens EC1	16	A4
Balfe Street N1	15	D1
Balfour Mews W1	19	E3
Balfour Place W1	19	E3
Balfour Street SE17	29	D3
Baltic Street EC1	16	C3
Bank End SE1	23	C3
Bankside SE1	22	C3
Banner Street EC1	17	C3
Barge House Street SE1	22	A3
Barlow Place W1	20	B3
Barnby Street NW1	14	B2
Barnham Street SE1	29	E1
Barnwood Close W9	3	A4
Baron Street N1	16	A1
Baron's Place SE1	28	A2
Barrett Street W1	19	E2
Barrie Street W2	18	B2
Barrow Hill Road NW8	13	C1
St Johns Wood High Street		
Barter Street WC1	21	D1
Barth Lane EC2	23	D1
Bartholomew Close EC1	22	B1
Bartholomew Square EC1	17	C3
Bartholomew Street SE1	29	D3
Bartlett Court EC4	22	A1
Barton Street SW1	27	D2
Basil Street SW3	25	D2
Basinghall Avenue EC2	23	D1
Basinghall Street EC2	23	C1
Basinghouse Yard E2	17	E2
Bastwick Street EC1	16	B3
Bateman Street W1	21	C2
Bateman's Row EC2	17	E3
Bath Place N1	17	D3
Bath Street EC1	17	C3
Bath Terrace SE1	28	C3
Bathurst Mews W2	18	B2
Bathurst Street W2	18	B2
Battersea Bridge Road SW11	30	C4
Battersea Bridge SE3 & SW11	30	C3
Battersea Church Road SW11	31	C4
Battersea Park Road SW11	32	B4
Battle Bridge Lane SE1	29	D1
Battle Bridge Road NW1	15	D1
Bayley Street WC1	21	C1
Baylis Road SE1	28	A2
Beak Street W1	20	B2
Bear Gardens SE1	22	C3
Bear Lane SE1	28	B1
Bear Street WC2	21	C2
Cranbourn Street		
Beauchamp Place SW3	25	D3
Beauchamp Street EC1	16	A4
Leather Lane		
Beaufort Gardens SW3	25	D2
Beaufort Street SW3	30	B2
Beaumont Mews W1	13	E4
Beaumont Place W1	14	B3
Beaumont Street W1	13	E4
Bedale Street SE1	29	D1
Borough High Street		
Bedford Avenue WC1	21	C1
Bedford Court WC2	21	D2
Bedford Place WC1	15	D4
Bedford Row WC1	15	E4
Bedford Square WC1	15	C4
Bedford Street WC2	21	D2
Bedford Way WC1	15	C3

165

London: Street index

Street	Page	Grid
Bedfordbury WC2	21	D3
Beech Street EC2	16	C4
Beeston Place SW1	25	A3
Belgrave Mews North SW1	25	E2
Belgrave Mews South SW1	25	E2
Belgrave Mews West SW1	25	E2
Belgrave Place SW1	25	E3
Belgrave Road SW1	32	B1
Belgrave Square SW1	25	E2
Belgrove Street WC1	15	D2
Bell Lane E1	23	E1
Bell Street NW1	13	C4
Bell Yard WC2	22	A1
Belvedere Buildings SE1	28	B2
Belvedere Road SE1	27	E1
Bendall Mews W1	13	D4
Benjamin Street EC1	16	B4
Bennet Street SW1	20	B3
Bennett's Yard SW1	27	D3
Bentinck Mews W1	20	A1
Marylebone Lane		
Bentinck Street W1	20	A1
Berkeley Mews W1	19	E1
Berkeley Square W1	20	A3
Berkeley Street W1	20	B3
Bermondsey Square SE1	29	E2
Long Lane		
Bermondsey Street SE1	29	E1
Bernard Street WC1	15	D3
Berners Mews W1	20	B1
Berners Street W1	20	B1
Berry Street EC1	16	B3
Berwick Street W1	20	C2
Bessborough Street SW1	32	C2
Bethnal Green Road E1 & E2	17	D3
Betterton Street WC2	21	D1
Bell Lane E1	23	E1
Bell Street NW1	13	C4
Bell Yard WC2	22	A1
Belvedere Buildings SE1	28	B2
Belvedere Road SE1	27	E1
Bendall Mews W1	13	D4
Benjamin Street EC1	16	B4
Bennet Street SW1	20	B3
Bennett's Yard SW1	27	D3
Bentinck Mews W1	20	A1
Marylebone Lane		
Bentinck Street W1	20	A1
Berkeley Mews W1	19	E1
Berkeley Square W1	20	A3
Berkeley Street W1	20	B3
Bermondsey Square SE1	29	E2
Long Lane		
Bermondsey Street SE1	29	E1
Bernard Street WC1	15	D3
Berners Mews W1	20	B1
Berners Street W1	20	B1
Berry Street EC1	16	B3
Berwick Street W1	20	C2
Bessborough Street SW1	32	C2
Bethnal Green Road E1 & E2	17	D3
Betterton Street WC2	21	D1
Bevenden Street N1	17	D2
Bevin Way WC1	16	A2
Bevis Marks EC3	23	E1
Bickenhall Street W1	13	D4
Bidborough Street WC1	15	D2
Billing Place SW10	30	A3
Billing Road Sw10	30	A3
Billing Street SW10	30	A3
Billiter Square EC3	23	E2
Fenchurch Avenue		
Billiter Street EC3	23	E2
Bina Gardens SW5	30	A1
Bingham Place W1	13	E4
Binney Street W1	20	A2
Birchin Lane EC3	23	D2
Bird Street W1	20	A2
Birdcage Walk SW1	26	C2
Birkenhead Street WC1	15	D2
Bishop's Court EC4	22	B1
Old Bailey		
Bishop's Court WC2	22	A1
Chancery Lane		
Bishop's Terrace SE11	28	A3
Bishops Bridge Road W2	18	A1
Bishopsgate EC2	23	D2
Bittern Street SE1	28	C2
Black Swan Yard SE1	29	E1
Blackall Street EC2	17	D3
Blackburne's Mews W1	19	E2
Blackfriars Bridge EC4 & SE1	22	B3
Blackfriars Lane EC4	22	B2
Blackfriars Passage EC4	22	B2
Blackfriars Road SE1	22	B3
Blacklands Terrace SW3	31	D1
Blandford Square NW1	13	D3
Blandford Street W1	19	E1
Blantyre Street SW10	30	B4
Bleeding Heart Yard EC1	16	A4
Greville Street		
Blenheim Street W1	20	A2
New Bond Street		
Blenheim Terrace NW8	12	A1
Bletchley Street N1	17	C1
Bletsoe Walk N1	17	C1
Blomfield Road W9	12	A4
Blomfield Villas W2	12	A4
Bloomburg Street SW1	32	C1
Vauxhall Bridge Road		
Bloomfield Place W1	20	A2
Bourdon Street		
Bloomfield Terrace SW1	31	E1
Bloomsbury Court WC1	21	D1
High Holborn		
Bloomsbury Place WC1	15	D4
Southampton Row		
Bloomsbury Square WC1	15	D4
Bloomsbury Street WC1	21	C1
Bloomsbury Way WC1	21	D1
Blossom Street E1	17	E4
Bolsover Street W1	14	B4
Bolt Court EC4	22	A1
Bolton Gardens Mews SW10	30	A2
Bolton Gardens SW5	30	A1
Bolton Street W1	20	A3
Bonhill Street EC2	17	D4
Boot Street N1	17	D3
Booth's Place W1	20	B1
Wells Street		
Boreas Walk N1	16	B1
Nelson Place		
Borough High Street SE1	29	C1
Borough Road SE1	28	B2
Boscobel Place SW1	26	A3
Boscobel Street NW8	12	B4
Boston Place NW1	13	D3
Boswell Court WC1	15	D4
Boswell Street		
Boswell Street WC1	15	E4
Botolph Lane EC3	23	D2
Boundary Road SE1	28	B1
Boundary Street E2	17	E3
Bourdon Place W1	20	A2
Bourdon Place		
Bourdon Street W1	20	A2
Bourlet Close W1	20	B1
Bourne Street SW1	31	E1
Bouverie Street EC4	22	A2
Bow Lane EC4	22	C2
Bow Street WC2	21	D2
Bowling Green Lane EC1	16	A3
Bowling Green Place SE1	29	D1
Newcomen Street		
Bowling Green Walk N1	17	D2
Boyfield Street SE1	28	B2
Boyle Street W1	20	B2
Savile Row		
Brackley Street EC1	16	C4
Brad Street SE1	28	A1
Bradmead SW8	32	B4
Braidwood Street SE1	29	E2
Bramerton Street SW3	30	C2
Bray Place SW3	31	D1
Bread Street EC4	22	C2
Bream's Buildings EC	22	A1
Brechin Place SW7	30	B1
Bremner Road SW7	24	B2
Brendon Street W1	19	D1
Bressenden Place SW1	26	B2
Brewer Street W1	20	C2
Brewers' Green SW1	26	C2
Caxton Street		
Brick Street W1	26	A1
Brick Court EC4	22	A2
Middle Temple Lane		
Bridewell Place EC4	22	B2
Bridford Mews W1	14	A4
Bridge Place SW1	26	B3
Bridge Street SW1	27	D2
Bridge Yard SE1	23	D3
Bridgeman Street NW8	13	C1
Bridgewater Street EC2	16	C4
Beech Street		
Bridgewater Street NW1	14	C1
Bridle Lane W1	20	B2
Bridport Place N1	17	D1
Brill Place NW1	15	C1
Briset Street EC1	16	B4
Bristol Gardens W9	12	A4
Bristol Mews W9	12	A4
Britannia Street WC1	15	E2
Britannia Walk N1	17	D2
Britten Street SW3	31	C2
Britton Street EC1	16	B4
Broad Court WC2	21	D2
Broad Sanctuary SW1	27	D2
Broad Walk W2	25	E1
Broadbent Street W1	20	A2
Broadley Street NW8	12	C4
Broadley Terrace NW1	13	C3
Bucknall Street WC2	21	D1
Budge's Walk W2	18	B3
Bullwharf Lane EC4	23	C2
Kensington Park Road		
Bulstrode Place W1	20	A1
Marylebone Lane		
Bulstrode Street W1	20	A1
Bunhill Row EC1	17	D3
Bunhouse Place SW1	31	E1
Burbage Close SE1	29	D3
Burdett Street SE1	28	A2
Burgh Street N1	16	B1
Burgon Street EC4	22	B2
Carter Lane		
Burleigh Street WC2	21	E2
Burlington Arcade W1	20	B3
Burlington Gardens W1	20	B3
Burnaby Street SW10	30	B3
Burne Street NW1	13	C4
Burnsall Street SW3	31	D2
Burrell Street SE1	22	B3
Burrows Mews SE1	28	B1
Bursar Street SE1	29	E1
Tooley Street		
Burton Place WC1	15	C3
Burton Street		
Burton Street WC1	15	C3
Burwood Place W2	19	C1
Bury Court EC3	23	E1
Bury Place WC1	21	D1
Bury Street EC3	23	E1
Bury Street SW1	20	B3
Bury Walk SW3	30	C1
Bush Lane EC4	23	D2
Bute Street SW7	30	B1
Butler Place SW1	26	C2
Buckingham Gate		
Buttesland Street N1	17	D2
Byng Place WC1	15	C4
Byward Street EC3	23	E3
Bywater Street SW3	31	D1
Cabbell Street NW1	19	C1
Cadogan Gardens SW3	31	D1
Cadogan Gate SW1	25	E3
Cadogan Lane SW1	25	E3
Cadogan Place SW1	25	E2
Cadogan Square SW1	25	D3
Cadogan Street SW3	31	D1
Cahill Street EC1	17	C3
Dufferin Street		
Caledonia Street N1	15	D1
Cale Street SW3	31	C1
Caleb Street SE1	28	C1
Marshalsea Road		
Caledonian Road N1 & N7	15	D1
Callcott Street W8	24	A3
Callow Street SW3	30	B2
Calshot Street N1	15	E1
Calthorpe Street WC1	15	E3
Cambridge Circus WC2	21	C2
Cambridge Gate Mews NW1	14	A3
Albany Street		
Cambridge Gate NW1	14	A3
Cambridge Place W8	24	A2
Cambridge Square W2	19	C1
Cambridge Street SW1	32	B1
Cambridge Terrace Mews NW1	14	A3
Chester Gate		
Cambridge Terrace NW1	14	A3
Outer Circle		
Camera Place SW10	30	B3
Camlet Street E2	17	E3
Camley Street N1	15	D1
Camomile Street EC3	23	E1
Candover Street W1	14	B4
Foley Street		
Canning Passage W8	24	A2
Canning Place W8	24	A2
Cannon Row SW1	27	D1
Cannon Street EC4	22	C2
Canvey Street SE1	22	B3
Capland Street NW8	12	C3
Capper Street WC1	14	B4
Carburton Street W1	14	B4
Cardington Street NW1	14	B2
Carey Lane EC2	22	C1
Carey Street WC2	21	E1
Carlisle Avenue EC3	23	E2
Carlisle Lane SE1	27	E3
Carlisle Place SW1	26	B3
Carlos Place W1	20	A2
Carlton Gardens SW1	26	C1
Carlton Hill NW8	12	A1

London: Street index

Street	Page	Grid
Carlton House Terrace SW1	20	C3
Carlton Street SW1	20	C3
Carlyle Square SW3	30	C2
Carmelite Street EC4	22	A2
Carnaby Street W1	20	B2
Caroline Place Mews W2	18	A2
Caroline Terrace SW1	31	E1
Carpenter Street W1	20	A3
Carriage Drive East SW11	32	A4
Carriage Drive North SW11	31	D4
Carriage Drive West SW11	31	D4
Carrington Street W1	26	A1
Shepherd Street		
Carter Lane EC4	22	B2
Carteret Street SW1	27	C2
Carthusian Street EC1	16	B4
Carting Lane WC2	21	E3
Cartwright Gardens WC1	15	D3
Castle Baynard Street EC4	22	B2
Castle Lane SW1	26	B2
Castle Yard SE1	22	B3
Cathcart Road SW10	30	A3
Cathedral Piazza SW1	26	B3
Cathedral Street SE1	23	D3
Winchester Walk		
Catherine Place SW1	26	B2
Catherine Street WC2	21	E2
Catherine Wheel Alley E1	23	E1
Catton Street WC1	21	E1
Cavaye Place SW10	30	B2
Cavendish Avenue NW8	12	B1
Cavendish Close NW8	12	C2
Cavendish Mews North W1	14	A4
Hallam Street		
Cavendish Place W1	20	A1
Cavendish Square W1	20	A1
Cavendish Street N1	17	D1
Caversham Street SW3	31	D2
Caxton Street SW1	26	C2
Cayton Place EC1	17	C2
Cayton Street		
Cayton Street EC1	17	C2
Cecil Court WC2	21	D2
St Martin's Lane		
Centaur Street SE1	27	E2
Central Avenue SW11	31	E4
Central Street EC1	16	C2
Chadwell Street EC1	16	A2
Chadwick Street SW1	27	C3
Chagford Street NW1	13	D3
Chalton Street NW1	14	C1
Chancel Street SE1	28	B1
Chancery Lane WC2	22	A1
Chandos Place WC2	21	D2
Chandos Street W1	20	A1
Chapel Market N1	16	A1
Chapel Place W1	20	A1
Chapel Street NW1	13	C4
Chapel Street W1	26	A2
Charing Cross Road WC2	21	C2
Charlbert Street NW8	13	C1
Charles II Street SW1	20	C3
Charles Lane NW8	12	C1
Charles Square N1	16	C3
Charles Street W1	20	A3
Charlotte Place W1	20	B1
Goodge Street		
Charlotte Road EC2	17	E3
Charlotte Street W1	14	B4
Charlwood Street SW1	32	B2
Charrington Street NW1	14	C1
Chart Street N1	17	D2
Charterhouse Square EC1	16	B4
Charterhouse Street EC1	22	A1
Chatham Street SE17	29	C3
Cheapside EC4	22	C2
Chelsea Bridge Road SW1	31	E2
Chelsea Bridge SW1 & SW8	32	A2
Chelsea Embankment SW3	31	C3
Chelsea Manor Gardens SW3	31	C2
Chelsea Manor Street SW3	31	C2
Chelsea Park Gardens SW3	30	B3
Chelsea Square SW3	30	C2
Cheltenham Terrace SW3	31	D1
Cheney Road NW1	15	D1
Chenies Mews WC1	14	C4
Chenies Place NW1	15	C1
Chenies Street WC1	14	C4
Chequer Street EC1	17	C3
Cherbury Street N1	17	D1
Chesham Place SW1	25	E3
Chesham Street SW1	25	E3
Chester Close North NW1	14	A2
Chester Close South		
Chester Close South NW1	14	A2
Chester Court NW1	14	A2
Albany Street		
Chester Gate NW1	14	A2
Chester Mews SW1	26	A2
Chester Place NW1	14	A2
Chester Road NW1	14	A2
Chester Row SW1	31	E1
Chester Square SW1	26	A3
Chester Street SW1	26	A2
Chester Terrace NW1	14	A2
Chesterfield Gardens W1	20	A3
Chesterfield Hill W1	20	A3
Chesterfield Street W1	20	A3
Cheval Place SW7	25	C2
Cheyne Gardens SW3	31	D3
Cheyne Row SW3	31	C3
Cheyne Walk SW3 & SW10	30	B4
Chicheley Street SE1	27	E1
Chichester Rents WC2	22	A1
Chancery Lane		
Chichester Road W2	12	A4
Chichester Street SW1	32	B2
The Highway		
Chiltern Street W1	13	E4
Chilworth Mews W2	18	B1
Chilworth Street W2	18	B2
Chiswell Street EC1	17	D4
Chitty Street W1	14	B4
Christchurch Street SW3	31	D2
Christopher Street EC2	17	D4
Church Place SW1	20	B3
Piccadilly		
Church Street NW8	12	B4
Churchill Gardens Road SW1	32	A2
Churchway NW1	15	C2
Churton Street SW1	32	B1
Circus Place EC2	23	D1
Circus Road NW8	12	B2
City Garden Row N1	16	B1
City Road EC1	16	B2
Clabon Mews SW1	25	D3
Hordle Promenade West		
Clare Market WC2	21	E2
Claremont Close N1	16	A2
Claremont Square N1	16	A2
Clarence Gardens NW1	14	B2
Clarence Passage NW1	15	D1
Pancras Road		
Clarendon Close W2	19	C2
Clarendon Gardens W9	12	B3
Clarendon Place W2	19	C2
Clarendon Street SW1	32	B1
Clarendon Terrace W9	12	B3
Clareville Grove SW7	30	B1
Clareville Street SW7	30	B1
Clarges Mews W1	20	A3
Clarges Street W1	20	A3
Clarke's Mews W1	14	A4
Clavert Avenue E2	17	E3
Claverton Street SW1	32	B2
Clay Street W1	13	E4
Clearwell Drive W9	12	A4
Cleaver Street SE11	43	A2
Clement's Inn WC2	21	E2
Clements Lane EC4	23	D2
Clennam Street SE1	28	C1
Clenston Mews W1	19	D1
Clere Street EC2	17	D3
Clerkenwell Close EC1	16	A3
Clerkenwell Green EC1	16	A4
Clerkenwell Road EC1	16	A4
Cleveland Gardens W2	18	A2
Cleveland Mews W1	14	B4
Cleveland Row SW1	26	B1
Cleveland Square W2	18	A2
Cleveland Street W1	14	B3
Cleveland Terrace W2	18	A1
Clifford Street W1	20	B2
Clifton Gardens W9	12	A4
Clifton Place W2	18	C2
Clifton Road W9	12	B3
Clifton Street EC2	17	D4
Clifton Villas W9	12	A4
Clink Street SE1	23	C3
Kinburn Street		
Clipstone Mews W1	14	B4
Clipstone Street W1	14	B4
Cliveden Place SW1	31	E1
Cloak Lane EC4	23	C2
Cloth Fair EC1	16	B4
Cloth Street EC1	16	C4
Clunbury Street N1	17	D1
Cluny Place SE1	29	E2
Cobb Street E1	23	E1
Cobourg Street NW1	14	B2
Cochrane Street NW8	12	C1
Cock Lane EC1	22	B1
Cockpit Yard WC1	15	E4
Cockspur Street SW1	21	C3
Coin Street SE1	22	A3
Colbeck Mews SW7	30	A1
Colchester STREET	E121A1	
Whitechapel High Street		
Coldbath Square EC1	16	A3
Roseberry Avenue		
Cole Street SE1	29	C2
Colebrooke Row N1	16	B1
Coleman Street EC2	23	D1
Coley Street WC1	15	E3
College Hill EC4	23	C2
College Street		
College Street EC4	23	C2
Collier Street N1	15	E1
Collingham Gardens SW5	30	A1
Collingham Road SW5	30	A1
Collinson Street SE1	28	C2
Colnbrook Street SE1	28	B3
Colombo Street SE1	22	B3
Colonnade WC1	15	D4
Commercial Street E1	17	E4
Compton Passage EC1	16	B3
Compton Place WC1	15	D3
Compton Street EC1	16	B3
Concert Hall Approach SE1	27	E1
Conduit Mews W2	18	B2
Conduit Street W1	20	B2
Connaught Place W2	19	D2
Connaught Square W2	19	D2
Connaught Street W2	19	D2
Cons Street SE1	28	A1
Constitution Hill SW1	26	A1
Conway Street W1	14	B4
Coombs Street N1	16	B2
Cooper Close SE1	28	A2
Cooper's Row EC3	23	E2
Hordle Promenade West		
Copperfield Street SE1	28	B1
Copthall Avenue EC2	23	D1
Coptic Street WC1	21	D1
Coral Street SE1	28	A2
Coram Street WC1	15	D3
Cork Street W1	20	B3
Corlett Street NW1	12	C4
Bell Street		
Corner House Street WC2	21	D3
Northumberland Street		
Cornhill EC3	23	D2
Cornwall Gardens SW7	24	A3
Cornwall Gardens Walk SW7	24	A3
Cornwall Mews South SW7	24	A3
Cornwall Road SE1	28	A1
Cornwall Terrace NW1	13	D3
Coronet Street N1	17	D2
Corporation Row EC1	16	A3
Corsham Street N1	17	D2
Cosmo Place WC1	15	D4
Southampton Row		
Cosser Street SE1	27	E3
Cosway Street NW1	28	A3
Cosway Street NW1	13	C4
Cottesmore Gardens W8	24	A2
Cotton's Gardens E2	17	E1
Cottons Lane SE1	23	D3
Coulson Street Sw3	31	D1
Counter Street SE1	29	D1
County Street SE1	29	C3
Cousin Lane EC4	23	C3
Coventry Street W1	20	C3
Cowcross Street EC1	16	B4
Cowley Street SW1	27	D3
Cowper Street EC2	17	D3
Crace Street NW1	14	C2
Cramer Street W1	19	E1
Cranbourn Street WC2	21	C2
Cranleigh Street NW1	14	B1
Cranley Gardens SW7	30	B1
Cranley Mews SW7	30	B1
Cranley Place SW7	30	B1
Cranmer Court SW3	31	D1
Cranwood Street EC1	17	D3
Craven Hill Gardens W2	18	A2
Craven Hill Mews W2	18	B2
Craven Hill W2	18	B2
Craven Road W2	18	B2
Craven Street WC2	21	D3
Craven Terrace W2	18	B2
Crawford Passage EC1	16	A3
Crawford Place W1	19	C1
Crawford Street W1	19	D1
Creasy Street SE1	29	E3
Swan Mead		
Creechurch Lane EC3	23	E2
Creechurch Place EC3	23	E1
Creed Lane EC4	22	B2
Cremer Street E2	17	E2
Cremorne Road SW10	30	B4
Crescent Place SW3	25	C3
Crescent Row EC1	16	C3
Cresswell Place SW10	30	A1
Crestfield Street WC1	15	D2
Kennington Park Road		
Crimscott Street SE1	29	E3
Crinan Street N1	15	D1

167

London: Street index

Street	Page	Grid
Cringle Street SW8	32	B3
Cripplegate Street EC1	16	C4
Viscount Street		
Crispin Street E1	17	E4
Cromer Street WC1	15	D2
Crompton Street W2	12	B4
Cromwell Gardens SW7	24	C3
Cromwell Mews SW7	24	B3
Cromwell Place SW7	24	B3
Crondall Street N1	17	E2
Cropley Street N1	17	D1
Crosby Row SE1	29	D2
Cross Keys Close W1	19	E1
Marylebone Lane		
Cross Lane EC3	23	E3
Crosswall EC3	23	E2
Crown Court WC2	21	D2
Crown Office Row EC4	22	A2
Crucifix Lane SE1	29	E1
Cruikshank Street WC1	16	A2
Crutched Friars EC3	23	E2
Cubitt Street WC1	15	E3
Culford Gardens SW3	31	D1
Cullum Street EC3	23	E2
Culross Street W1	19	E3
Culworth Street NW8	13	C1
Cumberland Gardens WC1	15	E2
Great Percy Street		
Cumberland Gate W1 & W2	19	D2
Cumberland Market NW1	14	B2
Cumberland Street SW1	32	A2
Cumberland Terrace Mews NW1	14	A1
Albany Street		
Cumberland Terrace NW1	14	A1
Cumming Street N1	15	E1
Cundy Street SW1	32	A1
Cunningham Place NW8	12	B3
Cursitor Street EC4	22	A1
Curtain Road EC2	17	E3
Curtis Street SE1	29	E3
Curzon Gate W1	25	E1
Curzon Place W1	26	A1
Curzon Street W1	26	A1
Cuthbert Street W2	12	B4
Cutler Street E1	23	E1
Cynthia Street N1	15	E1
Cyrus Street EC1	16	B3
D'arblay Street W1	20	C2
D'oyley Street SW1	25	E3
Dacre Street SW1	27	C2
Dallington Street EC1	16	B3
Danbury Street N1	16	B1
Dane Street WC1	21	E1
Dante Road SE11	28	B3
Danvers Street SW3	30	C3
Dartmouth Street SW1	27	C2
Darwin Street SE17	29	C3
Daventry Street NW1	13	C4
Davidge Street SE1	28	B2
Davies Mews W1	20	A2
De Vere Gardens W8	24	A2
De Walden Street W1	19	E1
Westmorland Street		
Deacon Way SE17	28	C3
Dean Bradley Street SW1	27	D3
Dean Farrar Street SW1	27	C2
Dean Ryle Street SW1	27	D3
Dean Stanley Street SW1	27	D3
Millbank		
Dean Street W1	20	C2
Dean Trench Street SW1	27	D3
Dean's Court EC4	22	B2
Carter Lane		
Dean's Mews W1	20	A1
Deanery Street W1	19	E3
Decima Street SE1	29	E2
Delamere Terrace W2	12	A4
Denbigh Street SW1	32	B1
Denman Street W1	20	C2
Denmark Place WC2	21	C1
Charing Cross Road		
Denmark Street WC2	21	C1
Denning Close NW8	12	B2
Denyer Street SW3	31	D1
Derby Gate SW1	27	D1
Derby Street W1	26	A1
Dereham Place EC2	17	E3
Dering Street W1	20	A2
Deverell Street SE1	29	D3
Devereux Court WC2	22	A2
Strand		
Devonshire Close W1	14	A4
Devonshire Mews South W1	14	A4
Devonshire Mews West W1	14	A4
Devonshire Place Mews W1	13	E4
Devonshire Place W1	14	A4
Devonshire Row EC2	23	E1
Devonshire Row Mews W1	13	D4
Devonshire Street		
Devonshire Square EC2	23	E1
Devonshire Street W1	13	E4
Devonshire Terrace W2	18	B2
Diadem Court W1	20	C1
Dean Street		
Diana Place NW1	14	B3
Dickens Square SE1	29	C2
Dilke Street SW3	31	D3
Dingley Place EC1	17	C2
Dingley Road EC1	16	C2
Disney Place SE1	29	C1
Disney Street SE1	29	C1
Redcross Way		
Distaff Lane EC4	22	C2
Distillery Lane W6	37	B2
Distillery Road W6	37	B2
Distin Street SE11	43	A1
West Lane		
Dock Hill Avenue SE16	34	E1
Dodson Street SE1	28	A2
Dolben Street SE1	28	B1
Dombey Street WC1	15	E4
Domingo Street EC1	16	C3
Old Street		
Dominion Street EC2	17	D4
Donegal Street N1	15	E1
Donne Place SW3	25	C3
Doon Street SE1	22	A3
Doric Way NW1	14	C2
Dorrington Street EC1	16	A4
Leather Lane		
Dorset Close NW1	13	D4
Dorset Mews SW1	26	A2
Dorset Rise EC4	22	A2
Dorset Square NW1	13	D4
Dorset Street W1	13	E4
Doughty Mews WC1	15	E3
Doughty Street WC1	15	E3
Douglas Street SW1	32	C1
Douro Place W8	24	A2
Torrington Place		
Dove Mews SW5	30	A2
Dove Walk SW1	31	E1
Dovehouse Street SW3	30	C1
Dover Street W1	20	B3
Dowgate Hill EC4	23	D2
Down Street W1	26	A1
Downing Street SW1	27	D1
Drake Street WC1	15	D4
Draycott Avenue SW3	31	D1
Draycott Place SW3	31	D1
Draycott Terrace SW3	31	D1
Druid Street SE1	29	E1
Drummond Crescent NW1	14	C2
Drummond Street NW1	14	B3
Drury Lane WC2	21	D1
Dryaton Gardens SW10	30	A1
Dryden Street WC2	21	D2
Drysdale Place N1	17	E2
Drysdale Street N1	17	E2
Duchess Mews W1	20	A1
Duchess Street W1	20	A1
Duchy Street SE1	22	A3
Dudley Street W2	18	B1
Dudmaston Mews SW3	30	C1
Dufferin Street EC1	17	C3
Dufour's Place W1	20	B2
Duke Of Wellington Place SW1	26	A1
Duke Of York Street SW1	20	C2
Duke Street Hill SE1	23	D3
Duke Street St. James's SW1	20	B3
Duke Street W1	19	E1
Duke's Mews W1	19	E1
Duke's Place EC3	23	E1
Duke's Road WC1	15	C3
Duke's Yard W1	20	A2
Duke Street		
Duncan Street N1	16	B1
Duncan Terrace N1	16	B1
Duncannon Street WC2	21	D3
Dunraven Street W1	19	E2
Dunstable Mews W1	14	A4
Dunster Court EC3	23	E2
Dunsterville Way SE1	29	D2
Duplex Ride SW1	25	E2
Durham House Street WC2	21	D3
Durweston Street W1	13	D4
Crawford Street		
Dyott Street WC1	21	D1
Dysart Street EC2	17	D4
Eagle Court EC1	16	B4
Eagle Street WC2	21	E1
Eagle Wharf Road N1	17	C1
Eamont Street NW8	13	C1
Earl Street EC2	17	D4
Earlham Street WC2	21	D2
Earlstoke Street EC1	16	B2
Spencer Street		
Earnshaw Street WC2	21	C1
Easley's Mews W1	20	A1
East Harding Street EC4	22	A1
West Smithfield		
East Poultry Avenue EC1	16	B4
East Road N1	17	D2
Eastbourne Mews W2	18	B1
Eastbourne Terrace W2	18	B1
Eastcastle Street W1	20	B1
Eastcheap EC3	23	D2
Easton Street WC1	16	A3
Eaton Gate SW1	25	E3
Eaton Mews North SW1	25	E3
Eaton Mews South SW1	25	A3
Eaton Place SW1	25	E3
Eaton Square SW1	25	E3
Eaton Terrace SW1	31	E1
Ebenezer Street N1	17	D2
Ebor Street E1	17	E3
Ebury Bridge Road SW1	32	A2
Ebury Bridge SW1	32	A2
Ebury Mews East SW1	25	A3
Ebury Mews SW1	26	A3
Ebury Square SW1	32	A1
Ebury Street SW1	31	E1
Eccleston Bridge SW1	26	A3
Eccleston Mews SW1	25	A3
Eccleston Place SW1	32	A1
Eccleston Square Mews SW1	32	B1
Eccleston Square SW1	32	A1
Eccleston Street SW1	26	A3
Eckford Street N1	16	A1
Penton Street		
Edgware Road W2	12	B4
Edinburgh Gate SW1	25	D2
Edith Grove SW10	30	A3
Edith Terrace SW10	30	A3
Edward Mews W1	19	E1
Edward Street NW1	14	A2
Egerton Crescent SW3	25	C3
Egerton Gardens Mews SW3	25	C3
Egerton Terrace		
Egerton Gardens SW3	25	C3
Egerton Place SW3	25	C3
Egerton Terrace		
Egerton Terrace SW3	25	C3
Elba Place SE17	29	C3
Elcho Street SW11	31	C4
Elder Street E1	17	E4
Eldon Road W8	24	A3
Eldon Street EC2	17	D4
Elephant And Castle SE1	28	B3
Elephant Road SE17	28	C3
Elgin Mews North W9	12	A2
Elgin Mews South W9	12	A2
Elia Street N1	16	B1
Elim Street SE1	29	D2
Elizabeth Bridge SW1	32	A1
Elizabeth Close W9	12	B3
Elizabeth Street SW1	26	A3
Elliott's Row SE11	28	B3
Ellis Street SW1	25	E3
Elm Park Gardens SW10	30	B2
Elm Park Lane SW3	30	B2
Elm Park Road SW3	30	B2
Elm Place SW7	30	B2
Elm Street WC1	15	E4
Elm Tree Close NW8	12	B2
Elm Tree Road NW8	12	B2
Elms Mews W2	18	B2
Elnathan Mews W9	12	A4
Elvaston Mews SW7	24	B3
Elvaston Place SW7	24	A3
Elverton Street SW1	26	C3
Ely Place EC1	22	A1
Elystan Place SW3	31	D1
Elystan Street SW3	31	C1
Emba Street SE16	33	B2
Embankment Gardens SW3	31	E3
Embankment Place WC2	21	D3
Emerald Street WC1	15	E4
Emerson Street SE1	22	C3
Emery Hill Street SW1	26	C3
Emery Street SE1	28	A2
Emperor's Gate SW7	24	A3
Endell Street WC2	21	D1
Endsleigh Gardens WC1	14	C3
Endsleigh Place WC1	15	C3
Endsleigh Street WC1	15	C3
Enford Street W1	13	D4
Ennismore Garden Mews SW7	25	C2
Ennismore Gardens SW7	24	C2
Ennismore Mews SW7	25	C2
Ensor Mews SW7	30	B1
Epworth Street EC2	17	D3
Errol Street EC1	17	C4

Street	Page	Grid	Street	Page	Grid	Street	Page	Grid	Street	Page	Grid
Essex Street WC2	22	A2	Folgate Street E1	17	E4	Gerridge Street SE1	28	A2	Great Chapel Street W1	20	C1
Europa Place C1	16	C3	Fore Street Avenue EC2	23	D1	Gertrude Street SW10	30	B3	Great College Street SW1	27	D2
Euston Road NW1	14	B3	Fore Street EC2	23	C1	Gilbert Place WC1	21	D1	*Seymour Street*		
Euston Square NW1	14	C2	Formosa Street W9	12	A4	Gilbert Street W1	20	A2	Great Cumberland Mews W1	19	D2
Euston Street NW1	14	B3	Forset Street W1	19	D1	Gildea Street W1	14	B4	Great Cumberland Place W1	19	D1
Evelyn Gardens SW7	30	B2	Forston Street N1	17	C1	Gillingham Street SW1	26	B3	Great Dover Street SE1	29	C2
Evelyn Walk N1	17	D1	Fortune Street EC1	17	C4	Gilston Road SW10	30	A2	Great Eastern Street EC2	17	E3
Evelyn Yard W1	20	C1	Fosbury Mews W2	18	A3	Giltspur Street EC1	22	B1	Great George Street SW1	27	D2
Gresse Street			Foster Lane EC2	22	C1	Gladstone Street SE1	28	B3	Great Guildford Street SE1	28	C1
Eversholt Street NW1	14	B1	Foubert's Place W1	20	B2	Glasgow Terrace SW1	32	B2	Great James Street WC1	15	E4
Ewer Street SE1	28	C1	Foulis Terrace SW7	30	B1	Glasshill Street SE1	28	B1	Great Marlborough Street W1	20	B2
Exeter Street WC2	21	E2	Fox And Knot Street EC1	16	B4	Glasshouse Street W1	20	B3	Great New Street EC4	22	A1
Exhibition Road SW7	24	C2	*Charterhouse Square*			Glebe Place SW3	31	D2	Great Newport Street WC2	21	D2
Exmouth Market EC1	16	A3	Frampton Strt NW8	12	B3	Gledhow Gardens SW5	30	A1	*Newport Street*		
Exton Street SE1	28	A1	Francis Street SW1	26	B3	Glendower Place SW7	30	B1	Great Ormond Street WC1	15	E4
Eyre Court NW8	12	B1	Franklin's Row SW3	31	E1	Glentworth Street NW1	13	D3	Great Percy Street WC1	15	E2
Eyre Street Hill EC1	16	A4	Frazier Street SE1	28	A2	Globe Street SE1	29	C2	Great Peter Street SW1	27	C3
			Frederick Close W2	19	D2	Gloucester Court EC3	23	E3	Great Portland Street W1	14	A4
			Frederick Street WC1	15	E2	Gloucester Gate Mews NW1	14	A1	Great Pulteney Street W1	20	C2
			Fredericks Row EC1	16	B2	*Albany Street*			Great Queen Street WC2	21	D2
			Goswell Road			Gloucester Gate NW1	14	A1	Great Russell Street WC1	21	C1
Fair Street SE1	29	E1	French Ordinary Court EC3	23	E2	Gloucester Mews W2	18	B2	Great Scotland Yard SW1	21	D3
Falcon Close SE1	22	B3	*Hart Street*			Gloucester Mews West W2	18	A2	Great Smith Street SW1	27	C2
Falkirk Street N1	17	E2	French Place E1	17	E3	Gloucester Place Mews W1	19	D1	Great St. Helen's EC3	23	E1
Falmouth Road SE1	29	C3	*Dereham Place*			Gloucester Place NW1 & W1	13	D3	Great St. Thomas Apostle EC4	23	C2
Fann Street EC1	16	C4	Friar Street EC4	22	B2	Gloucester Road SW7	24	A3	*Queen Street*		
Fanshaw Street N1	17	E2	*Carter Lane*			Gloucester Square W2	18	C2	Great Suffolk Street SE1	28	B1
Fareham Street W1	20	C1	Friday Street EC4	22	C2	Gloucester Street SW1	32	B2	Great Sutton Street EC1	16	B3
Dean Street			Friend Street EC1	16	B2	Gloucester Terrace W2	18	A1	Great Titchfield Street W1	20	B1
Farm Street W1	20	A3	Frith Street W1	21	C2	Gloucester Way EC1	16	A2	Great Titchfield Street W1	14	B4
Farnham Place SE1	28	B1	Frying Pan Alley E1	23	E1	Godfrey Street SW3	31	D1	Great Tower Street EC3	23	E2
Farringdon Lane EC1	16	A4	Fullwood's Mews N1	17	D2	Godliman Street EC4	22	B2	Great Trinity Lane EC4	23	C2
Farringdon Road EC1	16	A4	Furnival Street EC4	22	A1	Godson Street N1	16	A1	*Garlick Hill*		
Farringdon Street EC4	22	B1	Fynes Street SW1	27	C3	Golden Lane EC1	16	C3	Great Turnstile WC1	21	E1
Fawcett Street SW10	30	A3				Golden Square W1	20	B2	*High Holborn*		
Featherstone Street EC1	17	D3				Goldington Street NW1	14	C1	Great Winchester Street EC2	23	D1
Fen Court EC3	23	E2				Goldsmith Street EC2	22	C1	Great Windmill Street W1	20	C2
Fenchurch Avenue EC3	23	E2				Goodge Place W1	14	B4	Greek Street W1	21	C2
Fenchurch Buildings EC3	23	E2	Galen Place WC1	21	D1	Goodge Street W1	14	B4	Green Street W1	19	E2
Fenchurch Street			Galway Street EC1	17	C3	Goods Way NW1	15	D1	Green Walk SE1	29	D3
Fenchurch Place EC3	23	E2	Gambia Street SE1	28	B1	Gordon Square WC1	15	C3	Greenberry Street NW8	13	C1
Fenchurch Street			Ganton Street W1	20	B2	Gordon Street WC1	14	C3	Greencoat Place SW1	26	B3
Fenchurch Street EC3	23	E2	Garbutt Place W1	13	E4	Gore Street SW7	24	B2	Greencoat Row SW1	26	C3
Fendall Street SE1	29	E3	*Moxon Street*			Goring Street E1	23	E1	Greenwell Street W1	14	B4
Fenning Street SE1	29	D1	Gard Street EC1	16	B2	*Bevis Marks*			Greet Street SE1	28	A1
St Thomas Street			Garden Road NW8	12	B2	Gorsuch Place E2	17	E2	Grendon Street SW8	13	C3
Fernsbury Street WC1	16	A2	Garden Row SE1	28	B3	Gosfield Street W1	14	B4	Grenville Place SW7	24	A3
Fernshaw Road SW10	30	A3	Gardeners Lane EC4	22	C2	Goslett Yard WC2	21	C1	Grenville Street WC1	15	D3
Fetter Lane EC4	22	A1	*High Timber Street*			Goswell Road EC1	16	B2	Gresham Street EC2	22	C1
Field Street WC1	15	E2	Garlick Hill EC4	23	C2	Gough Square EC4	22	A1	Gresse Street W1	20	C1
Finch Lane EC3	23	D2	Garnault Mews EC1	16	A2	Gough Street WC1	15	E3	Greville Road NW6	12	A1
Finsbury Avenue EC2	17	D4	Garnault Place EC1	16	A3	Gower Place WC1	14	C3	Greville Street EC1	16	A4
Finsbury Circus EC2	23	D1	*Rosebery Avenue*			Gower Street WC1	14	C3	Greycoat Place SW1	26	C3
Finsbury Pavement EC2	17	D4	Garrett Street EC1	16	C3	Gracechurch Street EC3	23	D2	Greycoat Street SW1	26	C3
Finsbury Square EC2	17	D4	Garrick Street WC2	21	D2	Grafton Mews W1	14	B3	Greystoke Place EC4	22	A1
Finsbury Street EC2	17	D4	Gaspar Close SW5	24	A3	Grafton Place NW1	15	C2	*Fetter Lane*		
First Street SW3	25	D3	Gaspar Mews SW5	30	A1	Grafton Street W1	20	B3	Grigg's Place SE1	29	E3
Fish Street Hill EC3	23	D2	Gate Street WC2	21	E1	Grafton Way W1	14	B4	Groom Place SW1	26	A2
Fisher Street WC1	21	E1	Gatliff Road SW1	32	A2	Graham Street N1	16	B1	Grosvenor Crescent Mews		
Fisherton Street NW8	12	B3	Gaunt Street SE1	28	B2	Granby Terrace NW1	14	B1	SW1	25	E2
Fitzalan Street SE11	28	A3	Gayfere Street SW1	27	D3	Grand Avenue EC1	16	B4	Grosvenor Crescent SW1	25	E2
Fitzhardinge Street W1	19	E1	Gaywood Street SE1	28	B3	Grange Court WC2	21	E2	Grosvenor Gardens SW1	25	A3
Fitzmaurice Place W1	20	A3	Gee Street EC1	16	C3	Grange Road SE1	29	E3	Grosvenor Gate W1	19	E3
Fitzroy Square W1	14	B4	Gees Court W1	20	A2	Grant Street N1	16	A1	*Park Lane*		
Fitzroy Street WC1	14	B4	Geffrye Street E2	17	E1	Granville Place W1	19	E2	Grosvenor Hill W1	20	A2
Flaxman Terrace WC1	15	C3	George Court WC2	21	D3	Granville Square WC1	15	E2	Grosvenor Place SW1	26	A2
Fleet Lane EC4	22	B1	George Mews NW1	14	B3	Granville Street WC1	15	E2	Grosvenor Road SW1	32	A2
Fleet Square WC1	15	E3	George Street W1	19	D1	*Granville Square*			Grosvenor Square W1	20	A2
Fleet Street EC4	22	A2	George Yard EC3	23	D2	Grape Street WC2	21	D1	Grosvenor Street W1	20	A2
Fleur De Lis Street E1	17	E4	George Yard W1	19	E2	Gravel Lane E1	23	E1	Grove End Road NW8	12	B2
Flitcroft Street WC2	21	C1	Gerald Road SW1	31	E1	Gray Street SE1	28	A2	Grove Gardens NW8	13	C2
Flood Street SW3	31	D2	Geraldine Street SE11	28	B3	Gray's Inn Road WC1	15	D2	Grove Hall Court NW8	12	B2
Flood Walk SW3	31	D2	Gerrard Place W1	21	C2	Great Castle Street W1	20	B1	Guildhall Buildings EC2	23	C1
Floral Street WC2	21	D2	Gerrard Road N1	16	B1	Great Central Street NW1	13	D4	*Basinghall Street*		
Foley Street F1	14	B4	Gerrard Street W1	21	D2				Guildhall Yard EC2	23	C1

169

London: Street index

Street	Page	Grid	Street	Page	Grid	Street	Page	Grid	Street	Page	Grid
Guildhouse Street SW1	32	B1	Harrowby Street W1	19	D1	Holywell Row EC2	17	E4	Ivy Street N1	17	E1
Guilford Place WC1	15	E3	Hart Street EC3	23	E2	Homefield Street N1	17	E1	Ixworth Place SW3	31	C1
Guilford Street			Harwood Road NW1	13	D4	*Hoxton Street*					
Guilford Street WC1	15	D4	Hasker Street SW3	25	D3	Homer Row W1	19	D1			
Gun Street E1	17	E4	Hastings Street WC1	15	D2	Homer Street W1	13	D4			
Gunter Grove SW10	30	A3	Hatfields SE1	22	A3	Honduras Street EC1	16	C3			
Guthrie Street SW3	30	C1	Hatherley Street SW1	32	B1	*Old Street*			James Street W1	20	A2
Gutter Lane EC2	22	C1	Hatton Garden EC1	16	A4	Hop Gardens WC2	21	D2	James Street WC2	21	D2
Guy Street SE1	29	D1	Hatton Street NW8	12	B4	*St Martin's Lane*			*Long Acre*		
			Hatton Wall EC1	16	A4	Hopkins Street W1	20	C2	Jay Mews SW7	24	B2
			Haunch Of Venison Yard W1	20	A2	Hopton Street SE1	22	B3	Jermyn Street SW1	20	B3
			Brook Street			Horse Guards Avenue SW1	27	D1	Jerome Crescent NW8	13	C3
			Haverstock Street N1	16	B2	Horse Guards Road SW1	27	C1	Jerrold Street N1	17	E2
Haberdasher Street N1	17	D2	Hay Hill W1	20	B3	Horse Ride SW1	26	A1	*Falkirk Street*		
Hackney Road E2	17	E2	Hay's Lane SE1	23	D3	Horseferry Road SW1	26	C3	Jerusalem Passage EC1	16	B3
Half Moon Court EC1	16	C4	Hay's Mews W1	20	A3	Hortensia Road SW10	30	A3	Jewry Street EC3	23	E2
Bartholomew Close			Hayes Place NW1	13	D4	Hosier Lane EC1	22	B1	Joan Street SE1	28	B1
Half Moon Street W1	26	A1	Hayles Street SE11	28	B3	Houghton Street WC2	21	E2	Jockey's Fields WC1	15	E4
Halkin Place SW1	25	E2	Haymarket SW1	21	C3	*Aldwych*			John Adams Street WC2	21	D3
Halkin Street SW1	25	E2	Hayne Street EC1	16	B4	Houndsditch EC3	23	E1	John Aird Court W2	12	B4
Hall Gate NW8	12	B2	Hayward's Place EC1	16	B3	Howard Place SW1	26	B3	John Carpenter Street EC4	22	A2
Hall Place W2	12	B4	Hazel Way SE1	29	E3	*Carlisle Street*			John Princes Street W1	20	B1
Hall Road NW8	12	B2	Headfort Place SW1	26	A1	Howick Place SW1	26	B3	John Street WC1	15	E4
Hall Street EC1	16	B2	Hearn Street EC2	17	E4	Howie Street SW11	31	C4	John's Mews WC1	15	E4
Hallam Mews W1	14	A4	Heathcote Street WC1	15	E3	Howland Street W1	14	B4	Johnson's Place SW1	32	B2
Hallam Street W1	14	A4	Heddon Street W1	20	B2	Howley Place W2	12	B4	Joiner Street SE1	29	D1
Halsey Street SW3	25	D3	Helmet Row EC1	16	C3	Hoxton Market N18	17	D2	Jubilee Place SW3	31	D1
Hamilton Close NW8	12	B3	Henderson Drive NW8	12	B3	Hoxton Square N1	17	E2	Jubilee Terrace N1	17	D1
Hamilton Gardens NW8	12	B2	Heneage Place EC3	23	E1	Hoxton Street N1	17	E2	Judd Street WC1	15	D2
Hamilton Place W1	26	A1	Henniker Mews SW3	30	B2	Hudson's Place SW1	26	B3	Juer Street SW11	31	D4
Hamilton Square SE1	29	D1	Henrietta Place W1	20	A1	Huggin Hill EC4	22	C2	Junction Mews W2	19	C1
Hamilton Terrace NW8	12	A2	Henrietta Street WC2	21	D2	*Upper Thames Street*			Juxon Street SE11	27	E3
Hampden Close NW1	15	C1	Henshaw Street SE17	29	D3	Hugh Street SW1	32	A1			
Hampstead Road NW1	14	B3	Herbal Hill EC1	16	A4	Hull Street EC1	16	C2			
Handel Street WC1	15	D3	Herbert Crescent SW1	25	D2	Hunt's Court WC2	21	C3			
Hanover Gate NW1	13	D2	Herbrand Street WC1	15	D3	Hunter Close SE1	29	D3			
Hanover Place WC2	21	C2	Hercules Road SE1	27	E3	*Priores Street*			Kean Street WC2	21	E2
Long Acre			Hereford Square SW7	30	B1	Hunter Street WC1	15	D3	Keeley Street WC2	21	E1
Hanover Square W1	20	B2	Hermit Street EC1	16	B2	Huntley Street WC1	14	C4	Kelso Place W8	24	A3
Hanover Street W1	20	B2	Hermitage Street W2	18	B1	Huntsworth Mews NW1	13	D3	Kemble Street WC2	21	D2
Hanover Terrace Mews NW1	13	D3	Hertford Street W1	26	A1	Hutton Street EC4	22	A2	Kemp's Court W1	20	C2
Hanover Terrace NW1	13	D2	Hester Road SW11	31	C4	Hyde Park Corner W1	26	A1	Kendal Street W2	19	C2
Hans Crescent SW1	25	D2	Hewett Street EC2	17	E3	Hyde Park Crescent W2	19	C2	Kendall Place W1	19	E1
Hans Place SW1	25	D3	Hide Place SW1	32	C1	Hyde Park Gardens Mews W2	18	C2	Kenrick Place W1	13	E4
Hans Road SW3	25	D2	High Holborn WC1	21	E1	Hyde Park Gardens W2	18	C2	Kensington Court Place W8	24	A3
Hans Street SW1	25	D3	High Timber Street EC4	22	C2	Hyde Park Gate SW7	24	A2	Kensington Court W8	24	A2
Hanson Street W1	14	B4	Hill Road W9	12	B2	Hyde Park Square W2	19	C2	Kensington Gate W8	24	A2
Hanway Place W1	21	C1	Hill Street W1	20	A3	Hyde Park Street W2	19	C2	Kensington Gore SW7	24	B2
Hanway Street W1	20	C1	Hills Place W1	20	B1				Kensington Road W8 & SW7	24	A2
Harbert Road W2	18	C1	Hillside Close NW8	12	A1				Kent Passage NW1	13	D3
Harcourt Street W1	13	D4	Hind Court EC4	22	A1				Kent Terrace NW1	13	D3
Harcourt Terrace SW10	30	A2	Hinde Street W1	19	E1				Kenton Street WC1	15	D3
Hardwick Street EC1	16	A2	Hobart Place SW1	26	A2	Idol Lane EC3	23	E2	Keppel Row SE1	28	C1
Hardwidge Street SE1	29	E1	Hobury Street SW10	30	B3	Ifield Road SW10	30	A3	Keppel Street WC1	15	C4
Hare Walk N1	17	E1	Hogarth Court EC3	23	E2	India Street EC3	23	E2	Keystone Crescent N1	15	D1
Harewood Avenue NW1	13	D4	*Fenchurch Street*			Ingestre Place W1	20	C2	Keyworth Street SE1	28	B2
Harewood Place W1	20	A2	Hogsden Close N1	17	C1	Inglebert Street EC1	16	A2	Killick Street N1	15	E1
Harley Gardens SW10	30	B2	Holbein Mews SW1	31	E1	Ingram Close SE11	27	E3	King Charles Street SW1	27	D1
Harley Place W1	20	A1	Holbein Place SW1	31	E1	Inigo Place WC2	21	D2	King Edward Street EC1	22	B1
Harley Street W1	14	A4	Holborn Circus EC1	22	A1	*Bedford Street*			King Edward Walk SE1	28	A2
Harp Alley EC4	22	B1	Holborn EC1	22	A1	Inner Circle NW1	13	D2	King James Street SE1	28	B2
Farringdon Street			Holborn Viaduct EC1	22	B1	Inner Temple Lane EC4	22	A2	King John Court EC2	17	E3
Harp Lane EC3	23	E3	Holford Place WC1	15	E2	Insurance Street WC1	16	A2	King Square EC1	16	B2
Cross Lane			Holford Street WC1	16	A2	Inverness Mews W2	18	A2	King Street EC2	23	C1
Harper Road SE1	29	C2	Holland Street SE1	22	B3	Inverness Place W2	18	A2	King Street SW1	20	B3
Harpur Street WC1	15	E4	Hollen Street W1	20	C1	Inverness Terrace W2	18	A2	King Street WC2	21	D2
Harriet Street SW1	25	D2	*Wardour Street*			Ireland Yard EC4	22	B2	King William Street EC4	23	D2
Harriet Walk SW1	25	D2	Holles Street W1	20	A1	*St Andrew's Hill*			King's Bench Walk EC4	22	A2
Harrington Gardens SW7	30	A1	Holly Mews SW10	30	B2	Ironmonger Lane EC2	23	C1	King's Cross Road WC1	15	E2
Harrington Road SW7	30	B1	*Drayton Gardens*			Ironmonger Row EC1	16	C3	King's Mews WC1	15	E4
Harrington Square NW1	14	B1	Hollywood Mews SW10	30	A2	Irving Street WC2	21	C3	King's Road SW3,SW6'SW10	30	A3
Harrington Street NW1	14	B2	Hollywood Road SW10	30	A2	Isabella Street SE1	28	B1	Kinghorn Street EC1	16	B3
Harrison Street WC1	15	D2	Holmead Road SW6	30	A4	Islington High Street N1	16	A1	*Cloth Fair*		
Harrow Place E1	23	E1	Holyrood Street SE1	29	E1	Ives Street SW3	31	C1	Kingly Street W1	20	B2
Harrow Road Bridge W2	12	B4	Holywell Lane EC2	17	E3	Ivor Place NW1	13	D3	Kings Arms Yard EC2	23	D1

London: Street index

Street	Page	Grid
Kings Bench Street SE1	28	B1
Kingscote Street EC4	22	B2
Kingsland Road E2?E8	17	E2
Kingsmill Terrace NW8	12	C1
Kingsway WC2	21	E1
Kinnerton Street SW1	25	E2
Kipling Street SE1	29	C1
Kirby Grove SE1	29	D1
Kirby Street EC1	16	A4
Kirtling Street SW8	32	B3
Knightrider Street EC4	22	B2
Knightsbridge Green SW1	25	D2
Lamb's Passage		
Knightsbridge SW1 & SW7	25	C2
Knox Street W1	13	D4
Kynance Mews SW7	24	A3
Kynance Place SW7	24	A3
Lackington Street EC2	17	D4
Lamb Street E1	17	E4
Lamb Walk SE1	29	E2
Lamb's Buildings EC1	17	C4
Lamb's Conduit Street WC1	15	E4
Lamb's Passage EC1	17	C4
Lambeth Bridge SW1 & SE11	27	D3
Lambeth Hill EC4	22	C2
Lambeth Palace Road SE1	27	E3
Lambeth Road SE1	27	E3
Lamlash Street SE11	28	B3
Lamont Road SW10	30	B3
Lanark Place W9	12	B3
Lanark Road W9	12	A2
Lancaster Gate W2	18	B2
Lancaster Mews W2	18	B2
Lancaster Place WC2	21	E2
Lancaster Street SE1	28	B2
Lancaster Terrace W2	18	B2
Lancaster Walk W2	18	B3
Lancelot Place SW7	25	D2
Langford Close NW8	12	B1
Langford Place NW8	12	B1
Langham Place W1	20	A1
Langham Street W1	20	B1
Langley Street WC2	21	D2
Langton Close WC1	15	E3
Langton Street SW10	30	B3
Lansdowne Row W1	20	A3
Lansdowne Terrace WC1	15	D3
Lant Street SE1	28	C2
Launcelot Street SE1	28	A2
Lower Marsh		
Launceston Place W8	24	A2
Laurence Pountney Hill EC4	23	D2
Canon Street		
Laurence Pountney Lane EC4	23	D2
Lavender Close SW3	30	C3
Laverton Place SW5	30	A1
Lavington Street SE1	28	B1
Lavinia Grove N1	15	E1
Wharfdale Road		
Law Street SE1	29	D2
Lawrence Lane EC2	23	C1
Trump Street		
Lawrence Street SW3	31	C3
Laxton Place NW1	14	B3
Laystall Street EC1	16	A4
Leadenhall Place EC3	23	E2
Leadenhall Street EC3	23	E2
Leake Street SE1	27	E1
Leather Lane EC1	16	A4
Leathermarket Street SE1	29	D2
Lecky Terrace SW1	30	B2
Leeke Street WC1	15	E2
Lees Place W1	19	E2
Leicester Court WC2	21	C2
Cranbourn Street		
Leicester Place WC2	21	C2
Lisle Street		
Leicester Square WC2	21	C3
Leicester Street WC2	21	C2
Leigh Hunt Street SE1	28	C1
Leigh Street WC1	15	D3
Leinster Gardens W2	18	A2
Leinster Mews W2	18	A2
Leinster Place W2	18	A2
Leinster Terrace W2	18	A2
Lennox Gardens Mews SW1	25	D3
Lennox Gardens SW1	25	D3
Leonard Street EC2	17	D3
Leroy Street SE1	29	E3
Lever Street EC1	16	B3
Leverett Street SW3	31	D1
Mossop Street		
Lewisham Street SW1	27	C2
Lexington Street W1	20	C2
Leyden Street E1	23	E1
Library Street SE1	28	B2
Lidlington Place NW1	14	B1
Ligonier Street E2	17	E3
Lilestone Street NW8	13	C3
Lime Street EC3	23	E2
Limerston Street SW10	30	B3
Lincoln Street SW3	31	D1
Lincoln's Inn Fields WC2	21	E1
Lindsey Street EC1	16	B4
Linhope Street NW1	13	D3
Lisle Street W1	21	C2
Lisson Grove NW1 & NW8	12	C3
Lisson Street NW1	13	C4
Litchfield Street WC2	21	D2
Little Albany Street NW1	14	A2
Little Argyll Street W1	20	B2
Regent Street		
Little Britain EC1	22	B1
Little Chester Street SW1	26	A2
Little College Street SW1	27	D3
Little Dorrit Close SE1	29	C1
Little George Street SW1	27	D2
Great George Street		
Little Marlborough Street W1	20	B2
Kingly Street		
Little New Street EC4	22	A1
New Street Square		
Little Newport Street WC2	21	C2
Little Portland Street W1	20	B1
Little Russell Street WC1	21	D1
Little Sanctuary SW1	27	D2
Broad Sanctuary		
Little Smith Street SW1	27	D3
Little St. James's Street SW1	26	B1
Little Titchfield Street W1	20	B1
Little Trinity Lane EC4	23	C2
Liverpool Road N1 & N7	16	A1
Liverpool Street EC2	23	E1
Livonia Street W2	20	C2
Lizard Street EC1	17	C3
Lloyd Baker Street WC1	16	A2
Lloyd Square WC1	16	A2
Lloyd's Avenue EC3	23	E2
Lloyd's Row EC1	16	B2
Lodge Road NW8	12	C3
Lollard Street SE11	27	E3
Loman Street SE1	28	B1
Lombard Lane EC4	22	A2
Temple Lane		
Lombard Street EC3	23	D2
London Bridge EC4 & SE1	23	D3
London Bridge Street SE1	29	D1
London Road SE1	28	B2
London Street EC3	23	E2
London Street W2	18	B1
London Wall EC2	22	C1
Long Acre WC2	21	D2
Long Lane EC1	16	B4
Long Lane SE1	29	D2
Long Street E2	17	E2
Long Walk SE1	29	E2
Long Yard WC1	15	E4
Longford Street NW1	14	A3
Longmoore Street SW1	32	B1
Longville Road SE11	28	B3
Lord North Street SW1	27	D3
Lordship Place SW3	31	C3
Lawrence Street		
Lorenzo Street WC1	15	E2
Lothbury EC2	23	D1
Lots Road SW10	30	A4
Loudoun Road NW8	12	B1
Lovat Lane EC3	23	D2
Love Lane EC2	23	C1
Lovers' Walk W1	19	E3
Lower Belgrave Street SW1	25	A3
Lower Grosvenor Place SW1	26	A2
Lower James Street W1	20	B2
Lower John Street W1	20	B2
Lower Marsh SE1	28	A2
Lower Sloane Street SW1	31	E1
Lower Thames Street EC3	23	D3
Lowndes Place SW1	25	E3
Lowndes Square SW1	25	E2
Lowndes Street SW1	25	E2
Loxham Street WC1	16	D2
Cromer Street		
Lucan Place SW3	31	C1
Ludgate Broadway EC4	22	B2
Pilgrim Street		
Ludgate Circus EC4	22	B2
Ludgate Court EC4	22	B2
Ludgate Hill		
Ludgate Hill EC4	22	B2
Ludlow Street EC1	16	C3
Gee Street		
Luke Street EC2	17	E3
Lumley Street W1	19	E2
Brown Hart Garden		
Lupus Street SW1	32	A2
Luton Street NW8	12	C3
Luxborough Street W1	13	E4
Lyall Street SW1	25	E3
Lygon Place SW1	25	A3
Lyons Place NW8	12	B3
Mabledon Place WC1	15	D2
Macclesfield Road EC1	16	C2
Mackennal Street NW8	13	C1
Macklin Street WC2	21	D1
Mackworth Street NW1	14	B2
Maddox Street SW1	20	B2
Magdalen Street SE1	29	E1
Maida Avenue W2	12	B4
Maiden Lane WC2	21	D2
Makins Street SW3	31	D1
Malet Street WC1	15	C4
Mallord Street SW3	30	B2
Mallory Street NW8	13	C3
Mallow Street EC1	17	D3
Malta Street EC1	16	B3
Maltravers Street WC2	21	E2
Manchester Square W1	19	E1
Manchester Street W1	19	E1
Manciple Street SE1	29	D2
Mandeville Place W1	19	E1
Manette Street W1	21	C1
Manningford Close EC1	16	B2
Manresa Road SW3	30	C2
Mansfield Mews W1	20	A1
Mansfield Street		
Mansfield Street W1	20	A1
Mansion House Place EC4	23	D2
St Swithun's Lane		
Manson Mews SW7	30	B1
Manson Place SW7	30	B1
Maple Street W1	14	B4
Marble Arch W1	19	D2
Marchmont Street WC1	15	D3
Margaret Court W1	20	B1
Margaret Street		
Margaret Street W1	20	B1
Margaretta Terrace SW3	31	C2
Margery Street WC1	16	A3
Mark Lane EC3	23	E2
Market Court W1	20	B1
Oxford Street		
Market Entrance SW8	32	B4
Market Mews W1	26	A1
Market Place W1	20	B1
Markham Square SW3	31	D1
Markham Street SW3	31	D1
Marlborough Place NW8	12	A1
Marlborough Road SW1	26	B1
Marlborough Street SW3	31	C1
Marshall Street W1	20	B2
Marshalsea Road SE1	28	C1
Marsham Street SW1	27	C3
Martin Lane EC4	23	D2
Martin's Street WC2	21	D2
Martlett Court WC2	21	C2
Bow Street		
Marylebone High Street W1	13	E4
Marylebone Lane W1	19	E1
Marylebone Mews W1	20	A1
Marylebone Road NW1	13	D4
Marylebone Street W1	13	E4
Mason's Place EC1	16	B2
Mason's Yard SW1	20	B3
Duke Street St James's		
Matthew Parker Street SW1	27	C2
Maunsel Street SW1	27	C3
May's Court WC2	21	D3
St Martin's Lane		
Mayfair Place W1	20	B3
McAuley Close SE1	28	A2
McCleod's Mews SW7	24	A3
Mead Row SE1	28	A2
Meadow Row SE1	28	C3
Meard Street W1	20	C2
Mecklenburgh Place WC1	15	E3
Mecklenburgh Street WC1	15	E3
Mecklenburgh Street WC1	15	E3
Mecklenburgh Square		
Medburn Street NW1	14	C1
Medway Street SW1	27	C3
Melbourne Place WC2	21	E2
Aldwych		
Melbury Terrace NW1	13	D4
Melcombe Place NW1	13	D4
Melcombe Street NW1	13	D4
Melina Place NW8	12	B2
Melior Place SE1	29	D1
Snowfields		
Melior Street SE1	29	D1
Melton Street NW1	14	C3
Memel Court EC1	16	C3
Baltic Street		

171

London: Street index

Street	Page	Grid
Mepham Street SE1	27	E1
Mercer Street WC2	21	D2
Meredith Street EC1	16	B3
Merlin Street WC1	16	A2
Mermaid Court SE1	29	D1
Mermaid Row SE1	29	D1
Merrick Square SE1	29	C2
Meymott Street SE1	28	B1
Micawber Street N1	17	C2
Middle Street EC1	16	C4
Middle Temple Lane EC4	22	A2
Middle Yard SE1	23	D3
Middlesex Street E1	23	E1
Midford Place W1	14	B2
Tottenham Court Road		
Midhope Street WC1	15	D2
Midland Road NW1	15	D2
Milborne Grove SW10	30	B2
Milcote Street SE1	28	B2
Milford Lane WC2	22	A2
Milk Street EC2	23	C1
Mill Street W1	20	E2
Millman Street WC1	15	E4
Milman's Street SW10	30	B3
Milner Street SW3	25	D3
Milton Court EC2	17	D4
Milton Street EC2	17	C4
Mincing Lane EC3	23	E2
Minera Mews SW1	25	E3
Mint Street SE1	28	C1
Mintern Street N1	17	D1
Mitchell Street EC1	16	C3
Mitre Road SE1	28	A1
Mitre Street EC3	23	E2
Molyneux Street W1	19	D1
Monck Street SW1	27	C3
Moncorvo Close SW7	24	C2
Monkton Street SE11	28	A3
Monkwell Square EC2	23	C1
Monmouth Street WC2	21	D2
Montagu Mansions W1	13	E4
Montagu Mews North W1	13	D4
Montagu Mews South W1	19	D1
Montagu Mews West W1	19	D1
Montagu Place W1	19	D1
Montagu Row W1	13	E4
Montagu Square W1	19	D1
Montagu Street W1	19	D1
Montague Close SE1	23	D3
Montague Place WC1	15	C3
Montague Street WC1	15	D4
Montpelier Mews SW7	25	D2
Montpelier Place SW7	25	D2
Montpelier Square SW7	25	D2
Montpelier Street SW7	25	E2
Montpelier Walk SW7	25	C2
Montreal Place WC2	21	E2
Montrose Court SW7	25	D2
Montrose Place SW1	25	E2
Monument Street EC3	23	D2
Moor Lane EC2	17	D4
Moor Street W1	21	C2
Moore Street SW3	25	D3
Old Compton Street		
Moorfields EC2	17	D4
Moorgate EC2	23	D1
Mora Street EC1	17	C2
Moravian Place SW10	30	B3
Moreland Street EC1	16	B2
Moreton Place SW1	32	B1
Moreton Street SW1	32	C1
Moreton Terrace SW1	32	B1
Morgan's Lane SE1	29	E1
Morley Street SE1	28	A2
Mornington Crescent NW1	14	B1
Mornington Place NW1	14	B1
Mornington Street NW1	14	A1
Mornington Terrace NW1	14	B1
Morocco Street SE1	29	E2
Morpeth Terrace SW1	26	B3
Mortimer Market WC1	14	B4
Capper Street		
Mortimer Street W1	15	E4
Morwell Street WC1	21	C1
Mossop Street SW3	31	D1
Motcomb Street SW1	25	E2
Mount Pleasant WC1	16	A3
Mount Row W1	20	A3
Mount Street W1	19	E3
Moxon Street W1	13	E4
Mulberry Walk SW3	30	B2
Mulready Street NW8	13	C3
Mulvaney Way SE1	29	D2
Mumford Court EC2	23	C1
Milk Street		
Mundy Street N1	17	E2
Munro Terrace SW10	30	B3
Munster Square NW1	14	A3
Munton Road SE17	29	C3
Murphy Street SE1	28	A2
Murray Grove N1	17	C2
Muscovy Street EC3	23	E2
Museum Street WC1	21	D1
Myddelton Passage EC1	16	A2
Myddelton Square EC1	16	A2
Myddelton Street EC1	16	A2
Mylne Street EC1	16	A2
Myrtle Walk N1	17	E2
Napier Grove N1	17	C1
Nash Street NW1	14	A2
Nassau Street W1	20	B1
Navarre Street E2	17	E3
Nazrul Street N2	17	E2
Neal Street WC2	21	D2
Neathouse Place SW1	26	B3
Wilton Road		
Nebraska Street SE1	29	C2
Nelson Passage EC1	17	C2
Mora Street		
Nelson Place N1	16	B2
Nelson Square SE1	28	B1
Nelson Terrace N1	16	B2
Netherton Grove SW10	30	A3
Netley Street NW1	14	B2
Neville Street SW7	30	B1
Neville Terrace SW7	30	B1
New Bond Street W1	20	A2
New Bridge Street EC4	22	B2
New Broad Street EC2	23	D1
New Burlington Mews W1	20	B2
Hart Street		
New Burlington Place W1	20	B2
New Burlington Street W1	20	B2
New Cavendish Street W1	20	A1
New Change EC4	22	C2
New Compton Street WC2	21	D1
New Fetter Lane EC4	22	A1
New Inn Street EC2	17	E3
New Inn Yard EC2	17	E3
New Kent Road SE1	29	D3
New London Street EC3	23	E2
New North Place EC2	17	E3
New North Road N1	17	D1
New North Street WC1	15	E4
New Oxford Street WC1	21	C1
New Quebec Street W1	19	E1
New Ride SW7	24	C2
New Row WC2	21	D2
New Square WC2	21	E1
New Street EC2	23	E1
New Street Square EC4	22	A1
New Turnstile WC1	21	E1
New Wharf Road N1	15	D1
Wharfdale Road		
Newburgh Street W1	20	B2
Newbury Street EC1	16	B4
Newcastle Place W2	12	C4
Newcomen Street SE1	29	D1
Newcourt Street NW8	13	C1
Newgate Street EC1	22	B1
Newington Causeway SE1	28	B3
Newman Street W1	20	C1
Newman's Row WC2	21	E1
Lincoln's Inn Fields		
Newnham Terrace SE1	28	A2
Newnhams Row SE1	29	E2
Newport Place WC2	21	C2
Newton Street WC2	21	D1
Nicholson Street SE1	28	B1
Nile Street N1	17	D2
Nine Elms Lane SW8	32	B3
Noble Street EC2	22	C1
Noel Road N1	16	B1
Noel Street W1	20	B1
Norfolk Crescent W2	19	C1
Norfolk Place W2	18	C1
Norfolk Square W2	18	B1
Norman Street EC1	16	C3
Norman's Buildings EC1	16	C3
Norris Street SW1	20	C3
North Audley Street W1	19	E2
North Bank NW8	13	C2
North Carriage Drive (The Ring) W2	19	C2
North Crescent WC1	14	C4
North Gower Street NW1	14	B3
North Mews WC1	15	E4
North Ride W2	19	C2
North Row W1	19	E2
North Terrace SW3	25	C3
North Wharf Road W2	18	B1
Northampton Road EC1	16	A3
Northampton Row EC1	16	A3
Exmouth Market		
Northampton Square EC1	16	B3
Northburgh Street EC1	16	B3
Northdown Street N1	15	E1
Northington Street WC1	15	E4
Northumberland Alley EC3	23	E2
Northumberland Avenue WC2	21	D3
Northumberland Street WC2	21	D3
Northwick Close NW8	12	B3
Northwick Terrace NW8	12	B3
Norton Folgate E1	17	E4
Norwich Street EC4	22	A1
Nottingham Place W1	13	E4
Nottingham Street W1	13	E4
Nugent Terrace NW8	12	A2
Nutford Place W1	19	D1
O'meara Street SE1	29	C1
Oak Tree Road NW8	12	C2
Oakfield Street SW10	30	A2
Oakley Crescent EC1	16	B2
Oakley Gardens SW3	31	D2
Oakley Square NW1	14	B1
Oakley Street SW3	31	C2
Oat Lane EC2	23	C1
Ogle Street W1	14	B4
Old Bailey EC4	22	B1
Old Bond Street W1	20	B3
Old Broad Street EC2	23	D1
Old Burlington Street W1	20	B3
Old Cavendish Street W1	20	A1
Old Church Street SW3	30	B2
Old Compton Street W1	21	C2
Old Gloucester Street WC1	15	D4
Old Jewry EC2	23	D1
Old Marylebone Road NW1	19	C1
Old Mitre Court EC4	22	A2
Fleet Street		
Old Nichol Street E2	17	E3
Old North Street WC1	15	E4
Theobalds Road		
Old Palace Yard SW1	27	D2
Old Paradise Street SE11	27	E3
Old Park Lane W1	26	A1
Old Pye Street SW1	27	C3
Old Quebec Street W1	19	E2
Old Queen Street SW1	27	C2
Old Seacoal Lane EC4	22	B1
Old Square WC2	22	A1
Old Street EC1	17	D3
Oldbury Place W1	13	E4
Olivers Yard EC1	17	D3
Onslow Gardens SW7	30	B1
Onslow Mews SW7	30	B1
Onslow Square SW7	30	C1
Onslow Street EC1	16	A4
Saffron Street		
Ontario Street SE1	28	B3
Orange Street WC2	21	C3
Orchard Street W1	19	E2
Orchardson Street NW8	12	B3
Orde Hall Street WC1	15	E4
Ordnance Mews NW8	12	C1
St Ann's Terrace		
Ormond Yard SW1	20	B3
Ormonde Gate SW3	31	D2
Ormsby Street E2	17	E1
Orsett Terrace W2	18	A1
Osbert Street SW1	32	C1
Osnaburgh Street NW1	14	A3
Osnaburgh Terrace NW1	14	A3
Albany Street		
Ossington Buildings W1	13	E4
Moxon Street		
Ossulston Street NW1	15	C2
Osten Mews SW7	24	A3
Oswin Street SE11	28	B3
Outer Circle NW1	13	D1
Ovington Gardens SW3	25	D3
Ovington Square SW3	25	D3
Ovington Street SW3	25	D3
Owen Street EC1	16	A2
Oxendon Street SW1	21	C3
Coventry Street		
Oxford Square W2	19	C1
Oxford Street W1	19	E2
Paddington Green W2	12	B4
Paddington Street W1	13	E4
Page Street SW1	27	D3
Page's Walk SE1	29	E3
Paget Street EC1	16	B2
Pakenham Street WC1	15	E3
Palace Avenue W8	24	A1
Palace Gate W8	24	A2

London: Street index

Street	Page	Grid	Street	Page	Grid	Street	Page	Grid	Street	Page	Grid
Palace Place SW1	26	B2	Carter Lane			Prestwood Street N1	17	C1	Radstock Street SW11	31	C4
Palace Street SW1	26	B2	Petersham Lane SW7	24	A3	Wenlock Road			Railway Approach SE1	23	D3
Pall Mall East SW1	21	C3	Petersham Mews SW7	24	A3	Price's Street SE1	22	B3	Railway Street N1	15	C1
Pall Mall SW1	20	C3	Petersham Place SW7	24	A3	Prideaux Place WC1	15	E2	Rainsford Street W2	18	C1
Palmer Street SW1	26	C2	Peto Place NW1	14	A2	Primrose Hill EC4	22	A2	Ralston Street SW3	31	D2
Palmerston Way SW8	32	B4	Petty France SW1	26	C2	Hutton Street			Ramillies Place W1	20	B2
Bradmead			Petyward SW3	31	D1	Princeton Street EC2	17	E4	Ramillies Street W1	20	B1
Pancras Lane EC4	23	C2	Phene Street SW3	31	C3	Prince Albert Road NW1 &			Randolph Crescent W9	12	A3
Pancras Road NW1	15	C1	Philpot Lane EC3	23	D2	NW1	13	C2	Randolph Mews W9	12	B4
Panton Street SW1	21	C3	Phipp Street EC2	17	E3	Prince Consort Road SW7	24	B2	Randolph Road W9	12	A4
Paradise Walk SW3	31	D2	Charing Cross Road			Prince Of Wales Drive SW8 &			Ranelagh Bridge W2	18	A1
Paragon Mews SE1	29	C3	Phoenix Place WC1	15	E3	SW11	32	A4	Ranelagh Grove SW1	32	A1
Searles Road			Phoenix Road NW1	14	C2	Prince Of Wales Terrace W8	24	A2	Ranelagh Road SW1	32	B2
Pardon Street EC1	16	B3	Phoenix Street WC2	21	C2	Kensington Road			Ranston Street NW1	13	C4
Darlington Street			Piccadilly W1	26	A1	Prince's Gardens SW7	24	C2	Raphael Street SW7	25	D2
Pardoner Street SE1	29	D2	Pickard Street EC1	16	B2	Prince's Gate Mews SW7	24	C2	Ratcliff Grove EC1	17	C2
Paris Garden SE1	22	B3	Pickwick Street SE1	28	C2	Prince's Gate SW7	24	C2	Rathbone Street W1	20	C1
Park Crescent Mews East W1	14	A4	Picton Place W1	19	E1	Princes Street EC2	23	D1	Rathbone Street W1	20	C1
Park Crescent Mews West W1	14	A4	Pilgrim Street EC4	22	B2	Princes Street W1	20	B2	Ravey Street EC2	17	E3
Park Crescent W1	14	A4	Pilgrimage Street SE1	29	D2	Princess Street SE1	28	B3	Rawlings Street SW3	31	D1
Park Lane W1	19	E2	Pimlico Road SW1	31	E1	Princeton Street WC1	15	E4	Rawstone Place EC1	16	B3
Park Place SW1	20	B3	Pindar Street EC2	17	E4	Printer Street EC4	22	A1	Rawstorne Street		
Park Place Villas W2	12	B4	Pindock Mews W9	12	A3	Prioress Street SE1	29	D3	Rawstorne Street EC1	16	B2
Park Road NW1?NW8	13	D3	Pine Street EC1	16	A3	Priory Walk SW10	30	B2	Ray Street EC1	16	A3
Park Square East NW1	14	A3	Pitfield Street N1	17	D2	Procter Street WC1	21	E1	Red Lion Square WC1	15	E4
Park Square Mews W1	14	A3	Pitt's Head Mews W1	26	A1	Providence Court W1	19	E2	Red Lion Street WC1	15	E4
Harley Street			Platina Street EC2	17	D3	Province Street N1	16	C1	Red Place W1	19	E2
Park Square West NW1	14	A3	Platt Street NW1	14	C1	Provost Street N1	17	D2	Redburn Street SW3	31	D2
Park Street SE1	22	C3	Playhouse Yard EC4	22	B2	Pudding Lane EC3	23	D2	Redchurch Street E2	17	E3
Park Street W1	19	E2	Pleydell Street EC4	22	A2	Puddle Dock EC4	22	B2	Redcliffe Mews SW10	30	A2
Park Village East NW1	14	A1	Bouverie Street			Purbrook Street SE1	29	E2	Redcliffe Place SW10	30	A3
Park Village West NW1	14	A1	Plough Place EC4	22	A1	Purcell Street N1	17	E1	Redcliffe Road SW10	30	A2
Park Walk SW10	30	B3	Fetter Lane			Purchese Street NW1	15	C1	Redcliffe Square SW10	30	A2
Park West Place W2	19	C1	Plough Yard EC2	17	E4				Redcliffe Street SW10	30	A2
Parker Street WC2	21	D1	Plumtree Court EC4	22	A1				Redcross Way SE1	29	C1
Parkfield Street N1	16	A1	Plymton Place NW8	13	C3				Redesdale Street SW3	31	D2
Liverpool Road			Plympton Street			Quebec Mews W1	19	D1	Redhill Street NW1	14	A2
Parkgate Road SW11	31	C4	Plymton Street NW8	13	C3	Queen Anne Mews W1	20	A1	Reece Mews SW7	30	B1
Parliament Square SW1	27	D2	Pocock Street SE1	28	B1	Chandos Street			Reeves Mews W1	19	E3
Parliament Street SW1	27	D1	Poland Street W1	20	B2	Queen Anne Street W1	20	A1	Regan Way N1	17	E1
Passmore Street SW1	31	E1	Pollitt Drive NW8	12	B3	Queen Anne's Gate SW1	26	C2	Regency Street SW1	27	C3
Pastor Street SE1	28	B3	Polygon Road NW1	14	C2	Queen Square WC1	15	D4	Regent Street SW1	15	D3
Paternoster Row EC4	23	C1	Pond Place SW3	30	C1	Queen Street EC4	23	C2	Regent Street W1 & SW1	20	B1
Paternoster Square EC4	22	B1	Pont Street Mews SW1	25	D3	Queen Street Place EC4	23	C2	Regnart Buildings W1	14	B2
Paul Street EC2	17	D3	Pont Street SW1	25	D3	Queen Street W1	20	A3	Euston Street		
Paultons Square SW3	30	C3	Pope Street SE1	29	E2	Queen Victoria Street EC4	22	B2	Relton Mews SW7	25	D2
Paveley Drive SW11	30	C4	Poplar Place W2	18	A2	Queen's Circus SW8	32	A4	Remington Street N1	16	B2
Paveley Street NW8	13	C3	Poppins Court EC4	22	B1	Queen's Gardens SW1	26	B2	Remnant Street WC2	21	E1
Pavilion Road SW1	25	D2	Fleet Street			Queen's Gardens W2	18	A2	Kingsway		
Pavilion Street SW1	25	D3	Porchester Gardens W2	18	A2	Queen's Gate Gardens SW7	24	A3	Rempstone Mews N1	17	D1
Peabody Avenue SW1	32	A2	Porchester Place W2	19	C1	Queen's Gate Mews SW7	24	B2	Jubilee Terrace		
Pear Tree Court EC1	16	A3	Porchester Road W2	18	A1	Queen's Gate Place Mews			Rennie Street SE1	22	B3
Pear Tree Street EC1	16	B3	Porchester Square W2	18	A1	SW7	24	B3	Rephidim Street SE1	29	D3
Pearman Street SE1	28	A2	Porchester Terrace W2	18	A1	Queen's Gate Place SW7	24	B3	Reston Place SW7	24	A2
Pearson Street E2	17	E1	Porchester Terrace N W2	18	A2	Queen's Gate SW7	24	B2	Retford Street N1	17	E2
Peerless Street EC1	17	D2	Porlock Street SE1	29	D1	Queen's Gate Terrace SW7	24	B2	Rewell Street SW6	30	A4
Pelham Crescent SW7	30	C1	Porter Street W1	13	E4	Queen's Walk SW1	26	B1	Rex Place W1	19	E3
Pelham Place SW1	30	C1	Porteus Road W2	12	B4	Queenhithe EC4	23	C2	Richard's Place SW3	25	D3
Pelham Street SW7	30	C1	Portland Place W1	14	A4	Queensberry Mews West SW7	24	B3	Richbell Place WC1	15	E4
Pemberton Row EC4	22	A1	Portman Close W1	19	E1	Queensberry Place SW7	24	B3	Emerald Street		
Penfold Place NW1	12	C4	Portman Mews South W1	19	E1	Harrington Street			Richmond Buildings W1	20	C2
Penfold Street NW1 & NW8	12	C4	Portman Square W1	19	E1	Queensborough Way SW7	24	B3	Dean Street		
Penryn Street W1	14	C1	Portman Street W1	19	E2	Queensborough Mews W2	18	A2	Richmond Mews W1	20	C2
Penton Rise WC1	15	E2	Portpool Lane EC1	16	A4	Queensborough Terrace W2	18	A2	Richmond Terrace SW1	27	D1
Penton Street N1	16	A1	Portsea Place W2	19	D1	Queenstown Road SW8	32	A3	Ridgmount Gardens WC1	14	C4
Pentonville Road N1	15	E2	Portsmouth Street WC2	21	E1	Quick Street N1	16	B1	Ridgmount Street WC1	15	C4
Pepper Street SE1	28	C1	Portugal Street						Riding House Street W1	20	B1
Pepys Street EC3	23	E2	Portugal Street WC2	21	E1				Riley Road SE1	29	E2
Percival Street EC1	16	B3	Potier Street SE1	29	D3	Radnor Mews W2	18	C2	Riley Street SW10	30	B3
Percy Circus WC1	15	E2	Potter's Fields SE1	29	E1	Radnor Place W2	18	C1	Risborough Street SE1	28	B1
Percy Street W1	20	C1	Poultry EC2	23	D2	Radnor Street EC1	17	C3	Risinghill Street N1	16	A1
Perkin's Rents SW1	27	C3	Praed Street W2	18	B1	Radnor Place W2	18	C1	River Street EC1	16	A2
Peter Street W1	20	C2	Pratt Walk SE11	27	E3	Radnor Street EC1	17	C3	Riverside Walk SE1	22	A3
Peter's Lane EC1	16	B4	President Street EC1	16	C2	Radnor Walk SW3	31	D2	Rivington Street EC2	17	E3
Peters Hill EC4	22	C2	Central Street						Robert Adam Street W1	19	E1

173

London: Street index

Street	Page	Grid
Robert Close W9	12	B3
Robert Street NW1	14	B2
Robert Street WC2	21	D3
Robinson Street SW3	31	C2
Flood Street		
Rochester Row SW1	26	B3
Rochester Street SW1	26	C3
Rockingham Street SE1	28	C3
Rocliffe Street N1	16	B1
Rodmarton Street W1	19	E1
Rodney Place SE17	29	C3
Rodney Street N1	15	E1
Roger Street WC1	15	E4
Roland Gardens SW7	30	B1
Roland Way SW7	30	B1
Rolls Buildings EC4	22	A1
Rolls Passage EC4	22	A1
Romilly Street W1	20	C2
Romney Street W1	27	D3
Rood Lane EC3	23	E2
Ropemaker Street EC2	17	D4
Roper Lane SE1	29	E2
Rosary Gardens SW7	30	A1
Roscoe Street EC1	17	C3
Rose Alley SE1	22	C3
Rosebery Avenue EC1	16	A2
Rosemoor Street SW3	31	D1
Rosoman Place EC1	16	A3
Rosoman Street		
Rosoman Street EC1	16	A3
Rossmore Road NW1	13	D3
Rotary Street SE1	28	B2
Rothsay Street SE1	29	D3
Rotten Row SW7 & SW1	24	C1
Roupell Street SE1	28	A1
Royal Avenue SW3	31	D1
Royal Exchange Buildings EC2	23	D2
Cornhill		
Royal Hospital Road SW3	31	D3
Royal Opera Arcade SW1	21	C3
Royal Street SE1	27	E2
Rufus Street N1	17	C2
Rugby Street WC1	15	E4
Rumbold Road SW6	30	A4
Rupert Street W1	20	C2
Rushton Street N1	17	D1
Rushworth Street SE1	28	B2
Russell Square W1	15	D4
Russell Street WC2	21	E2
Russia Row EC2	23	C1
Rutherford Street SW1	27	C3
Rutland Gardens SW7	25	C2
Rutland Gate SW7	25	C2
Rutland Place EC1	16	B4
Rutland Street SW7	25	C2
Ryder Street SW1	20	B3
Rysbrack Street SW3	25	D2
Sackville Street W1	20	B3
Saffron Hill EC1	16	A4
Saffron Street EC1	16	A4
Sage Way WC1	15	E2
Sail Street SE11	27	E3
Salem Road W2	18	A2
Salisbury Court EC4	22	A2
Salisbury Place W1	13	D4
Salisbury Square EC4	22	A2
Salisbury Court		
Salisbury Street NW8	12	C4
Samford Street NW8	12	C3
Sanctuary Street SE1	29	C2
Marshalsea Road		
Sandell Street SE1	28	A1
Sandland Street WC1	15	E4
Sandwich Street WC1	15	D3
Sandys Row E1	23	E1
Sans Walk EC1	16	A3
Sarah Street N1	17	E2
Sardinia Street WC2	21	E1
Savage Gardens EC3	23	E2
Pepys Street		
Savile Row W1	20	B2
Savona Street SW8	32	B4
Savoy Hill WC2	21	E3
Savoy Way		
Savoy Place WC2	21	E3
Savoy Row WC2	21	E2
Savoy Street		
Savoy Steps WC2	21	E2
Savoy Way		
Savoy Street WC2	21	E2
Savoy Way WC2	21	E3
Sawyer Street SE1	28	C1
Scala Street W1	14	C4
Scoresby Street SE1	28	B1
Scotswood Street EC1	16	A3
Sans Walk		
Scott Ellis Gardens NW8	12	B2
Scovell Road SE1	28	C2
Scrutton Street EC2	17	D3
Seacoal Lane EC4	22	B1
Seaford Street WC1	15	E3
Searles Close SW11	31	C4
Searles Road SE1	29	D3
Sebastian Street EC1	16	B3
Secker Street SE1	28	A1
Sedding Street SW1	31	E1
Sloane Square		
Seddon Street WC1	15	E3
Sedley Place W1	20	A2
Woodstock Street		
Seething Lane EC3	23	E2
Sekforde Street EC1	16	B3
Selwood Place SW7	30	B2
Semley Place SW1	32	A1
Serle Street WC2	21	E1
Serpentine Road W2	25	C1
Seven Dials WC2	21	D2
Seville Street SW1	25	D2
Knightsbridge		
Seward Street EC1	16	B3
Seymour Mews W1	19	E1
Seymour Place W1	13	D4
Seymour Street W2	19	D2
Seymour Walk SW10	30	A2
Shaftesbury Avenue W1 & WC2	20	C2
Shaftesbury Street N1	17	D1
Shafto Mews SW1	25	D3
Shalcomb Street SW10	30	B3
Shand Street SE1	29	E1
Shawfield Street SW3	31	D2
Sheffield Street WC2	21	E1
Portugal Street		
Shelton Street WC2	21	D2
Shenfield Street N1	17	E2
Shepherd Market W1	26	A1
Shepherd Street W1	26	A1
Shepherdess Place N1	17	C2
Shepherdess Walk		
Shepherdess Walk N1	17	C2
Sheraton Street W1	20	C1
Wardour Street		
Sherlock Mews W1	13	E4
Sherwood Street W1	20	C2
Shillibeer Place W1	13	D4
Shoe Lane EC4	22	A1
Shoreditch High Street E1	17	E3
Short Street SE1	28	A1
Short's Gardens WC2	21	D1
Shouldham Street W1	19	D1
Shroton Street NW1	13	C4
Sicilian Avenue WC1	21	D1
Vernon Place		
Siddons Lane NW1	13	D3
Sidmouth Street WC1	15	E3
Silbury Street N1	17	D2
Silex Street SE1	28	B2
Silk Street EC2	17	C4
Silvester Street SE1	29	C2
Singer Street EC2	17	D3
Sise Lane EC4	23	C2
Pancras Lane		
Skinner Street EC1	16	A3
Skinners Lane EC4	23	C2
Queen Street		
Skipton Street SE1	28	B3
Slaidburn Street SW10	30	B3
Sleaford Street SW8	32	B4
Slingsby Place WC2	21	D2
Sloane Avenue SW3	31	D1
Sloane Court East SW3	31	E1
Sloane Court West SW3	31	E1
Sloane Gardens SW1	31	E1
Sloane Square SW1	31	E1
Sloane Street SW1	25	D2
Sloane Terrace SW1	31	E1
Smart's Place WC2	21	D1
Smith Square SW1	27	D3
Smith Street SW3	31	D2
Smith Terrace SW3	31	D2
Smithfield Street EC1	22	B1
Snow Hill EC1	22	B1
Snowden Street EC2	17	E4
Snowsfields SE1	29	D1
Soho Square W1	21	C1
Soho Street W1	20	C1
Somers Close NW1	14	C1
Somers Crescent W2	18	C2
Somers Mews W2	18	C1
South Audley Street W1	19	E3
South Bolton Gardens SW5	30	A2
South Carriage Drive (The Ring) SW7 & SW1	24	C2
South Crescent WC1	14	C4
Store Street		
South Eaton Place SW1	25	E3
South End Row W8	24	A2
South End W8	24	F2
South Molton Lane W1	20	A2
South Molton Street W1	20	A2
South Parade SW3	30	B2
South Place EC2	17	D4
South Street W1	19	E3
South Terrace SW7	24	C3
South Wharf Road W2	18	B1
Southampton Buildings WC2	22	A1
Southampton Place WC1	21	D1
Southampton Row WC1	15	D4
Southampton Street WC2	21	D2
Southern Street N1	15	E1
Southwark Bridge EC4 & SE1	23	C3
Southwark Bridge Road SE1	28	B2
Southwark Street SE1	22	B3
Southwell Gardens SW7	24	A3
Southwick Place W2	18	C2
Southwick Street W2	18	C1
Hyde Park Crescent		
Spafield Street EC1	16	A3
Exmouth Market		
Spanish Place W1	19	E1
Spencer Street EC1	16	B2
Spenser Street SW1	26	B2
Spital Square E1	17	E4
Sprimont Place SW3	31	D1
Spring Gardens SW1	21	D3
Spring Mews W1	13	E4
Spring Street W2	18	B2
Spur Road SW1	26	B2
Spurgeon Street SE1	29	D3
St. Alban's Grove W8	24	A2
St. Alban's Street SW1	20	C3
St. Albans Mews W2	12	C4
St. Alphage Garden EC2	23	C1
St. Andrew Street EC4	22	A1
St. Andrew's Hill EC4	22	B2
St. Andrew's Place NW1	14	A3
Outer Circle		
St. Ann's Lane SW1	27	C3
St. Ann's Street SW1	27	C2
St. Ann's Terrace NW8	12	C1
St. Anne's Court W1	20	C2
St. Anselm's Place W1	20	A2
St. Barnabas Street SW1	32	A1
St. Botolph Street EC3	23	E1
St. Bride Street EC4	22	B1
St. Chad's Place WC1	15	E2
St. Chad's Street WC1	15	D2
St. Christopher's Place W1	20	A1
St. Clare Street EC3	23	A2
St. Clement's Lane WC2	21	E2
St. Cross Street EC1	16	A4
St. Dunstan's Court EC4	22	A1
Fleet Street		
St. Dunstan's Lane EC3	23	E2
St Mary at Hill		
St. Dunstans Alley EC3	23	E2
St Dunstans Hill		
St. Ermins Hill SW1	26	C2
St. George Street W1	20	B2
St. George's Drive SW1	32	A1
St. George's Road SE1	28	B3
St. George's Square Mews SW1	32	C2
St. George's Square SW1	32	C2
St. Giles High Street WC2	21	C1
St. Helen's Place EC3	23	E1
St. Helena Street WC1	16	A2
St. James's Court SW1	26	B2
St. James's Market SW1	20	C3
Haymarket		
St. James's Place SW1	26	B1
St. James's Row EC1	16	B3
St. James's Square SW1	20	C3
St. James's Street SW1	20	B3
St. James's Walk EC1	16	B3
St. John Street EC1	16	A1
St. John's Lane EC1	16	B4
St. John's Place EC1	16	B4
St. John's Square EC1	16	B4
St. John's Wood High Street NW8	12	C1
St. John's Wood Road NW8	12	B3
St. John's Wood Terrace NW8	12	C1
St. Katherine's Precinct NW1	14	A1
Outer Circle		
St. Katherine's Row EC3	23	E2
Fenchurch Street		
St. Leonard's Terrace SW3	31	D2
St. Loo Avenue SW3	31	D3
St. Luke's Street SW3	31	C1
St. Margaret's Street SW1	27	D2
St. Mark's Grove SW10	30	A3
St. Martin's Court WC2	21	D2
St Martin's Lane		

174

London: Street index

Street	Page	Grid
St. Martin's Lane WC2	21	D2
St. Martin's Place WC2	21	D3
St. Martin's Street WC2	21	C3
St. Martin's-le-grand EC1	22	C1
St. Mary At Hill EC3	23	E2
St. Mary Axe EC3	23	E1
St. Mary's Gardens SE11	28	A3
St. Mary's Mansions W2	12	B4
St. Mary's Square W2	12	B4
St. Mary's Terrace W2	12	B4
St. Mary's Walk SE11	28	A3
St. Matthew Street SW1	26	C3
St. Michael's Street W2	18	C1
St. Paul's Churchyard EC4	22	B2
St. Peter's Street N1	16	B1
St. Swithin's Lane EC4	23	D2
St. Thomas Street SE1	29	D1
St. Vincent Street W1	19	C1
Stable Yard Road SW1	26	B1
Stacey Street WC2	21	D2
Stadium Street SW10	30	B4
Staff Street EC1	17	D2
Vince Street		
Stafford Place SW1	26	B2
Stag Place SW1	26	B2
Stainer Street SE1	29	D1
Staining Lane EC2	22	C1
Stalbridge Street NW1	13	C4
Stamford Street SE1	28	A3
Stanford Road W8	24	A2
Stanford Street SW1	32	C1
Stanhope Gardens SW7	24	B3
Stanhope Gate W1	19	E3
Hertford Street		
Stanhope Mews East SW7	24	B3
Stanhope Mews South SW7	30	B1
Stanhope Mews West SW7	24	A1
Stanhope Place W2	19	D2
Stanhope Row W1	26	A1
Stanhope Street NW1	14	B2
Stanhope Terrace W2	18	C2
Stanley Passage NW1	15	D1
Stanway Street N1	17	E1
Staple Inn Buildings WC1	22	A1
Staple Street SE1	29	D2
Star Street W2	18	C1
Star Yard WC2	22	A1
Starcross Street NW1	14	B3
Stephen Mews W1	20	C1
Gresse Street		
Stephen Street W1	20	C1
Stephen's Row EC4	23	D2
Walbrook		
Stephenson Way NW1	14	B3
Sterling Street SW7	25	C2
Montpelier Place		
Sterry Street SE1	29	D2
Stevens Street SE1	29	E2
Steward Street E1	17	F4
Stewart's Grove SW3	30	C1
Stewart's Road SW8	32	C4
Stillington Street SW1	26	B3
Stone Buildings WC2	21	E1
Chancery Lane		
Stonecutter Street EC4	22	B1
Stones End Street SE1	28	C2
Stoney Lane E1	23	E1
Stoney Street SE1	23	C3
Store Street WC1	14	C4
Storey's Gate SW1	27	C2
Stourcliffe Street W1	19	D1
Strand WC2	21	D3
Stratford Place W1	20	A2
Strathearn Place W2	18	C2
Hyde Park Square		

Street	Page	Grid
Stratton Street W1	20	B3
Streatham Street WC1	21	D1
Strutton Ground SW1	26	C3
Stukeley Street WC2	21	D1
Sturge Street SE1	28	C2
Sturt Street N1	17	C1
Sudeley Street N1	16	B1
Sudrey Street SE1	28	C2
Suffolk Lane EC4	23	D2
Suffolk Place SW1	21	C3
Suffolk Street		
Suffolk Street SW1	21	C3
Sullivan Road SE1	28	A3
Summers Street EC1	16	A4
Back Hill		
Sumner Place Mews SW7	30	B1
Sumner Place SW7	30	B1
Sumner Street SE1	22	B3
Sun Street EC2	17	D4
Surrey Row SE1	28	B1
Surrey Street WC2	21	E2
Sussex Gardens W2	18	C1
Sussex Place NW1	13	D3
Sussex Place SW7	18	B2
Sussex Square W2	18	B2
Sussex Street SW1	32	A2
Sutherland Row SW1	32	A1
Sutherland Street		
Sutherland Street SW1	32	A1
Sutton Row W1	21	C1
Swallow Street W1	20	B3
Swan Alley EC2	23	D1
Swan Lane EC4	23	D3
Swan Mead SE1	29	E3
Swan Street SE1	29	C2
Swan Walk SW3	31	D3
Swinton Street WC1	15	E2
Sycamore Street EC1	16	C3
Sydney Mews SW3	30	C1
Sydney Place SW7	30	C1
Sydney Street SW3	30	C1
Symons Street SW3	31	E1
Tabard Street SE1	29	C1
Tabernacle Street EC2	17	D3
Tachbrook Street SW1	32	B1
Tadema Road SW10	30	B4
Talbot Square W2	18	B2
Tallis Street EC4	22	A2
Tankerton Street WC1	15	D2
Cromer Street		
Tanner Street SE1	29	E2
Taplow Street N1	17	C2
Taunton Mews NW1	13	D4
Balcombe Street		
Taunton Place NW1	13	D3
Tavistock Place WC1	15	C3
Tavistock Square WC1	15	C3
Tavistock Street WC2	21	D2
Taviton Street WC1	14	C3
Tedworth Square SW3	31	D2
Telegraph Street EC2	23	D1
Temple Avenue EC4	22	A2
Temple Lane EC4	22	A2
Temple Place WC2	21	E2
Tenison Court W1	20	B2
Regent Street		
Tenison Way SE1	28	A3
Tennis Street SE1	29	C1
Tenterden Street W1	20	A2
Terminus Place SW1	26	B3

Street	Page	Grid
Tetcott Road SW10	30	A4
Thackeray Street W8	24	A2
Thanet Street WC1	15	D2
Thavies Inn EC4	22	A1
Thayer Street W1	19	E1
The Boltons SW10	30	A2
The Broad Walk NW1	13	E1
The Broadwalk W8	18	A3
The Cut SE1	28	A1
The Dial Walk W8	24	A1
The Flower Walk SW7	24	B1
The Grange SE1	29	E3
The Lane NW8	12	A1
The Little Boltons SW10 & SW5	30	A2
The Mall SW1	26	C1
The Parade SW11	31	E3
The Piazza WC2	21	D2
The Vale SW3	30	B2
Theed Street SE1	28	A1
Theobold's Road WC1	15	E4
Theseus Walk N1	16	B1
Rocliffe Street		
Thessaly Road SW8	32	B4
Thirleby Road SE1	26	B3
Thistle Grove SW10	30	B1
Thomas Doyle Street SE1	28	B2
Thomas More Street E1	21	A3
Thoresby Street N1	16	C2
Thorndike Close SW10	30	A4
Thorney Crescent SW11	30	C4
Thorney Street SW1	27	D3
Thornton Place W1	13	D4
Thrale Street SE1	29	C1
Threadneedle Street EC2	23	D2
Three Kings Yard W1	20	A2
Throgmorton Avenue EC2	23	D
Throgmorton Street EC2	23	D1
Thurloe Close SW7	25	C3
Thurloe Place Mews SW7	24	C3
Thurloe Place SW7	24	C3
Thurloe Square SW7	24	C3
Thurloe Street SW7	24	C3
Tidbury Court SW8	32	B4
Tilney Street W1	19	E3
Timber Street EC1	16	C3
Titchborne Row W2	19	C2
Tite Street SW3	31	D2
Tiverton Street SE1	28	C3
Tokenhouse Yard EC2	23	D1
Tolmers Square NW1	14	B3
Tonbridge Street WC1	15	D2
Took's Court EC4	22	A1
Tooley Street SE1	23	D3
Tooley Street SE1	29	D1
Topham Street EC1	16	A3
Torrens Street EC1	16	A1
Torrington Place WC1	14	C4
Tothill Street SW1	27	C2
Tottenham Court Road W1	14	B4
Tottenham Street W1	14	B4
Toulmin Street SE1	28	C2
Tower Bridge Road SE1	29	E2
Tower Court WC2	21	D2
Monmouth Street		
Tower Hill EC3	23	E3
Tower Street WC2	21	D2
Trafalgar Square WC2	21	D3
Trebeck Street W1	26	A1
Tregunter Road SW10	30	A2
Tresham Crescent NW8	13	C3
Treveris Street SE1	28	B1
Bear Lane		
Trevor Place SW7	25	D2

Street	Page	Grid
Trevor Square SW7	25	D2
Trevor Street SW7	25	D2
Trinity Church Square SE1	29	C2
Trinity Square EC3	23	E2
Trinity Street SE1	29	C2
Trio Place SE1	29	C2
Triton Square NW1	14	B3
Trump Street EC2	23	C1
Tryon Street SW3	31	D1
Tudor Street EC4	22	A2
Tufton Street SW1	27	D3
Turk's Row SW3	31	E1
Turnmill Street EC1	16	A4
Turpentine Lane SW1	32	A2
Twyford Place WC2	21	E1
Kingsway		
Tyers Gate SE1	29	E2
Tysoe Street EC1	16	A3
Udall Street SW1	32	C1
Ufford Street SE1	28	A1
Ulster Place NW1	14	A3
Undershaft EC3	23	E1
Underwood Row N1	17	C2
Shepherdess Walk		
Underwood Street N1	17	C2
Union Street SE1	28	B1
Union Walk E2	17	E2
University Street WC1	14	B4
Upbrook Mews W2	18	B2
Upcerne Road SW10	30	A4
Upper Belgrave Street SW1	26	A2
Upper Berkeley Street W1	19	D1
Upper Brook Street W1	19	E2
Upper Cheyne Row SW3	31	C3
Upper Grosvenor Street W1	19	E3
Upper Ground SE1	22	A3
Upper Harley Street NW1	14	A3
Upper James Street W1	20	B2
Upper John Street W1	20	B2
Upper Marsh SE1	27	E2
Upper Montagu Street W1	13	D4
Upper St. Martin's Lane WC2	21	D2
Upper Street N1	16	A1
Upper Tachbrook Street SW1	32	B1
Upper Thames Street EC4	22	B2
Upper Wimpole Street W1	14	A4
Upper Woburn Place WC1	15	C3
Uverdale Road SW10	30	B4
Vale Close W9	12	A2
Valentine Place SE1	28	B1
Valentine Row SE1	28	B2
Vandon Passage SW1	26	C2
Vandon Street SW1	30	C2
Vandy Street EC2	17	E4
Vane Street W1	26	C3
Varndell Street NW1	14	B2
Vauxhall Bridge Road SW1	26	B3
Venables Street NW8	12	B4
Vere Street W1	20	A1
Vernon Place WC1	21	D1
Vernon Rise WC1	15	E2
Vernon Square WC1	15	E2
Verulam Street WC1	16	A4
Vestry Street N1	17	D2
Victoria Avenue EC2	23	E1
Victoria Embankment SW1, WC2 & EC4	27	D2

175

London: Street index

Street	Page	Grid
Victoria Grove W8	24	A2
Victoria Road W8	24	A2
Victoria Street SW1	26	B3
Victory Place SE17	29	D3
Vigo Street W1	20	B3
Villiers Street WC2	21	D3
Vince Street EC1	17	D3
Vincent Square SW1	26	C3
Vincent Terrace N1	16	B1
Vine Lane SE1	29	E1
Vine Street Bridge EC1	16	A4
Farringdon Lane		
Vine Street EC3	23	E2
Vine Street W1	20	B3
Vineyard Walk EC1	16	A3
Pine Street		
Vintner's Place EC4	23	C2
Violet Hill NW8	12	A1
Virgil Street SE1	27	E2
Virginia Road E2	17	E3
Viscount Street EC1	16	C4
Waithman Street EC4	22	B2
Pilgrim Street		
Wakefield Mews WC1	15	D3
Wakefield Street		
Wakefield Street WC1	15	D3
Wakley Street EC1	16	B2
Walbrook EC4	23	D2
Walcot Square SE11	28	A3
Walnut Tree Walk SE11	28	A3
Walpole Street SW3	31	D1
Walton Place SW3	25	D2
Walton Street SW3	25	C3
Wandon Road SW6	30	A4
Wardour Street W1	20	C1
Warner Street EC1	16	A3
Warren Street W1	14	B3
Warrington Crescent W9	12	A3
Warrington Gardens W9	12	A4
Warwick Crescent W2	12	A4
Warwick House Street SW1	21	C3
Warwick Lane EC4	22	B1
Warwick Place W9	12	A4
Warwick Row SW1	26	B2
Warwick Square EC4	22	B1
Warwick Square SW1	32	B1
Warwick Street W1	20	B2
Warwick Way SW1	32	A1
Watergate EC4	22	B2
New Bridge Street		
Watergate Walk WC2	21	D3
Villiers Street		
Waterloo Bridge WC2 & SE1	21	E3
Waterloo Place SW1	21	C3
Waterloo Road SE1	21	E3
Waterson Street E2	17	D2
Watling Street EC4	22	C2
Waverley Place NW8	12	B1
Waverton Street W1	20	A3
Weavers Lane SE1	29	E1
Webb Street SE1	29	E3
Webber Row SE1	28	A2
Webber Street SE1	28	B2
Weighouse Street W1	20	A2
Welbeck Street W1	20	A1
Welbeck Way W1	20	A1
Well Court EC4	23	C2
Queen Street		
Weller Street SE1	28	C1
Wellers Court NW1	15	D1
Pancras Road		
Wellesley Terrace N1	17	C2
Wellington Place NW8	12	C2
Wellington Road NW8	12	B1
Wellington Square SW3	31	D2
Wellington Street WC2	21	E2
Wells Mews W1	20	B1
Wells Square WC1	15	E2
Wells Street W1	20	B1
Wenlock Road N1	16	C1
Wenlock Street N1	17	C1
Werrington Street NW1	14	C1
Wesley Street W1	13	E4
Weymouth Street		
West Carriage Drive (The Ring) W2	18	C3
West Central Street WC1	21	D1
New Oxford Street		
West Eaton Place SW1	25	E3
West Halkin Street SW1	25	E2
West Poultry Avenue EC1	22	B1
West Smithfield		
West Road SW4	31	E2
West Smithfield EC1	22	B1
West Square SE11	28	B3
West Street WC2	21	D2
Westbourne Crescent W2	18	B2
Westbourne Street W2	18	B2
Westbourne Terrace Mews W2	18	A1
Westbourne Terrace Road W2	12	A4
Westbourne Terrace W2	18	A1
Westgate Terrace SW10	30	A2
Westland Place N1	17	D2
Westminster Bridge Road SE1	27	E2
Westminster Bridge SW1 & SE1	27	D2
Westmoreland Place SW1	32	A2
Westmoreland Street W1	14	A4
Westmoreland Terrace SW1	32	A2
Weston Rise WC1	15	E2
Weston Street SE1	29	D2
Wetherby Gardens SW5	30	A1
Wetherby Place SW7	30	A1
Weymouth Mews W1	14	A4
Weymouth Street W1	14	A4
Wharf Road N1	16	C1
Wharfdale Road N1	15	D1
Wharton Street WC1	15	E2
Wheatley Street W1	13	E4
Marylebone Street		
Wheler Street E1	17	E4
Whetstone Park WC2	21	E1
Whidborne Street WC1	15	D2
Whiskin Street EC1	16	B2
Whitcomb Street WC2	21	C3
White Conduit Street N1	16	A1
Chapel Market		
White Horse Street W1	26	A1
White Kennet Street E1	23	E1
White Lion Hill EC4	22	B2
White Lion Street N1	16	A1
White's Grounds SE1	29	E2
White's Row E1	23	E1
Whitecross Place EC2	17	D4
Whitecross Street EC1	17	C3
Whitefriars Street EC4	22	A2
Whitehall Court SW1	27	D1
Whitehall Place SW1	27	D1
Whitehall SW1	21	D3
Whitehaven Street NW8	13	C4
Whitehead's Grove SW3	31	D1
Whitfield Place W1	14	B3
Whitfield Street		
Whitfield Street W1	14	B4
Whittaker Street SW1	31	E1
Whittington Avenue EC3	23	E2
Leadenhall Street		
Whittlesey Street SE1	28	A1
Wicklow Street WC1	15	E2
Widegate Street E1	23	E1
Miiddlesex Street		
Wigmore Place W1	20	A1
Wigmore Street W1	19	E1
Wilbraham Place SW1	25	E3
Wilcox Place SW1	26	B3
Wild Court WC2	21	E1
Wild Street WC2	21	E1
Wild's Rents SE1	29	D2
Wilfred Street SW1	26	B2
Wilks Place N1	17	E1
William IV Street WC2	21	D3
William Mews SW1	25	E2
William Road NW1	14	B3
William Street SW1	25	E2
Willow Place SW1	26	B3
Willow Street EC2	17	D3
Willow Walk SE1	29	E3
Wilmington Square WC1	16	A3
Wilmington Street WC1	16	A3
Wilson Street EC2	17	D4
Wilton Crescent SW1	25	E2
Wilton Mews SW1	26	A2
Wilton Place SW1	25	E2
Wilton Road SW1	26	B3
Wilton Row SW1	25	E2
Wilton Street SW1	25	A2
Wilton Terrace SW1	25	E2
Wimbourne Street N1	17	D1
Wimpole Mews W1	14	A4
Wimpole Street W1	20	A1
Winchester Square SE1	23	D3
Winchester Walk		
Winchester Street SW1	32	A1
Winchester Walk SE1	23	C3
Windmill Street W1	20	C1
Windmill Walk SE1	28	A1
Windsor Terrace N1	17	C2
Wine Office Court EC4	22	A1
Winnett Street W1	20	C2
Rupert Street		
Winsland Mews W2	18	B1
Winsland Street W2	18	B1
Winsley Street W1	20	B1
Winterton Place SW10	30	B3
Woburn Place WC1	15	D3
Woburn Square WC1	15	C3
Woburn Walk WC1	15	C3
Upper Woburn Place		
Wood Street EC2	23	C1
Wood's Mews W1	19	E2
Wood's Place SE1	29	E3
Woodbridge Street EC1	16	B3
Woodfall Street SW3	31	D2
Woodstock Mews W1	14	A4
Westmoreland Street		
Woodstock Street W1	20	A2
Wootton Street SE1	28	A1
Worfield Street SW11	31	D4
Wormwood Street EC2	23	E1
Worship Street EC2	17	D4
Wren Street WC1	15	E3
Wybert Street NW1	14	B3
Wyclif Street EC1	16	B3
Wyndham Street W1	13	D4
Wynyatt Street EC1	16	B2
Wythburn Place W1	19	D1
Yardley Street WC1	16	A3
Yarmouth Place W1	26	A1
Yeoman's Row SW3	25	D3
York Bridge NW1	13	E3
York Buildings WC2	21	D3
York Gate NW1	13	E3
York Road SE1	27	E1
York Street W1	13	D4
York Terrace East NW1	13	E3
York Terrace West NW1	13	E3
York Way N1 & N7	15	D1
Zoar Street SE1	22	C3